ISRAEL
THE
CHURCH
AND THE
MIDDLE
EAST

A BIBLICAL RESPONSE TO THE CURRENT CONFLICT

In Celebration of Israel's 70ᵗʰ Anniversary

ISRAEL
THE
CHURCH
AND THE
MIDDLE
EAST

A BIBLICAL RESPONSE TO THE CURRENT CONFLICT

Darrell L. Bock and Mitch Glaser, Editors

Kregel
Publications

This volume of essays is dedicated to the nation of Israel in honor of her 70ᵗʰ birthday. It commemorates the creation of the modern Jewish state that rose out of the ashes of the Holocaust in 1948—a mere three years after the conclusion of World War II as the mass destruction of 6 million Jews was uncovered and revealed to a horrified world. Had Hitler been victorious, the entirety of world Jewry may very well have perished. Yet, the God of Israel would not allow the people of Israel to be destroyed.

As the prophet Jeremiah promised,

Thus says the LORD, Who gives the sun for light by day and the fixed order of the moon and the stars for light by night, Who stirs up the sea so that its waves roar; The LORD of hosts is His name: "If this fixed order departs From before Me," declares the LORD, "Then the offspring of Israel also will cease From being a nation before Me forever" (Jeremiah 31:35–36, NASB).

By honoring Israel in this milestone year, we pay homage to the pioneers who created the modern State of Israel out of rock, dust, and sand. But more importantly, we honor the God of Abraham, Isaac, and Jacob who has promised to preserve his people for the sake of his everlasting glory.

Pray for the peace of Jerusalem:
"May they prosper who love you."
                    —Psalm 122:6, NASB

CONTENTS

PART 4: CURRENT CHALLENGES TO PEACE IN ISRAEL

THE LIFEWAY SURVEY

EDITORS AND CONTRIBUTORS

Richard E. Averbeck (Ph.D., Annenberg Research Institute) is Professor of Old Testament and Semitic Languages and Director of the Ph.D. program in Theological Studies at Trinity Evangelical Divinity School in Deerfield, Illinois.

Mark L. Bailey (Ph.D., Dallas Theological Seminary) is the President and Senior Professor of Bible Exposition at Dallas Theological Seminary. For more than forty years he has served in theological education, pastored various churches, and led numerous tours to Israel and the Middle East.

Craig Blaising (Ph.D., University of Aberdeen, Scotland) is Executive Vice President and Provost, Professor of Theology, and Jesse Hendley Chair of Biblical Theology at Southwestern Baptist Theological Seminary, and has written many articles on Israel and the Church.

Darrell Bock (Ph.D.,University of Aberdeen) is Research Professor of New Testament Studies at Dallas Theological Seminary, a Humboldt Scholar (Tübingen University in Germany), former President of the Evangelical Theological Society, and corresponding editor-at-large for *Christianity Today*.

Mike Brown (Ph.D., New York University) is a Messianic Jewish apologist and author of various books, such as the five-volume series *Answering Jewish Objections to Jesus*. He has served as visiting and/or adjunct professor at many schools and seminaries, including Gordon-Conwell Theological Seminary, Denver Theological Seminary, Regent University (Virginia Beach), and Trinity (Deerfield, IL).

Tom Doyle (Th.M., Dallas Theological Seminary) is the Vice President and Middle East Director of e3 Partners, a licensed guide for the State of Israel, and has authored eight books including two best sellers.

Mitch Glaser (Ph.D., Fuller Theological Seminary) is President of Chosen People Ministries and speaks and writes widely on Jewish evangelism and Messianic Judaism. He is coeditor with Darrell Bock of five academic volumes published by Kregel Publications, including *To the Jew First: The Case for Jewish Evangelism in Scripture and History.*

Walter C. Kaiser, Jr. (Ph.D., Brandeis University) is the Colman M. Mockler Distinguished Professor of Old Testament and former President of Gordon-Conwell Theological Seminary. Throughout his career, he has published considerably in the field of biblical studies.

Craig Parshall (J.D., Marquette University Law School) is a constitutional lawyer serving as Special Counsel to the American Center for Law and Justice (ACLJ) on Supreme Court matters and an author who frequently writes on Israel and the Middle East.

Michael Rydelnik, (D.Miss., Trinity International University) is Professor of Jewish Studies and Bible at Moody Bible Institute and Host/Bible teacher on Open Line with Dr. Michael Rydelnik, answering listener Bible questions every Saturday morning for more than 230 stations on Moody Radio. He also is the coeditor of and a contributor to The Moody Bible Commentary, author of *Understanding the Arab-Israeli Conflict*, as well as other books. He has also contributed to numerous books, journals, and study Bibles.

Erez Soref (Psy.D., Wheaton College) is the President of One for Israel, based in Netanya, Israel. He also serves on the board of directors of several Israeli and international NGOs.

Michael J. Vlach (Ph.D., Southeastern Baptist Theological Seminary) is Professor of Theology at The Master's Seminary and specializes in the areas of Systematic Theology, Historical Theology, Apologetics, and World Religions.

Mark Yarbrough (Ph.D., Dallas Theological Seminary) is Vice President for Academic Affairs, Academic Dean, and Associate Professor of Bible Exposition at Dallas Theological Seminary and has been published in various magazines and written several books.

INTRODUCTION

DR. MITCH GLASER & DR. DARRELL BOCK

THE RELATIONSHIP BETWEEN THE CHURCH and Israel has been the source of passionate debate among Christians throughout much of Church history. More recently, however, the issue has moved beyond the exegetical and theological spheres to encompass the political realm, with the publication of a number of books by evangelical authors who champion the Palestinian cause and are highly critical of both Israel and Christian support for the Jewish state. The debate surrounding the relationship between the Church and Israel has evolved from mere disagreement over doctrine and now includes areas of both historical and political debate regarding the current Middle East that further divides Christians.

In recent years it has become apparent that the traditional pro-Israel stance of evangelicals has come under fire by those who support the Palestinian cause, calling for a new perspective and more nuanced approach by Christians who believe that the Land of Israel belongs to the Jewish people by virtue of God's covenants and promises. As the apostle Paul writes, about the Jewish people of his day:

As regards the gospel, they are enemies for your sake. But as regards election, they are beloved for the sake of their forefathers. For the gifts and the calling of God are irrevocable (Rom. 11:28–29).

The books, articles, and videos of resources has, by and large, been limited to the popular sphere, so that there is a notable paucity of academic works by evangelicals advocating the view that God retains a plan and purpose for the Jewish people (and by extension a divine interest in the Jewish state and the wider Middle East conflict). There is also a significant lack of objective academic responses to books by Christian authors critical of Israel and Christian Zionism. In addition, those that do defend Israel are sometimes not sensitive to or aware of the legitimate concerns of Palestinians, especially those who are Evangelicals. This book is an effort to bring balance to these topics.

The debate over how the Church should respond to the situation in the Middle East has produced volumes of literature that are polarized and pejorative toward both sides, which is unfortunate as many Christians are seeking guidance on how to better understand the Middle East crisis and more particularly, the conflict between Israel and the Palestinians, including the believers on both sides of the debate.

Therefore, the editors seek to provide readers with an alternative approach. The proposed volume will challenge the Supersessionist drift of the modern Church, arguing that God retains a plan and purpose for the Jewish people while also addressing a number of the divisive issues raised by authors critical of Israel, including justice-related issues which so many of young adults are concerned with regarding the Middle East conflict.

The book will explore hermeneutical issues touching upon God's plan and purpose for the Jewish people as well as the wider effects of the conflict, such as the growing antipathy within the Church toward the evangelization of the Jewish people. The authors will also attempt to discover whether support for Israel has hurt efforts to reach Muslims, and whether adequate attention has been given to the question of reconciliation between the offended parties. Given how extremes on both sides are driving the current debate at times, an important aim of the book is to provide readers with an interdisciplinary and nuanced treatment of the issues. It attempts to eschew partisanship, in a way that is irenic and respectful in tone.

The book is directed toward pastors and global Christian leaders as well as theological students, together with lay Christians who are actively seeking guidance and resources regarding the Middle East conflict. It may also be of interest to anyone interested in how a significant group of Christians see discussion about the region. Contributors have been invited who represent a broad evangelical spectrum and yet no single denomination or tradition is dominant. The book appeals to as wide a readership as possible, although the authors share a common view regarding the ongoing election of the Jewish people.

PART 1: BIBLICAL FOUNDATIONS

The editors believe this is the proper way to begin a book of this nature. All too often, believers in Jesus develop a set of political or even ethical and moral beliefs but fail to ground these beliefs in the Bible and to further allow themselves to be influenced by Scripture. Therefore, it is important to make sure that we square our perspective on controversial issues, like the Middle East conflict, with a solid understanding of Scripture. We still might come to the table with differing views, but at least we have plumbed the depth of Scripture on the topic; and then, as brothers and sisters in the common faith, we will be able to have more irenic and productive discussions about our differences.

The Bible must impact and inform our views on contemporary issues, like the Israeli/Palestinian conflict. We asked six well-qualified authors to help us delve deeper into what the Bible teaches us about the conflict. The authors leave it up to the individual to then try and apply what was learned to the ways in which we process the opinions, news reports and to evaluate the positions of those who on both sides of the conflict.

Dr. Richard Averbeck writes on the topic, "Israel, the Jewish People, and God's Covenants." This is a theological core to the conflict under discussion. It deals with the traditional ways in which the role of Jews and Gentiles in God's plan and, in particular, the biblical understanding of the Land; it's ownership, sharing and future are understood. Covenant theology traditionally believes the Land promises to be fulfilled in one way or another in the Church, and Dispensationalism views ethnic Israel as the literal recipients of the Land's promises. Averbeck takes a more biblical-theological tact rather than systematic approach to these questions. He presents the promises and treats the fulfillment of them through the great covenants God made with His people. This provides a superior way to examine the role of Israel in God's plan and her relationship to the Land. Looking at these issues through the lens of God's covenants enables the student of Scripture to go beyond a particular theological system. An approach through biblical theology proves useful for uncovering some of the core issues in the Israel/Palestinian conflict.

Dr. Walter Kaiser draws our attention to the biblical question of "Israel and Her Neighbors: Isaiah 19." He examines God's purposes for Israel in relationship to the nations of the world—especially Israel's current neighbors. Drawing on Isaiah 19, he argues that God's ultimate goal for Israel and the nations consists of an Israeli state present and at peace in the land. Furthermore, a day will come when Israel and her neighbors will live in harmony, worshiping the same Lord and King. This chapter of Isaiah is largely unexplored within academic theological circles, yet arguably should have an important impact on how Christians today might view and respond to the Middle East conflict. As believers in Jesus, we live life today in the shadow of the future.

Dr. Mark Yarbrough believes that without understanding "Israel and the Story of the Bible," we are missing a piece of the very heart of Scripture. The story of the Bible, beginning in Genesis and concluding in the Book of Revelation, is the expression of God's love for humanity. It is important to understand the grand sweep of Scripture and to understand the different elements of the narrative in light of the whole. Themes of redemption, kingdom, regeneration, and holiness build upon one another. As the story progresses so does the ongoing significance of Israel, the Jewish people, and the unfolding of God's plan throughout time and Scripture.

We are provided with a necessary tool to unlock the mystery of the current conflict in the Middle East and beyond by understanding the breadth of His story and focusing on the role of Israel, the Jewish people, the fulfillment of prophecy, the destructive nature of sin, and the emergence of the Jewish Savior.

Dr. Michael Rydelnik covers the critical issues of biblical interpretation in his chapter, "The Hermeneutics of the Conflict," answering key questions that span both testaments about the relationship of the Jewish people to the Land of Israel. For example, does the Abrahamic covenant promise a particular land to the Jewish people, or is the Promised Land to be viewed more universally?

How are the boundaries outlined in the Book of Genesis to be understood? Are there passages of Scripture which point to the Jewish people returning to the land after dispersion? Can today's state of Israel be the fulfillment in part of these land promises? Why is the land of Israel rarely mentioned in the New Testament? Did the land promises pass to the Church in a spiritual sense, or should we expect that the land promises are literal and would be fulfilled in a regathered Israel? Are there additional land promises to be fulfilled in the future and if so, for whom and under what conditions? Will non-Jews have access to the land promises or even be able to live in the Land of Israel?

Dr. Rydelnik all of answers these questions, but also helps the Bible student understand the principles of Bible interpretation that enables the reader to study Scripture and answer these questions more effectively for themselves.

PART 2: THEOLOGY AND THE CONFLICT

The second part of the book focuses on the theological interpretations of those biblical foundations covered in the first part of the book.

Dr. Craig Blaising develops a more in-depth "Theology of Israel and the Church" by tracing the theme of God's ongoing calling, purpose, and plan for the Jewish people. He works from ancient times throughout Scripture to the present and into the future. He covers issues such as the use and understanding of the term "Israel" in the Old and New Testaments; the election, mission, and ongoing calling of the Jewish people; and the place of the land of Israel in the promises of God.

The relationship of the Church and Israel is developed throughout the Bible, especially in the Pauline epistles. Passages such as Romans 9–11, Ephesians 2–3, as well the prayers of Jesus and Paul describe a unity within diversity that is at the very heart of the Gospel. Resolving conflicts, reconciliation, and living in unity is important to God, but this cannot be achieved without a fundamental understanding of the particular roles God determined for the Jewish people, the nations, and the Church.

This chapter attempts to articulate the unique roles God has given to both Jews and Gentiles in the Body of Christ and the expanded relationship that the nation of Israel and the Church have to one another. By understanding these roles and relationships we will better be able to parse our way through the Middle East conflict. Most importantly, this chapter will answer the question as to whether or not the God of Israel has completed the purposes for which He created the nation of Israel, or if in fact the role of Israel in the plan is God is yet to be completed with the promised venue for completion in the land of Israel.

Dr. Mitch Glaser addresses the almost hidden issue of replacement theology in his chapter, "The Dangers of Supersessionism." He focuses on the ways in which this view has shaped the Palestinian narrative and the views of those who tend to be pro-Palestinian while opposing the modern state of Israel. Unfortunately, these views have widened the chasm between Israeli and Palestinian believers, but are not often sufficiently discussed to show their negative impact.

This chapter focuses on the impact modern Supersessionism has on today's Church in Israel, the Middle East, and the West. The author zeroes in on the negative impact Supersessionism has had on the Jewish people. This impact is especially the case with Jewish evangelism over the past century. Issues covered will include how negative portrayals of Israel by some sectors of the Church have a detrimental impact on Jewish responses to the Gospel, and how a high view of Israel aids Jewish evangelism. The writings of some of the better-known Supersessionist authors of our day receive particular attention and analysis. Solid principles emerge that might lead toward less acrimonious, healthier dialogue.

Dr. Mike Vlach specializes in how the Church Fathers understood the Bible regarding Israel, the Church, and the land. So he explores the topic, "Israel and the Land in the Writings of the Church." Many have charged that the relationship of Israel and the land in the writings of many theologians are "new" or recent theological concepts and therefore invalid. Dr. Vlach ably responds to these challenges.

His chapter explores the ways the promise of the land has been understood throughout Church history. Modern Supersessionism argues—on the basis of writings from the early and medieval Church—that the Church is now Israel, while also claiming that the concept of God's continued plan and purpose for the Jewish people (together with Christian Zionism) is a relatively modern invention. The chapter will challenge and critique such views, exploring how certain Church Fathers were influenced by their culture, as well as tracing support for the view that God retains a plan and purpose for the Jewish people throughout the Church's history. This demonstrates how such a view is not limited to a particular millennial viewpoint or doctrinal tradition or more recent time period. The reader will better understand the ways in which some Church Fathers, and those influenced by them, dispensed with the land promises of the Old Testament.

PART 3: YESHUA IN THE MIDST OF THE CRISIS

The third part of the book focuses on the practical issues related to the conflict, especially the relationships between Israeli and Palestinian believers.

Dr. Erez Soref writes on "The Messianic Jewish Movement in Modern Israel," giving a brief overview of the today's growing Messianic movement in Israel. This includes a focus on the views Israeli Messianic Jews have on the state of Israel, their relationships with Palestinian believers, and other aspects of the Middle East crisis; as well as providing the most up-to-date survey-based projection as to how many Jewish believers there are in Israel today. In preparation for this chapter, a professional study of the leaders of Israeli Messianic congregations was undertaken, and the results of this survey are shared and discussed in the chapter. Dr. Soref leads us to a better understanding of the state of the indigenous Israeli movement for Yeshua within Israel.

Tom Doyle spends months each year serving both Palestinians (both believers and nonbelievers) and Israeli Jewish believers. He writes about his experiences in his chapter entitles, "The 21st-Century Palestinian Church within Israel." The editors chose an American missionary to the Middle East to gain the perspective of how a pro-Israel Westerner could appreciate and deeply love the Palestinians, yet still be favorable toward Israel.

Tom describes the growth of the Palestinian churches on both the West Bank and in Gaza, and to some degree within Israel as well. The chapter also focuses on the internal struggles of the Palestinian church and how they relate to Israel and the Jewish people on a spiritual and political level. Does the Palestinian church reach out to Jewish people? Do they sympathize with the Palestinian Authority or with Hamas? How do the individual Palestinian churches get along with one another? What is the general view of the Palestinian church regarding the variety of solutions under consideration?

Are there Palestinian believers who deeply care about the Jewish people and the state of Israel? Tom introduces us to a variety of opinions on this topic in a warm and very personal way that has much experience behind it. He tells these stories through interviews and his own reflections.

Dr. Darrell Bock investigates the biblical teaching on reconciliation in his chapter, "Biblical Reconciliation for Jews and Arabs." He develops a theology of reconciliation from both the Old and New Testaments and applies these principles to the Middle East crisis, providing guidance for those who want to pray for and support reconciliation efforts. The chapter will also outline and discuss some of the "good things" that are happening between Jewish and Arab Christians in Israel to give the readers more hope and optimism. Yet, this chapter does not avoid the very real issues that make reconciliation difficult (e.g. Israel's security, the demonization of Israel, Arab hostility, the ideology behind settler activity, and the common minority status of both Jewish and Palestinian Christians).

Dr. Bock is a New Testament theologian and a Jewish believer in Jesus, who has had many experiences with both Palestinian and Israeli Jewish believers. Having been on both sides of the wall, he writes with both biblical authority and practical experience on this most difficult issue.

PART 4: CURRENT CHALLENGES TO PEACE IN ISRAEL

The fourth section of the book explores the more profound historical, theological, and practical issues that need to be solved, or at least better understood by both sides in the conflict. Additionally, those who love Israel and the Palestinians also need to be made aware of the complex issues that are ingrained within the cultures of Jewish people and Palestinians embroiled within the conflict. All too often, those outside of the situations have "easy answers" and solutions to the conflicts between others of a different culture. In order to become better peacemakers and to serve as more effective prayer partners, the difficult everyday issues that impact the conflict needs to better understood. This section attempts to do this by exploring the historical and theological issues that divide Israelis and Palestinians, especially within the church.

Those of us who care about the conflict but live outside of Israel will benefit greatly from this section. One of the key questions covered in this section will be to help Christians better understand the Jewish side of the narrative. Can you be "for Palestinians" and "for Israelis"? We propose a both/and solution in this book, and believe this section will be helpful in guiding us toward this end. Yet, in the current climate where the church in the West has become so influenced by those impacted by a more "pro-Palestinian" narrative—especially among our younger generations of Jesus followers—it is critical to gain a better understanding of the Jewish Israeli narrative as well. This narrative which influenced the Church during previous, post-World War II generations is being lost and needs to be recast without being tied to a more extreme Christian Zionism. That retelling allows for a greater concern for all those who live in the Holy Land.

Mark Bailey engages with the church to discover a more balanced approach to the conflict in his chapter "Should Christians Support the Modern State of Israel?"

Dr. Bailey explores the convergence of theology and politics, addressing issues that answer provocative questions, including to what extent can one be biblically and even politically supportive of Israel, yet not necessarily affirm every action of the Israeli government. It critiques the "Israel right or wrong" approach, and how this has impacted the witness of the Western church to Muslims and Palestinians. He explores the contribution of Jews to the world and reviews the biblical account of Israel's role in the world.

Human rights attorney Craig Parshall, in "The Legal Challenges at the Nexus of the Conflict," covers the many of the legal issues at the very heart of the conflict. This chapter calls for a rehearsal of the history of the various agreements leading to the Balfour Declaration and onward that gave the Jewish people a legal right to the land. Also examined are the attempts to forge some type of accord through negotiations between the parties, as brokered by the United States and other nations.

A critique emerges with an assessment of more recent arguments against Israel in the International Court of Justice and the United Nations, in a reversal of a previous pro-Israel position. The chapter effectively examines the sweep of history regarding Israel and their legal right to the land. Readers should then be able to share the key points in the arguments with others.

Finally, Dr. Michael Brown discusses the very controversial topic, "Is It Sinful to Divide the Land of Israel?" The two-state solution is still a possible solution to the conflict. Many Bible-believing Christians are against this solution, of dividing the land God gave to the Jewish people. They see it as an anathema. Therefore, believers find the two-state solution problematic; they view the modern state of Israel as the fulfillment of prophecies predicting the land would be given to the Jewish people in the last days. On the other side, there are followers of Jesus who are in favor of the two-state solution, as they believe this solution is a political necessity for the present—and that eventually, the Jewish people will enjoy the full Abrahamic boundaries at a future date when Jesus returns to reign as King. The chapter examines these options without making a decision on the matter. By reading this chapter, a Bible-believer should be able to understand the issues and the arguments both for and against the two-state solution, from a biblical and even practical perspective.

The editors are hopeful that the book will lead to greater unity at many levels: in the Body of Christ between Jews and Arabs, between Supersessionists and those who are not, between those who want to reach Muslims and those who want to reach Jewish people, and for those who want to reach all these groups. The book's conclusion will also call upon all sides to make sure their politics are subservient to their view of Scripture. Our prayer is that you will learn much, enjoy the journey, and be better equipped to think about and discuss the role of Israel, the church, and the nations in the Middle East!

—Dr. Mitch Glaser

—Dr. Darrell Bock

PART 1
BIBLICAL FOUNDATIONS

ISRAEL, THE JEWISH PEOPLE, AND GOD'S COVENANTS

RICHARD E. AVERBECK

IT IS A DELIGHT TO PARTICIPATE IN THIS very important discussion of God's promises to Israel, as part of the celebration of the seventieth anniversary of the modern State of Israel. The main concern of this essay is the significance of the biblical covenants for the ongoing claim that the land of Israel was promised to them and is still part of God's plan for them. "Covenant," of course, is very important in the Bible. It will not be possible, of course, to treat the covenants in full detail in this short essay. The focus here is on the Abrahamic, Mosaic, Davidic, and New covenants, with a brief glance at the Noahic covenant as well.

These are *not* the major covenants of the theological system known as "covenant theology." This theological system is built on two major covenants, neither of which are explicitly referred to as covenants in the Bible, although some would argue that such a designation can be justified anyway. The first of these is the covenant of works, or covenant of creation, or the Adamic covenant associated with Genesis 1 and 2. The name chosen for this covenant varies between different covenant theologians, but it is pre-fall in any case. The second covenant in covenant theology as a system is the covenant of grace in Genesis 3, after the fall. Within covenant theology, the explicitly historical Abrahamic, Mosaic, Davidic, and New covenants are considered to be "dispensations" of the proposed covenant of grace in Genesis 3. Historically, covenant theologians have also held to a "covenant of redemption," which envisions a covenant between God the Father and the God the Son in eternity past, committing to the work of redemption.[1]

---

1. For a clear, brief introduction to covenant theology, see Gerard Van Groningen, "Covenant," in *Evangelical Dictionary of Biblical Theology*, ed. Walter A. Elwell (Grand Rapids: Baker, 1996), 124–32, esp. pp. 125–27. See also Vern S. Poythress, *Symphonic Theology: The Validity of Multiple Perspectives in Theology* (Grand Rapids: Zondervan, 1987), 31. As a well-known covenant theologian, Poythress refers to covenant as a recurring pattern in the Bible based on the explicit covenants in the Bible, referring specifically to the Abrahamic, Mosaic, Davidic, and New Covenants. He also points out that covenant theology as a system expands the use of the term "covenant" wherever we find a "pattern of promise,

The system of theology known as "dispensational theology" describes the historical biblical covenants as subsumed under a set of dispensations in God's program of redemption, some of which are directly related to one of the biblical covenants and others not. For example, there is a close relationship between the dispensation of promise and the Abrahamic covenant, and between the dispensation of law and the Mosaic covenant. The newer "progressive dispensationalism" relaxes some of the features of the classical form and, in my view, is a vast improvement.[2] Necessary adjustments are being made within covenant theology as well. For example, some are less sanguine about replacement theology, where the church replaces Israel in God's program, and are even willing to consider a version of premillennial eschatology. I see these movements within and between the two systems of theology to be healthy adjustments to what the Bible actually says.

There is, of course, much more to this discussion, but these systems of theology are not my concern in this essay. The treatment of covenants in the present essay does *not* rely on, and should *not* be confused with, either of these two theological systems. In fact, that is one of the reasons this brief introduction to these systems is provided—to distance the approach taken in this chapter from both of these traditional views. The goal in this essay is to allow the major biblical texts for the historical biblical covenants, and the relationships between them, to carry the discussion, and especially to see how the land promises fit into the historical and theological progression of these explicitly biblical covenants.

Although there are other important covenants in the Bible (see, e.g., the priestly covenant in Numbers 25:10–13), there are actually five major covenants that give substance and structure to God's program of redemption overall: the Noahic, Abrahamic, Mosaic, Davidic, and New covenants. God initiated the covenantal land promise to Israel in the Abrahamic covenant,

---

command, human obedience or disobedience, and reward or punishment" in the Bible, so that it "sees all of God's relations with human beings in terms of the perspective of covenant."

It is helpful to observe the interchange over this extended use of the term "covenant" between John H. Stek, "'Covenant' Overload in Reformed Theology," *Calvin Theological Journal* 29 (1994):12–41, and Craig G. Bartholomew, "Covenant and Creation: Covenant Overload of Covenantal Deconstruction," *Calvin Theological Journal* 30 (1995): 11–33. Both are covenant theologians. As would be expected, Stek's critique provoked a negative reaction. Bartholomew raises some important objections. I would not agree with some of Stek's points about the nature of covenants and related matters, but, in spite of Bartholomew's objections to the contrary, in my view, Stek has underlined a very real problem in covenant theology as a system.

For the newer form of covenant theology referred to as "progressive covenantalism," see for example, Peter J. Gentry and Stephen J. Wellum, *Kingdom through Covenant: A Biblical-Theological Understanding of the Covenants* (Wheaton, IL: Crossway, 2012); and Stephen J. Wellum and Brent E. Parker, eds., *Progressive Covenantalism* (Nashville: B&H Academic, 2016).

2. See the helpful discussion of the term "dispensation" and the history of "dispensationalism" as a system of theology in Craig A. Blaising and Darrell Bock, *Progressive Dispensationalism* (Wheaton, IL: BridgePoint, 1993), 112–27. This book and Robert L. Saucy, *The Case for Progressive Dispensationalism: The Interface between Dispensational and Non-Dispensational Theology* (Grand Rapids: Zondervan, 1993) are also helpful treatments of the engagement of dispensationalism with covenant theology and its important results.

but the first covenant in the Bible and in history is the Noahic covenant. We will treat the Noahic covenant briefly, and then focus most of our attention on the latter four covenants and the promise of the land.

THE NOAHIC COVENANT

The Noahic covenant is unlike the others in that it articulates a covenant between God and all air-breathing creatures, including humanity, but not just humanity. There are actually two Noahic covenants, or at least two parts to the one covenant. The first comes before the flood as God's promise to bring Noah and his family through the flood, along with representative pairs of animals: "I am going to bring floodwaters on the earth to destroy all life under the heavens, every creature that has the breath of life in it. Everything on earth will perish. But I will establish my covenant (וַהֲקִמֹתִי אֶת־בְּרִיתִי) with you, and you will enter the ark—you and your sons and your wife and your sons' wives with you" (Gen. 6:17–18). This is the first occurrence of the word "covenant" in the Bible. The second is in Genesis 9, after the flood, where the Lord promised to never again bring such a flood upon the earth: "I now establish my covenant (וַאֲנִי הִנְנִי מֵקִים אֶת־בְּרִיתִי) with you and with your descendants after you and with every living creature that was with you—the birds, the livestock and all the wild animals, all those that came out of the ark with you—every living creature on earth. I establish my covenant (וַהֲקִמֹתִי אֶת־בְּרִיתִי) with you: Never again will all life be destroyed by the waters of a flood; never again will there be a flood to destroy the earth" (Gen. 9:9–11).

The point of the Noahic covenant(s), therefore, was to preserve the natural order of humanity and land animals through the flood, and perpetuate it after the flood. It did not focus on Israel in particular, but established relative stability in the natural order. It is a "creation covenant," so to speak, but not the creation covenant proposed by the system of covenant theology introduced above. God had judged the corruption of the world by means of the flood, and afterward he committed to never dealing with this corruption in the same way again. He remains fully engaged in working his kingdom program in the world, but he will carry it forward in a different way. This perpetual commitment was anticipated in Genesis 8:21–22, right after Noah exited the ark and made his sacrifice to God: "As long as the earth endures, seedtime and harvest, cold and heat, summer and winter, day and night will never cease" (cf. Isa. 54:9).

Thus, God maintained the natural world order until the generations and his redemptive program have run their course, issuing in the new heavens and new earth (see, e.g., Isa. 66:22–24; Rev. 21–22). In the meantime, he is working his covenant program of redemption in the midst of the world amid the groaning of creation and humanity for redemption (Rom. 8:18–30). God still steps in to judge at certain points along the way, as he did at the Tower of Babel in Genesis 11, and in Days of the Lord described throughout biblical history (see, e.g., Amos 5:18–27, referring to the exile of the northern kingdom of Israel, and the exile of the southern kingdom Judah in Zephaniah 2:1–3, etc.). Above all, however, he has selected a line of promise through which he is working out his program of redemption through time, up till today, and beyond. Of course, he had this in mind all along, as we can see from passages like Genesis 3:15, where he promised that the seed of the woman will defeat the seed of the serpent. This lays the foundation for all the biblical, historical, and theological developments carried by the "seed" of Abraham, Israel, David, and the church.

WHAT IS A "COVENANT"?

So, what exactly is a covenant? Basically, *a covenant is a solemn and formal means of establishing and defining a relationship.* There are at least two parties to a covenant and, in one way or another, the issue at hand is always the making and doing of relationship between them. When the term is used for the relationship between God and people it is intended as a way to help us understand how the holy God engages in a relationship with us as a fallen and sinful people. We also need to keep in mind, however, that the term "covenant" is a metaphor, one of many important and theologically loaded metaphors in the Bible. It is metaphorical language, a figure of speech, an analogy (see more on this below). We know this is true because of the many instances where this same terminology is used from Genesis onwards to designate a treaty, alliance, grant, loyalty oath, or something similar between people.

For example, Abraham made a treaty/covenant with Abimelek in Genesis 21 (note esp. v. 32), and the terminology for making the treaty used is the same as when the Lord made his covenant with Abraham in Genesis 15 (note esp. v. 18, and see more on this passage below). The concept comes from that world and has analogs in the surrounding ancient Near Eastern (ANE) world of that day.[3] Abraham already knew what a covenant was when the Lord first used it as a solemn way of establishing and defining their relationship in Genesis 15. As a matter of fact, Abraham already had a treaty/covenant with the leaders of Hebron in Genesis 14, where the same word for treaty/covenant appears (Genesis 14:13, they were "allied with Abram," Hebrew וְהֵם בַּעֲלֵי בְרִית־אַבְרָם lit. "they were lords of the treaty of Abram"; his name was changed from "Abram" to "Abraham" in Genesis 17:5, another important Abrahamic covenant passage, see below).

Oftentimes critical points of biblical theology are expressed through figures of speech, like "covenant," that carry a set of implications important

---

3. See the brief discussion and literature cited in Richard E. Averbeck, "Law," *Cracking Old Testament Codes: A Guide to Interpreting the Literary Genres of the Old Testament* (Nashville: Broadman and Holman, 1995), 125–128, and the more complete summary treatments in Kenneth A. Kitchen, *On the Reliability of the Old Testament* (Grand Rapids: Eerdmans, 2003), 241–312; and Samuel Greengus, "Covenant and Treaty in the Hebrew Bible and in the Ancient Near East," in *Ancient Israel's History: An Introduction to Issues and Sources,* eds. Bill T. Arnold and Richard S. Hess (Grand Rapids: Baker Academic, 2014), 91–126. For comprehensive presentation and discussion of virtually all the ANE texts available, see now Kenneth A. Kitchen and Paul J. N. Lawrence, *Treaty, Law, and Covenant in the Ancient Near East,* 3 vols. (Wiesbaden: Harrassowitz, 2012). The ceremonial features of making covenants is discussed, for example, in Menahem Haran, "The *Běrît* 'Covenant': Its Nature and Ceremonial Background," in *Tehillah le-Moshe: Biblical and Judaic Studies in Honor of Moshe Greenberg,* eds. Mordechai Cogan, et al. (Winona Lake, IN: Eisenbrauns, 1997), 203–219.

to the context in which they appear and to biblical theology as a whole. Each takes a certain point of view on our relationship with God. By speaking of "covenant" as a metaphor, we are not suggesting that the term or relationship it describes is less important. Actually, a metaphor or analogy is a way of talking about a person, place, or circumstance that highlights a certain feature (or features) and thereby makes it more concrete, real, and comprehensible. Such figures of speech are pervasive in the Bible and are of key importance in a truly biblical theology.[4]

For example, God is the father and we are his children. This has certain implications for how we should understand our relationship with the Lord, and certain passages of scripture draw them out (e.g., Ps. 103:13–14; Heb. 12:4–13). Sometimes the Bible uses other kinds of familial language or images such as "adoption" (e.g., Rom. 8:15–17, 31–39) or "marriage" (Jer. 31:32, "though I was a husband to them"; cf. also, e.g., Hos. 1–3 and Ezek. 16:8–14). Similarly, he is the bridegroom and we are the bride (e.g., Rev. 19:7–10; 21:2, 9). Other metaphors include, for instance, the Lord is the shepherd and we are the sheep (e.g., Ps. 23; John 10:1–18). He is the king and we are the people of his kingdom (e.g., Ps. 2:8–9; Isa. 9:6–7; Matt. 2; 4:17; 5:3 etc.; Rev. 2:27; 12:5). He is the master and we are the servants/slaves (e.g., Lev. 25:55; Isa. 52:13–53:12; 1 Pet. 2:18–25). He is the head and we are the body (e.g., Rom. 12:4–5; 1 Cor. 12:12–31). He is the potter and we are the clay (e.g., Jer. 18:1–12; Rom. 9:21–23). The list is extensive. Such images are all pervasive in Scripture, carrying a great deal of significance for believers.

THE ABRAHAMIC COVENANT

God's call and commission of Abram in Genesis 12:1–3 is, of course, a key passage, even though it is not in the form of a covenant. That comes later in Genesis 15 and 17. The rendering offered here of the Genesis 12 commission takes certain Hebrew grammatical features into consideration:

> The LORD said to Abram, "**Go forth** (לֶךְ־לְךָ) from your country, your people and your father's household and go to the land I will show you, **in order that** I may make you into a great nation, and bless you, make your name great. And **be a blessing, in order that** I may bless those who bless you and curse those who curse you, **so that** all peoples on earth may be blessed through you" (my translation).

There is a twofold command and purpose sequence in the passage: the Lord says "do this . . . in order that I may do this . . .," first in vv. 1–2a and second in vv. 2b–3a. The whole commission ends with a result clause, "so that all peoples on earth may be blessed through you" (v. 3b). The Lord called Abram to trust him, and step outside of his own comfort and safety with his

---

4. For a helpful explanation of the meaning and significance of metaphor in biblical and theological studies see Ian Paul, "Metaphor," in *Dictionary for Theological Interpretation of the Bible*, ed. Kevin J. Vanhoozer (Grand Rapids: Baker 2006), 507–510.

family and clan to go to another place. In that place and situation he would have no choice but to fully trust and depend on the Lord himself. The result of living by this kind of faith in the Lord would make Abram the historical pivot man for all the families and peoples that multiplied and occupied the earth after the flood (cf. Gen. 11:32). Biblical faith has a very close relationship to courage—a willingness to step outside one's own comfort zone to follow the Lord and find comfort only in him amid such steps of faith. This passage makes Abraham "the father of faith," and today all who have this kind of faith in the true God through *Yeshua Hamashiakh*, Jesus the Christ, are the children of Abraham by faith (Gal. 3:7–9; cf. also John 9:31–47; Rom. 3:9–16; Gal. 3:29, etc.).

This same core principle of faith anticipates the first passage, in which the Abrahamic relationship with God is put into covenant form. The first section of Genesis 15 is all about the "seed" of Abram. Sarah was barren and they had been in the land for a long time by then, long enough to have made a treaty (i.e., covenant) with the people around Hebron (Gen. 14:13, see above). Abram was becoming concerned about dying without a physical offspring, but the Lord promised him "Look up at the sky and count the stars— if indeed you can count them." Then he said to him, "So shall your offspring be" (v. 5b). Abram's response was to trust the Lord's promise. As verse 6 puts it, "He believed the Lord, and He credited it to him as righteousness." As is well-known, this verse became a primary Old Testament text for the apostle Paul undergirding his argument in Galatians 3 and Romans 4 that salvation comes through faith, not by circumcision or keeping the Old Testament law. After all, according to Genesis 15:6, Abram was reckoned as righteous before either circumcision or the law had been instituted.

The second section of Genesis 15 brings us to the first time God promised the land to Abraham and his seed in the form of a covenant, which is the main concern of this essay. The Lord promises, "I am the Lord, who brought you out of Ur of the Chaldeans to give you this land to take possession of it." Abram's immediate response was, "Sovereign Lord, how can I know that I will gain possession of it?" (v. 8). The Lord does not take this as an unwillingness to believe, but simply a request for an oath guarantee, which he was ready, willing, and able to supply. He instructs Abram to bring some animals, divide them in two (except for the two birds), and lay the halves opposite one other with a path between them. We cannot go into all the details here, but later in this scene the Lord himself passed between the parts of the animals in the form of "a smoking firepot with a blazing torch" (v. 17). For the Israelite readers of Moses' day this would have recalled the glory cloud with the pillar of fire in it by night that led them out of Egypt (Exod. 13:20–22; cf. also Exod. 14:19, 24; 24:16; 33:9–10; 34:5; 40:38; Num. 9:16; 12:5; 14:14; Deut. 1:33; Neh. 9:12, 19; Ps. 78:14; 99:7; 105:39; Isa. 4:5; 1 Cor. 10:1). As vv. 18–21 put it, "On that day the Lord made a covenant with Abram (כָּרַת יְהוָה אֶת־אַבְרָם בְּרִית) and said, 'To your descendants I give this land, from the Wadi of Egypt to the great river, the Euphrates—the land of the Kenites, Kenizzites, Kadmonites, . . .'" etc.

There is a parallel to this procedure in Jeremiah 34, where the Lord had a made a covenant with the people of that day to release the debts of the economically depressed within Israel. They violated their covenant commitment, so the Lord addresses them as "those who have violated my covenant and have not fulfilled the terms of the covenant they made before me." Therefore, he would treat them "like the calf they cut in two and then walked between its pieces" (Jer. 34:18). So "Their dead bodies will become food for the birds and the wild animals" (v. 20). You may recall that, when Abram cut the animals in two and set their parts across from each other in Genesis 15, the birds of prey came down and tried to eat the carcasses, "but Abram drove them away" (v. 11). The verb here means "to blow," probably suggesting a kind of blowing, whistling, hissing, or shewing sound. We are not certain, but it would seem that this chasing away of the birds symbolically represents enemies that would threaten the covenant between God and Israel, perhaps leading into the Egyptian threat in vv. 13–14.

The most likely interpretation of the rite as a whole is that when the Lord passed between the parts of the animals in the form of "a smoking firepot with a blazing torch" he was taking upon himself a self-curse to the effect that if he did not fulfill this covenant may the birds of prey consume his dead corpse, so to speak.[5] Although some are repulsed and react against this interpretation because it sounds sacrilegious to them,[6] in reality it is very much like what the Lord actually did when the Son of God died on the cross for our sins. Our Lord goes to great extremes in his commitment to redeem and restore us to himself. In Genesis 15 this was the Lord's way of solemnly swearing to Abram that his covenant commitment to giving the promised-land to his seed was absolute and guaranteed by the Lord himself.

The next statement of the Abrahamic covenant comes in Genesis 17. After an introduction the passage begins with something very similar to Genesis 12:1–3. God begins with two imperatives commanding Abram: "walk before me faithfully and be blameless" (v. 1b), and follows with purpose clauses, "in

---

5. See, e.g., the discussion in Claus Westermann, *Genesis 12-36: A Commentary*, trans. John J. Scullion S. J. (Minneapolis: Augsburg, 1985), 225, 228; Allen P. Ross, *Creation and Blessing: A Guide to the Study and Exposition of the Book of Genesis* (Grand Rapids: Baker, 1988), 312; and most recently, Tremper Longman III, *Genesis*, The Story of God Bible Commentary (Grand Rapids: Zondervan, 2016), 203–205.

Richard E. Averbeck, "The Egyptian Sojourn and Deliverance from Slavery in the Framing and Shaping of the Mosaic Law," in *"Did I Not Bring Israel Out of Egypt?" Biblical, Archaeological, and Egyptological Perspectives on the Exodus Narratives*, Bulletin of Biblical Research Monograph Series, eds. James Hoffmeier, et al. (Winona Lake, IN: Eisenbrauns, 2016), 146–47, points to the similarities between the terminology for covenant ratification rituals on the shores of Moab in Deuteronomy 29:9–15 and the similar terminology in Genesis 15 and Jeremiah 34 treated here.

6. See, e.g., G. J. Wenham, "The Symbolism of the Animal Rite in Genesis 15: A Response to G. F. Hasel, *JSOT* 19 (1981): 61–78 and Richard S. Hess, "The Slaughter of the Animals in Genesis 15: Genesis 15:18–21 and its Ancient Near Eastern Context," in *He Swore an Oath: Biblical Themes in Genesis 12–50*, eds. R. S. Hess, et al., second edition (Grand Rapids: Baker, 1994), 55–65 and the literature cited in those places. See also, e.g., Victor P. Hamilton, *The Book of Genesis Chapters 1–17*, NICOT (Grand Rapids: Eerdmans, 1990), 430–33 and 436–37.

order that I may institute my covenant (וְאֶתְּנָה בְרִיתִי) between me and you and greatly increase your numbers" (v. 2). After Abram fell down on his face, God proclaimed his covenant commitment to Abram, and even changed his name from Abram "exalted father" to Abraham "father of a multitude," in accordance with the promise just affirmed in v. 2b (cited just above). Abraham would become "the father of a multitude of nations" (v. 4). In vv. 6b–7 the Lord promises, "I will make you very fruitful; I will make nations of you, and kings will come from you. I will establish my covenant as a permanent covenant (לִבְרִית עוֹלָם) between me and you and your descendants (זַרְעֲךָ) after you for the generations to come, to be your God and the God of your descendants after you (וּלְזַרְעֲךָ אַחֲרֶיךָ)."

In the very next verse God proclaims, "The whole land of Canaan, where you now reside as a foreigner, I will give as a permanent possession (לַאֲחֻזַּת עוֹלָם) to you and your descendants after you (וּלְזַרְעֲךָ אַחֲרֶיךָ); and I will be their God" (v. 8). I have rendered עוֹלָם "permanent" in both verses to try to capture the effect of the passage. The point is that here both the seed promise and the land promise are said to be "permanent."

The promise of the land to Israel is in the forefront of this critical covenant passage. Some have argued that there are really two Abrahamic covenants, the one in Genesis 15 about the "great nation" Israel, promised in Genesis 12:2, and the other in Genesis 17 where the focus is on "all the peoples of the earth" in Genesis 12:3.[7] According to this view, Genesis 15 "was only the preliminary stage in God's unfolding plan of redemption."[8] The second stage is about "how Abraham, through the great nation descended from him, would mediate blessings to 'all peoples on earth,'" which is the focus of Genesis 17 and 22, according to this view. Moreover, the promises to Israel as a great nation will eventually be subsumed under the New Covenant in the new creation to come in Revelation 21 and 22.[9]

I have no objection to much of what is said in these works about the fact that God gave both national and universal promises to Abraham as both elements are in the text. The misstep comes when these authors argue that

---

7. Consider, for example, Paul R. Williamson, *Abraham, Israel and the Nations: The Patriarchal Promise and its Covenantal Development in Genesis*, JSOTSup 315 (Sheffield, England: Sheffield Academic Press, 2000); idem, *Sealed with an Oath: Covenant in God's Unfolding Purpose*, NSBT 23 (Downers Grove, IL: InterVarsity Press, 2007), 85–93 and 195–99; idem, "Covenant," in *Dictionary of the Old Testament: Pentateuch* (Downers Grove, IL: InterVarsity Press, 2003), 139–55; idem, "Covenant," in *NIV Study Bible*, second edition (Grand Rapids: Zondervan, 2015), 2646–48. Williamson is following the lead of his dissertation supervisor, T. Desmond Alexander, "Further Observations on the Term 'Seed' in Genesis," *Tyndale Bulletin* 48 (1997), 63–67, and "Royal Expectations in Genesis to Kings: Their Importance for Biblical Theology," *Tyndale Bulletin* 49 (1998): 191–212, esp. pp, 196–209; and most recently idem, *From Paradise to the Promised Land: An Introduction to the Pentateuch*, third edition (Grand Rapids: Baker, 2012), 134–72.

8. Williamson, *NIV Study Bible* second edition, 2646. I will use this concise statement of the position in the *NIV Study Bible* to highlight the main points and conclusions of this line of argument. Of course, his other sources cited in the previous note make the same point.

9. Ibid., 2647–48.

the national promises of seed and land in Genesis 12 and 15 give way to the universal promises to "all peoples on earth" (Gen. 12:3), which is ostensibly the distinct focus of Genesis 17 and 22. Accordingly, the conclusion is that the national promises are actually eliminated when the universal promises take the stage in the church.

However, the land promise to Israel extends from Genesis 12 to 15 to 17 and far beyond. As shown above, the Genesis 17 passage portrays the land promise as permanent in the same way as the seed promise. It is telling that those who argue for the elimination of the national promises to Israel rush past this point so quickly that it is hardly noticed in their treatment of the passage. This seems to be an attempt to muffle the text by saying, for example, "Even though the promise of nationhood is not altogether absent in Genesis 17 (cf. v. 8), stress is placed on 'nations,' 'kings,' and a perpetual divine-human relationship with Abraham's offspring (Gen. 17:4–8, 16–21)."[10] This position minimizes the importance of the promise of the land and does not do justice to the explicit emphasis in the text. It does not allow the focus of Genesis 15 to come to influence Genesis 17. Yet, the text clearly joins the promise of the "seed," and even the "universal" seed (v. 6), with the promise of the "land" (v. 8). The one is as permanent as the other.

Moreover, among many other passages, even the New Covenant passage in Jeremiah 31:31–37 highlights God's permanent commitment to Israel as a nation when he promises that his commitment to them as a nation is as enduring as his decrees for the sun, moon, and stars: "'Only if these decrees vanish from my sight,' declares the LORD, 'will Israel ever cease being a nation before me'" (v. 36, cf. the remarks on the Noahic covenant above). Unfortunately, we all too often interpret Jeremiah 31:31–34 without considering verses 35–37. The reality is that the promises of seed, land, as well as blessing to all the peoples of the earth, accumulate as the text progresses from the Book of Genesis onward. Some passages focus one of the promises, and others a combination of them.

Some units of the text use the terminology of covenant and some continue the language of the commission in Genesis 12. Genesus 22 is of the latter type. It is often referred to as the "Aqedah," for the verb used in Hebrew for the binding of Isaac in verse 9. The term "covenant" never appears in Genesis 22. Of course, as is well known, a passage does not need to use the actual term "covenant" for the concept to be invoked. However, in Genesis 22 the language explicitly recalls Genesis 12:1–3. For example, in Genesis 22:2a God commands Abraham, "Take *your son, your only son, whom you love—Isaac—*and *go forth* (וְלֶךְ־לְךָ) to the region of Moriah. Sacrifice him there as a burnt offering on a mountain I will show you." This recalls the very similar threefold progression and pattern found in Genesis 12:1a, "Go forth from your country, your people and your father's household." In both cases the intensity and the intimacy of what is at stake increases step by step.

---

10. Ibid., 2646.

Moreover, when Genesis 22:2 says "and go forth to the region of Moriah," it uses the same verbal expression as Genesis 12:1, לֶךְ־לְךָ "go forth." In Jewish circles today the Genesis 12 passage is also known as לֶךְ־לְךָ, and the connection to Genesis 22:2 gives shape to the whole unit of the Abrahamic narratives and the work of God in and through Abraham's life as a whole. Then at the end of the chapter it comes back again to the beginning of the Abraham narratives to tie it all together: "I will surely bless you and make your descendants as numerous as the stars in the sky and as the sand on the seashore. Your descendants will take possession of the cities of their enemies, and through your offspring all nations on earth will be blessed, because you have obeyed me" (Gen. 22:17–18).[11] The following verses (vv. 19–24) conclude the narrative with Abraham returning to Beersheba and, finally, a continuation of the genealogical line from Genesis 11:27–30, forming an inclusio for the unit as a whole, from Genesis 12–22. More could be said about the details, but the reason the land promise is not treated in Genesis 22 is not to deemphasize this part of the covenant, but because the seed is the focus in this passage. The land promise is not secondary and is still part of the long-term plan of God.

FROM ABRAHAM TO JESUS AND THE NEW COVENANT

So how do we get from Abraham to Jesus, the New Covenant, and the church? One of the best ways is to follow the historically progressive sequence of God's redemptive covenants from the Abrahamic covenant to the Mosaic, Davidic, and New covenants. I have found it useful to illustrate this with an "umbrella chart" designed to clarify the relationships and progressions from one to the next (see the figure below). The first one is the Abrahamic covenant. As noted above, the Noahic covenant is actually a covenant with all creation, and relates ultimately to the redemption of all creation in the new heaven and earth, something which the whole creation longs for. Romans 8:18–22 highlights this, and verse 23 binds this redemption of creation to the culmination of God's program of redemption for those whom God created in his own image and likeness: "we ourselves, who have the firstfruits of the Spirit, groan inwardly as we wait eagerly for our adoption to sonship, the redemption of our bodies." This brings us to the historical

---

11. Alexander's argument for "seed" as collective plural in Genesis 22:17a but singular in Genesis 22:17b–18, referring the singular line that leads ultimately to Christ, is highly questionable to say the least. He himself argues that "there is nothing here to indicate a change number" between 17b and 18, but this cuts both ways, since there is nothing here to indicate a change in number between 17a and 17b either. All the verbs are singular except when referring "all the nations of the earth" in v. 18a. Alexander's analysis presses too hard to find a way to drive a wedge between the national promises and the universal promises of God to Abraham. See his discussion in Alexander, "Further Observations on the Term Seed," 364–66 (cf. also idem, "Royal Expectations in Genesis and Kings," 202–203 and idem, *From Paradise to the Promised Land*, esp. pp. 153 and 171–72). His arguments are not convincing. Moreover, we do not need this interpretation of Genesis 22:17–18 to support the singular seed from generation to generation through the OT into the NT as a universal promise to Abraham. There is plenty of support for this truth elsewhere in Genesis, as Alexander himself and others have shown.

and sequential accumulation of the Abrahamic, Mosaic, Davidic, and New covenants as one important way of following the development of the pattern of God's redemptive plan for those who know him through the scriptures.

In the chart below, the Abrahamic Covenant is the overarching umbrella under which the Mosaic Covenant fits, and the Davidic Covenant fits under both the Mosaic and Abrahamic covenants. The New Covenant umbrella stretches out to include them all because it fulfills the promise that God would bless all the peoples of the earth through Abraham. The dotted lines down the sides of the chart from the earlier covenants to the New Covenant are intended to indicate that each of the three earlier covenants have continuity into the New Covenant. The diagonal lines through the cross at the peak of the New Covenant umbrella indicate that these earlier covenants come through into the New covenant in ways that are transformed in the New Covenant. Jesus the Messiah initiated and ratified this New Covenant for a new community of the faithful known as the church in the New Testament. However, many of the national features of the Old Testament covenants are not directly relevant to the church. Instead, the New Covenant people are not a nation in the usual sense of the word, but rather communities of faith proliferating among the nations.

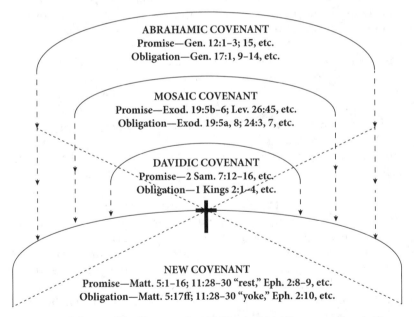

NOTE: Both "promise" (yielding peace) and "obligation" (yielding purpose) are built into the very organic nature of God's redemptive program. One makes no sense and will not work without the other. Our "rest" depends upon the combination of the two.

Under each umbrella there are passages cited to indicate that each of these covenants combines both promise and obligation, by which I mean *permanent* promise and *ongoing* obligation. It has been common, at least in some circles, to distinguish between conditional and unconditional covenants. The Abrahamic and Davidic covenants are often considered unconditional or grant covenants, and the Mosaic and sometimes the New Covenant are considered conditional or administrative covenants. There has been much written on this through the centuries and even in recent years. As it turns out, however, this is not a good way to treat the covenants. First, the text does not support it because, in some instances, the so-called unconditional covenants are articulated in the Bible as if they are conditional, and vice versa. Second, the ancient Near Eastern textual support that is often called forth to support this distinction cannot bear the weight that some scholars have put upon it.[12]

God engages in covenant relationship with his people through a combination of permanent promise and ongoing obligation. Permanent promise assures those who know him of his covenant faithfulness to them. Ongoing obligation challenges those who know him to live in reciprocal covenant faithfulness. Both are essential to the way God enacts a covenant relationship with us in our fallen condition.

God made the Abrahamic Covenant with the head of a family, so it was a family-level covenant meant to regulate and guide a family as they walked with the Lord. By the time God delivered the Israelites from Egypt, however, the family had grown into a nation, so the Mosaic Covenant became a national covenant. It was designed to guide and regulate the nation in their relationship with the Lord. Similarly, the Davidic Covenant fits under both the Abrahamic and Mosaic covenants. The *family* had grown into a *nation* that needed a *king*. So this adds a dynastic element to the covenant program. The Davidic kings were expected to have Abrahamic faith in the Lord and rule the nation according to the law of Moses. In fact, according to Deuteronomy 17:18–20, when a new king ascended to the throne he was to write his own copy of the law under the supervision of the Levitical priests so that he could read and study the law all the days of his life, and rule according to it.

We cannot discuss all the various passages of scripture this chart is intended to illustrate. Four key points are essential to the present discussion. The first has to do with the OT law and the relationship to the New Covenant believer in Jesus the Christ, whether Jew or Gentile. We will treat the New Covenant passage in Jeremiah 31:31–37 in more detail below, but for now it is important to recognize that the law of God in the Mosaic law is anything but left behind in the New Covenant: "I will put My law within them and on their heart I will write it" (Jer. 31:33). He has done essentially the same thing with circumcision, which was instituted under the Abrahamic covenant: "circumcision is circumcision of the heart, by the Spirit, not by the written code" (Rom. 2:29; cf. Gal. 5:6 with Lev. 26:41; Deut. 10:16; Jer. 4:4).

---

12. See, e. g., the critique and the literature cited in Gary N. Knoppers, "Ancient Near Eastern Royal Grants and the Davidic Covenant: A Parallel?" *JAOS* 116 (1996): 670–97.

So what does the apostle Paul mean when he writes that we are not "under the law" (e.g., 1 Cor. 9:20; Gal. 3:23, 25; 4:4–5, 21, etc.)? To begin with, it means that we are no longer under "the curse of the Law" (Gal. 3:13, cf. v. 10). The law cannot condemn us because we have been justified by God by accepting by faith the work of Jesus Christ on the cross. Moreover, the law was never designed to give anyone spiritual life in the first place: "For if a law had been given that could impart life, then righteousness would certainly have come by the law" (Gal. 3:21). The law was given as a guide to those who already had Abrahamic faith, whether in the OT or the NT. Paul refers to it as a "tutor" (Gal. 3:24–25), and we are no longer "under" a tutor.

Furthermore, spiritual life comes through the work of the Holy Spirit in the person who has Abrahamic faith. From a biblical point of view, Abraham kept the law as a man of faith (Gen. 15:6) before the law was even given: "Abraham obeyed Me and kept My charge, My commandments, My statutes and My laws" (Gen. 26:5; cf. Deut. 6:2; 11:1; etc.).[13] Similarly, we keep the law as people of Abrahamic faith (Gal. 3:14) even as we are not "under the law." As Paul puts it later in Galatians 5:14, "For the entire law is fulfilled in keeping this one command: 'Love your neighbor as yourself.'" Of course, this goes back to Jesus' two great commandments (see Matt. 22:34–40 and parallels) and is part of "the law of Christ" as Paul labels it in 1 Corinthians 9:21, "To those not having the law I became like one not having the law (though I am not free from God's law but am under Christ's law). . . ." The "law of Christ" is the way the OT law is mediated to us in Christ in an internalized way, described in Scripture as "written on the heart." When Jesus gave the two great commandments, both of which come from the OT law itself, he added at the end, "All the Law and the Prophets hang on these two commandments" (Matt. 22:40). God has always desired the same from everyone: a love for God and a love for people. The Ten Commandments and the entirety of the law given in the Pentateuch are all about how to live out the two great commandments as a nation of Abrahamic believers in ancient context.

As noted above, the diagonal dotted lines that cross through the covenant chart indicate that the Old Testament covenants and their features enter the New Covenant transformed by the work of the Messiah on the cross, the coming of the Spirit on Pentecost, and the nature of the New Covenant community of faith. Changes were made because the laws of the national covenant with Israel do not match the needs and nature of a community of faith. In fact, even in the Old Testament, the law itself changes within the Pentateuch, especially to manage situational shifts that took place when the life of Israel in the wilderness shifted to the life of Israel in the land after the conquest. See, for example, Leviticus 17 where all eating of meat was limited

---

13. See, e.g., the remarks in Longman, *Genesis*, 341–42; Ross, *Creation and Blessing*, 458–59. Moses wrote the Law long after Abraham was dead, but since he was a righteous man before God in his own day, he could be labeled a keeper of the law in terms that the later Israelite readers, who had the Law in their day, would have understood.

to animal sacrifice at the tabernacle while they were in the wilderness, but this had to change when they were spread out in the land after the conquest, according to Deuteronomy 12, so "profane slaughter" for eating meat was instituted, just as long as they did not eat the blood of the slaughtered animal but poured it out on the ground (Deut. 12:15–25).[14] The law always included a degree of flexibility in order to meet the needs of the covenant people for whom the Law guided their life of Abrahamic faith. This is true in the New Testament as well.

The second key point comes from Leviticus 26:40–45, the conclusion to the blessings and curses of the Mosaic covenant made at Sinai. The Mosaic covenant fits under the Abrahamic umbrella because there would be no Mosaic covenant if it were not for the covenant commitment God made to Israel's patriarchal fathers. The assumption is that the nation of Israel would consist of a people known for their Abrahamic faith. Of course, historically, this was not the case, which is the reason the prophets so often railed against the chosen people with oracles of judgment. Leviticus 26 anticipates the time when Israel would violate the Mosaic covenant so severely that they would be banished from the Holy Land and taken into exile. In hindsight, we know the above passage has the Babylonian captivity in mind. The passage begins this way:

> But if [when they are in captivity] they will confess their sins and the sins of their ancestors—their unfaithfulness and their hostility toward me, which made me hostile toward them so that I sent them into the land of their enemies—then when their uncircumcised hearts are humbled and they pay for their sin, I will remember my covenant with Jacob and my covenant with Isaac and my covenant with Abraham, and I will remember the land (Lev. 26:40–42).

The passage reminds us that even when the Jewish people are in captivity because of their sin, the Lord will still remain committed to the covenant he made with the Patriarchs through the Abrahamic covenant. The passage continues:

> For the land will be deserted by them and will enjoy its sabbaths while it lies desolate without them. They will pay for their sins because they rejected my laws and abhorred my decrees (Lev. 26:43).

Since the children of Israel had not have given the land its seventh-year sabbatical rest, they would spend a commensurate amount of time in captivity. The land will then enjoy its sabbatical years all at once. The passage concludes with this reminder:

---

14.   See Richard E. Averbeck, "The Cult in Deuteronomy and Its Relationship to the Book of the Covenant and the Holiness Code," *Sēpher Tôrat Mōšeh: Studies in the Interpretation of Deuteronomy*, eds. Daniel I. Block and Richard L. Schultz. Peabody, MA: Hendrickson, 2017), 235–36, 239–41, 254–56.

> Yet in spite of this, when they are in the land of their enemies, I will not reject them or abhor them so as to destroy them completely, breaking my covenant with them. I am the Lord their God. But for their sake I will remember the covenant with their ancestors whom I brought out of Egypt in the sight of the nations to be their God. I am the Lord' " (Lev. 26:44–45).

The covenant that God made when he brought their ancestors out of Egypt was the Mosaic Covenant, which will break. Yet, he still will not destroy them completely, even when they break their covenant with him. God would remain committed to his covenant. Our God is not a fickle God and remains faithful to his covenant people even when they are not faithful, but also chastises them when necessary. In this sense, the Mosaic Covenant is just as permanent as the Abrahamic. How could it be otherwise, since the people of the Mosaic Covenant were the descendants of Abraham and heirs of that covenant as well?

This brings us to a third key point. The Lord's promises to Abraham's seed in the Abrahamic and Mosaic covenants continue through the New Covenant era. Although the Mosaic Covenant itself does not continue because of the shift to the New Covenant explicit in the move from Jeremiah 31:31 to verse 32 (the New Covenant is "*not* like the covenant which I made with their fathers in the day I took them by the hand to bring them out of the land of Egypt"), the same passage highlights the importance of God's permanent covenant commitment to Israel.

The New Covenant itself is articulated in Jeremiah 31:31–34 and initiated by Jesus through his death, burial, and resurrection (see, e.g., Luke 22:20; cf. 1 Cor. 11:25):

> "The days are coming," declares the LORD,
>> "when I will make a new covenant with the people of Israel
>>> and with the people of Judah.
> *It will not be* like the covenant I made with their ancestors
>> when I took them by the hand to lead them out of Egypt, . . .
> "This is the covenant I will make with the people of Israel after that time,"
>> declares the LORD.
> "I will put my law in their minds and write it on their hearts.
> I will be their God, and they will be my people.
> No longer will they teach their neighbor, or say to one another, 'Know the LORD,'
>> because they will all know me. . . .

As noted above, from the point of view of this important passage, God's law in the Mosaic covenant is written on the heart of the New Covenant believer. It is not left behind, although it has been transformed in order to guide the New Covenant believer into all righteousness as a Jewish or Gentile follower of Christ who lives in the church.

Furthermore, the point that is most important to our discussion here actually comes from the verses that immediately follow:

This is what the LORD says, he who appoints the sun to shine by day,
    who decrees the moon and stars to shine by night,
    who stirs up the sea so that its waves roar— the LORD Almighty is his name:
"Only if these decrees vanish from my sight," declares the LORD,
    "will Israel *ever cease* being *a nation* before me."
This is what the LORD says: "*Only if the heavens above can be measured*
    and the foundations of the earth below be searched out
    will I reject all the descendants of Israel because of all they have done,"
    declares the LORD (Jer. 31:35–37).

Even in the New Covenant era, the Lord continues to emphasize the permanence of his covenant commitment to Israel as a nation. It extends throughout redemptive history. This commitment to Israel as a nation endures as long as God's commitment to maintaining the natural order (cf. Gen. 8:22).

CONCLUSION

This essay comes to a close with a look at a fourth key point based in Romans 9–11. In Romans 9:4–5, amid his great anguish about the fact that most of the Jews had rejected the Gospel, Paul lists a number of great works of redemptive grace God has historically worked through Israel, including the covenants: "Theirs is the adoption to sonship; theirs the divine glory, *the covenants*, the receiving of the law, the temple worship and *the promises*. Theirs are *the patriarchs*, and from them is traced the human ancestry of the Messiah, who is God over all, forever praised! Amen." He then makes note of the fact that "not all who are descended from Israel are Israel. Nor because they are his descendants are they all Abraham's children" (Rom. 9:6–7). His basic point is that not all of the Israelites had Abrahamic faith, which was the main point of concern in the redemptive covenant sequence from the start (Gen. 15:6). He follows with a long explanation of how this has all happened.

Then in Romans 11 he turns to the situation in his own day as it relates to Jews and Gentiles, and the kingdom of God. A few salient points from this chapter will be sufficient. The first point the apostle Paul makes here is that there is a remnant of the Jews already in the church. He is one of them. "What the people of Israel sought so earnestly they did not obtain. The elect among them did, but the others were hardened" (v. 7). That's the second point: By and large, the Jews were temporarily hardened, so that "salvation has come to the Gentiles" (v. 11). He likens the kingdom of the redeemed to an olive tree: "some of the (natural) branches [Jews] have been broken off, and you [Gentiles], though a wild olive shoot, have been grafted in among the others and now share in the nourishing sap from the olive root" (v. 17). These Gentile branches have been grafted in only because of their faith and they need to remember this: "You do not support the root, but the root supports you" (v. 18).

Finally, "if they do not persist in unbelief, they will be grafted in, for God is able to graft them in again" (v. 23). After all, they are the natural branches. They belong attached to the tree. Paul continues, "I do not want you to be ignorant of this *mystery*, brothers and sisters, so that you may not be conceited: Israel has experienced a hardening in part until the full number of the Gentiles has come in, and in this way *all Israel will be saved*" (vv. 25–26). The meaning of "all Israel" is much debated. Some have gone back to Romans 9 to find the meaning, since there we find the notion that not all Israel is the true Israel of the faith of Abraham. But in Romans 11, Paul has already made the point that there is a remnant of Jewish believers in Jesus already joined to the church. He is speaking of the so-called "natural branches," the Jewish people, being grafted back in. This is more than a remnant.

There is a "mystery" here according to verse 25. The term used is the same as that the same apostle Paul used in Ephesians 3 for the "mystery" of the church that was not known to previous generations. That mystery is the inclusion of the Gentiles as heirs of God's kingdom work through the Jews. No one saw that coming in the way God made it happen through Jesus. The Book of Acts attests to this. Here in Romans 11, the mystery is reversed. It is about grafting the Jews back into their own kingdom tree. How will God do this, and what will it look like? I suspect that we will all be surprised. The following verses, however, make it clear that it is accordance with God's previous covenant commitments: "As far as the gospel is concerned, they are enemies for your sake; but as far as election is concerned, they are loved on account of the patriarchs, for God's gifts and his call are irrevocable" (vv. 28–29).

In my view, based on the analysis of Abrahamic Covenant promise texts and other covenant texts presented above, this will include the land promises since they are as "irrevocable" as the seed promises. It goes hand in hand with the promise that through Abraham's seed shall all the peoples of the earth be blessed. Ultimately, this Israel will be made up of those who have put their faith in Jesus Christ, their Messiah, the Son of God, and the Savior of both Jews and Gentiles. As the apostle Paul put it, this is the Gospel, the "Good News," which is "the power of God that brings salvation to everyone who believes: first to the Jew, then to the Gentile" (Rom. 1:17).

ISRAEL AND HER NEIGHBORS: ISAIAH 19

WALTER C. KAISER, JR.

INTRODUCTION TO THE PROPHECY ABOUT EGYPT

NO OTHER NATION ON THE FACE OF THE EARTH is so bound up with the history of Israel and the kingdom of God through the ages as the nation of Egypt. There are in excess of seven hundred references to Egypt in the Bible, with some 125 of those references found alone in the formula: "I am the LORD your God who brought you up from the land of Egypt."

This passage in Isaiah 19 preserves for us one of the most amazing expressions, not only of international understanding found in the Bible, but one that specifically envisages the divine use of heavy judgment on that nation for the purpose of bringing about that nation's healing and conversion as a people.

Isaiah 19 is found in the midst of a group of prophecies to ten nations in Isaiah 13–23. Very little attention is usually given to the twenty-five chapters dealing with prophecies to these nations in the three major prophets of Isaiah, Jeremiah, and Ezekiel (Isa. 13–23; Jer. 46–51; Ezek. 25–32). All told, fourteen nations are mentioned in 680 verses and twenty-five chapters, which total more verses than in all of the Pauline prison epistles in the New Testament. How, then, can believers today afford to neglect what God had to say in these passages?

But how shall we interpret these passages dealing with Gentile nations other than Israel? Most have treated this chapter in a symbolical, mystical, or even in an allegorical way. Thus the early Church Fathers, Eusebius, Cyril, Jerome, and Calvin in Reformation times saw this chapter as depicting the conversion of Egypt to Christianity. Later, the Reformed theologian named Cocceius (1603–1669) understood "Egypt" to mean "Rome" or the "Roman Empire," and therefore took the chapter as a synopsis of all of Church History from the conversion of Constantine to the end of this age! Martin Luther went in the opposite direction: "Egypt" stood for the idolatry of the Roman Church. But all this time, there stood the nation of "Egypt," waiting for a straightforward interpretation.

But notice the Biblical context for these prophecies against these nations. They are enveloped or bracketed on the front side before Isaiah 13 with the Book of Immanuel in chapters 7–12, which describes the First Advent of our Lord, while chapter 23 (the last of the eleven chapters of Isaiah 13–23) is followed by the Little Apocalypse or the Little Book of Revelation in chapters 24–27. Surely that signals that this great collection of prophecies to the nations is not one that is completed some time in past history, but is one that encompasses God's work in the last days. The scope of God's purpose, therefore, is as inclusive as the entire universe and as specific as all the families and nations on this globe—especially for those specified by name! The Bible does not indulge in wasteful and foolish banter when it opens the first eleven chapters of Genesis with its worldwide scope and its build-up of naming some seventy particular nations in Genesis 10. Neither has the Bible wasted its space later on by devoting twenty-five of its precious chapters in the writings of these three prophets of God's concern for Israel to be a light to all of the rest of the nations of the world.

The magnitude of the scope and details of God's plan for the nations and empires that have been part of "His-story" of salvation, which God sent at first through one woman, Eve, and then through one man, Abraham, is finally fully fleshed out in Daniel 2 and 7, where the four great empires on earth are portrayed over against the coming, but final rule and reign of our Sovereign Lord.

A Short History of Egypt. Egypt is a nation with a history dating all the way back to 4000 BC or more! The last native dynasty/house of the Pharaohs fell in 341 BC to the Persians, who themselves were later replaced by the Greeks, Romans, Byzantines and Arabs. At first the Greek Macedonians ruled through the Ptolemies for three hundred years, to about thirty years before the first coming of Christ, when it became a province of the Roman Empire, only to come later under the rule of Constantinople in AD 641 as the Saracens ruled. In 1250 the Mamelukes (a military caste of Caucasian origin) took over and brought on one of Egypt's cruelest periods of history. Finally in 1517, Egypt became tributary to the Turks, with the Mamelukes still exercising oppressive power. In 1882 British rule came as the Turkish Sultan was deposed and exiled from Egypt. King Farouk began his reign in April 28, 1936. Gamel Abder Nasser led a military junta in a bloodless coup in July 23, 1952. He was the oldest of four sons with a father of pure Arabian stock, so he too was not of pure Egyptian extraction. He died in 1970, and Vice President Anwar Sadat replaced him, only to be assassinated on October 6, 1981. Hosni Mubarak replaced him and several times escaped assassination himself. Mubarak resigned as president on February 14, 2011, in the Egyptian Revolution of 2011. The vacant office was fulfilled by the chairman of the Supreme Council of the Armed Forces, Field Marshall Mohammed Hussein Tantawi. Mohamed Morsi took office on June 30, 2012, after he was elected by the people. However, he too was deposed in a *coup d'etat* on July 3, 2013 with masses of Egyptians calling for his resignation.

He was succeeded by Adly Mansour, the head of the Supreme Constitutional Court of Egyptian July 4, 2013. On July 8, 2014 Abdel Fattah el-Sisi took office as president, whose mandate expires on June 8, 2018.

I. AN ANNOUNCEMENT OF GOD'S JUDGMENT (19:1)

The first verse of this chapter states the theme of the passage: The Lord will execute judgment on the nation of Egypt. The message is called the "burden of Egypt," for it carries a heavy word of judgment that will spell out, at least at first, a grievous word for that people over whom it is announced. The word "burden"[1] occurs in prophetic speeches twenty-seven times, usually threatening some act of judgment. Others rendered it as "oracle," but it is never followed by the genitive of the speaker, such as "the word of the Lord."

The fact that the Lord is "rid[ing] on a swift cloud" as he comes to Egypt is an analogy that often appears with divine epiphanies in the Bible (cf. Deut. 33:26; Ps. 18:11 [Eng 10]; 68:34 [Eng 33]; 104:3), a phrase that is also used in the Ugaritic tablets from Syria of the Canaanite storm god, Baal. But whatever the original source of the expression, it certainly signaled a coming storm.

The idols are graphically depicted as fearing and trembling before him as they at least begin to totter and wobble on their bases of their pedestals, or fall over before the strong storm winds that accompany the clouds. The Hebrew word used for the "idols" is literally the "nothings;" they are regarded as nonentities in every sense of the word. Then even the "hearts of the Egyptians melt within them." In the face of this onslaught, finally as the Egyptians sense their powerlessness, their hearts begin to dissolve, for they sense the approaching storm signals the divine judgment from God, as if he rode on a literal war chariot.

II. THREE DISASTERS ANNOUNCED OVER EGYPT (19:2-15)

A. A Political Disaster (19:2–4)

It would appear that internal strife, civil war, and anarchy break out as Egyptian city goes to war with Egyptian city, as neighbor goes out against neighbor, and kingdom (or "nome" as they were called in Egypt) tangles with kingdom (v. 2). The Egyptians begin to lose their way as they see their plans evaporate into nothing. The only alternative that seems to be left for them is to go to the netherworld and see if any wisdom can be obtained from consulting "spirits of the dead," "mediums, or spiritists."

For a people who were so renown for the gift of wisdom (1 Kings 4:30), it is amazing to see them reduced to depending on the spirit world for information and wisdom. Bereft of the shrewd wisdom given to them by God as a gift of common grace, they act as if they are at their wits' end. So depressed is

---

1.   See Walter C. Kaiser, Jr., "Nasi," in *Theological Wordbook of the Old Testament*, eds. R. Laird Harris, Gleason L. Archer, Jr., Bruce K. Waltke, 2 vols. (Chicago: Moody Press, 2003) 2:601–602.

the nation that it descends into magical quackery as a new, but false, source of wisdom.

Finally God hands Egypt over into "the power of a cruel master and a fierce king" (v 4). There is no word given on the identity of this person, but he does not seem to be a conqueror, but apparently some type of national Egyptian despot. No other clues are given as to who he is or will be, so it will be no good to try to guess who he is until he appears.

B. An Economic Disaster (19:5–10).

No factor was as important to the life of Egypt than the Nile River. It was literally the life-stream of the nation. The references to the water, streams, the deep, sea, water courses, channels, and/or the Nile in the three chapters in Isaiah 18–20, dealing the prophecies of the Egypto-Ethiopian kingdom, mount up to forty-five different references to the Nile and related bodies of water. No wonder that Herodotus said that Egypt was indeed the "gift of the Nile."

Amazingly, however, verse 5 says that "the waters of the river will dry up and the riverbed will be parched and dry." However, each year, for time and memoriam, the Nile River has faithfully flooded the Nile Valley, that is until the Aswan Dam was completed in 1971 at the first cataract on the Nile at Aswan, Egypt. Previously, on average, an annual deposit of 130 million tons of rich soil spilled over the banks of the Nile River to provide rich soil for a country that depended on agriculture as some of its top exports.

However, with the construction of the new dam, it was hoped that the newly created Lake Nasser that backed up south behind the dam would supply enough hydroelectrical power to take Egypt into the modern era as a new industrial nation, and that the water itself would irrigate a million acres of land. The dam itself is truly a modern marvel, for it is many times higher than the tallest pyramid in Egypt (which is more than 750 feet tall) and took eleven years to build at the cost of nearly $1 billion. The dam required forty million cubic meters of rock-filled material, and a workforce of 35,000 workers to construct it.

However, Aswan Dam has ever since been an ecological and an economical disaster. For example, because of the winds blowing over the surface of the five-hundred-mile-mile long Lake Nasser, desiccation on the surface of the lake and mud build up on its bottom continues to grow at the rate of 100 million tons of silt a year—both factors together meaning that the dam will probably never fill up with water as had been planned. Meanwhile, below the dam, the Nile River floor has been scoured, lowering the water table as it deepens the bottom of the river. Meanwhile, the lack of silt at the mouth of the river in the Mediterranean Sea, from the now trapped mud behind the dam, has left serious erosion with the result that salt water from the Mediterranean Sea has deeply invaded the fresh water of the river. Likewise, the former run off branches and channels leading to the Nile are now left dry and have helped spread malaria and a parasite known as schistosomiasis, which gets into the bloodstream causing exhaustion (and often death in some cases) in one of every ten Egyptians today (19:6).

The dam has also affected the fishing, linen and cotton exports as each was severely reduced in output by issues caused by the dam (19:7–10). For example, with erosion at the mouth of the Nile, saltwater has flowed into the Nile and the Sardine exports have shrunken. With high irrigation, there has come a salt build up in the soil and thereby affected the crops and the need for commercial fertilizers.

C. An Intellectual Disaster (19:11–15)

Whereas in the past "officials" and "counselors" have given wise advice and exhibited wisdom, the national gift of God's grace to Egypt, suddenly the wise men of Egypt appear to be little more than "fools" who "give sense-less advice" (19:11). The "princes of Zoan" (vv. 11, 13; an ancient capital of Egypt in the northeastern part of the delta, also known as Tanis, the city nearest Palestine) and the "wise counselors of Pharaoh," previously renowned for their gift of wisdom (1 Kings 4:30) are no match for the judgments from God. The idea of "folly" forms an inclusion in verses 11 and 13.

Those who formerly were regarded as wise can no longer read the signs of the times. No longer are they able to see the foolishness of their own actions and advice. No one seems to be able to show them or to disclose what the Lord Almighty has planned to do in Egypt (v. 12). "Memphis" (also called Noph) was another former capital in southern Egypt, near Cairo; thus, from one end of the former centers of government to the other (north to south), everyone is stymied and looks downright stupid.

The reason for this is that the Lord has imparted "a spirit of dizziness" or bewilderment among the people of Egypt (vv. 14–15). All her leaders "stagger," as they have no idea which way to turn. They cannot tell one end from the other (v. 15). In the permissive will of God, he allows the presumed wisdom of Egypt's leaders and wise men to backfire. Nothing works! No one knows a way of escape.

III. A BRIDGE SECTION: TRANSITION FROM JUDGMENT TO DELIVERANCE (19:16–17)

The events of the final section of chapter 19 all seem to be set "in that day." Six times (vv. 16, 18, 19, 21, 22, 24) the prophet clearly sets the action he is to announce as commencing in the end of times in the eschaton, the last days or time of the end. To look for a final fulfillment in history past would be to overlook the sixfold signal given in the text.

Two events signal a shift in history. First, Egypt will "shudder with fear at the uplifted hand of the Lord" (v. 16). In place of respect and fear for their idols, it is the "Lord Almighty" whom they shall now fear. That surely makes a major change.

The second major shift in history is that "the land of Judah will bring terror to the Egyptians" (v. 17). Here is a strange statement indeed. For more than two thousand years and more, Egypt was never afraid of Judah. What is more, Judah did not even exist as an independent kingdom for most of that time. But the earliest event that could possibly fit this situation was probably the Six-Day War from June 5–10, 1967, or perhaps even prior to that, Israel's invasion of Egypt's Sinai Peninsula on October 29, 1956. For the first time Egypt had to call on the world's powers to help them against the armies of Israel. But note that it is not the people of Israel or Judah that are the cause of Egypt's terror; it is from the Lord himself and from the land of Judah—where the Lord will have his seat of his universal kingdom in Zion—that the deepest of terrors arises.

IV. FIVE ANNOUNCEMENTS OF SALVATION AND DELIVERANCE FOR EGYPT (19:18-25)

It must be kept in mind that each of the five paragraphs that follow are set "in that day," a time of judgment and salvation in connection with the second coming of our Lord. [2]

A. God Plans for the Conversion of Egypt (19:18)
A time in the future is coming when "five cities in Egypt will speak the language of Canaan." It is not altogether certain whether this refers to Egypt's startling allegiance to Yahweh or if it means there will be a large number of Jews in Egypt, but the text is about the Egyptians. It is true that during the Hellenistic period of Alexander the Great, the Greek language became the lingua Franca of Egypt, as it did for Israel/Canaan. Was that but a foretaste of a coming revival that Egypt would experience in the future? But the amazing thing is that the Egyptians will "swear allegiance to the LORD Almighty." This seems to speak of coming revival to the modern nation of Egypt—which had, of course, been a Christian nation up to the fourth Christian century.

One of the five Egyptian cities is mentioned by name, "The city of Destruction," but a number of versions, including the Dead Sea Scrolls, would more correctly appear to read "City of the Sun," which would be the city of Heliopolis. The difference between the two names in Hebrew is only one letter.

B. God Plans to Receive Worship from Egypt and Send a Deliverer (19:19–20)
The Egyptians would erect a pillar at the border of their land as a "sign" and a "witness" to the fact that the Lord Almighty was indeed in their land. This pillar has the feel about it that the Statue of Liberty has for Americans, which greets them and their visitors as they come into the New York harbor.

---

2. See For full definition of "Day of the Lord," Walter C. Kaiser, Jr, "The Arrival of the Day of the Lord," Joel 2:28–3:21," in Preaching and Teaching the Last Things, Old Testament Eschatology for the Life of the Church," Grand Rapids, MI.: Baker Academic, 2011, pp. 77–88.

Surely it will be erected by the Egyptians to commemorate some great future meeting that they will have had by that time with God. No such pillar or memorial, however, currently exists as yet.

The altar that will be placed in the heart of the land of Egypt signals worship of the Lord God himself. This would be a sign that the request for God's provision of forgiveness and the worship of him alone will be another new change in this nation.

Finally, they will also cry out for "a savior and defender" (v. 20) to deliver them, just as God did for Israel in the days of the judges send to Israel one judge after another to deliver them. This "savior and defender" would seem to be the counter-mover to the "cruel master, and a fierce king" (v. 4).

C. God Plans to Make Himself Known throughout All Egypt (19:21–22)

As the Lord makes himself known in Egypt, this nation that has been an Islamic nation since AD 640 will suddenly turn and acknowledge the Lord God who made them and provided redemption for them. Similar to Zephaniah 2:11 and Malachi 1:11, the persons who are now offering sacrifices to God are not the priests in Jerusalem, but believers all across the face of the globe are worshipping the Lord, as the Egyptians symbolized and as Scriptures clearly foretold in advance of it happening.

Even though Egypt will have experienced the revival fires of conversion, there still will be a need for dealing with their residual sins. Thus the "LORD will strike Egypt with a plague," but he will "heal them" (v. 22). Just as God had promised he would do for Israel in Leviticus 26:44, so Egypt too will receive the same blessings from God.

D. God Plans to Bring Iraqis and Egyptians Together to Worship Him (19:23)

The fourth promised act of deliverance that God announced here is that he will make a "highway from Egypt to Assyria," which today is modern Iraq. But what is meant here goes beyond the existence of an international roadway that connects the old Mesopotamian Valley nation with Egypt; it no doubt included trade and cultural interaction, but now it would involve especially the joint worship of these three nations, who have had a record of bitter hostility and violence with one another throughout history.

Imagine representatives of currently Muslim countries participating in joint worship services to the Lord God of Israel! The direction of the flow of worshipers will go in both directions: from Iraq to Egypt and from Egypt to Iraq—and both with Israel!

E. God Plans to Make Egypt, Israel, and Iraq a Blessing to All the World (19:24–25)

This final announcement seems to be more breathtaking than all of the previous promises: These same three nations who up to this point in history have been at such terrible odds with each other and the great disturbers of the peace of the rest of the world will turn around and suddenly become a blessing on earth (v. 24). What is more, God will bless each of the three nations individually. He will call Egypt "My people;" Assyria/ Iraq will be named "My handiwork;" and Israel will be known by God as "My inheritance," v. 25). Those are names that had at one time or another been the exclusive names for Israel, but now were being shared with her former enemies!

We are familiar with the call of Abraham, where God promised that he and his descendants would be a blessing to all the nations/families of the earth (Gen. 12:3), but now God promises something similar to these three former bitter enemies who will now be "third[s]" together in the kingdom of God. Amazing!

Instead, God now uses names he had previously reserved for Israel/Judah to describe the other two nations. Thus, Israel was the "work of [God's] hands" in Isaiah 43:1, 15; 44:2, 24; 45:11, including Deuteronomy 32:6; Psalm 100:3. In the same way Israel had been declared God's "inheritance" in Deuteronomy 4:20; Psalm 28:9; 47:5; 94:5; Micah 7:14. But these titles are now shared with Israel's former enemies "in that day."

CONCLUSION

The picture God paints as to what will happen in the final days as we come into the days leading up to the millennium are startling, to say the least. The three formerly deadlocked nations, set on seeing at least the complete genocide of Israel, will be changed by the grace of God to function as a blessing to all the world. The harvest of Gentile nations will be as great as the harvest in those last days when all Israel will be saved as well (Rom. 11:26).

God will include all the nations of the world in his triumph. Even Egypt, that hostile and bitter nation, that was once most hospitable to Israel, will be converted in the end times as Jews and Arabs go to the house of God together. What a day that will be!

ISRAEL AND THE STORY OF THE BIBLE

MARK YARBROUGH

After a recent trek to the movie theatre, my kids returned home raving about the flick. I asked them to describe it at a *high level*—reminding them to be careful to avoid the needed "spoiler alert," nor to divulge the cinematic magic that made it so grand in their eyes. After pondering how to do that, my son said with a wily grin: "Here's the scoop, Dad. They introduced us to the characters; then there was a problem. The problem was addressed; then it was all resolved." Then he winked and said, "Is that high-level enough?" Fresh off a high school English lit class, he knew what he was doing. In one breath he described, at its macro-structure, what is true about *any* movie, play, or novel—there is a general pattern to most every chronicled account. That is one of the reasons we all love stories; they stick with us and penetrate our hearts in unexplainable ways. N. T. Wright is correct: "Tell someone to do something and you change their life—for a day; tell someone a story and you change their life."[1]

THE BIG PICTURE AS OVERVIEW

Whether it is an aerial view of real estate, a lookout tower at a national park trail, or a box top to a puzzle, seeing the big picture allows one to have a framework for the whole. It helps frame the voyage, but it does not present the details that direct the nuances of the movement. However, it paints instructively a picture of the general direction. And that is extremely valuable in regard to the Bible.

Recent attention in evangelical work has focused on articulating how the Bible is one contiguous account, connected together with skill, and presented in a cohesive manner. A host of material, including digital production, attempts to tell the Bible succinctly, yet with continuity. Just search on "The Bible Story" on the Internet, and you will find hundreds of professional works intent on communicating the grand narrative of Scripture. One such

---

1. N. T. Wright, *The New Testament and the People of God* (Minneapolis: Fortress, 1992), 40..

production, *The Greatest Story Ever Told—The Whole Bible in 3 Minutes*, produced by Gateway Service, presents an animated account of the Bible covering the primary biblical acts from Genesis to Revelation.[2]

A vast array of books and articles also have been written in an attempt to explore this topic.[3] In their book, *Living God's Word: Discovering Our Place in the Great Story of Scripture*, J. Scott Duvall and J. Daniel Hays make this connection to the grand narrative of Scripture:

> Your typical story opens with things going well. The author introduces the characters, gives us the necessary background information, and sets the scene. Generally, everything is good at the beginning. Then a problem or crisis arises that threatens one or more of the characters. Much of the story focuses on solving the problem (i.e., conflict resolution). Usually during the resolution phrase there is a climax where everything rushes to a critical point and the overall story turns in one direction or the other. Finally, the resolution is worked out so that, in the end, things are even better than they were in the beginning. Not all stories work this way, but many do. If there is no happy ending, we label the story a tragedy. Here is how the Bible unfolds as a Great Story:

- Opening—Genesis 1–2
- Problem—Genesis 3–11
- Resolution—Genesis 12 through Revelation 18
- Climax to resolution—The life, ministry, death, and resurrection of Jesus Christ
- Closing—Revelation 19–22[4]

Others have noted that the whole of Christian theology, and in particular the grand message of the Christian story, has mirrored a traditional "hero cycle."[5] In this regard, Holsteen and Svigel state,

> With the same foundational pattern, storytellers throughout history have gripped their audiences by tapping into universal experiences—elements common to most or all individual cultures:

---

2. See https://www.youtube.com/watch?v=niCJoqY_IGw&t=13s

3. See D. A. Carson, *The God Who Is There: Finding Your Place in God's Story* (Grand Rapids: Baker Books, 2010); Tim Chester, *From Creation to New Creation: Making Sense of the Whole Bible Story* (Purcellville, VA: The Good Book Company, 2010); Wayne Grudem, *Understanding the Big Picture of the Bible: A Guide to Reading the Bible Well* (Wheaton, IL: Crossway, 2012); David R. Helm, *The Big Picture Story Bible* (Wheaton, IL: Crossway, 2010); Max Lucado and Randy Frazee, *The Story: The Bible as One Continuing Story of God and His People* (Grand Rapids: Zondervan, 2011); William H. Marty, *The Whole Bible Story: Everything That Happens in the Bible in Plain English* (Minneapolis: Bethany House, 2011); Vaughan Roberts, *God's Big Picture: Tracing the Storyline of the Bible* (Downers Grove, IL: InterVarsity Press, 2002).

4. J. Scott Duvall and J. Daniel Hays, *Living God's Word: Discovering Our Place in the Great Story of Scripture* (Grand Rapids: Zondervan, 2012), 5.

5. Donald McCullough, *If Grace Is So Amazing, Why Don't We Like It? How God's Radical Love Turns the World Upside Down* (San Francisco: Jossey-Bass, 2005), 19.

- an experience of personal conflict between good and evil
- frustration with the present world
- anxieties about the future
- a sense of a greater purpose and meaning
- the conviction that this world isn't the way it's supposed to be
- the hope that things will one day be better than they are[6]

When one has a general understanding of the biblical presentation, this makes sense. There clearly is conflict between good and evil, personal and national frustration because of sin, questions about future and meaning, a general presentation of the chaos, and hope that someone will fix the mess of the world—at least by some. One can make points of connection to this type of description with Christ Jesus himself as the "hero" that paves a scarlet path of redemption through the muck and mire of sin. Amen!

One of the most common presentations coming out of evangelicalism today is succinct and presents the grand narrative of the Bible in four acts:

Act 1: Creation (Genesis 1–2)
Act 2: Fall (Genesis 3–Malachi)
Act 3: Redemption (Gospels and Epistles)
Act 4: Restoration (Revelation)

While the exact origin of this general phrasing may be untraceable, it appears to be missiologically driven. David Nelson states, "In order to build a biblical-theological framework for understanding God's mission, the church's mission, and the church's mission to the nations, one must first understand the unified biblical narrative, including its four major plot movements—creation, fall, redemption, and restoration."[7] Many others have attempted to unpack this language as a defensible model of the Bible's presentation.[8] Again, the language explains the grand narrative in a story format. It presents God as Creator, followed by the fall. It identifies the failures as encompassing all of the Old Testament, and climaxes the story of redemption in Christ, while anticipating a promised time of restoration.

All of the aforementioned models, at some level, have merit. I am thankful that the people of God have given effort to connecting the dots of the biblical account. It is the greatest story ever told! And for many, growing up in a non-Christian environment, the Bible is a mystery—an unknown

---

6. Nathan D. Holsteen and Michael J. Svigel, general editors, *Exploring Christian Theology* (Minneapolis: Bethany House, 2015), 12.

7. David Nelson, "The Story of Mission: The Grand Biblical Narrative," in *Theology and Practice of Mission: God, the Church, and the Nations,* ed. Bruce Ashford (Nashville: B&H, 2011), 6.

8. See Holsteen and Svigel, *Exploring Christina Theology;* Trevin Wax, *Counterfeit Gospels* (Chicago: Moody, 2011), 31–40; Ed Stetzer, "The Big Story of Scripture: Creation, Fall, Redemption, Restoration," *Christianity Today,* November 2012, http://www.christianitytoday.com/edstetzer/2012/november/big-story-of-scripture-creation-fall-redemption.html.

quantity. Unfortunately, many longtime believers struggle when piecing it all together.

As I reflect on the significance of this discussion, two points arise. First, understanding and communicating the Bible builds *familiarity* with God's Word and diffuses the overwhelming feeling that many have because of its size and span of history. The Bible is big and can be intimidating to both believers and unbelievers. Unfortunately, the church has not always done the best job at explaining how the Bible is structured and how the narrative flows from one book to the next.

A second value of identifying and communicating the big picture of the Bible is that it assists in the area of *evangelism.* This obviously is tied to the value of familiarity, but it goes one step further—to the Gospel. Such tools, and high-level narratives, have the opportunity to emphasize both sin and salvation. Without question, "faith comes from hearing the message, and the message is heard through the word of Christ" (Rom. 10:17). The Bible tells the story of our problem, and of God's solution through Christ. To this end, we can appreciate the succinct presentation of the story that leads to a presentation of the Good News of the work of Christ.

BIG-PICTURE LIMITATIONS

It is not the attempt of this chapter to belittle any effort or enterprise that attempts to tell the biblical narrative in unique ways. I've already championed the value of presenting the big picture of the narrative of Scripture. We need those that frame the narrative in simple clarity. A child needs to hear (and mature adults as well!) that the Good Book says that "God sent Jesus to save us from our sins." We need to connect all sixty-six books in order to be reminded that the biblical message is interconnected, working toward one climactic end. We need to be reminded that this biblical account is leading the reader somewhere. The apostle John said it best: "But these are written that you may believe that Jesus is the Messiah, the Son of God, and that by believing you may have life in his name" (John 20:31).

This is true of the master narrative because as Jesus himself clarified— the Old Testament points to him. Remember the encounter on the road to Emmaus? After the two disciples described the events of the third day post-crucifixion Jesus said to them, "'How foolish you are, and how slow of heart to believe all that the prophets have spoken! Did not the Christ have to suffer these things and then enter his glory?' And beginning with Moses and all the Prophets, he explained to them what was said in all the Scriptures concerning himself" (Luke 24:25–27). So in one sense we need to present this message with simplicity, but also with purpose.

The problem that comes with the big picture is that *we are not supposed to stay where it leaves us.* The high-level assessment only shows us where we are going and provides a foundation in which the details reside. But here is an important point: biblical meaning is a product both of the macro-structure and the microstructure. That is why we believe that "All Scripture is God-breathed" (2 Tim. 3:16). Paul did not say that some passages are God breathed; he said *all* Scripture. If we tell the biblical story too concisely, we could end up with something like "God wins," and that would be void of necessary information for full understanding. In a culture that focuses on "just the facts" and the "Cliff Note version" of everything, we risk an incomplete understanding of the revealed Word of God and the theological truths that God intends for us to have in order to survive in this depraved world. Perhaps that is why Scripture used the metaphor of milk and meat.[9] Milk has a purpose, but it must lead us to meat, which produces growth and maturity.

My point? Our understanding of the story of the Bible cannot stay only at such an abbreviated version because it has built a problem: It risks missing the details that anchor the story to the words of Scripture, which lead to maturity in faith and practice. In short, the presentation of the biblical story must be anchored to the very words of the text that honor the theological thrust of the text, in order to demonstrate the connectedness of the entirety of Scripture. In so doing, we acknowledge that the Bible is a grand story that:

- utilizes narrative traits
- is a thoroughly Jewish contextualized presentation from beginning to end
- has as its epicenter the work and deliverance offered by the promised *Jewish* Messiah
- demonstrates God's sovereignty through individuals and the nations, for his glory

And I would contend that God chooses to use Israel as *the* strand that connects the biblical story together. The called-out nation is the lynchpin in the narrative flow, and to miss such a point lessens what is revealed, and potentially causes an abbreviated view to become distorted—and ultimately, confusing.

THE BIBLE AS STORY

By now you may be asking: "Is it even permissible to reference the Bible as a story?" I believe it is. I have found that many believers are hesitant to think in terms of literary categories when it comes to the Bible because most Christ followers have been trained to ask pragmatic questions such as how the Bible applies to them. Understandably, followers of Yeshua long to apply the text to life. It is God's written communication to the world, and it tells us of the sacrifice of his Son. That's a life changing event! And Scripture has a purpose—to equip believers to know these things. That is why the text must be real, practical, applicable, and valued. But to call the Bible a "story" almost seems irreverent, doesn't it?

To engage the Bible literarily might seem to be an attempt to humanize the divine book; but make no mistake about it, Christians *do* believe the

---

9. Cf. 1 Corinthians 3:1–4 and Hebrews 5:11–14.

Bible is a divine book! That conviction is a firmly held position of Christian orthodoxy. All Christ followers, in all places and at all times, have the conviction that the Bible is the Word of God. To be specific, we believe that "the Bible, made up of both Old and New Testaments, is the written Word of God, recorded through human authors under the direction of the Holy Spirit. The books were composed without error in the original autographs, and the Bible as a whole is authoritative for Christian living. It discloses God's redemptive plan for humanity through Christ."[10] Believers support this conviction by citing specific biblical texts that articulate this claim.[11] However, many of the same texts cited for the purpose of establishing sound doctrine also remind us that the Bible was written by human authors who "though human, spoke from God as they were carried along by the Holy Spirit" (2 Peter 1:21). God chose to use people, created in his image, to carry out his written record to the world through the working of his Spirit. So the Bible is a divine book that reflects human pattern and subsequent creativity. Not only does this add variety; these literary genres unlock the actual message itself. And narrative (i.e., story), in particular, unlocks it all.

NARRATIVE AND NARRATIVE TRAITS

Four significant genres make up the majority of the Bible: narrative, poetry, prophecy, and letters. Categorically, narrative is the largest genre of literature in the Bible. Approximately forty percent of the Old Testament and sixty percent of the New Testament is narrative. Biblical narrative is defined as "an organized presentation of a historical event artistically advanced to recount God's working in his creation and through his people."[12] It is a specific genre. It has traits, characteristics, and patterns just like any other genre. It can be evaluated with specificity to an individual account recorded in the Bible. However, it is also the most impactful genre in Scripture. All other genres are contained within the grand framework of the biblical narrative. The opening thrust of the Bible casts the entire account in a story motif. Throughout the sacred text, continuity is woven together through narrative. One could argue that all other genres have no bearing or connection without narrative. It is the thread that binds them to a progressive movement of God throughout the Bible and human history. So even though "narrative" is a technical literary term, it also is the tone of the entirety of Scripture. To understand the technical traits of the genre will assist in understanding the message of the Bible itself.

Leland Ryken, in his classic *Words of Delight*, states, "The stories of the Bible, like stories generally, are made up of three basic elements—setting, plot or action, and character."[13] Most of us, like my son, learned this in a high-

---

10.   Mark Yarbrough, *How to Read the Bible Like a Seminary Professor* (New York: FaithWords, 2016), 7.

11.   Cf. 1 Corinthians 2:12–13; 2 Timothy 3:16; 2 Peter 1:21; 3:15.

12.   Yarbrough, *How to Read the Bible Like a Seminary Professor*, 175.

13.   Leland Ryken, *Words of Delight* (Grand Rapids: Baker, 1992), 53.

school literature class, and we likely think in those categories whether we realize it or not. We naturally assess the surroundings that are presented when we enter into a story. We orient ourselves as to how the scene opens and the events develop. We assess the characters as they are revealed and we connect to how each one is portrayed. Then we pay attention to the actions of each character. Thus, the reader is drawn to all three categories in a story and the connection is made. This is what makes the narrative real. Biblical stories, like all stories, have these components as well; and it is a sound interpretive strategy to identify their presence in any given account. After all, the Bible is literature, and simply stated, "Literature is an interpretive presentation of experience in artistic form."[14] Many of the self-contained short stories in the Bible are literary masterpieces. That is why C. S. Lewis says: "There is a . . . sense in which the Bible, since it is literature cannot be properly read except as literature; and the different parts of it as the different sorts of literature they are."[15] The meaning itself, of such stories, is "found in what the author willed to teach his reader by recalling this incident."[16] However, don't confuse the art of biblical narrative literature with fiction. These accounts, and the presentation of the Bible as a whole, are true. We believe these events actually happened.

DETAILS MATTER, TOO

The primary messaging of the biblical story in recent years has been presented as four acts (Creation, Fall, Redemption, Restoration [CFRR]), each corresponding to perceived dominant moves in the grand narrative. Again—this may be helpful to build large-scale familiarity with the biblical text and/or tell the grand narrative evangelistically, but it is void of significant details that take up considerable real estate in the biblical canon. Note the significant gap between what is articulated as "Fall" and that of "Redemption." This presentation moves from the Garden . . . to Jesus. Are they connected? Certainly. And, of course, no high-scale overview can cover the details. But that's the point. We must understand and remember that any abbreviated summary of the Bible story omits significant detail. In this case, this summary moves from Genesis to the Gospels, with 38 important books in between, which deserve to be understood for the picture to be completely whole.

Ryken is correct in that narratives exist around the interchange between setting, plot, and character. The most noticeable observation in the CFRR model is the *emphasis* on plot and the *omission* of setting and character. Think of what is affirmed and missed. One certainly cannot disagree with the macro-narrative entrance into the story of the Bible; God is the Creator and He creates a place of peace. All is right with the world, and the created order. It is very good. And we know the story quickly moves: Sin enters, and all of creation falls. Hence Creation (Act 1) and Fall (Act 2) cover the first

---

14. Leland Ryken, *The Literature of the Bible* (Grand Rapids: Zondervan, 1974), 13.

15. C. S. Lewis, *Reflections on the Psalms* (New York: Harcourt, Brace and World, 1958), 3.

16. Robert Stein, *A Basic Guide to Interpreting the Bible* (Grand Rapids: Baker, 1994), 18.

three chapters of Genesis. But Act 3 in the CFRR model moves to Jesus and the Gospels. To do so misses at least three critical points.

First, it is agreed that Genesis 3 is a turning point in the grand narrative. It states the problem of the story and casts the plot in motion. When sin entered with God's warning of death (Gen. 2:17), that is what happens. Genesis 4 demonstrates that truth because Cain kills Abel. That is followed by a genealogy of death (Gen. 5), the story of the wickedness of the world and the grace of God (Gen. 6–9), the table of nations (Gen. 10), and the account of Babel (Gen. 11). But what happens next is stunning. The narrative slows when the Creator intervenes in a new way. He calls Abram and makes a commitment. The focused reader observes that the problem (sin) finds the beginnings of a solution in the fact that the Creator is a covenant God. The language of covenant (ברית) is a critical part of the narrative flow because this is something that God does. He makes promises. In the promise given to Abram, one sees his character and learns that he is a God who keeps his word. He promised that sin would lead to death, but he now promises to a nomadic Semite that he will one day be the father of a 1) *nation*, that would reside in a particular 2) *land*, and would have a seed that would 3) *bless the nations*. Obviously any macro-presentation of the Bible would be unable to present *all* the details, including such models as CFRR, but all models should attempt to be consistent in the narrative movement and not miss critical revelations *in* the narrative. While Jesus is that ultimate fulfillment of Abram's seed (Gal. 3:16), that fulfillment cannot be conceived without the fact that it occurs because of God's covenant with Abraham. So the first critical point that cannot be avoided is that the story is anchored not in a sinful humanity (Fall) but in the fact that God has revealed himself as a covenant God (Gen. 12, 15, 17, et.al.). This also means that God will fulfill all of his covenants, because he cannot void his Word (cf. 2 Kings 13:23).

The second critical point that cannot be omitted is an argument related to characterization. *The* major character in the grand story of Scripture is a people, the nation of Israel. The story of Scripture is thoroughly Jewish. To de-emphasize or omit this part of the story is to misunderstand the covenants and the manner in which God blesses all people through his Messiah. He does this by promises to the Jewish people and the nation of Israel. Just think about it. How can the grand story of the Bible be presented without its Jewish context? The line of Abraham, as seen in the nation of Israel, is the main earthly character in the entirety of the Old Testament. It is their history throughout the Old Testament that we follow through times of judgment, yet with a constant reminder of the eternal, everlasting promises of God's covenants. The entirety of the Old Testament is centered around this unfolding story. Major emphasis must be given to the role that Israel plays in God's desire to bless the nations, and this is rooted in the covenant promises. As McDermott states:

> The purpose of the covenant with Abraham and his progeny was to bless them so that they in turn would bring blessing to the world. God did great things for Israel in order

to educate the nations. Israel came to know God so that in turn the nations might come to know Israel's God. Hence the covenant of election was not simply soteriological (to bless and save Israel) but also missional (to bring blessing to the nations).[17]

Any such presentation is responsible for acknowledging the role of the covenantal promises to Israel—which occurs at least 350 times in the Hebrew Bible. Tied to this is the overwhelming volume of references of the land in regard to the covenants. "The land appears more than one thousand times in the Jewish Bible and is even more common than the word 'covenant,' which scholars agree is fundamental to the Bible. In more than 70 percent of the places where 'covenant' appears, it is linked to the land promises."[18] As Gerhard von Rad said, "Of all the promises made to the patriarchs it was that of the land that was the most prominent and decisive."[19]

Connected to this is the third point that is critical when telling the story of the Bible. It is simple, yet pertinent: Jesus was and is the *Jewish* Messiah. The implications of this are many in *how* the story is told. It forces the interpreter to understand a variety of things such as:

- the language of the covenants; those that are conditional and those that are unconditional
- the promise of an earthly Messiah that will rule on planet earth, in Jerusalem
- the clear delineation of the two Messianic advents
- the distinct offer of a kingdom, by the Jewish Messiah Jesus, and the implications *on* the two Messianic advents
- the unfulfilled covenantal promises yet anticipated in regard to land, worship, and the messianic era

In summary, the story of the Bible, when told briefly, is valuable for familiarity and evangelism. Yet for disciples, it must not stay there. While many such accounts are true, they fail to engage the enormity of material that God chose to reveal in Scripture. The details of the story lead to the final conclusion. Obviously, from this perspective, the central character of the master narrative is that of Israel, with Israel's Messiah as the hero of the grand story. To miss this perspective, either by persuasion of others or by lack of personal analysis, is to avoid large portions of Old Testament scriptures and focus on personalized salvation in Christ. While the latter is true and essential, the total story is much more. God's redemptive process is one of total reclamation based on his promises. That is why we wait for his return, in this

---

17. Gerald McDermott, *Israel Matters* (Grand Rapids: Brazos Press, 2017), 48. This book is highly recommended.

18. Ibid., 49.

19. Gerhard von Rad, *The Problem of the Hexateuch and Other Essays*, trans. E. W. Trueman Dicken (London: Oliver & Boyd, 1966), 79.

current mess and state of confusion, to bring a kingdom where Jesus, as the righteous King reigns. That is what is missed when one replaces Israel with the church.[20]

A NOTE ABOUT HERMENEUTICS, DESCRIPTIVE LANGUAGE, AND PRESENTATION

The entirety of this subject, and the entirety of this book, models a particular hermeneutical perspective. It is not the intent of this chapter to argue for or teach the fundamentals of hermeneutics, but it is at the core of the discussion. When teaching the story of the Bible, people inevitably ask, and rightfully so, about hermeneutics—or the nature of interpretation. It has long been said that biblical hermeneutics is a science and an art.[21] In our context, this means that students of the Word must faithfully employ basic rules (science) for interpretation, and then apply (art) those rules consistently while synthesizing the grand narrative of the Bible. This means at least three practical things. First it means we must study the language used to record the account. This will force us to make observations about words, sentences and syntax. Second, it means we must know the background—both the historical account, and the theological underpinnings that envelop that account. Third, it means we must work within the type of literature in which the passage exists. In other words, we must understand the genre and look for the literary clues that direct our interpretive decisions. This hermeneutic is frequently alluded to as the historical, grammatical, and literary approach to understanding scripture. The conclusions in this chapter and book are based on such an approach. One must resolve to tell the story of the Bible in adherence to basic principles of interpretation. This provides boundaries that will lead to consistency of thought and thus prevent error of application.

A Bible teacher will make decisions on how many details to present when communicating the story of the Bible, and also the language used to walk through the biblical narrative. I approach hermeneutics from a historical, grammatical, and literary perspective that leads to my conviction, on a technical front, to embrace a dispensational, premillennial understanding of Scripture. However, when speaking on this subject outside of the classroom

---

20. Gerald McDermott, in *Israel Matters* (Grand Rapids: Brazos Press, 2017), 1, states, "Most Christians for most of Christian history have been wrong about Israel. They have believed in what scholars call 'supersessionism.' This is the view that the Church has superseded Israel. According to this view, after most of Israel rejected Jesus' claim to be the Messiah, God revoked his covenant with the biblical Israel and transferred the covenant to those who believed in Jesus. The Church has become the New Israel." This citation occurs in the opening statement in a chapter appropriately titled "Getting the Big Story Wrong." In it, McDermott provides a sweeping historical survey, including a quick assessment of several early church fathers, leading to the spiritualization of covenants and promises that ultimately has led to the supersessionist position. For an extended look at this issue, see McDermott, ed., *The New Christian Zionism: Fresh Perspectives on Israel and the Land* (Downers Grove, IL: IVP Academic, 2016).

21. See Milton Terry, *Biblical Hermeneutics*, 2nd ed. (1883; reprint ed., Grand Rapids: Zondervan, n.d.), 20.

environment, I very rarely use such theological language. I have found it valuable to think through more palatable ways to communicate the same truths without sacrificing conviction.[22] At the same time, the nontechnical presentation opens dialogue in ways that technical terminology do not. Obviously some specialized words cannot and should not be avoided, and a consistency of wording assists in presenting the biblical story both for communication and memorization.

In the last couple of years I have developed a new course that has been taught at the graduate level, undergraduate level, and in a non-credit form in the local church, entitled "The Story of Scripture." The description of the course is as follows: "An exposition of the biblical narrative of Scripture from Genesis to Revelation with emphasis on the relationships between the content of all 66 books and the unity of what God is doing and saying throughout the entirety of canonical and biblical history."[23] I explore ways to mitigate the concerns I have discussed in this chapter about communicating the grand narrative of Scripture. While any course is always in development, I am currently presenting twelve distinct moves when teaching the story of the Bible. It is an attempt to reframe the grand narrative in a way that embraces all sixty-six books, demonstrates their interconnectedness, presents a hermeneutically consistent yet memorable high-level narrative with ample detail, and tells the greatest story ever told. The twelve categories are as follows:

1. *The Creator God of Shalom*
   Emphasis: God is the Creator God, and what he creates is good. Humanity, created in his image, is the apex of the created order. This perfect world is shalom. It is the world for which all humanity yearns.

2. *The Problem*
   Emphasis: Adam and Eve rebel against the Creator. Sin enters and devastates shalom, and there are consequences for sin. Where there is sin there is death. Cain kills Abel. All humanity dies, and the entire world is under sin. Even with Noah's new start, sin reigns. Humanity's chief goal is to make its name great.

3. *The Solution*
   Emphasis: YHWH is a covenant God. He gives unconditional covenants, and conditional covenants. God gives an unconditional covenant, a promise, to Abram. He will be the father of a great nation

---

22. For example, instead of using millennial kingdom (which may lend some to tune out based on previous engagements with those who hold such truths), I will speak of the "physical reign of the Messiah on planet earth in the era to come." Instead of using the word rapture (a loaded term to many), I will address key passages in regard to the timing of the resurrections—a topic all serious students of the Word cannot avoid.

23. BE201 Story of Scripture syllabus, Dallas Theological Seminary, 2017. Unpublished.

that will dwell in a designated land, and whose offspring will bless the nations. God's promises are reiterated from one generation to the next because God is a Covenant God.

4. *Covenant Obedience*
   Emphasis: The descendants of Abraham were miraculously led out of captivity by Moses and are directed to the land of promise, sworn to Abraham. God gave his Law to his people, but they rebelled, causing a forty-year desert wandering. God demonstrated His holiness and grace through the sacrificial system. The second generation entered the land of promise, with the giving of a conditional covenant that would lead to blessings or curses based upon their obedience to the Law, or lack thereof. God reminded them that he alone should be followed.

5. *Covenant King*
   Emphasis: Joshua led the people into the land, dividing it to the twelve tribes of Jacob. Years later the people suffered the consequences of disobedience, eventually crying out to God, who in turn sent judges of deliverance. Later rebellion led to a desire for a king. God gave them Saul, but he did not yearn for God. David was God's choice. He too was a sinner, but God promised David's line an eternal King and kingdom. This promised Messiah and kingdom was yet to come. Upon David's death, Solomon reigned and built a temple for God, but Solomon's heart was not always wise in the ways of God.

6. *Covenant Worship*
   Emphasis: For the people of God, worship was important. The Psalms, in particular, are expressions of worship for both individual and corporate participation. Through such expression, the people were taught that fearing the Lord is the beginning of wisdom. God cares about his people's relationship to him, and to each other.

7. *Covenant Consequences*
   Emphasis: Upon Solomon's death, a civil war ensued, dividing the nation. The kingdom of the north, Israel, spiraled downward due to faithless kings. The kingdom of the south, Judah, had a few good kings that attempted to lead the nation in covenant faithfulness, but to no avail. During this time, God sent prophets. Their message of repentance was strong, but not heeded. Even with judgment looming, the prophets foresaw Messiah as suffering for his people, who one day would be established as the conquering King. But even this hope did not change the nation's heart. Judgement came in accordance to the promises of Deuteronomy 28. Israel fell to the Assyrians in 722 BC, and Judah to the Babylonians in 586.

8. *Covenant Love*
   Emphasis: In the midst of judgement, God did not forget his promises. He preserved his people told in Daniel and Esther. Even during
   Jerusalem's fall God spoke of a coming "new covenant" that would
   bring true forgiveness of sin. God eventually brought his people
   back to the land. Three groups of captives returned under Zerub-
   babel, Ezra, and Nehemiah; however, things were not the same. No
   Davidic king sat on the throne. Persecution continued. Societal in-
   justices prevailed. The only hope was in Messiah.

9. *The King Has Come*
   Emphasis: Jesus is the Jewish Messiah that has come in fulfillment of
   Old Testament prophecies. He is God in flesh—full deity and perfect
   humanity. His message was a call to the kingdom of God, and entrance is through repentance of sin and trust in him. But the religious
   leaders desired rescue from Rome, not sin. As Gabriel had announced,
   Jesus had come to save his people from their sins. At this first advent,
   Messiah came to die on a cross for the sins of humanity. This narrative
   climax is the apex of human history. It is Jesus who fulfills the blessing
   to the world as promised first to Abraham, then to all by the power
   of his resurrection. Death is defeated for all who believe in him. The
   curse of sin has been broken, and the New Covenant is inaugurated.

10. *All the King's Men*
    Emphasis: The book of Acts is Luke, part 2. The emphasis is upon the
    continuing work of Messiah, though now ascended, in and through
    those who are his by the working of the Holy Spirit. The Church,
    made up of both believing Jews and Gentiles, is a product of Yeshua's
    reconciling work. The narrative chronicles the message of the Gos-
    pel from Jerusalem, to Judea and Samaria, to the ends of the earth.
    YHWH's love for the nations is found in Messiah, and his people
    anticipate his return to complete the promised covenantal promises.

11. *Living for the King*
    Emphasis: The twenty-one letters in the New Testament, written to
    individuals or churches address a variety of issues. While each one is
    unique in content, they collectively present an encompassing frame-
    work for faith and practice. In such records, followers of Messiah
    understand both orthodoxy (Christian doctrine) and orthopraxy
    (Christian practice).

12. *The King Is Coming*
    Emphasis: The Revelation culminates the Old and New Testaments
    since it completes the story begun in Genesis. As the apocalypse is
    written to seven churches to warn against falling away, it assures all

readers that ultimate victory exists for those who are in Christ. John records this prophecy of the end of time and reveals God's ultimate triumph over all the forces of evil, the demise of Satan, the completion of all covenants, and the culmination of the eternal reign of Messiah in a new heaven and earth.

A SURPRISE NARRATIVE TWIST
YOU DON'T WANT TO MISS

So where does this leave us? While there are great advantages in presenting the story of the Bible in a short, succinct format, those presentations are best suited toward environments where the goal is to build *familiarity* of the biblical message or for *evangelism*. There is great value in this. However, followers of Messiah must not stay at such levels in their maturation of understanding. To do so will overlook critical, conviction-forming details such as the literary points of the story line, the language and centrality of covenants, the promise of an earthly messianic reign, the primacy of Jesus' coming as the *Jewish* Messiah, and the anticipated fulfillment of all covenant promises. Summaries are difficult at best, but such works must provide ample details to inform the substance of the story—not just the highlights. It is a challenge to all students of the Bible to evaluate how they frame the narrative and what language is used in order to tell the story of scripture. After teaching through the twelve anchor points listed above, I usually provide the following statement:

> The master narrative allows us to see beauty, followed by sin and its consequences. However, God moves forward making a Covenant Promise to Abraham, guaranteeing that through him will come a nation (the Jews) in a land (Israel) that will bless the world (through Jesus Christ). Fulfillment of that Covenant Promise appears to follow a winding course.

> Through Moses (and the Mosaic Covenant), God reveals his Law. This Law demonstrates that man is a sinner in need of God's grace and cannot survive without deliverance. While the nation failed miserably and received severe judgment as promised in the Law and reinforced by the prophets, God's unconditional promises were never in jeopardy. Despite Israel's failures, God promised David that an ultimate deliverer, the Messiah, would establish an everlasting Kingdom. In this Kingdom, God's people would enjoy the benefits of a New Covenant that is eternal and would receive complete forgiveness of sin.

> The New Testament writers focused on showing the fulfillment of all the covenants in the person of Jesus Christ. Jesus is the Messiah of the Davidic line who fulfills the Covenant Promises to Abraham. Jesus, as complete deity and perfect humanity, lived out the Mosaic Covenant flawlessly—doing what Israel could not do. Jesus, through his death and resurrection, inaugurated the New Covenant. While all covenants are completed in Jesus, Jesus has yet to complete all covenants. That is why we await the

second advent of Christ, when he will return and finish what has been started.[24]

The response of this statement usually leads to two questions: Why has God preserved the Jews throughout history? And, what covenant promises remain to be fulfilled? If I have done my job well, students answer their own questions. God is sovereign and the covenants that still await fulfillment are the great promises to Israel regarding her land, forgiveness, and King. All will occur when the covenant people embrace Yeshua as Messiah.

From a New Testament perspective, there is a surprising twist that simply can't be missed: The Word became flesh and dwelt among us. Messiah came into our mire and muck in order to pull us out. Shockingly, God has brought us to the story to be amazed by his grace. In fact, everyone who embraces the Savior is a product of that grace. Gentiles have been invited to the party as "spiritual Israel" (Galatians 3:29). But here is the icing on the cake: *A believer's life of grace reflects what he one day will do with his literal, covenant people.* The apostle Paul makes this clear when he states, "I ask then: Did God reject his people? By no means! I am an Israelite myself, a descendant of Abraham, from the tribe of Benjamin. God did not reject his people, whom he foreknew" (Rom. 11:1–2). Later, he added, "Again, I ask: Did they [Israel] stumble so as to fall beyond recovery? Not at all! Rather, because of their transgression, salvation has come to the Gentiles to make Israel envious. But if their transgression means riches for the world, and their loss means riches for the Gentiles, how much greater riches will their full inclusion bring!" (Rom. 11:11–12). Paul concludes his teaching on God's sovereignty when he states, "As far as the gospel is concerned, they are enemies for your sake; but as far as election is concerned, they are loved on account of the patriarchs, for God's gifts and his call are irrevocable" (Rom. 11:28–29).

And so we wait for the consummation of God's promises to Israel. This is a pinnacle of grace in the grand story of Scripture. God is good at his Word, and this is the story we have to tell.

> *I love to tell the story*
> *'Twill be my theme in glory!*
> *To tell the old, old story*
> *Of Jesus and his love.*[25]

---

24. Yarbrough, *How to Read the Bible Like a Seminary Professor*, 56–57.
25. Arabella K. Hankey, "I Love to Tell the Story," 1866.

THE HERMENEUTICS
OF THE CONFLICT

MICHAEL RYDELNIK

"MICHAEL IS PRESENTING THE OLD TESTAMENT view of the land promise to Israel; I'm presenting the Christian view. His view is based on the Old Testament while mine is based on the New Testament." Those are the words of a college professor who joined me on a radio forum to discuss our differing perspectives on the Bible's teaching about the land of Israel. My interlocutor's basic proposition with regard to God's territorial grant to the Jewish people was that the New Testament does not affirm the Old and in fact expands the meaning of the biblical land promise in terms of its receptors and scope.[1] His view of the land promise was founded on three premises:

1. The land promise to Israel is never mentioned in the New Testament or by Jesus, so it is no longer operative as it once was in the Old Testament.

2. The land promise to Israel is no longer the inheritance of the Jewish people at large (ethnic Israel) but it has been transferred (or expanded) to the Church, composed of all true followers of the Lord Jesus, most of whom are not Jewish, but including a small number of Jewish believers.

3. The land promise has been enlarged or universalized so it is no longer about the historic land of Israel but rather refers to the whole world, which is the inheritance of the Church.

My response to this colleague was that I did not want to take an Old Testament view versus the New Testament view of the land promise, nor a Jewish view versus a Christian. Rather, I wanted to adopt an integrated bibli-

---

1. In a sense, this creates a canon within the canon—a problematic idea, because it gives the New Testament greater authority than the Old Testament.

cal perspective, recognizing that the Bible progresses in its presentation of revelation, without canceling the previous revelation or canceling the commitments God has previously made. This chapter will be based on this point of view: that the Old Testament and the New Testament present a harmonious and consistent view of the land promises to Israel. To do that, I will try to survey the land promise from the perspective of both the Hebrew Scriptures and the New Testament.

THE LAND PROMISE IN THE HEBREW BIBLE

This section will examine how the Hebrew Bible (Old Testament) answers the question, "To whom does the biblical land of promise truly belong?" The approach will be to state four propositions and consider the biblical evidence for each of them.[2] Then, based on those propositions, some conclusions will be drawn from the evidence.

1. God promised the land of Israel to Abraham, Isaac, Jacob, and their descendants.

This proposition is derived from the covenant God made with Abraham, called the Abrahamic Covenant. To begin, God made a promise to Abraham and then reiterated and expanded it several times. When the Scriptures are repetitious, the biblical author's intent is to have readers mark the recurrence as important.

The first record of God's promise to Abraham is found in Genesis 12:1–7. There Abram (Abraham's original name; see Genesis 17:3–5) was told to leave his native country of Ur and go to the land the Lord would show him (12:1). When Abram finally arrived in the land of Canaan (as it was called then), the Lord told him, "To your descendants I will give this land" (12:7, NASB). This promise is repeated in the next chapter after the story of the dispute between the herdsmen of Abram and his nephew Lot (Genesis 13:7). To preserve the peace, Abram told Lot to select any part of the land that he wished, thus assuring Lot that Abram would go elsewhere (vv. 8–10). In a sense, this put God's promise to Abram in jeopardy. If he gave up the land to his nephew, how could God fulfill His previous promise? So, God assured Abram that despite this sacrificial attitude, all the land of Canaan would one day be his. The Lord said, "Now lift up your eyes and look from the place where you are, northward and southward and eastward and westward; for all the land which you see, I will give it to you and to your descendants forever" (vv. 14–15, NASB).

A significant recurrence of the land promise is found in Genesis 15:1–21. Following immediately upon Abram's rescue of Lot from Sodom (Gen. 14), the king of Sodom offered Abram all the spoils of battle. But Abram refused, lest it be said that the wicked king of Sodom made Abram rich (14:21–23). Now, once again Abram demonstrated a sacrificial attitude and

---

2. This section is derived from my book, *Understanding the Arab-Israeli Conflict: What the Headlines Haven't Told You,* revised and updated (Chicago: Moody Publishers, 2007), 152–58. Used with permission.

entrusted himself to the Lord's provision. In light of this, the Lord reiterated His covenant with Abram, assuring him that he would indeed have an heir. To confirm the covenant, the Lord caused Abram to fall into a deep sleep, and then He walked among the animal sacrifices (Gen. 15:12, 17).

This action was important: By passing alone between the pieces of the sacrifices, God showed that this covenant did not depend on Abram but on the Lord alone. The covenant that was established was unconditional subject only to the will and power of the God of Abram, not Abram at all. [3] Then, having established the absolute nature of the covenant, God told Abram, "To your descendants I have given this land, from the river of Egypt as far as the great river, the river Euphrates" (15:18, NASB).

The Lord repeated the land promise in the context of establishing circumcision as an outward sign of the covenant, in Genesis 17. The Lord assured Abram, "I will establish My covenant between Me and you and your descendants after you throughout their generations for an everlasting covenant, to be God to you and to your descendants after you. "I will give to you and to your descendants after you, the land of your sojournings, all the land of Canaan, for an everlasting possession; and I will be their God." (17:7–8, NASB).

Furthermore, God made it clear in this passage that the land would go to Abram's descendants through Isaac, not Ishmael. Although Abraham (renamed, v. 5) pled for Ishmael, the Lord refused and told Abraham, "But My covenant I will establish with Isaac" (v. 21, NASB). Today many modern Arabs consider themselves to be descendants of Ishmael. Even if that were true, this passage makes it clear that the descendants of Abram, to whom God gave the land, are to be traced through Isaac and not Ishmael. [4]

The Lord did repeated the promise of the land to Isaac (26:3), just as he assured Abraham he would, and later God repeated it to Isaac's son Jacob (35:12).

Clearly, the land grant of the Abrahamic Covenant as found in Genesis, the first book of the Bible, was given to Abraham, Isaac, and Jacob, and then to the twelve tribes of Israel. Moreover, the land promise is reiterated in multiple passages throughout the Hebrew Scriptures. Additionally, the land promise is restated to all the people of Israel in 1 and 2 Chronicles, the last book of the Hebrew canon. [5] In 1 Chronicles 16:8–18, the psalmist David

---

3. For another similar perspective, but nuanced differently, see Richard Averbeck's chapter in this volume: "Israel, the Jewish People, and God's Covenants."

4. The Bible does make promises to Ishmael and his descendants (Genesis 17:20) but they are not the land promises given to Abraham, Isaac, Jacob, and their descendants. Moreover, even the biblical promises given to Ishmael do not necessarily apply to the Arabs. As S. D. Goitein writes, "To be sure, there is no record in the Bible showing that Ishmael was the forefather of the Arabs" (S. D. Goitein, *Jews and Arabs: Their Contact through the Ages* [New York: Schocken, 1964], 21). The idea that the Arab peoples descended from Ishmael is a much later Jewish tradition that was given life in the Qur'an rather than in the Scriptures.

5. The order of the books in the English Bible is different from the order in the Hebrew Bible. First and 2 Chronicles close the canon of the Hebrew Bible, and is considered one book.

praises God for giving His covenant to Abraham, Isaac, and Jacob, and so "to Israel as an everlasting covenant, saying, 'To you I will give the land of Canaan, as the portion of your inheritance'" (vv. 17–18, NASB). Also, in 2 Chronicles 20:7 Jehoshaphat prayed, "Did you not, O our God, drive out the inhabitants of this land before your people Israel and give it to the descendants of Abraham your friend forever?" So the Hebrew Bible, from the beginning to the end, recognizes that God gave the promise of the land to Abraham, Isaac, Jacob, and their descendants.

How did God have the right to give the land to the Jewish people when the Canaanites were obviously already there? The answer to this question is given by Rashi, the great medieval Jewish commentator (1040–1105) at the very inception of his commentary on the Torah.[6] From Rashi's point of view, the Sinai Covenant and its laws form the substance of the Torah and are foundational to Judaism. Therefore, he asks why the Torah does not begin with the first commandment given at Sinai but rather begins with the creation of the heavens and the earth. His answer is most telling when he says Creation is tied to the land of promise:

> Why does [the Torah] begin with "In the beginning [referring to the book of Genesis and the story of creation]?" . . . Thus, should the nations of the world say to Israel, "You are robbers, for you have taken by force the lands of the Seven Nations [who inhabited the land of Canaan]"? They [Israel] will say to them: "All the earth belongs to God. He created it and gave it to whomever He saw fit. It was His will to give it to them and it was His will to take it from them and give it to us."[7]

Rashi's explanation is quite helpful. Certainly, the author of the Torah did not include the creation of the world merely to satisfy his readers' curiosity. Instead, Moses wrote this account as a prologue to the Torah, establishing God's authority to give the land of His creation to His people Israel. Otherwise, the Canaanites or any other people that lived there might have a grievance. But the Creator and Owner of the land chose to give it to Abraham, Isaac, Jacob, and all teir descendants forever as was His divine right.

2. God defined the boundaries of the land of Israel.

In Genesis 15:18, God established the boundaries of the land given to Abraham "from the river of Egypt as far as the great river, the Euphrates" (NASB). There is a dispute regarding the identification of the southwestern boundary, the river of Egypt. Some identify this as the Wadi El-Arish, a river bed in the northern part of the Sinai Peninsula, that is dry in summer and filled with water during the rainy winter season. If this is correct, it would exclude the Sinai Desert from the land grant. Others identify it as

---

6.   *Torah* is the Hebrew word for Law, and refers to the Pentateuch, i.e., Genesis through Deuteronomy.

7.   Rashi, "Bereishis," *The Metsudah Chumash/Rashi,* vol. 1, trans. Avrohom Davis (Hoboken, NJ: Ktav, 1993), 1.

the Nile River. If this is correct, the Sinai Desert would be part of the land given to Israel.

It is unclear which view is correct. According to Exodus 23:31, the southern border is associated with the Red Sea, lending support to the Nile River view. But according to Numbers 34:4, the southern border is associated with Kadesh Barnea and the Wilderness of Zin, bolstering the Wadi El-Arish view. At this point, the evidence for either position is inconclusive but appears to favor the Wadi El-Arish as the southern border of the Promised Land.

In the north and east, the boundary is the Euphrates River, extending the land up to what is today's Lebanon, Syria, and Iraq. Obviously, Israel never obtained their entire land grant, either in the past or today; even at the zenith of David and Solomon's rule, the land they governed did not match the land grant God gave Abraham. Nevertheless, God's promise is faithful; thus, at some future time these certainly will be the boundaries of Israel. This promise is foundational to the expectation of the literal future messianic kingdom when the land grant will be fulfilled in its entirety. This should be expected, as all future hope should be shaped by the promises of Scripture.

3. God gave the land of Israel to the Jewish people as an eternal inheritance.

Both Genesis 13:15 and 2 Chronicles 20:7 state that God gave the land to the nation of Israel as an inheritance "forever." Nevertheless, it is possible that the Hebrew word used in these passages (*olam*), translated "forever," does not necessarily mean "for all eternity." For example, it is used in Exodus 21:6 of a slave who willingly accepts service to his master. When his ear is pierced, "he shall serve him forever [*olam*]" (author's translation). Clearly, Moses did not mean "for all eternity" but rather for the rest of his life or perhaps only until the year of jubilee. Therefore, since *olam* is the word used to describe the land grant, it could possibly mean that God gave the land to Israel for a long time, but not forever.

But there is yet another Hebrew phrase used to describe eternity—it is *min olam v'ad olam,* commonly translated "forever and ever" or "from everlasting to everlasting."[8] As a general rule, the phrase is used of matters pertaining to God alone. For example, it is used to describe the eternal blessedness of God (e.g., 1 Chronicles 16:36, NASB: "Blessed be the Lord, the God of Israel, from everlasting to everlasting").[9] The phrase declares the lovingkindness of God to be eternal (Ps. 103:17), and God's existence to be eternal (Ps. 90:2). Daniel uses the equivalent phrase in Aramaic to describe God's kingdom as existing "for all ages to come" (7:18, NASB). *"Min olam v'ad olam"* is the strongest expression in Hebrew to describe perpetuity and eternality. And, for the most part, it refers to God and his eternal nature.

---

8.   I am indebted to Stuart Dauermann, Ph.D., for this word study and the insights into the meaning of the phrase *min olam v'ad olam.*

9.   See also 1 Chronicles 29:10; Psalm 41:13; 106:48; Daniel 2:20; Nehemiah 9:5.

There are only two exceptional usages in which the phrase does not refer to God. In both cases it refers to the nation of Israel's eternal possession of the land of Israel. In Jeremiah 7:7, God promises Israel, "I will let you dwell in this place, in the land that I gave to your fathers *forever and ever*" (NASB). The prophet also uses the same phrase in Jeremiah 25:5, telling Israel that they will "dwell on the land which the Lord has given to you and your forefathers *forever and ever*" (NASB, emphasis added).

Biblical Hebrew usage simply has no stronger way to indicate eternality. Thus, Jeremiah's words could not be any clearer. God has give the land of Israel to the people of Israel as a perpetual and eternal inheritance.

4. God made total enjoyment and guaranteed habitation of the land of Israel contingent on Israel's faithfulness.

God's promise of the land as an eternal inheritance to Israel did not preclude the possibility that Israel might be temporarily removed from the Promised Land. In fact, God warned the nation that disobedience could, and would, lead to their exile and dispersion. In Leviticus 26:27–33, God alerted Israel. His warning included these words: If "you do not obey Me, but act with hostility against Me" (v. 27, NASB), God would indeed discipline them. After advising the nation that he would make the land of Israel desolate, he admonished them as follows: "You, however, I will scatter among the nations and will draw out a sword after you, as your land becomes desolate and your cities become waste" (v. 33, NASB).

This severe warning passage does not end without hope. Despite Israel's disobedience to God's commands and the discipline of dispersion, God assured:

> Yet in spite of this, when they are in the land of their enemies, I will not reject them, nor will I so abhor them as to destroy them, breaking My covenant with them; for I am the Lord their God. But I will remember for them the covenant with their ancestors, whom I brought out of the land of Egypt in the sight of the nations, that I might be their God. I am the Lord (Lev. 26: 44–45, NASB).

In Deuteronomy 4:40, Moses clarified the link between Israel's obedience to God and their enjoyment of the land. He commanded Israel to keep God's statutes and commandments "that it may go well with you and with your children after you, and that you may live long on the land which the Lord your God is giving you for all time" (NASB). According to this verse, there is an ongoing paradox to the Jewish people's relationship to the land. On the one hand, God said that he is giving the land to the Jewish people for all time. On the other hand, the Jewish people's enjoyment and guaranteed tenancy of the land would be contingent on their obedience to God. Nevertheless, the Jewish people can be exiled from the land without forfeiting or nullifying the gift of the land as their eternal inheritance.

History confirms the accuracy of these warnings. After the failure of the Jewish revolts against Rome, the people of Israel gradually did go into exile.

Although the land was never totally without any Jewish people, by the time of the birth of modern Zionism, Jewish people formed a tiny minority in a land that had indeed become desolate. Nevertheless, the promise of God, as recorded in the Scriptures indicates Israel's ownership or title to the land remains eternal and unconditional. It belongs to them for all time, because the land grant was not dependent on Israel's obedience but on God's faithfulness to His oath.

Because Israel is still in disobedience (i.e., the vast majority of the Jewish people do not yet believe in Jesus), some commentators have offered a different position. John Piper has argued:

> A non-covenant-keeping people does not have a divine right to the present possession of the land of promise. Both the experience of divine blessing and the habitation of the land are conditional on Israel's keeping the covenant God made with her. . . . Israel has no warrant to a present experience of divine privilege when she is not keeping covenant with God. . . . Israel as a whole today rejects her Messiah, Jesus Christ, God's Son. This is the ultimate act of covenant-breaking with God.[10]

This position is plainly untenable. The land grant was both unconditional and eternal. Although the Jewish people might be disciplined with dispersion, their right to the land will never be removed. It belongs to them for all time (or "forever and ever"). Therefore, even in unbelief, the land is theirs. Anytime the Lord returns the Jewish people to the land, it is theirs by right of the Abrahamic Covenant land grant. This is why God could promise to return the Jewish people to the land of Israel in unbelief (see Ezek. 36:24–25; 37:1–14) as a precursor to their end of days return to the Lord (Deut. 4:29). At that time, *all* the Jewish people will trust in their Messiah Jesus, and the remaining Jewish people in dispersion will all be returned to the land (see Isa. 11:11; Zech. 12:10; Matt. 23:37–39).

The point is, that according to the Hebrew Bible, that despite the disobedience and unbelief of the Jewish people, the land of Israel belongs to them, whether they are brought back to the land by God in faith or unbelief. This is by virtue of the Lord's unconditional and eternal land grant found in the Abrahamic Covenant. The Jewish people may indeed lose the enjoyment and habitation of the land of Israel temporarily, but they never can lose the title to the land.[11]

The Hebrew Bible is clear about the land grant to Israel, but does the New Testament sustain the same idea? This is the question which must be answered next.

---

10. John Piper, "Land Divine?" *World*, May 11, 2002.

11. Despite the frequent assertion that Israel's unbelief nullified the Jewish claim to the land, hardly anyone speaks of the unbelief of the Palestinians. More than ninety-five percent of Palestinians are Muslim. Certainly, they, too, have rejected Jesus as both Lord and Messiah. Moreover, the Palestinian Muslims never had any divine promises to claim. Therefore, a Bible-believer cannot justify transferring the right to the land from unbelieving Jewish people, who do have promises to claim, to unbelieving Arabs, who do not have any promise to the land.

THE LAND PROMISE AND THE NEW TESTAMENT

A fairly common view of the promise of the land in the New Testament is to see it through the lens of replacement theology. Although the name "replacement theology" is frequently rejected by its current adherents, they still hold to the basic categories of supersessionism.[12] Regardless of whether it is called "expansion" or "fulfillment" theology, it still alleges that the New Testament transforms the land promise, redefining the recipient of the promise, from the ethnic Jewish people to a spiritualized "Israel," a group consisting of all genuine followers of Jesus, predominantly Gentile Christians. The change also addresses the land itself, alleging that the promise does not pertain to the actual land of Israel but rather to the whole world, which is the inheritance of spiritual Israel (the Church). In summary, this view alleges that the New Testament rejects the Old Testament territorial promise to ethnic Israel and replaces it with a promise that Christ and his body, the Church, will inherit the world.[13] Although this theological view has been held for many years, recently, it has become foundational for political opposition to the state of Israel on the part of some Christians.[14]

As support for the view just stated, it is frequently alleged that the New Testament does not even mention the land promises as described in the Hebrew Bible. Contrary to that, this chapter will argue that although the New Testament does not assert the land promise as prominently as in the Hebrew Bible, it does indeed reaffirm the Hebrew Bible's grant of territory (i.e., the land of Israel) to ethnic/national Israel. Before examining the New Testament support for the land promise, it will be necessary to consider why the land promise to Israel is less prominent in the New Covenant Scriptures.

1. The New Testament is relatively quiet about the land promise.

Certainly, the New Testament does not articulate the land promise as clearly as the Hebrew Bible (although this is often overstated, as if the New Testament is absolutely silent on the land). Several points explain this relative quiet on this subject. First, an understanding of *antecedent theology* (the theology of the Old Testament that was understood and accepted by New Testament writers) should guide our reading of the New Testament. Walter C. Kaiser, Jr., author of the chapter on Isaiah 19 earlier in this volume, has shown the importance of remembering antecedent theology when reading the Bible. He maintains, "biblical theology need not repeat every single de-

---

12. See R. Kendell Soulen, *The God of Israel and Christian Theology* (Minneapolis: Fortress, 1996), 1–21.

13. Adherents of this view are dependent on W. D. Davies' seminal work, *The Gospel and the Land: Early Christianity and Jewish Territorial Doctrine* (Berkeley: University of California Press). Complementing this view is G. K. Beale, *The Temple and the Church's Mission: A Biblical Theology of the Dwelling Place of God*, New Studies in the Biblical Theology (Downers Grove, IL: IVP, 2004), and Nicholas Perrin, *Jesus the Temple* (Grand Rapids: Baker, 2010).

14. Authors who have used this view as a political argument against the state of Israel are Gary M. Burge, *Jesus and the Land: The New Testament Challenge to "Holy Land" Theology* (Grand Rapids: Baker, 2010) and Stephen Sizer, *Zion's Christian Soldiers: The Bible, Israel and the Church* (Downers Grove, IL: IVP, 2007).

tail of the canon in order to be authentic and accurate." Moreover, he says that different sections of the Bible "need to be informed by all the antecedent theology against which this small section may have been projected and especially on the whole theme of the canon."[15]

This is significant for understanding the land promise in the New Testament. The Old Testament needs to guide the understanding of the New Testament, and not vice versa. Therefore, the Old Testament promise of land to Israel ought to give primary direction for the theology of the New Testament writers regarding the land and people of Israel. Speaking directly to the New Testament's perceived reticence about the land promise, Kaiser cites antecedent theology as the explanation, arguing that in similar fashion, there are no laws against incest in the New Testament "but very few would contend that there is no teaching [from the Old Testament] that is relevant to the Christian believer."[16] When Paul wrote 2 Timothy 3:16: "All Scripture is inspired by God and profitable for teaching," he was referring to the Old Testament. In light of this, an inspired teaching that the apostle would have believed was that God had granted the land of Israel to the people of Israel as an eternal inheritanc. Whether he addressed this subject in detail or not, it certainly would have guided his understanding of it.

A second reason for the relative quiet of the New Testament about the land promise is the nature of the New Testament epistles as "occasional letters." As a general rule, authors of the epistles only wrote in response to specific issues that had arisen in the churches to which they wrote. Whether it was doctrinal error (Galatians), division (Philippians), persecution in the Diaspora (James and 1 Peter), or a multitude of problems (1 Corinthians), the apostles wrote to address the issues their audiences were facing. Since the early churches had not yet adopted the error of the transfer of land promises from ethnic Israel to the Church, the apostles did not have to address the issue. Had it been necessary, they certainly would have written about this issue in more detail. For example, when Paul learned that many Gentile Christians in Rome had adopted an incipient replacement theology, he corrected both their ignorance of the mystery of Israel and their arrogance toward the Jewish people (cf. Romans 9–11 generally, but specifically in Romans 11:1–32). Since the established theology of the land was derived from the Hebrew Bible, why would there be any need to discuss the land promise at all? The Jewish people were still present in their promised land and they had a measure of political autonomy under the Sanhedrin (despite Roman rule). The land promise was just not a subject that needed to be addressed.

---

15. Walter C. Kaiser, Jr., *Toward an Old Testament Theology* (Grand Rapids: Zondervan, 1991), 16. Not only does Kaiser argue for antecedent theology as a general principle, but he maintains it ought to be specifically understood as the basis for interpreting New Testament theology (cf. his comments on page 267).

16. Walter C. Kaiser, Jr., "The Land of Israel and the Future Return" in *Israel: The Land and the People*, ed. H. Wayne House (Grand Rapids: Kregel, 1998), 222.

A third reason for the New Testament not addressing the land promises to Israel as plainly as the Hebrew Bible does, has to do with the nature of New Testament application of the Old. Often those who hold to the transference view point out that the New Testament sees the fulfillment of the promises in a spiritual, symbolic, or typological way. They will cite the fulfillment language of Matthew's gospel, the symbolic language of John's gospel, and the book of Hebrews' use of typology. Craig Blaising has shown that just because Matthew sees a correspondence between ethnic Israel and her king, the Messiah Jesus, this does not mean that Matthew has repudiated the continued existence of ethnic Israel. Further, Blaising has also demonstrated that although the Gospel of John uses symbolic language about the Lord Jesus, nowhere does John ever redefine Israel or remove the expectation of a literal eschatological fulfillment of God's promises to ethnic Israel. Moreover, although the author of the book of Hebrews may use typology, specifically with reference to the tabernacle, Blaising shows that this is not an indication that God's gift of the land to Israel has been transferred. He argues correctly that Abraham was looking not for a heavenly city but a literal city that will come from heaven.[17] In addition to Blaising's arguments about Hebrews, the rest promised in Hebrews 4:1–11 refers to the literal, messianic kingdom, when God's promise to Israel, of rest in the land, will be fulfilled. To sum up: Although the New Testament may indeed make spiritual applications of the literal land promises, it does not negate the ultimate and literal fulfillment of God's promises to the Jewish people. In fact, the Hebrew Bible anticipated both spiritual and material fulfillment of its promises.

Despite the New Testament's relative quiet about the land promise, it is a mistake to say that it is silent. In fact, the New Testament does indeed reaffirm the land promise to Israel. It is to this positive case for the land promises in the New Testament to which we turn.

2. The New Testament does reaffirm the land promise.

Contrary to the allegations of some, the New Testament does indeed imply a reaffirmation of the land promise. This will be shown in the following four propositions.

a. The New Testament reaffirms that God's covenant promises presently belong to Israel.

The New Testament clearly indicates that the covenantal promises still belong to Israel, even while the nation does not recognize Yeshua (Jesus) as the Messiah. First, this is seen in Acts 3:25, where Peter is preaching to Jewish people, calling them "the sons of the prophets and of the covenant which God made with your Fathers." In the context, Peter called upon the people

---

17.   Craig Blaising, "Biblical Hermeneutics: How Are We to Interpret the Relation Between the Tanak and the New Testament on This Question?" in *The New Christian Zionism*, ed. Gerald R. McDermott (Downers Grove, IL: InterVarsity Press, 2016), 83–86.

of Israel to repent so that their "sins may be wiped away, in order that times of refreshing may come" (Acts 3:19), clearly indicating that these Jewish people were not yet believers in Yeshua. Obviously, in this passage Peter is addressing Jewish people who plainly do not yet believe in Yeshua after the establishment of the church (Acts 2). Yet he calls them the "sons of the covenant." Therefore, the apostle understands unbelieving Jewish people to be sons or heirs of the Abrahamic Covenant.

A second passage that recognizes that the Jewish people still have a national covenantal status derived from the Abrahamic Covenant is Romans 9:4–5. The context makes it clear that Paul is speaking of Israel in unbelief. In 9:1–3 the apostle makes plain his compassion and concern for the lost condition of his unbelieving brethren. So great was his love that he makes the remarkable statement that he would be willing to be accursed and separated from the Messiah, if this could provide spiritual life for his people. There is no question that Paul is speaking of unbelieving Israel here. Nevertheless, he describes them as having a significant national status: "They are Israelites, and to them belong the adoption, the glory, the covenants, the giving of the law, the temple service, and the promises. The ancestors are theirs, and from them, by physical descent, came the Messiah, who is God over all, praised forever. Amen" (HCSB).

The present tense verb in verse 4 demonstrates that all the benefits described still belong to Israel. As Thomas Schreiner writes, "The present tense verb ειоιν (*eisin*, they are) indicates that the Jews still 'are' Israelites and that all the blessings named still belong to them."[18] Of these benefits that God has granted to Israel,[19] two are significant to this discussion. The Jewish people still have covenants and promises to claim, both of which include God's grant of a specific territory. There is no way to separate the territorial promises found in the covenants or to think that Paul now views them as belonging to an alleged new spiritual Israel (the Church). Nor did he mean that these promises have been expanded to refer to the whole world and

---

18.   Thomas R. Schreiner, *Romans,* Baker Exegetical Commentary on the New Testament (Grand Rapids: Baker Books, 1998), 485. Similarly, Cranfield concludes that Paul is saying that his fellow Jews, even though they do not believe in Jesus as the Messiah, remain "the chosen people of God." C. E. B. Cranfield, *The Epistle to the Romans, Vol II,* The International Critical Commentary, eds. J. A. Emerton and C. E. B. Cranfield (Edinburgh: T & T Clark, 1979), 461.

19.   Paul states that these are the blessings of God that are Israel's: Theirs is the adoption, referring to Israel's national adoption by God (cf. Exod. 4:22); the glory, referring to God's visible manifestation of His own glory (Exod. 16:10; 24:16; 33:22, 40:34); the covenants, referring to the divine agreements God made with Israel, specifically the Abrahamic (Gen. 12:1–3; 15:1–21), Davidic (2 Sam. 7:12–16), and New covenants (Jer. 31:31–34); the giving of the Law, referring to the Sinai Covenant as a divine gift to Israel (Exod. 19:18–22); the temple service, referring to the establishment of priests and Levites to lead Israel in worship (Exod. 29:1–9); the promises, referring to the covenantal promises made to the Patriarchs of land, seed, and blessing, as well as the promises of the future Messiah and eschatological blessing; the Fathers (or Ancestors), referring to the three great patriarchs of Israel, Abraham, Isaac, and Jacob; and the Messiah by physical descent, indicating that the promised divine Messiah came as a Jewish man and will ever be so.

not the land of Israel. It seems Paul still believes that the God of Israel has granted the people of Israel covenants and promises, and thus that God has given them a specific territory.

The third crucial passage reaffirming Israel's covenant status is Romans 11:28–29: "Regarding the gospel, they are enemies for your advantage, but regarding election, they are loved because of the patriarchs, since God's gracious gifts and calling are irrevocable" (HCSB). Here are three observations to be derived from these verses. First, Paul is speaking of Israel in unbelief, a reference to the Jewish people who, for the most part, are opposed to the gospel. This does not mean that all Jewish people are clinging to unbelief as Paul has already identified a remnant of faithful Jewish people (Rom. 11:1–5) who are followers of Yeshua. Nevertheless, the majority of Jewish people do not believe Yeshua is the promised Messiah. God used this in an advantageous way for the Gentiles as Jewish nonbelief has mysteriously led to the gospel spreading to the Gentile world (Rom. 11:11).

Second, the Jewish people remain God's chosen people. The word "election" used here means "chosen." Therefore, the NASB translates it as "from the standpoint of God's *choice,*" indicating that the Jewish people remain chosen. This status is not based on merit but because of God's love (Deut. 7:6–8). "Love" and "hate" in Scripture are linked to the concepts of choice and rejection. God says, "I loved Jacob but I hated Esau" (Mal. 1:2–3), meaning he chose Jacob but rejected Esau. So, God has chosen the Jewish people because of His elective love, not because of the merit of the Patriarchs.[20] Rather, "because of the patriarchs" refers to Paul's confidence that God will be faithful to the covenant He made with the Fathers.

Third, God's gifts to Israel and His calling of the nation to be His special people are permanent expressions of God's love. These gifts were already described in Romans 9:4–5 (see above) and clearly include the gift of the land of Israel. The word translated "irrevocable" is "a legal term (cf. 2 Cor. 7:10) indicating the unbreakable nature of God's gifts and calling."[21]

Some find it objectionable that God has chosen the Jewish people and granted them irrevocable gifts. But this does not mean that God does not love the whole world—He clearly does (John 3:16). Moreover, it is not the world in a general undifferentiated way, but he loves the nations, and wants them to know him (Isa. 56:8). Nevertheless, God's love for the world does not negate that God has a distinctive and special love for Israel, through which he will ultimately bless the world (cf. Rom. 11:12, 15). As a college professor, I certainly love all my students and will always do all that I can for their good. Yet, when my son was a student in my class, I had a special,

---

20. The expression "because of the patriarchs" is not to be understood as referring to rabbinic literature's recognition of patriarchal merit. This would contradict all that Paul teaches of God's gracious gifting. Rather, this refers to God's faithfulness to his loving gift of the Abrahamic covenant to the three great patriarchs.

21. Schriener, *Romans,* 626.

distinctive love for him, different from my other students. One of the ways it was different was that I may have had a higher standard for him than the others. God's special distinctive, elective love for Israel ought not to raise objections but rather expectations of special blessings for the Gentiles when God fulfills all his promises to Israel.

Others may object that God has expanded his special love for Israel to all believers and expanded the land grant to include the whole world. An illustration some use is that of a father who may promise his children that he will take them to the park. Then, he might graciously choose not to take them to the park but to Disney World—and in fact, he brings the neighbors' children as well. The point of this illustration is that God expanded his promise, even if he will not fulfill it literally. The problem with this illustration is that while God may give his people far more than we anticipate, it does not depict the expansion of his promise. It would be more apropos to expansion theology to say that the father came home, did not take his own children to the park, but then took the neighbors' children to Disney World. What expansion theology is really saying is that God will take his promises that he gave to Israel, and give them to the church. And that is not expansion—it is betrayal.

The point in this section thus far is that the New Testament clearly reaffirms that God's national promises still belong to Israel. But the New Covenant Scriptures do more.

b. The New Testament reaffirms that God gave the land as an inheritance for Israel.

Three New Testament passages reiterate that God granted the land of Israel as an inheritance for the people of Israel. The first is Acts 7:5, in Stephen's speech, which states of Abraham, that God "didn't give him an inheritance it [the Land] . . . but He promised *to give it to him as a possession, and to his descendants after him*" (HCSB). Therefore, in a passage frequently cited as a repudiation of the land promises, Stephen recognizes the land grant to Abraham and his offspring forever.

A second New Testament passage is found in Peter's sermon to Cornelius. The apostle reminds his Gentile audience that they were already aware of "the thing which took place throughout all *Judea*, starting from *Galilee*. . . . We are witnesses of all the things He did both in the *land of the Jews and in Jerusalem*" (Acts 10:37, 39, HCSB). Speaking to the first Gentile convert, Peter does not speak of the land as formerly belonging to Jewish people or repudiate the land promise in any way. Rather, addressing a Roman centurion during a time of Roman occupation, Peter identifies the land of Israel as belonging to the Jewish people.

A third New Testament passage that views the land as the inheritance of Abraham and his offspring is Hebrews 11:8–10: "By faith Abraham, when he was called, obeyed and went out to a place he was going to receive as an inheritance. . . . By faith he stayed as a foreigner in *the land of promise*, living in tents with Isaac and Jacob, coheirs of the same promise. For he was looking forward to the city that has foundations, whose architect and builder is God" (HCSB). Abraham anticipated that the land was his by promise but he had not yet received the fulfillment. Still, he looked forward to receiving that city. Most New Testament interpreters have mistakenly seen that the contrast here is between the land of promise and heaven (the city with foundations). More likely the contrast is between Abraham "living in tents" and his anticipation of living in the city with foundations, the literal Jerusalem. Ultimately, in the New Creation, the New Jerusalem will descend from heaven and will be dwelling place of Abraham (Rev. 22:10). Although Abraham desired a heavenly city (Heb. 11:16), this refers to his anticipation of living in that city of Jerusalem which comes from heaven (not located in heaven). About the meaning of the phrase, "a better place—a heavenly one" George Wesley Buchanan has correctly maintained, "This does not mean it is not on earth any more than the 'sharers in [the] heavenly calling' (3:1) who had 'tasted the heavenly gift' (6:4) were not those who lived on earth. Indeed, it was the very land on which the patriarchs dwelt . . . but the expression means that it is a divine land which God himself has promised."[22]

These three passages show that the New Testament perspective is that in the past God gave the land to ethnic Israel as an inheritance (Acts 7:5), that it remains the land of the Jewish people in the present (Acts 10:37–39), and that it is the ultimate inheritance of ethnic Israel who will receive the land promise, literally, one day in the future (Heb. 11:8–16).

c. The New Testament reaffirms a future for the people of Israel in the land of Israel.

Not only does the New Testament recognize that the land of Israel remains the land of the Jewish people, it also predicts that the Jewish people will dwell in the land at the end of days. There are numerous passages which support this idea.

A future in the Land. When addressing events that will take place in the days just prior to the return of the Lord Jesus, the New Testament indicates that there will be Jewish people back in their land. For example, in Matthew 24:15–20, a passage that deals with the signs of Messiah's coming and the end of the age (Matt. 24:3),[23] it speaks of "the abomination that causes

---

22. George Wesley Buchanan, "To the Hebrews," *The Anchor Bible*, Vol. 36 (New York: Doubleday, 1972), 192. See all of Buchanan's excellent discussion of Abraham's anticipation of the literal fulfillment of the land promise in Hebrews 11:8–16 on pages 188–94. His reminder of the theology of Hebrews is especially crucial: "The author of Hebrews had basically one hope or aspiration: receiving the promised land in its full glory and prosperity, free from foreign rule or threat from enemies. This was called inheriting or the acquiring the promises (6:11, 1–17; 11:13, 33, 39) and entering into the 'rest' (3:11, 18; 4:1, 3, 5, 8, 11). The promise is that which was given to Abraham that his seed should inherit the land and be blessed with power, wealth and number (Gen 15). This is also the 'rest' (4:1), and the reception of the land was called an inheritance (11:8)" (194).

23. Some have argued that the Olivet Discourse (Matt. 24) is to be understood as solely referring to events fulfilled in the AD 70 destruction of Jerusalem (see J. M. Kik, *Matthew Twenty-Four: An*

desolation" (24:15, HCSB)—an end-of-days event foreseen by Daniel (9:27; 11:31)—and warns the people of Judea to flee (24:16). They are told to pray that their flight not be in winter (24:20) because it is the rainy season and travel is difficult. They are also to pray that they need not flee on Sabbath, when there is no public transportation available. This warning of the future is directed to Jewish people in their own land.

Another reference to the future in the land is the New Testament picture of the end-of-days campaign of Armageddon (Rev. 16:14–16). At that time, the kings of the whole world will muster "for the battle of the great day of God, the Almighty" (16:14, HCSB). The location of this gathering of armies is at Mt. Megiddo, overlooking the Jezreel Valley (16:16). When linked with the Hebrew Bible, it becomes clear that these armies will make their way to Jerusalem, in a final and failed attempt to destroy the Jewish people there (cf. Zech. 12:2–3; 14:2).

A future temple. Besides these end of days prophecies, the New Testament predicts that there will be a future temple built in Jerusalem. The "abomination that causes desolation" (Matt. 24:15, cited above) can only occur in a literal, future temple. Paul mentions this same event, stating that at the Day of the Lord, "the man of lawlessness [will be] revealed, the son of destruction." Then he describes the same abominable act, when the man of lawlessness, "opposes and exalts himself above every so-called god or object of worship, so that he sits in God's sanctuary, publicizing that he himself is

---

Exposition [Philadelphia: Presbyterian and Reformed, 1948] and R. V. G. Tasker, *The Gospel according to Matthew*, Tyndale New Testament Commentary [Grand Rapids: Eerdmans, 1961], 223–24) while others have proposed a partial fulfillment in AD 70 (24:4–25, 28, 35) and the rest referring to events at the return of the Messiah Jesus (24:26, 29, 36). A good example of this view is R. T. France, *The Gospel of Matthew*, New International Commentary on the New Testament (Grand Rapids: Eerdmans, 2007), 889–94. Yet others have proposed double fulfillment, indicating that the entire chapter pertains to both the destruction of Jerusalem in AD 70 and events at the return of Messiah (See D. A. Carson, "Matthew," *The Expositor's Bible Commentary* Vol. 8 [Grand Rapids: Zondervan, 1984], 488–95, and D. L. Turner, *Matthew*, Baker Exegetical Commentary on the New Testament [Grand Rapids: Baker, 2008], 566–67). Another approach is to view the passage as only referring to the time of the end (See Stanley D. Toussaint, *Behold the King* [Portland, OR: Multnomah Press, 1980], 266–69). It seems best to view Matthew 24 as referring solely to the end of days and the return of the Messiah Jesus (although Luke does indeed include a prediction of the AD 70 siege and destruction of Jerusalem in Luke 21:20–24, a part of Jesus' discourse not included by Matthew). The disciples' question regarding the time of the destruction of Jerusalem is not referring to AD 70 but to their perception of the end of days desolation of Jerusalem described in Zechariah (12:1–3; 14:1–2; similarly, Toussaint, 269). The passage is to be read as a chiasm, with the first question being "when will these things be" and the second being "what are the signs?" Then the answers are given in reverse order, with the second question answered first, in 24:4–35 and the first question answered second (in 24:36–44). Additional reasons for reading this as referring to events at the end of days rather than AD 70 include Jesus shift of the discussion to the end-of-days restoration of Israel at his return in the previous paragraph (Matt. 23:37–39; See R. H. Gundry, *A Commentary on His Literary and Theological Art* [Grand Rapids: Eerdmans, 1982], 474), the worldwide scope of the events described (e.g., 24:3, 7, 14, 21–22, 27, 30–31, 40–41; See M. G. VanLaningham, "Matthew," in *The Moody Bible Commentary* [Chicago: Moody Publishers, 2014], 1497–98) and the reference to an end-time abomination of desolation (24:15).

God" (2 Thess. 2:3–4, HCSB). Once again, the New Testament foresees a Jewish temple in the land of Israel at the end of days.

A future restoration. John Stott stated, "[T]he Old Testament promises about the land are nowhere repeated in the New Testament, except possibly in Luke 21:24."[24] Although this verse does not fit his presuppositions, Stott recognizes that Luke 21:24 does indeed anticipate a future restoration of the Jewish people to their land. This verse says "Jerusalem will be trampled by the Gentiles until the times of the Gentiles are fulfilled" (HCSB). Clearly the Lord Jesus is predicting the long oppression of Jerusalem under Gentile governments, but he does not view this as a permanent situation. This will only last *until* the time of Gentile domination is fulfilled. The simplest meaning of this verse is that when the times of the Gentiles end, God will restore Jerusalem to the Jewish people.[25]

There are several more verses in the New Testament that speak of Israel's restoration, despite Stott's assertion that Luke 21:24 is the one possible exception to his presupposition. For example, in Matthew 23:37–39, when speaking of Jerusalem's rejection of his Messiahship, the Lord Jesus not only expresses his sorrow and longing to have gathered the people of Israel to himself, but he also anticipates a day when the nation will accept him. Saying Israel will not see him again until they welcome him with the Hebrew greeting, "Blessed is He who comes in the Name of the Lord" (NASB). The Lord Jesus prophecies of a day when the Jewish people will receive him. This is an allusion to Zechariah 12:10, which will be fulfilled in Jerusalem at the end of days.

Another New Testament allusion to Zechariah 12:10 is found in the Olivet discourse. There, speaking of His return, Jesus says, "Then the sign of the Son of Man will appear in the sky, and then all the peoples of the earth will mourn; and they will see the Son of Man coming on the clouds of heaven with power and great glory" (Matt. 24:30, HCSB). The phrase "peoples of the earth" literally says, "all the tribes of the land," a reference to the Jewish people in the land of Israel at the return of Jesus. That these tribes "mourn" indicates that this is an allusion to Israel's actions at the return of the Lord to Jerusalem in Zechariah 12:10.

The apostle Paul also speaks of this day, when the nation of Israel will call for the return of the Lord Jesus to save them. He writes, "And in this way all Israel will be saved, as it is written: The Deliverer will come from Zion; He will turn away godlessness from Jacob. And this will be My covenant with them, when I take away their sins" (HCSB). The "all Israel" that

---

24. As cited by A. Boyd Luter, "The Continuation of Israel's Land Promise in the New Testament: A Fresh Approach," *Eruditio Ardescens* (Spring, I:2):3.

25. For a more detailed exposition of this passage and the parallel verses in Luke 13:34–35, see Darrell Bock, "Israel in Luke-Acts" *The People, the Land and the Future of Israel* (Grand Rapids: Kregel, 2014), 103–15. For, another exceptional exegetical discussion of the Lukan material, showing the continuing land promise to Israel, see Mark Kinzer, "Zionism in Luke-Acts: Do the People of Israel and the Land of Israel Persist as Abiding Concerns in Luke's Two Volumes?" *The New Christian Zionism*, ed. Gerald R. McDermott (Downers Grove, IL: InterVarsity Press, 2016), 141–65.

will be saved refers not to all the Jewish people for all time, but to the Jewish national acceptance of Jesus the Messiah at His return (cf. Matt. 23:37–39; 24:30; Zech. 12:10). The leadership of the Jewish people will turn to the Messiah Jesus as the armies of Armageddon attempt to crush Jerusalem. Then, the Messianic King, the Lord Jesus will return to save them. Specifically, this prophecy states that "the Deliverer will come from Zion." The Messiah Jesus will return to Jerusalem (cf. Zech 14:3) and from there save His people.

A future kingdom. The New Testament also predicts that there will indeed be a kingdom for Israel. For example, in Acts 1:6–7, the disciples, after forty days of instruction about the kingdom of God, ask their Messiah, "Lord, at this time are you restoring the kingdom to Israel?" Jesus' reply is, "It is not for you to know the times or periods that the Father has set by His own authority" (HCSB). Clearly, the disciples had not abandoned their anticipation of a literal messianic kingdom for the Jewish people in the land of Israel.

Gary Burge has explained Jesus' correction this way: "[It] should not be taken to mean that Jesus acknowledges the old Jewish worldview and that its timing is now hidden from the apostles. Instead Jesus is acknowledging their incomprehension. He in effect says, 'Yes I will restore Israel—but in a way you cannot imagine.'"[26] Although this interpretation fits the presuppositions of those who reject any New Testament reaffirmation of the land promise, it certainly does not fit the words of this text. Jesus plainly says the apostles cannot know "the times or periods" that the Father will set for the future kingdom. However, he does not in any way repudiate their expectation of that future kingdom for the Jewish people in the land of Israel, nor does he redefine their expectation in a way that is contrary to Old Testament revelation. The job of the apostles will be to preach the gospel. The responsibility of the Father is to set the day when the Lord will indeed restore the kingdom to Israel. The confirmation of this interpretation is in the text itself. When the Lord Jesus ascended from the Mount of Olives, the angels told the disciples that He would return in the same way (1:11). This is an allusion to Zechariah 14:3, which reveals that when the Messiah comes, his feet will stand on the literal Mount of Olives, in the literal land of Israel, just east of the literal city of Jerusalem, from whence he will save the literal people of Israel.

The Messiah Jesus also speaks of the Messianic age to his disciples in Matthew 19:28. Therein recognizing their sacrifices to follow him, the Lord tells them, "I assure you: In the Messianic Age, when the Son of Man sits on His glorious throne, you who have followed Me will also sit on 12 thrones, judging the 12 tribes of Israel" (HCSB). This anticipates that the 12 disciples, as leaders of the faithful remnant of Israel will govern the 12 tribes of Israel in the future Messianic kingdom.[27]

---

26. Burge, *Jesus and the Land*, 61.

27. This is not a conflation of the church and Israel. Rather, there needed to be twelve disciples, so they could govern Israel in the future messianic kingdom. For this reason, the disciples could not wait

The New Testament is not silent about the land promises. Rather, it presumes that these promises will be fulfilled. Therefore, the fulfillment of the land promise becomes the canvas upon which the New Testament paints its eschatology.

d. The New Testament does not redefine the people of Israel, nor the nature of the land promise.

The view that the New Testament has redefined both the people of Israel and the land promise is based on a mistaken understanding of two verses of Scripture. Therefore, these passages should be examined to show they do not allow New Testament interpretation that contradicts the original intent of the Old Testament author.

Galatians 3:16. This verse states "Now the promises were spoken to Abraham and to his seed. He does not say 'and to seeds,' as though referring to many, but referring to one, and to your seed, who is Christ" (HCSB). Paul emphatically states that the promise was made "to Abraham and to his seed," specifying that the word "seed" is not plural but "referring to one . . . who is Christ." Some have argued that the promises of the Abrahamic Covenant are no longer applicable to ethnic Israel but to the one true recipient, the Israel "par excellence," Jesus Christ.[28] Moreover, it is argued that since all followers of Jesus are in Christ (Gal. 3:29), it is the Church that is now the sole beneficiary of the Abrahamic promises. Further, the Church does not take over the land promises God made with Israel, but rather these promises have been spiritualized and "de-territorialize[d]" (with any territorial aspect removed) and fulfilled in connection with Christ and his people.[29]

The above interpretation of Galatians 3:16. fails to recognize that the context has only one specific aspect of the Abrahamic promise in mind, namely, the promise of the Spirit for the Gentiles (Gal. 3:15). This is a reference to the promise that in Abraham's seed all families of the earth would be blessed (Gen. 12:3). It also misunderstands the Abrahamic Covenant, and therefore misinterprets Paul's use of it.

The word "seed" is always singular in form, but may refer to an individual or a collective group. In Genesis 22:16–18, there appears to be an oscillation between the collective use, referring to the physical descendants of Abraham who would be as numerous as the stars and sand (Gen. 22:16–17a), and the individual sense, referring to the Messiah who will bless the whole world.[30] Therefore, the Abrahamic Covenant includes national prom-

---

for Paul, the apostle to the Gentiles, to be the twelfth apostle. Instead, they chose Matthias, one of their own, to replace Judas as the twelfth apostle to Israel.

28. Donald Guthrie, "Galatians," *New Century Bible* (London: Oliphants, 1974), 102.

29. See Gary M. Burge, *Whose Land? Whose Promise?* (Cleveland, OH: Pilgrim Press, 2003), 184.

30. The explanation of this oscillation is explained in my comment in the Moody Bible Commentary: "As a result of Abraham's faith, God reaffirmed the Abrahamic covenant, promising to bless Abraham and "greatly multiply [his] seed" (v. 17a). In this sentence, Abraham's seed is obviously to be

ises for the descendants of Abraham, Isaac, and Jacob, including the promise of the land of Israel for the people Israel (cf. Gen. 12:1, 7; 13:14–15; 15:18; 17:7–8; 26:2–3; 28:13; 35:12; 1 Chr. 16:16–18; 2 Chr. 20:6–7). The covenant promise also includes blessings for the world through an individual offspring of Abraham, the Messiah. But the blessing of the nations of the world does not necessitate the rejection of the land promises made to Israel.

In Galatians 3:16, Paul specifies that he is not referring to the corporate promises (made "to many," i.e., Israel) but to the individual "seed" ("who is Christ") and the universal blessings He brings to the nations as predicted in the OT. Paul is not changing the object of the Abrahamic promises or spiritualizing the land promises, but rather recognizing that God always intended the Messiah to provide salvation and spiritual blessing to the nations, not just for Israel. This verse is not even speaking of the physical and national promises to Abraham's physical descendants but is rather emphasizing the universal spiritual promises, that "the Scripture, foreseeing that God would justify the Gentiles by faith, preached the gospel beforehand to Abraham, saying, "All the nations will be blessed in you" (Gal. 3:8).

Romans 4:13. Paul states that the "the promise to Abraham or to his descendants that he would inherit the world was not through the law, but through the righteousness that comes by faith" (HCSB). This verse is frequently cited as proving that the New Testament view of the land promises refers to the whole world and no longer to the land of Israel alone. Burge states,

> Romans 4:13 is the only place where the apostle refers explicitly to the promises for the land given to Abraham and in this case Paul fails to refer to Judea. Paul writes that the promise to Abraham indicates that the patriarch would inherit *the world* (Gk *kosmos*). The universalizing intent of Paul has now shifted from the Gentiles to the domain of Gentile life. In Genesis Abraham was to inherit the Holy Land. In Romans 4:13, his claim is on the world.[31]

---

taken in a collective sense, since they will be as numerous "as the stars of the heavens and as the sand . . . on the seashore." Then, God promised that Abraham's "seed shall possess the gate of their [literally "his"] enemies" and in that "seed all the nations of the earth shall be blessed" (vv. 17b–18). This usage of seed appears to refer to an individual who will bless the whole world. This is evident in that the pronoun referring back to that seed is singular (lit. "shall possess the gate of *his* enemies"). T. D. Alexander has correctly proposed that this reflects an oscillation from a collective use of the word "seed" in verse 17a to an individual sense in verses 17b–18. His point is that although 22:17a uses "seed" in the collective sense, a new sentence begins in 22:17b (without a *vav consecutive*, typically used in Heb. for a continuation of thought but instead with a simple imperfect verb indicating the beginning of a completely new thought). This new sentence makes it likely that the word "seed" is being used in a new, individual sense. The significance of this is that this oracle looks forward to one particular descendant of Abraham who will rule over His enemies and bless the world. (T. Desmond Alexander, "Further Observations on the Term 'Seed' in Genesis," *Tyndale Bulletin* 48.2 [1997]): 363–367). Paul recognized that this individual seed was reference to the Messiah and fulfilled by Jesus of Nazareth (Gal. 3:8, 16)." See "Genesis," *The Moody Bible Commentary*, eds. Michael Rydelnik and Michael VanLaningham (Chicago: Moody Publishers, 2014), 82.

31. Burge, *Jesus and the Land*, 85.

Romans 4:13 does not appear to be about the land promise at all.[32] With regard to the Old Testament background to this verse, Abraham was promised that he would be "the father of many nations" (Gen. 17:5). This is clearly what Paul is discussing in the context, maintaining that Abraham was to be the physical and spiritual father of Jewish believers and the spiritual father of the Gentile believers (Rom. 4:9–12). Romans 4:13 asserts that Abraham is the heir of the world *of people*, not land. The word "world" (Gk. *kosmos*) in the New Testament is commonly understood to refer to the *world of people* (cf. John 1:29, 3:16; Rom. 3:19; 2 Cor. 5:19). Paul continues his discussion of Abraham and shows that he is speaking of Abraham being heir to the world *of people*. In Romans 4:16 he calls Abraham, "the father of us all," and in 4:17 he cites Genesis 17:5, "I have made you the father of many nations." Expanding the land promise from the land of Israel to the whole world is completely foreign to this context.

Despite the efforts of some to see a New Testament transference of the land promise to a newly defined "spiritual Israel" in Galatians 3:16 and an expanded territory encompassing the whole world in Romans 4:13, it does not appear that these two verses can easily carry this freight. A more literal interpretation of these two passages appears to be far more congruent with the promises of God to the Jewish people and is not only preferable, but more plausible, preserving the unity of the testaments with a greater degree of fidelity to both the Old and New Testament canon.

CONCLUSION

Once, I was at an academic conference with the great Old Testament scholar Walt Kaiser. I commented to him that I was surprised to see that he was giving a paper on the New Testament rather than the Old. Dr. Kaiser smiled and said, "I love the New Testament—it reminds me so much of the Old."

Dr. Kaiser's response is actually the point of this chapter. By using a hermeneutic that harmonizes the Old and New Testaments, it is possible to demonstrate that both testaments are consistent with regard to the land promise. The proposition that the New Testament does not reaffirm the literal nature of the Old Testament land promises and in fact repudiates them, is only possible by reading the New Testament through a supersessionst lens. However, if readers view the New Testament through their Old Testament spectacles, then what is seen becomes sharp and clear—the New Testament reaffirms the promise of the Old, that the God of Israel gave the land of Israel to the people of Israel, forever.

---

32. For a more detailed refutation of the interpretation that Romans 4:13 expands the land promise from the land of Israel to the whole world, see Nelson S. Hsieh, "Abraham as 'Heir of the World': Does Romans 4:13 Expand the Old Testament Abrahamic Land Promises?" *The Master's Seminary Journal* 26/1 (Spring 2015): 95–110.

PART 2
THEOLOGY AND THE CONFLICT

A THEOLOGY OF ISRAEL AND THE CHURCH

CRAIG BLAISING

A KEY QUESTION THAT UNDERLIES THE VARIOUS ARTICLES of this book is how to understand Israel and the church in the plan of God. This question must be answered in order to make sense of the story of the Bible from Old Testament to New Testament. To answer the question requires a theology of Israel and the church.

In order to sharpen the question, it is important to define Israel and the church within those portions of Scripture in which they are especially featured. In the Old Testament, Israel is an ethnic, national, territorial (ENT) reality that God created among the nations and to which He covenanted promises of everlasting ethnic, national, and territorial blessing. In the New Testament, the church is a Spirit-indwelt communion of individual Jews and Gentiles that is brought into existence in and through Jesus Christ with forgiveness of sins and the promise of everlasting life. The question is how to understand the relationship between Israel and the church as one traces the story of the Bible from the Old Testament to the New Testament. Are they ultimately the same thing? Is one simply a version of the other? Are they utterly different realities? Are they different but related in some way? Do they compete with one another? How do they fit into the ultimate plan of God?

Two well-known ways of understanding Israel and the church theologically are supersessionism and dispensationalism. Supersessionism sees Old Testament Israel as replaced (superseded) by another reality in the New Testament. As such, supersessionism is also known as *replacement theology*. Dispensationalism, traditionally understood, sees the New Testament church as a completely new people that is unrelated to Israel—a people that belong to a completely different story line in the Bible. While quite popular, supersessionism and traditional dispensationalism are both inadequate to explain the theological difference yet interconnection of Israel and the church in Scripture. However, in order to see this, some further explanation of each one is necessary.

While there are various forms of supersessionism, two may be highlighted here: ethnic supersessionism and economic supersessionism.[1] Ethnic supersessionism argues that Israel as a people has been replaced in the divine plan by Gentile peoples (some versions emphasize a particular Gentile people while others speak of Gentiles in general).[2] The reason for this replacement is said to be the failure of the Jews as a people to trust and obey God. As a result, God cancelled the promises made to Israel and turned to the Gentiles. The church, in this form of supersessionism, is a Gentile reality. When Christ returns, unbelieving Gentiles will be judged and only the Gentile church will remain to enter its consummate glory.[3] Accordingly, Jews who come to believe in Jesus lose their Jewish ethnicity and essentially become "Gentile" Christians. Obviously, ethnic supersessionism is strongly anti-Semitic, since in its view God has ultimately rejected the Jewish people as a people and has replaced them in the divine plan.

On the other hand, economic supersessionism argues that Israel, the "earthly" people of God in the Old Testament, has been replaced in the divine plan not by another "earthly" people or peoples, but by a "spiritual" people, the church of the New Testament.[4] In this form of supersessionism, Israel was never in God's mind more than a temporary reality ultimately to be superseded by "a new Israel," the church.[5] Accordingly, the ethnic, national, and territorial promises to Israel have to be spiritually interpreted in order to discern their true meaning.[6] Their fulfillment is to be found in the

---

1. A seminal work analyzing supersessionism is R. Kendall Soulen, *The God of Israel and Christian Theology* (Minneapolis, Fortress, 1996). Soulen's classification of different types of supersessionism has been adopted by others writing on this topic. A more recent work dependent on Soulen but developing the analysis further is Michael Vlach, *Has the Church Replaced Israel: A Theological Evaluation* (Nashville: B&H, 2010).

2. My category, *ethnic supersessionism*, refers to what Soulen and Vlach call *punitive supersessionism*. See Soulen, 30–31; Vlach, 13–14.

3. Not all forms of ethnic supersessionism expect a literal return of Christ. For purposes of comparison, this article will focus on those views that affirm a consummate state brought into existence by the personal return of Christ. Such views would also, of course, carry implications for the understanding of Christ and his messiahship.

4. The term *economic supersessionism* was proposed by Soulen and has been adopted by others. See Soulen, 29–30. Also see Vlach, *Has the Church Replaced Israel*, 13–16.

5. It should be noted that the adjective "economic" in this use carries the meaning of its Greek root, *oikonomia*, referring to an administrative or management order. This must be distinguished from the current, more limited use of the English word *economy* to refer to a financial order of money and wealth. Economic supersessionism refers to a change in God's administrative order of human beings, from a particular earthly structure to a universal spiritual order. This view of supersessionism is most common in traditional Christian theology.

6. Classical presentations of supersessionist hermeneutics may be found in: Oswald T. Allis, *Prophecy and the Church* (Philadelphia: Presbyterian and Reformed, 1947); and Patrick Fairbarn, *The Interpretation of Prophecy* (Edinburgh, T. and T. Clark, 1865). For a critique of supersessionist hermeneutics see Craig Blaising, "Israel and Hermeneutics," in *The People, the Land and the Future of Israel: A Biblical Theology of Israel and the Jewish People*, ed. Darrell L. Bock and Mitch Glaser (Grand Rapids: Kregel, 2014), 151–67; idem, "Biblical Hermeneutics: How Are We to Interpret the Relation Between the

spiritual realities of the church, not in a particular national and territorial future for ethnic Israel. While economic supersessionism allows a place for individual Jews in the church alongside Gentile believers, neither their ethnic identity nor that of any other peoples has any ultimate theological significance. In the consummation, the church replaces the entire multi-corporate (multi-national, multi-ethnic) structure of historical humanity. There will be only one "nation" of redeemed humanity, a "spiritual Israel" which replaces Israel and all Gentile nations. It should not be surprising that economic supersessionism has been criticized as anti-Semitic due to its rejection of the ENT aspects of corporate Israel, and this is not without consequence in the church's relationship with individual Jews.

Dispensationalism, traditionally understood, sees Israel, Gentiles, and church as distinct and exclusive groupings of humanity, each having its own purpose and place in the plan of God.[7] The church is a new people group that comes into existence in the New Testament as a spiritual or heavenly humanity formed from, but not in replacement of, the existing earthly peoples, Jews and Gentiles. The church is not a "new Israel." The church does not replace ENT Israel in the plan of God. It does not "spiritually fulfill" the promises covenanted by God to Israel. Rather, its appearance in history is more properly understood as an interruption in God's dealings with Israel. God's "earthly" plan for ENT Israel is temporarily suspended during the formation of the church.[8] In God's appointed time, the interruption will cease.

Tanak and the New Testament on This Question? In *The New Christian Zionism: Fresh Perspectives on Israel and the Land*, ed. Gerald R. McDermott (Downers Grove: IVP, 2016), 79–105. Also see, Barry Horner, "Israel and Christian Anti-Judaic Hermeneutics in History," and "Israel and Christian Anti-Judaic Hermeneutics Today," in *Future Israel: Why Christian Anti-Judaism Must Be Challenged* (Nashville: B&H, 2008); Vlach, *Has the Church Replaced Israel*, 79–120.

7. For an overview of dispensationalism, see Craig Blaising, "Dispensation, Dispensationalism" in *The Evangelical Dictionary of Theology*, ed. Daniel J. Treier and Walter A. Elwell, 3rd ed (Grand Rapids: Baker, 2017), 248–49; also see Craig A. Blaising and Darrell L. Bock, *Progressive Dispensationalism* (Wheaton, IL: Victor Books, 1993; reprint Baker Books). What is called traditional dispensationalism here can be further distinguished as classical and revised dispensationalism. The term "traditional dispensationalism" is used by many today to refer especially to what is described as revised dispensationalism. The term *traditional* is used primarily to distinguish an earlier dispensational theology from *progressive dispensationalism* which in this article is being called Redemptive Kingdom Theology. The book *Progressive Dispensationalism* presents this view in comparison and contrast to earlier forms of dispensationalism.

8. Seeing the church as an interruption of the divine plan for Israel is crucial for traditional dispensational theology. For some, it was not strong enough. Lewis Chafer preferred the term *intercalation* to emphasize the absolute disconnect between the church and Israel in the biblical narrative; Lewis Sperry Chafer, *Systematic Theology*, 8 vols. (Dallas: Dallas Seminary Press, 1948), 4:40. The church has no relationship to God's promises, plans, and providence for Israel. A consequence of this view is the utter disconnectedness of the New Testament theology of the church from covenant promises given in the Old Testament (although note some modifications of the dispensational view in *Progressive Dispensationalism*, 37–39). Traditional dispensationalists also decidedly rejected any connection between the church in New Testament theology and the kingdom of God in its holistic sense. This obviously creates problems for interpreting the many connections to Old Testament promise and prophecy found in the New Testament, see Darrell Bock, "Covenants in Progressive

The spiritual people will be removed (raptured) and God's purpose for the earthly people Israel will resume.[9] All three people groups, Israel, Gentiles, and the church, have a place in the consummation of the divine plan. When all is completed, redeemed humanity will be composed of church, Israel, and Gentiles. Consequently, all three, but especially Israel and the church, are of ultimate theological significance.

Understanding the church as a distinct people group is crucial for the traditional dispensational view. The term, people group, as it is used here would normally refer to an *ethne*, which might seem inappropriate for a "spiritual" people. However, in traditional dispensationalism, while Jews and the various Gentile peoples are distinct *ethnes*, the church is construed as a quasi-ethnic group in the sense that identity in the church is theologically exclusive of the ethnic identities of Jews and Gentiles. If one is part of the church, that one is neither Jew nor Gentile from a theological point of view. This was the traditional dispensational understanding of Paul's description of the "one new man" in Ephesians 2. Jew, Gentile, and church are mutually exclusive identities. One can only belong to one group. The consequences of this are most apparent in the case of Jewish believers. Jews who believe in Jesus, according to traditional dispensationalism, do not participate in the inheritance of Israel. As a part of the new people, the church, they have a separate place, a heavenly place, in the consummation of the divine plan apart from Israel per se.

A third way of viewing Israel and the church theologically may be described as Redemptive Kingdom Theology.[10] *Redemptive Kingdom Theology* has also been called *progressive dispensationalism* because of its similarity to and difference from traditional dispensationalism.[11] It is similar to traditional dispensationalism in its rejection of supersessionism. The church as a new

---

Dispensationalism," in *Three Central Issues in Contemporary Dispensationalism: A Comparison of Traditional and Progressive Views*, ed. Herbert W. Bateman IV (Grand Rapids: Kregel, 1999), 169–203, 211–23. It also creates an identity problem for Jewish believers in the church since it disassociates them from the inheritance of Israel.

9. Redemptive Kingdom Theology, explained below and also known as progressive dispensationalism, is not opposed to a pre-tribulational rapture. But, it would not see a pre-tribulational rapture as intrinsic to the definition of the church as is the case in traditional dispensationalism. For a defense of a pre-tribulational rapture from a Redemptive Kingdom standpoint, see Craig Blaising, "A Case for the Pretribulational Rapture," in *Three Views on the Rapture: Pretribulation, Prewrath, or Post-tribulation*, ed. Alan Hultberg (Grand Rapids: Zondervan, 2010), 25–73, see also pp. 103–08. For a traditional dispensational defense of the pretribulational rapture, see Paul D. Feinberg, "The Case for the Pretribulation Rapture Position," in *The Rapture: Pre-, Mid-, or Post-Tribulational?* Ed. Richard Reiter et al (Grand Rapids: Zondervan, 1984), 45–86.

10. The adjective *Redemptive* is necessary to distinguish this view from the use of the label *Kingdom Theology* by some to emphasize signs and wonders as indicative of kingdom presence. Redemptive Kingdom Theology sees the presence of the kingdom in the application of redemption to the peoples of the world who believe in Christ forming them into a spiritual communion which as such constitutes a present inaugural form of the coming Kingdom of God.

11. See Blaising and Bock, *Progressive Dispensationalism*, 46–54.

spiritual communion in the New Testament neither ethnically nor economically replaces or supersedes ENT Israel in the plan of God. However, RKT differs from traditional dispensationalism in that it does not see the church as a distinct people group, a quasi-ethnic people separate from the ethnic peoples of Israel and the Gentiles in the plan of God. To be included in the church does not mean exclusion from the inheritance of Israel for Jewish believers or exclusion of Gentile believers from God's plan of blessing for Gentile peoples or nations. Jews who believe in Jesus still belong to the people of Israel and have a heritage as redeemed Israel in the consummation of the divine plan. They are in fact evidence that Israel's redemption remains vital in the plan of God.

If the church is neither the divinely intended replacement of ethnic Israel nor a third people group designed to stand alongside ethnic Jews and Gentiles in the consummation, what is it? Redemptive Kingdom Theology would say that to answer this question, one must look to the Kingdom of God. The divine plan for Israel and for the Gentile peoples and nations is a future worldwide kingdom of nations—a multi-national kingdom—ruled and blessed by God through His Messiah on earth forever.[12] In this future kingdom, God's covenanted promises to Israel will be fulfilled and secured forever. Also, in that kingdom, under the reign of the messiah, Gentile peoples and nations likewise come under the everlasting blessing of God. This future worldwide kingdom is a progressively developed theme in biblical theology, which is linked to a future salvation prophesied for Israel and for all peoples.[13] The prophesied salvation makes possible the future fulfillment of Israel's promises. The extension of its benefits to Gentile peoples as well secures the stability of the kingdom forever.

The New Testament reveals two mysteries about the kingdom and the salvation associated with it. First is the appearance of an inaugural form of kingdom blessings after the ascension of Christ and prior to his return. These kingdom blessings are precisely the salvific blessings, which are now granted to Jews and Gentiles who believe in Jesus. They are granted to individual believers now in advance of the return of Jesus and the full establishment of his kingdom on earth over all nations. The second mystery concerns an

---

12. Redemptive Kingdom Theology does not deny a future millennial kingdom. But, contrary to some forms of premillennialism, it sees the final fulfillment of kingdom promises not in a temporary order but in one that is in fact everlasting. The millennial kingdom fulfills a line of prophecy predicting a future kingdom under mortal conditions as well as the explicit millennial vision of John in Revelation 20. However, the repeated prediction of an everlasting kingdom of nations and an everlasting messianic reign together with John's final vision of the new earth and new Jerusalem in Revelation 21–22 locates the final fulfillment of kingdom prophecy not in a penultimate order but in the final consummation. For a defense and framing of premillennialism that affirms both the future temporary (millennial) and eternal forms of the prophesied kingdom, see Craig A. Blaising, "Premillennialism," in *Three Views on the Millennium and Beyond*, ed. Darrell L. Bock (Grand Rapids: Zondervan, 1999), 155–227.

13. For a presentation on the development of the theme of the kingdom in Scripture, see *Progressive Dispensationalism*, 212–83.

aspect of these salvific blessings, the equal gifting of the Holy Spirit to Gentiles as well as Jews who believe in Christ. The equal gifting of the Holy
Spirit unites both Jewish and Gentile believers directly to Christ and to one
another forming a spiritual communion in Christ. This reveals something
new about the kingdom: God's plan is to dwell not only with but also in all
redeemed humanity. This in turn clarifies what makes the kingdom stable
and secure forever. And the appearance of this reality in its inaugural form
after the ascension of Christ is what the New Testament calls the church. The
church is the spiritual unity, the spiritual communion, of kingdom peoples.
It is the spiritual communion and unity in Christ of persons of various *ethnes*
and nations. It does not replace the multi-ethnic, multi-national corporate
reality of humanity but rather permeates it with the presence of God. It is a
spiritual unity that is intended to characterize an anthropologically diverse
worldwide kingdom, one in which the particular promises of God to the
particular people Israel are secured and fulfilled forever.[14]

THE KINGDOM OF GOD PROGRESSIVELY REVEALED IN CANONICAL THEOLOGY: ISRAEL, THE NATIONS, AND THE CHURCH

It is impossible within the scope of this article to fully develop the kingdom theme in canonical theology. However, a sketch of that development
may help elucidate the points made above about Redemptive Kingdom Theology. It is hoped that readers will take up the challenge to see the church as
an aspect of the greater revelation of a kingdom in which the promises and
purposes of God are fulfilled in Christ.

The Old Testament

The divine plan for a worldwide kingdom is first indicated in the creation mandate for human dominion over the earth (Gen. 1:26), a plan that
is renewed after the Fall with the promise of a future seed of the woman who
would crush the head of the serpent (Gen. 3:15). Further revelation of the
plan comes with the promise covenanted to Abraham, first to bless him and
his seed, forming of him and of them a people to be a great nation with a specific territorial location on earth as an everlasting possession, and secondly
to bless in him all the nations of the earth (Gen. 12:1–3; 18:18; 22:17–18).
Here the ENT promises to Israel are anchored, promises that are repeatedly
affirmed in the rest of Scripture.[15] However, the final element of the promise
to Abraham—the promise to "bless all nations in you"—expresses a universal
intent for all nations including Israel.[16] This intent comes to be described in

---

14. For the church as a phase of the kingdom, see ibid., 251–62.

15. The biblical data on this is too numerous to cite. For the covenant foundation and prophetic repetition of promises to ethnic, national, territorial Israel, see the treatment of the biblical covenants in
ibid., 130–73. See also Vlach, *Has the Church Replaced Israel*, 177–201.

16. The plan for universal blessing is expressed in the Old Testament side by side with the particular

the ongoing narrative as a multi-national kingdom whose rule is to be assigned to one from the tribe of Judah:

> The scepter shall not depart from Judah
> nor the ruler's staff from between his feet,
> until tribute comes to him;
> and to him will be the obedience of the peoples (Gen. 49:10).[17]

While Exodus and the subsequent books of the Old Testament develop the history of God's formation of ENT Israel, the next major step in the plan for a universal kingdom comes in the covenant with David (2 Sam. 7:8–17; 23:5; 1 Chron. 17:3–15; cf. Pss. 89; 110). To David of the tribe of Judah and his descendant God covenants the promise of an everlasting kingdom in which Israel will be secure and at peace with the nations (2 Sam. 7:9–11; 16). In Psalm 2, the Lord declares that the kingdom of His king, His messiah, His Son (cf. 2 Sam. 7:14), will be worldwide and multi-national:

> Ask of me, and I will make the nations your heritage
> and the ends of the earth your possession (Ps. 2:8).

The kings and rulers of the earth are warned to serve him and delight in him (Ps. 2:10–12) with the promise:

> Blessed are all who take refuge in him (Ps. 2:12).

Likewise, Psalm 72 sees the Abrahamic universal blessing channeled through the Davidic King:

> May people be blessed in him
> [May] all nations call him blessed! (Ps. 72:17).

Of course, the Old Testament also narrates the problem of sin and the threat it poses to the peoples of the world. Because of sin, the shroud of death lies upon all people. However, sin threatens not just individual persons, but also the corporate and collective dimensions of human life—the character and even the continual existence of whole peoples and nations. Because of sin, the entire human race save for one family perished in the flood of Genesis 6–9. Nations have come and gone on the face of the earth. Sin continually posed a threat to the people of Israel throughout their history—the people

---

divine plan for Israel. It is necessary to stress this point against misrepresentations of the biblical narrative as a transition from an Old Testament focus on a particular nation to a widened focus in the New Testament on all nations. This misrepresentation can be found even in recent publications by otherwise respected scholars who claim to present the theological narrative of Scripture.

17.   All citations of Scripture are from the English Standard Version.

who were called to be holy and who were warned that sin would destroy the nation and remove them from the promised land. Those warnings, of course, were realized climactically in the Assyrian and Babylonian destructions of the 8th and 6th centuries BC. The drama of Israel's failure on the national level was the object lesson chosen by God to reveal the gravity of sin. But Israel was also to be a people in and through whom God would reveal His mercy, His grace, and the truth of his covenant promises in national and territorial restoration. Their restoration, however, would require the redemption and spiritual renewal of the people. It would require the forgiveness of sins and a divinely instituted change of the human heart.

Three observations need to be noted concerning OT prophecy as the story of the Bible moves toward the New Testament. First, the kingdom plan revealed to the Patriarchs and then later covenanted to the house of David is restated and reaffirmed by the later prophets. Isaiah, Jeremiah, and the other prophets foresee a future Davidic king who will be given sovereignty over Israel and the Gentile nations to rule the world in righteousness and peace forever (e.g., Isa. 9:6–7; 11:1–12; Amos 9:11–15; Zech. 9:9–10). The same prophets clearly predicted that ENT Israel would be restored to be an essential feature of that kingdom, and they foresaw that the Gentiles would join themselves to the Lord and His messiah (Isa. 11:10–12; 49:14–52:10; 54:1–17; 60:1–62:12; Jer. 30:1–31:37; 32:36–33:26; Zech. 2:11; 8:7–15, 20–23; 10:8–10; 14:9, 16–19).

Second, the prophets speak of a coming redemption by means of a divinely provided atonement, the forgiveness of sins and renewal by the Holy Spirit. Isaiah speaks of a coming Servant who will bear "our transgressions" and "make many to be accounted righteous" (Isa. 53:4–12). Jeremiah predicts a new covenant in which God will write His law on the hearts of His people Israel and forgive their sins (Jer. 31:31–37). Ezekiel speaks of a cleansing from sin and the gift of a new heart (Ezek. 36:25–26). Isaiah speaks of the outpouring of the Holy Spirit giving life (Isa. 32:15; 44:1–5) and Ezekiel speaks of enablement by the gift of the indwelling Spirit (Ezek. 36:27).

Thirdly, these same prophets link the prophesied redemption to the restoration of ENT Israel and to the kingdom plan for all nations. The Servant who will bring redemption will not only restore Israel to God but will be a light to the Gentiles (Isa. 49:1–8). In Isaiah's prophecy, this Servant is the coming king of all the earth prophesied in Isaiah 11, the one who establishes righteousness on earth, restores Israel, and draws Gentiles to himself.

The New Testament

The New Testament carries forward and advances the theme of the coming eschatological kingdom and the redemption associated with it by identifying Jesus of Nazareth as the messiah, Son of David, Son of God. Jesus referred to himself as the Son of Man, referencing the figure of Daniel 7:13–14 who will receive an everlasting world-wide kingdom over all peoples and nations (Matt. 16:27–28; 24:30; 25:31–32). But he also linked the title to the prophesied servant who would give his life as a ransom for many (Matt. 20:28; Mark 10:45). Even before his birth, Jesus was designated by an angel in reference to both themes of redemption and kingdom:

> She will bear a son, and you shall call his name Jesus, for he will save his people from their sins (Matt. 1:21).

> He will be great and will be called the Son of the Most High. And the Lord God will give to him the throne of his father David, and he will reign over the house of Jacob forever, and of his kingdom there will be no end (Luke 1:32–33).

The kingdom was the theme of Jesus' preaching and ministry in the Gospels in anticipation of which he called people to repentance. It was what he taught people to seek above all else along with the righteousness that repeatedly describes it in Old Testament prediction (Matt. 6:33, cf Isa. 9:7; 11:4–6; Jer. 23:5–6; 33:15–16). To enter the kingdom, or even to see it, one would have to be born of the Spirit (John 3:3, 5). And rebirth by the Spirit would only be given to those who placed their faith in the redemptive death of Christ (John 3:14–16). Jesus explicitly described the future kingdom in Matthew 25 as a worldwide reign over all nations to be established at his coming in glory (Matt. 25:31–46; cf. 19:23–30). The commission at the end of Matthew to make disciples of all nations (Matt. 28:18–20)—a commission issued by the one who has all authority in heaven and on earth—is given in light of this previously announced reign over all nations.

The New Testament epistles develop the theology of redemption accomplished by Christ and given as a gift to those who trust in Him (e.g., Rom. 3:21–26). These are the blessings of the forgiveness of sins (Eph. 1:7; Col. 1:14; 1 John 2:12), imputation of righteousness (Phil. 3:7–11; Rom. 4:1–8; 2 Cor. 5:21), and adoption into the inheritance of Christ (Rom. 8:15–17, 23; Gal. 3:26; 4:5–7). They also include cleansing from sin (1 John 1:9; Eph. 5:26), regeneration (Titus 3:5; 1 John 2:29; 3:9; 4:7; 5:4, 18) and sanctification in Christ (1 Cor 1:2; 6:11) by the Holy Spirit who baptizes (1 Cor. 12:13), seals (2 Cor. 1:22; Eph. 1:13), and indwells believers (1 Cor. 3:16; 6:19; Rom. 8:1–27. Believers receiving these blessings of redemption are thereby said to be transferred presently into the kingdom of Christ (Col. 1:13–14) even though the kingdom in its fullness is still seen as coming with Christ in the future (1 Tim. 4:1).

The book of Acts presents the apostles of Jesus preaching the redemption accomplished by Christ and offered to those who believe in Him together with the forgiveness of sins and the gift of the Holy Spirit. However, all this takes place with respect to the coming kingdom. The kingdom theme is introduced at the beginning of the book where Jesus instructs his disciples for forty days on the topic (Acts 1:3). At the close of the book, we find Paul preaching the kingdom in Rome (Acts 28:30–31). The question raised by the apostles in Acts 1 regarding the restoration of the kingdom to Israel is discussed only as a matter of time (Acts 1:6–7). Prior to the restoration of the kingdom, the disciples will be empowered by the Holy Spirit for a mission from Jerusalem to the ends of the earth (Acts 1:7–8). The certainty of the future restoration of Israel in the prophesied consummation is proclaimed by Peter in his sermon in Acts 3 in two points: (1) Jesus will remain in heaven until the time for the restoration of all things predicted by the prophets (2) when Jesus comes, that restoration will take place (Acts 3:20–21).

The future restoration of Israel is also affirmed by Paul in Romans 11, the same epistle that clearly presents the redemption and justification of Jewish and Gentile believers in Jesus. Paul expects that "all Israel," that is, the corporate people Israel, will be saved when the Redeemer comes (Rom. 11:26). "He will banish ungodliness from Jacob" and "take away their sins" (Rom. 11:26–27) because "the gifts and the calling of God are irrevocable" (Rom. 11:29). The plan of God for Israel and the Gentiles will be fulfilled through Christ, as Paul says in Romans 15:8–9:

> For I tell you that Christ became a servant to the circumcised to show God's truth-fulness, in order to confirm the promises given to the patriarchs, and in order that the Gentiles might glorify God for his mercy.

Gentiles glorify God in accordance with kingdom prophecies in which they are featured (Rom. 15:9–12), including the noted prophecy of Isaiah 11, the coming Davidic king who will rule all nations on earth (Rom. 15:12; cf. Isa. 11:10).

Elsewhere, Paul speaks of the kingdom as a future inheritance (1 Cor. 6:9, 10; Gal. 5:21; Eph. 5:5; 1 Cor. 15:50), as that which is coming with Jesus (1 Tim 4:1) and into which the redeemed will enter (Acts 14:22). The kingdom is also seen as future in Hebrews (Heb. 12:28), James (James 2:5), and the book of Revelation.

In Revelation 1, John writes that the redemption accomplished by Christ has led to the present creation of a kingdom people. In Revelation 5:9–10, the Lamb has redeemed "a people for God from every tribe and language and people and nation" and has "made them a kingdom." But importantly, John adds, "they shall reign on the earth," pointing to the yet future manifesta-tion of that kingdom. The coming of the kingdom is delayed, but the delay will be ended "in the days of the trumpet call of the seventh angel" (Rev. 10:6–7) when it will be announced, "the kingdom of the world has become the kingdom of our Lord and of his Christ, and he shall reign forever and ever" (Rev. 11:15). Revelation 19:15 foresees Christ coming to rule the na-tions. Revelation 20:4–6 envisions the commencement of that reign in a millennial order. Revelation 21:22–22:5 concludes the prophecy with the eternal reign of God and the Lamb over the nations of earth from a new and holy Jerusalem (whose gates are always open to Israel and the nations; Rev. 21:12–13, 24–26), on a new earth (Rev. 21:1–2) with all things made new (Rev. 21:3–5). This is the kingdom that will be forever (Rev. 22:5).

To summarize to this point, the themes of a worldwide multi-national eschatological kingdom is progressively revealed and developed from the OT to the NT and is linked in the latter to the person of Jesus, the messiah predicted in the former. This kingdom is a redemptive kingdom, in that its establishment requires the redemption of peoples—Jews and Gentiles—by God from sin and death. Redemption is the key to the fulfillment of Israel's promises. It is a blessing extended to Gentiles as well. The full revelation of the kingdom over Israel and the Gentiles is linked to the future coming of Jesus the Messiah in glory.

The Church and the Kingdom

The church is not introduced in the New Testament as the completion of the kingdom plan or as a "spiritualization" of its expected reality but as a phase of its revelation. Jesus spoke before the cross of the church as something he would build *in the future* ("I will build my church," Matt. 16:18), and Ephesians speaks of the church as that which God brought into existence after the ascension of Christ "when he raised him from the dead and seated him at his right hand in the heavenly places far above all rule and authority and power and dominion . . . ." (Eph. 1:20–21):

> And he put all things under his feet and gave him as head over all things to the church, which is his body, the fullness of him who fills all in all (Eph. 1:22–23).

The church comes into existence in the present age subsequent to the death, resurrection, and ascension of Jesus Christ in keeping with a plan that God has "for the fullness of time, to unite all things in him [Christ], things in heaven and things on earth" (Eph. 1:10). The union of "all things on earth" in Jesus is the worldwide kingdom of biblical prophecy. The union of all things in heaven as well as on earth reveals a cosmic, angelic addition to that future kingdom anticipated in Christ's declaration that "all authority *in heaven* and on earth has been given to me" (Matt. 28:18). On the basis of that authority, he commissioned his followers to "make disciples of all nations [on earth]" (Matt. 28:19). Those disciples from all nations—Jews and Gentiles—are formed into a union that reveals to heavenly authorities "God's eternal purpose" (Eph. 3:10–11), that is, the union of all things in Christ. The kingdom can still be described as a future reality (Eph. 5:5). However, the church is being formed in the present time under the sovereign authority of Christ. And, in that sense, Paul can speak of believers in Christ in the present time as already members of Christ's kingdom:

> He has delivered us from the domain of darkness and transferred us to the kingdom of his beloved Son, in whom we have redemption, the forgiveness of sins (Col. 1:13–14).

What marks the church as a present form of the kingdom is its formation in Christ, under his sovereign authority, through the redemption accomplished by him, in accordance with the divine kingdom plan. The kingdom as an administration of the polities of Israel and the Gentile nations is yet to be instituted at the coming of Christ. But an inaugurated form of the spiritual communion that unites peoples of the kingdom—of whatever ethnicity or nationality—is now being revealed as the body of Christ, the church.[18]

The newness of the church is due to the fact that the blessings of the Holy Spirit given to those who believe in Christ are said to be new. John 7:39 says that the Spirit was not given prior to the glorification of Christ through the cross and the resurrection. In Acts 1, Jesus, just before his ascension into heaven, declared to his followers that they would soon be baptized by the Holy Spirit. After his ascension, Acts 2 records the giving of the Holy Spirit to believers on the day of Pentecost. Paul notes the significance of this gift of the Holy Spirit for the church in 1 Corinthians 12:13:

> For by one Spirit we were all baptized into one body—Jews or Greeks; slaves or free—and all were made to drink of one Spirit.

The church, the body of Christ, comes into existence by the Holy Spirit newly "baptizing" believers into Christ, joining them to Christ and thereby to one another. And this begins to take place after the ascension of Christ into heaven and exaltation over all authority (Eph. 1:20–23). Further, the Holy Spirit indwells the resultant union filling it with His presence. This new spiritual communion in Christ is the church.

A major question regarding the church and the kingdom can be raised at this point: Does the spiritual formation of Jewish and Gentile believers in Christ remove their ethnic identities so as to disassociate them from the ethnic and national promises of the kingdom. Do Jews lose their inheritance in Israel when they become Christians? Are Gentiles changed so as to no longer be Gentiles from a theological standpoint? What does Paul mean when he says of those who are baptized into Christ that "there is neither Jew nor Greek, there is neither slave nor free, there is neither male nor female, for you are all one in Christ Jesus" (Gal. 3:28)? Or again, he says that Christ created in himself "one new man in place of the two" (Eph. 2:15).

Two considerations may be brought to bear on this question. The first is the affirmation of ethnic diversity in the church given in the book of Acts on the basis of Old Testament kingdom prophecy. The spiritual communion in Christ was seen to transcend but not replace ethnic, national differences. In other words, while distinctions are recognized, such as the "Jewishness" of Jews, and the "Gentileness" of Gentiles, the distinctions are transformed in Christ (a "Christian" Jewishness and a "Christian" Gentileness) and are permeable by the spiritual communion instituted in and by Christ. The second consideration is the New Testament's affirmation of Israel's particular

---

18. This is why the book of Revelation speaks of believers already having been made into a kingdom (Rev. 1:6; 5:10) while yet expecting the kingdom to come on earth in the future when Jesus comes (Rev. 5:10; 11:15; 19:15; 20:4–6; 21:22–22:5).

election and future restoration, especially in Acts and in Paul. For, if the particular promises of Israel are yet to be fulfilled by Christ at his future coming, it can hardly be the case that redemption in Christ is meant to remove Jewish ethnicity or otherwise cancel out the multi-corporate aspects of the promised kingdom.

Consider, first of all, the theological explanation offered at the so-called "Jerusalem Council" in Acts 15 for the phenomenon of Gentile believers receiving the Holy Spirit. Pharisaic Jews saw salvation restricted to Jews and insisted that Gentiles, in order to be saved, must become Jews by proselyting into Judaism and being circumcised. In other words, they could not be saved as Gentiles. However, the apostolic decision was that *God had accepted the Gentiles as Gentiles in accordance with the Old Testament prophecy of a multi-national eschatological kingdom of ENT Israel and Gentile peoples under the name of the Lord.* The prophecy in Amos 9 speaks of the rebuilding of the Davidic house, the restoration of Israel (Amos 9:11, 14), and also of "all the nations who are called by my name" (Amos 9:12). God's cleansing of the hearts of Gentile believers in Jesus by the Holy Spirit without requiring them to become Jews was seen to be in accord with the plan to have *Gentiles as Gentiles* in the messianic kingdom (Acts 15:8–17a; cf., 11:1–18).

It would certainly have seemed strange to this early Christian church to question as some do today whether Jewish believers have an inheritance in the kingdom as Jews. It certainly would not have occurred to any of those at the Jerusalem Council. The kingdom prophecy which they cited for accepting Gentiles as Gentiles speaks of the restoration of Israel as Israel and could just as easily be cited for God's acceptance of Jews as Jews (Amos 9:14–15). While Jesus and Paul both clearly challenge and reject the particular way Jewish identity was being promoted by Jewish leaders at that time, their criticism does not constitute a rejection of Jewish ethnicity per se. Rather they point to a renewal of Jewish and Gentile identities in the new creation that is formed in Christ.

Galatians 3:28–29 speaks of being "one in Christ Jesus" which in Paul's argument is a development of the promise "in you shall all the nations be blessed" (Gal. 3:8). They are all blessed in Christ. However, there is no reason to think that "neither Jew nor Greek" means a removal of ethnicity from humanity any more than "neither male nor female" teaches androgyny in Christ. What Paul is referring to is the equal privilege of justification and reception of the Spirit by faith in Christ which he finds in the universal blessing revealed to Abraham (Gal. 3:8–9, 14, 22), the blessing to be fulfilled *in his seed.* All are blessed *in him.* The "him" referred to here is not Israel but the King of Israel and all nations, who was already being distinguished in biblical prophecy from the rest of Israel as early as Jacob's blessing on Judah in Genesis 49 and was later narrowed further to the house of David. Jews and Gentiles are blessed "in him," in that seed of Abraham not because they are amalgamated into a new Israel but because they are being prepared as people of his coming kingdom (Gal. 5:21). Both Jews and Gentiles are blessed in him, the king (Ps. 72:17; Isa. 11:12; 49:6; Amos 9:11–15).

The issue in Ephesians 2:13–21 is not genealogy per se but hostility and alienation. *Both Jews and Gentiles* are reconciled to God through the body of Christ and are thereby put at peace with God and with one another. Both have access through Christ to God in one Spirit. Both are together being built into a dwelling place for God. They have become *in Christ* "fellow heirs." They are being formed into a kingdom under the Lordship of Christ (Eph. 1:22–23), a kingdom that is yet coming in the future (Eph. 5:5), and they are being built into an extended "temple" (Eph. 2:21) permeated by the presence of God. Gentiles formally alienated from Israel are not being added to Israel, rather Jews and Gentiles are both being redeemed and re-made in Christ, transitioning from an old humanity into a new humanity (Eph. 2:15–16). The Old Testament predicted a unified multi-ethnic, multi-national eschatological kingdom at peace. The New Testament reveals how that unity and peace comes about in Christ. Jewish believers and all kinds of Gentile believers are "being built" together in Christ as they are redeemed by him and formed by Him into a new humanity that is united and sanctified by the indwelling Spirit to be a spiritual communion in Christ. In this way, the house which God builds for David coincides with the "house" that the Son of David builds for God (2 Sam. 7:11b–13).

The Church of the Kingdom and Its Local Expressions

What are the implications of Redemptive Kingdom ecclesiology for the church in its local expressions? Here we can only address one issue, which is much discussed in Evangelicalism. Is it biblical for a local congregation to be mono-ethnic in its composition? Or, do texts like Ephesians 2 and Galatians 3 require congregational composition always to be ethnically diverse?[19]

From the standpoint of Redemptive Kingdom Theology, both are possible. One has to note, first of all that a text like Ephesians 2 is not a prescription for the demographics of a local congregation. It speaks of the Body of Christ and the inaugurated spiritual communion that unites believers of whatever ethnic identity in the kingdom of Christ. But since ethnic identity is not just a personal matter but is also a collective reality, which is affirmed in the kingdom, the possibilities for local congregational composition are more varied than some allow. It is certainly possible to have a congregation of people who share a common ethnicity. The NT church located in Jerusalem was composed of Jews, although it had internal subgroupings of Hellenistic Jews, those of the Pharisaic party, etc. On the other hand, it is certainly possible to have congregations that are varied in their ethnic or social composition as some other NT churches demonstrate. The key, as noted in the Jerusalem debate about Gentile believers and developed especially by the Apostle Paul in his letters, is that even

---

19. This issue often debated with respect to this is the so-called "homogeneous unit principle" of church growth advanced by Donald McGavran and C. Peter Wagner. For a discussion of this matter both pro and con see "The Pasadena Consultation: Homogeneous Unit Principle," *Lausanne Occasional Paper 1*, accessed at https://www.lausanne.org/content/lop.lop-1.

in *de facto* homogeneous congregations, acceptance must be extended to any believer of whatever *ethne* who wishes to fellowship because the spiritual communion of the kingdom permeates all anthropological distinctions.

Consequently, Redemptive Kingdom Theology would affirm the existence of Messianic Jewish Congregations today and numerous churches composed of a majority Gentile ethnicity—not because the church is a particular ethnicity but because ethnicities are redeemed in the kingdom. A gathering of believers of a particular nationality or ethnicity in common worship reflects this reality. But RKT would also affirm the many multiethnic, multi-social, even inter-urban congregations as reflective also of a key reality of the Kingdom, the interconnection and interrelatedness of kingdom peoples of whatever ethnicity or nationality. The inter-ethnic relationality will especially be seen in the future Jerusalem (Rev. 21–22) where the nations and peoples of the earth gather in common worship. It is reflected now in many mixed ethnic social settings into which the gospel enters and begins reforming inter-ethnic relationships through the redemption that is in Christ. Inter-ethnic congregations reflect the trans-ethnic nature of the spiritual communion, which is in Christ. Congregations predominately mono-ethnic are to reflect the transformation that permeates collective identity. The commonality of kingdom identity in all these cases means that believers of whatever ethnicity or social group are welcomed into any fellowship at any time because of the unity that all have *in Christ*.

Israel, the Church, and the Kingdom

As has already been stated, Israel is an ethnic, national, territorial reality in Scripture. At times, Israel may exist as a people, an *ethne*, without national or territorial status, but by covenant grant, this condition is only temporary. A return to national and territorial status is repeatedly promised and prophesied in keeping with an eschatological consummation in which a redeemed Israel is a signature piece of the truth, mercy, and grace of God.

"I the LORD do not change; therefore you, O Jacob, are not consumed" (Mal. 3:1).

"For I know the plans I have for you, declares the LORD, plans for wholeness and not for evil, to give you a future and a hope" (Jer. 29:11).

This declaration of a future hope in Jeremiah is followed by promises that the Lord will "restore the fortunes" of his people by bringing them back to the land covenanted to them and restoring their national status. The prophets speak of a restoration in which Israel will be fully forgiven, cleansed from sin, indwelt by the Spirit of God, in accordance with a plan to renew all things, a plan which envisions a humanity united in a multi-personal, multi-corporate everlasting kingdom.

At this present time, Israel as a people exists partly in national and territorial identity and partly dispersed among the peoples of the world (the Gentiles). But they are also only partly a people of faith in Messiah and thereby only partly a people who know the forgiveness, cleansing, and renewal that is found in Christ. In this they are like the other peoples and nations of the world during the time of Christ's ascension in heaven. A national fullness for Israel is expected in the future coordinate with the fullness of the Gentiles and the return of Christ (Rom. 11:25–27).

The portion of Israel which is the Israel of faith is, in prophetic terminology, a remnant that signals hope for the whole of the people (Rom 11:1–16). It is also that part of Israel in which is found the inaugurated spiritual communion that connects Jewish believers to Christ, to one another, and to Gentile believers. This spiritual communion traverses ethnic and national boundaries to renew the distinctive personal and corporate differences of humanity while creating a Spirit-formed unity in Christ among the persons and communities so renewed. This Spirit-formed communion in Christ is the Body of Christ, the church, which manifests itself in local gatherings, local congregations or local churches, among the various *ethnes* into which it has penetrated. It is an inaugural form of the kingdom, which is coming with Jesus.

Theological clarity on Israel, the church, and the kingdom is necessary to understand the plan and purpose of God as it is progressively revealed in the story of the Bible. The church's own self-perception in this theology is necessary to avoid both misunderstanding and improper or inadequate relations to corporate Israel and other peoples on earth that are due to supersessionist or traditional dispensational ecclesiologies. Keeping the kingdom central in the redemptive work of God clarifies both the identity and the mission of the church that manifests and proclaims the love of God for persons (Jews and Gentiles) and peoples (Israel and Gentile peoples and nations) of the world.

Until the day that Jesus comes and the nations of the world, including Israel, come fully under his direct administration for a yet glorious manifestation of the presence of God, the church, the communion of kingdom peoples, has been given this mission to proclaim the good news of the kingdom. And in that proclamation, the power of God is at work, to bring salvation—forgiveness of and cleansing from sin, re-creation, renewal, enlivening by the Spirit of God, and sanctification for everlasting life. With redemption in Christ comes the inauguration of a peace among and between peoples, the peace of a kingdom that will endure forever, one in which all the promises of God—for Israel and Gentile peoples—will be affirmed, fulfilled, and established forever in Christ!

THE DANGERS OF SUPERSESSIONISM

MITCH GLASER

SUPERSESSIONISM IS ON THE RISE TODAY and capturing a new generation of adherents. This position asserts that the Jewish people no longer have a role in the plan of God for the ages, due to their disobedience and rejection of Christ at his first coming. This chapter will look at the impact of Supersessionism on a new generation of evangelicals, especially as reflected in the views of the anti-Christian Zionist movement. The anti-Christian Zionists, through their theological views and pro-Palestinian political perspective, have devalued the theological significance of Israel and the Jewish people causing Christians to be less concerned with missions to the Jewish people.

The views of British Anglican theologians Colin Chapman and Stephen Sizer, as well as American New Testament scholar Gary Burge, have done much to shape the views of mainline evangelicals on both sides of the Atlantic, toward the modern State of Israel and the Jewish people.[1] These three theologians typify the position of the anti-Christian Zionists that will be discussed throughout this chapter.

CHRISTIAN ZIONISM

It is important to begin by establishing some basic definitions.

Christian Zionism is the viewpoint of Christians who believe that the land of Israel belongs to the Jewish people and that followers of Christ should support the modern State of Israel. The movement also usually involves a belief in some type of prophetic future for Israel.

---

1. Colin Chapman's *Whose Promised Land?* (Grand Rapids: Baker, 2002) and *Whose Holy City?* (Oxford: Lion, 2004), and Stephen Sizer's *Christian Zionism* (Downers Grove, IL: IVP Academic, 2006) and *Zion's Christian Soldiers* (Downers Grove, IL: Inter-Varsity, 2007) have influenced the opinions of Christians, both theologically and politically. Gary Burge, who now teaches at Calvin College, has done much the same through two major books as well as numerous articles on the subject. His books are *Whose Land? Whose Promise?: What Christians Are Not Being Told about Israel and the Palestinians* (Cleveland: Pilgrim Press, 2003) and *Jesus and the Land: The New Testament Challenge to "Holy Land" Theology* (Grand Rapids: Baker, 2010). I have written about them in detail in Stanley Porter's (ed.) *The Future Restoration of Israel*, in the chapter, "The Impact of Supersessionism on Jewish Evangelism."

Darrell Bock defines Christian Zionism in Gerald McDermott's book *The New Christian Zionism*, as follows, "In one sense, all the term Christian Zionism means in the end is that Israel has a right to exist with the same human rights and security guarantees that other nations receive. But of course Christian Zionism is also more than that, for it makes a theological case for that right to exist, beyond a merely prudential one."[2] Bock believes that Israel, as a national entity, will inherit the promises of God, including the land.

He continues, "Christian Zionism argues that Israel has a corporate future in God's plan and as a nation has a right to land in the Middle East. Israel also has a right to function as a nation and be recognized as such in the world."[3]

McDermott adds that one does not need to be either a Christian Zionist or dispensationalist to believe that God's promises about the land will be literally given to the physical sons and daughters of Abraham, Isaac, and Jacob.[4] This is the foundation of *The New Christian Zionism*.

One commonality of those who affirm Israel's theological right to the land of promise, whatever theological system they embrace, is the belief that the Jewish people have an ongoing relationship with God through the Abrahamic Covenant, assuring ethnic Israel's ultimate possession of the land.[5]

Yet, not every premillennialist is certain that the modern State of Israel is the fulfillment of prophecy. Those who do usually distinguish between a future day of total *shalom,* as described by the prophet Isaiah (Isaiah 2:2–4, 9:6–7, 11:1–12) and return of the Jewish people to the land of Israel in unbelief—and therefore the modern State of Israel is the fulfillment of prophecy from this perspective (Ezekiel 36:22ff.). The best, so to speak, is yet to come!

Matthew Westbrook, who studies the rise of modern "revivalist" Christian Zionism—usually associated with the modern charismatic renewal movement—suggests that many of those who believe in a future for Israel enjoy a common theological heritage. He purports that dispensationalists had a strong influence on those who believe in God's ongoing work among the Jewish people and the nation of Israel. Yet Westbrook also asserts that Christian Zionism had a long history before the rise of modern dispensationalism.

---

2. Gerald R. McDermott, ed., *The New Christian Zionism: Fresh Perspectives on Israel and the Land* (Downers Grove, IL: InterVarsity Press, 2016), 308.

3. Ibid., 308–310.

4. Ibid., 74–75.

5. Bock concludes, "Unbelieving Israel has a right to the land because God gave it to all the nation and seed of Abraham initially as an act of his grace when he called Abraham to form a nation even before the patriarch trusted God. This future for Jewish people can be affirmed alongside the idea that Christ is also the heir of all promises, including promises about rule of the earth. This combination of ideas about hope means that although Christ is the center of the realization of promise, fulfillment in him does not nullify previous commitments God has made to ethnic Israel, which God will complete through the Christ. Christ comes as one who fulfills national goals for Israel as well as those he fulfills for all the world. Israel's current unbelief does not disqualify her from the covenant but makes her subject to covenant discipline from the Messiah—even if she does not recognize it. This can be seen in Jesus' declaration that Israel's house will be desolate until she recognizes the one who comes in the name of the Lord (Lk 13: 34–35; Mt. 23:37–39)." Ibid., 309.

The academic study of Christian Zionism has suffered from an over-reliance on premillennial dispensationalism in retellings of the roots of the phenomenon. In part, this is due to scholarly attention to only American sources of Christian Zionism dating from after the Civil War. It also results from a failure to define and then compare dispensationalist Zionism to the data observed. This error has resulted in the carrying-forward of assumptions based in the theology and philosophical presuppositions of dispensationalism into contemporary analysis of the phenomenon. As a result, most scholars have neglected sources of Christian Zionism that predate dispensational premillennialism and the inability to distinguish Christian Zionism not manifesting as dispensationalism. Differentiation of these streams is important because they potentially carry very different assumptions and ideological convictions, leading to very different practices and cultural, social and political outcomes.[6]

Today's anti-Christian Zionists generally paint all who believe in a future for Israel, with the brush of extremism, prophetic sensationalism and an attachment to an archaic and irrelevant form of dispensationalism. In fact, they would argue that all dispensationalism is passé without acknowledging the various nuances of the position.

Stephen Sizer, one of the chief spokespersons for the anti-Christian Zionist position, defines Christian Zionism as "a political form of philo-Semitism, and can be defined as Christian support for Zionism."[7] Note carefully that Sizer does not state, "Christian support for Israel," but rather for Zionism. This small

---

6. Matthew C. Westbrook, "The International Christian Embassy, Jerusalem, and Renewalist Zionism: Emerging Jewish-Christian Ethnonationalism" (Madison, NJ: Drew University Press, 2014), 312. Jerusalem is a primary lens into this global movement. The major finding in this dissertation is the contemporary emergence of a Jewish-Christian ethnonationalism, suggesting changes to the way nationalism is manifested in a global age, changes to certain segments of Christianity, and the emergence of a distinctive global political and religious culture centered on the existence of the State of Israel. Scholars of Christian Zionism have long associated the Christian Zionism with the largely American nineteenth-century theological movement known as premillennial dispensationalism. This association is erroneous in that it does not recognize earlier and different sources of Christian Zionism; nor does it recognize alternate, contemporary forms of the movement. Such undifferentiating associations have consequences for scholarly approaches to understanding the socio-political activities of Christian Zionism globally, the history of Christian Zionism, millennialist Christianity, and the Christian appropriation of the state of Israel and Jewish religion, culture, and even persons. Using the International Christian Embassy Jerusalem (ICEJ) as a primary example of renewalist Zionism, this dissertation examines the ways this Christian Zionism manifests in other historical and contemporaneous forms of renewalist Christianity. This work includes ethnography of the ICEJ's annual Feast of Tabernacles celebration held in Jerusalem, attended by thousands of Christians annually. A further ethnography of the ICEJ-USA's constructed pilgrimage and tour to Israel explores the expressions and practices of renewalist Zionism on the ground in Israel. The ways that charismatic authority is constructed; the interplay of text, contemporary political realities, and renewalist spirituality; and the role of global Christian media are also examined in detail. Furthermore, using the sociological theories of cultural globalization and social memory, Christian Zionism is theorized as a subjective ground for truth for its adherents in a relativizing, global age characterized by transnational flows and local, socio-political particularizations.

7. Stephen Sizer, *Christian Zionism: Roadmap to Armageddon* (Leicester: InterVarsity Press, 2004), 19.

difference will loom larger in importance as the chapter progresses. Sizer might be the most aggressive among Israel's evangelical critics. A few years ago, he was censured by his bishop for anti-Israel statements and activities.[8] His views are also well known within the British Jewish community and have fanned the ill feelings of some British evangelicals toward Israel and the Jewish people.

Sizer's public statements have shown greater restraint since his bishop censured him. Courageous actions like this may very well need to be administered on both sides of the issue. We are our brother's keepers and those who support Israel must also speak against those pro-Israel Christians who cross the line from support for Israel to advocating anti-Palestinian polemics.

ANTI-CHRISTIAN ZIONISM

The term "anti-Christian Zionism" is used to describe those who oppose Christian Zionism. Again, those who oppose Christian Zionism often broaden the definition of Christian Zionism to include all who believe God promised the land of Israel to the Jewish people and has ongoing covenantal purposes for Israel, essentially including all premillennialists. The anti-Christian Zionists fail to recognize that there is a broad continuum within the premillennial and Christian Zionist position and that many evangelicals who believe in Israel's present and future are uncomfortable with the appelation Christian Zionism. They would especially eschew the political extremes of eschatological sensationalism and anti-Palestinian attitudes.

Some evangelicals affirm the political views of Christian Zionists, yet would still accept the position that the land belongs to the Jewish people by right of covenant and believe that the modern State of Israel belongs to the Jewish people. They seek to avoid extremes, from their perspective, associated with Christian Zionism, including a pro-Israel political agenda, identification with more right-wing Israeli political parties such as Likud, the alleged mistreatment of Palestinians, and a sensationalist view of the fulfillment of prophecy. Some who affirm the "new" Christian Zionism also do not want to be identified with the dispensational roots of the modern Christian Zionist movement, which includes within its theological worldview some of the hallmarks of dispensationalism, including the pretribulation rapture of the church and building of a millennial temple.

Supersessionism, which underlies the theological worldview of most anti-Christian Zionists, makes all political or moral arguments for modern Israel's divine right to the land null and void. It really does not matter whether or not the modern State of Israel is the fulfillment of prophecy, since in the Supersessionist understanding of Scripture the land never really belonged to the Jewish people anyway. The arguments against modern Israel's right to the land due to Israeli secularism and poor treatment of the Palestinians are rendered

---

8.   See John Bingham, "Church Bans 9/11 Israel Conspiracy Priest from Using Social Media," *The Telegraph*, February 9, 2015, https://www.telegraph.co.uk/news/religion/11399986/Vicar-who-blamed-Israel-for-911-attacks-is-banned-from-writing-about-the-Middle-East.html.

irrelevant, because the overarching and damning charge against the Jewish people is that the nation rejected Christ in the first century and lost its divine election, including the land promises.

Supersessionists are critics of premillennialism in any form, as they do not believe the land of Israel belongs to the Jewish people by divine covenant. They do not believe that God will ever give the land to the Jewish people irrespective of Israel's current "moral condition." The promise of the land to Israel has been superseded, spiritualized, and given to the church. Michael J. Vlach, in his book, *Has the Church Replaced Israel?*, provides us with a description of classical supersessionism. He writes,

> Supersessionism, therefore, appears to be based on two core beliefs: (1) the nation Israel has somehow completed or forfeited its status as the people of God and will never again possess a unique role or function apart from the church, and (2) the church is now the true Israel that has permanently replaced or superseded national Israel as the people of God. In the context of Israel and the church, Supersessionism is the view that the NT Church is the new and/or true Israel that has forever superseded the nation Israel as the people of God.[9]

It is easy to see how supersessionism, which denies any theological present or future for the Jewish people, undergirds the views of anti-Christian Zionists who deem the modern State of Israel as theologically illegitimate.

THE UNIVERSALIZATION OF THE LAND PROMISES

Supersessionism makes any debate over what is either called the "territories" or "occupied territories" of Judea and Samaria to be moot, since according to classical supersessionism, the Jewish rejection of the Messiah cost the Jewish people their "covenantal" future without the possibility of restoration. The future repentance of ethnic Jewish people, as Romans 11 teaches, enfolds the "converted" nation into the church. They do not inherit the land with any particularity nor do they enjoy some type of special relationship to God in a literal earthily kingdom as predicted in the Hebrew Scriptures. (Amos 9:11–15; Zech. 14:12–21)

According to supersessionists, the land promises are universalized and belong to a redeemed humanity—the church. The universalization of the land promises is based upon the interpretation of the phrase τὸ κληρονόμον αὐτὸν εἶναι κόσμου, found in Romans 4:13, "For the promise to Abraham or to his descendants that he would be *heir of the world* was not through the Law, but through the righteousness of faith." David Rudolph, in his chapter "Zionism in Pauline Literature" in *The New Christian Zionism*, responds to the idea that the land promises of the Abrahamic covenant are universalized as claimed by the anti-Christian Zionists.

---

9. Michael J. Vlach, *Has the Church Replaced Israel?* (Nashville: B & H Publishing Group, 2014), 12.

In his book *Jesus and the Land*, Gary Burge claims that Christ universalized the Promised Land and that this is explicitly stated in Paul's words, "For the promise that he would inherit the world did not come to Abraham or to his descendants through the law but through the righteousness of faith" (Rom 4:13). Burge, building on [N. T.] Wright, reasons that Paul's use of the expression "inherit the world" rather than "inherit the land of Judea" indicates that the land promise was reconfigured and no longer in force: "The formula that linked Abraham to Jewish ethnic lineage and the right to possess the land has now been overturned in Christ.[10]

For Burge and other supersessionists, the question of Jewish possession of the land of Israel, both today and in the future, is political in nature—as according to the anti-Christian Zionists, the Jewish people have no biblical claim to the land of Israel. Neither the land within the 1948 borders nor the alleged "occupied territories" belong to Israel, according to the supersessionist interpretation of the Abrahamic covenant.[11]

THE PALESTINIAN VOICES

Western anti-Christian Zionists reflect the position held by a group of Palestinian evangelical theologians, who accept a historical and theological metanarrative that is both definitively supersessionist and politically pro-Palestinian. One voice that is perhaps more resolute than others is that of Bethlehem Bible College board member Hind Khoury, the general secretary of Kairos Palestine and former Palestinian Liberation Organization representative to France. Khoury reflects the values and views of many Bethlehem Bible College leaders in a message to a United Methodist church group in North Carolina, where she calls the establishment of settlements in the West Bank a "war crime."[12] Khoury also petitions the church group to pressure the International Court of Justice and the UN to condemn the security wall. And although she does not agree with suicide bombing as an appropriate response to what she calls "Israeli aggression," she does describe the suicide bombers as martyrs for the Palestinian cause.[13]

Khoury's position is a complex mix of politics and theology founded upon a combination of supersessionist theology and anti-Israel politics. Through the popularity of conferences such as *Christ at the Checkpoint*, this anti-Israel perspective now heavily influences the ways in which many younger evangelicals view the Israeli-Palestinian conflict. Hundreds of

---

10.   McDermott, *The New Christian Zionism*, 171.

11.   This charge is also well answered by Dr. Dick Averbeck and Dr. Mark Yarborough in their chapters found in this volume.

12.   Hind Khoury, "An Evening with Hind Khoury," YouTube video, 14:30, North Carolina Conference of the Middle East Church, October 30 2015, https://www.youtube.com/watch?v=ai4KNGfcfCM.

13.   Hind Khoury, "Forty Shades (Israel/ Palestine)," YouTube video, 1:50, interview by the Irish Arts Council, May 8, 2011, https://www.youtube.com/watch?v=IPna6K_RMjY.

Christian college students have attended this conference and now view the Israeli-Palestinian conflict through the Palestinian metanarrative without having been presented with an alternative. As one younger millennial suggests, "They think they know the alternative—the wreckage of their parents' prophecy-by-newspaper politicization of eschatology. So they are not merely blank slates being presented with one opinion—they are swinging the pendulum to the opposite side."[14]

THE KAIROS PALESTINE DOCUMENT

Yohana Katanacho, author and advisor to the faculty at Bethlehem Bible College, in his recent book *The Land of Christ: A Palestinian Cry*, follows the argumentation of the Kairos Palestine Document, which lists the alleged offenses of Israel against the Palestinian peoples, including the occupation of Palestinian "territories" and the "separation" wall. His brief book shows how a Palestinian evangelical syncretizes a politically militant pro-Palestinian metanarrative with a Supersessionist perspective on Scripture.

The Kairos Palestine Document was penned in Bethlehem on December 11, 2009, by the Global Kairos Network and includes members of both evangelical and historic churches. According to its website, the document advocates a form of Palestinian liberation theology.[15] The full document should be read, but the following statements summarize the essential tone and content of the document,

> We proclaim our word based on our Christian faith and our sense of Palestinian belonging—a word of faith, hope and love. We declare that the military occupation of Palestinian land constitutes a sin against God and humanity. Any theology that legitimizes the occupation and justifies crimes perpetrated against the Palestinian people lies far from Christian teachings. We urge the international community to stand with the Palestinian people in their struggle against oppression, displacement, and apartheid. We demand that all people, political leaders and decision-makers put pressure on Israel and take legal measures in order to oblige its government to end its oppression and disregard for international law.[16] We hold a clear position that non-violent resistance to this injustice is a right and duty for all Palestinians, including Christians. We support Palestinian civil society organizations, international NGOs and religious institutions that call on individuals, companies and states to

---

14. Personal note from Brian Crawford, 10/6/2017

15. The Kairos Palestine Document was launched in Bethlehem on December 11, 2009, and endorsed by patriarchs and heads of churches in Jerusalem, December 15, 2009; cf. appendix, signatories, and authors. Since then, several individual churches and ecumenical bodies in the ecumenical family have studied and endorsed the document and called their constituencies to listen to the voice of Palestinian Christians. The original language of the document is Arabic; it has been translated into more than ten languages. See "The Kairos Palestine Document," *IROM International Review of Mission* 99, no. 2 (2010): 278–92; as well as http://www.kairospalestine.ps or http://www.oikoumene.org/es/documentacion/documents/other-ecumenical-bodies/documento-kairos-palestina.html.

16. These charges are carefully refuted in the chapter by Craig Parshall in this volume.

engage in boycotts, divestment and sanctions against the Israeli occupation. "Everything that happens in our land, everyone who lives there, all the pains and hopes, all the injustice and all the efforts to stop this injustice, are part and parcel of the prayer of the Palestinian Church and the service of all her institutions."[17]

Dr. Katanacho, who was on the committee that wrote the document, uses the Kairos statement to express his views regarding Israel. Katanacho quotes from section 1.1.1 of the Kairos document: "The separation wall erected on Palestinian Territory, a large part of which has been confiscated for this purpose, has turned our towns and villages into prisons, separating them from one another, making them dispersed and divided cantons."[18] The document also states:

> While the separation wall divides Palestinian neighborhoods, Jerusalem continues to be emptied of its Palestinian citizens, Christians, and Muslims. Their identity cards are confiscated, which means the loss of their right to reside in Jerusalem. Their homes are demolished or expropriated. Jerusalem, the city of reconciliation, has become a city of discrimination and exclusion, a source of struggle rather than peace.[19]

The document then lists the following concerns: the cruel treatment of the citizens of Gaza during the December 2008 war, the blockade of Gaza, checkpoints, separation of families, restrictions on visiting holy sites, issues related to Palestinian refugees, the number of Palestinians in Israeli prisons, the dividing of Jerusalem, and the loss of rights by Palestinians in East Jerusalem. Katanacho continues to list the charges found in the Kairos document, where Israel is accused of ignoring international law, violating the human rights of Palestinians, regularly discriminating against the nearly two million Israeli Arab citizens, and causing the emigration of young Palestinians from Israel to seek a better life. The document calls for an end of the occupation as the solution to a new day of peace and reconciliation in Israel.

Katanacho also quotes from section 1.4 of the document:

> In the face of this reality, Israel justifies its actions as self-defense, including occupation, collective punishment and all other forms of reprisals against the Palestinians. In our opinion, this vision is a reversal of reality. Yes, there is Palestinian resistance to the occupation. However, if there were no occupation, there would be no resistance, no fear and no insecurity. This is our understanding of the situation. Therefore, we call on the Israelis to end the occupation. Then they will see a new world in which there is no fear, no threat but rather security, justice and peace.[20]

---

17. "Kairos Palestine," accessed October 19, 2017, http://www.kairospalestine.ps.
18. Yohanna Katanacho, *The Land of Christ: A Palestinian Cry* (Eugene, OR: Pickwick Publications, 2013), 74.
19. Ibid., 75.
20. Ibid., 76.

These litany of charges need to be carefully evaluated, as they are disputed by both Israelis and Palestinians. Yet, they are presented as the alleged facts at the heart of the pro-Palestinian narrative and are laced throughout the writings of Western advocates for the position. Responses to the accusations and details of the document are widely available, including Robert Nicholson's excellent presentation in *The New Christian Zionism*.[21]

Nothing is said in the document, as we would expect, about the history of the Palestine Liberation Organization's violent attacks against noncombatant Israelis and the Israel Defense Forces that may have caused the government of Israel to take measures to protect her citizens. Also, the Kairos document fails to condemn as wrong and immoral the firing of missiles from Gaza and the indiscriminate personal terrorist attacks on Israeli citizens. This is an astounding omission in a document claiming to be Christian in nature. Unfortunately, the document extols the virtues and sacrifice of those Palestinians who died for their country, which would include suicide bombers and those who committed acts of terrorism.

> Resistance to the evil of occupation is integrated, then, within this Christian love that refuses evil and corrects it. It resists evil in all its forms with methods that enter into the logic of love and draw on all energies to make peace. We can resist through civil disobedience. We do not resist with death but rather through respect of life. We respect and have a high esteem for all those who have given their lives for our nation. And we affirm that every citizen must be ready to defend his or her life, freedom and land.[22]

The Kairos Palestine Document is a politically pro-Palestinian document written by Christians, but in essence, it is a political document. It has become a major information and rhetoric resource for the argumentation of Western anti-Christian Zionists. In reading the document, it becomes apparent that our Western critics, including Sizer and Burge, use these arguments prolifically. The document portrays Israelis as monsters and aggressors, which is especially repugnant to our younger and more justice-sensitive evangelical young adults—especially in the West. Unfortunately, the Kairos Palestine Document comes with little explanation or balance and is communicated with passion and fervor, shaping the attitudes of young evangelical adults who do not know the full story.

Where is the moral conscience of Palestinian Christians who refuse to

---

21. Anglican Friends of Israel, "A Response to the Kairos Document," The Emmaus Group UK, March 1, 2013, http://www.anglicanfriendsofisrael.com/2013/03/a-response-to-the-kairos-document; Malcolm Lowe, "'Kairos Palestine': From Mendacity to Megalomania," The Gatestone Institute, December 23, 2011, https://www.gatestoneinstitute.org/2697/kairos-palestine. Also see the chapter in this volume by Craig Parshall; and Robert Nicholson, "Theology and Law: Does the Modern State of Israel Violate Its Call to Justice in the Covenant by Its Relation to International Law?" in McDermott, *The New Christian Zionism*, 249–280.

22. Katanacho, *The Land of Christ*, 85.

decry the terror tactics employed by Palestinian terrorists, in rewarding suicide bombers and honoring those who murder innocent Israelis?

The supersessionism undergirding the Kairos Document is evident, as the view of God's choice of Israel is negated and described as outdated. Katancacho suggests that God's Word, when taken literally, is "out of date" and a perversion of God's love:

> Our Lord Jesus Christ came, proclaiming that the Kingdom of God was near. He provoked a revolution in the life and faith of all humanity. He came with "a new teaching" (Mark 1:27), casting a new light on the Old Testament, on the themes that relate to our Christian faith and our daily lives, themes such as the promises, the election, the people of God and the land. We believe that the Word of God is a living Word, casting a particular light on each period of history, manifesting to Christian believers what God is saying to us here and now. For this reason, it is unacceptable to transform the Word of God into letters of stone that pervert the love of God and His providence in the life of both peoples and individuals. This is precisely the error in fundamentalist Biblical interpretation that brings us death and destruction when the word of God is petrified and transmitted from generation to generation as a dead letter. This dead letter is used as a weapon in our present history in order to deprive us of our rights in our own land.[23]

The above is obviously describing those Christians who believe that the Jewish people have a right to the land by divine covenant. Yet this statement undermines the authority of Scripture and suggest that the Bible should adapt to our current political realities. This approach to the Bible causes many evangelicals to wonder about those who affirm the Kairos document regarding the authority of Scripture. Furthermore, it is hypocritical to demand that Jewish Israelis live according to the moral principles of God's Word without calling upon Palestinians to denounce terrorism.

A better path to peace in the Middle East is to accept one another as God has fashioned us—which would include, at minimum, a new respect for fellow Jesus disciples who believe that the Jewish people are God's chosen people and that the land belongs to the Jewish people. There can be no authentic dialogue without respect. The language of the document is patently dismissive of the views of those who believe that God's plan for Israel continues.

THE IMPACT ON RECONCILIATION AMONG BELIEVERS

Reconciliation not only needs to take place between Israeli and Palestinian believers but also between Western Christians on both sides of the conflict. Christian Zionists and premillennialists (especially those who are in one way or another Dispensational) feel unfairly demeaned and attacked

---

23.   Ibid., 74; cf. Kairos Palestine Document, 2.2.2.

by the anti-Christian Zionists for their view of Israel's divine right to the land by covenant. In effect, supersessionism nails shut the coffin of Jewish covenantal existence for all eternity. This viewpoint is a major impediment to reconciliation and peace between Arab and Israeli believers in Israel. Additionally, there is a deep concern that the anti-Christian Zionists is damaging the image of Israel within the church and causing a new generation of evangelical young people to have a poor attitude toward Israel. This rhetoric would not be acceptable if pro-Israel evangelicals were causing fellow Christians to think poorly of Palestinians.

We must ask ourselves whether or not peace between Palestinian and Messianic Jews is even possible with one side believing that Israel lost her theological right to exist? Can Israeli believers especially, and those who affirm God's plan for Israel and the Jewish people easily fellowship with those who are generally orthodox in beliefs and yet "write Israel out" of the biblical story? I doubt it. The Kairos Palestine Document reflects the personal and theological disdain that permeates the evangelical Palestinian communities who affirm the contents of the document. Unfortunately, unless the Kairos document is revisited and rewritten, most reconciliation efforts between Messianic Jews and Palestinians are doomed to failure.

True reconciliation is only possible when Palestinian evangelicals and anti-Christian Zionists show respect for those who believe the Jewish people are God's chosen people and that the land was given to the Jewish people by covenant. Dr. Darrell Bock challenges anti-Christian Zionists to transcend political obstacles for the sake of the Gospel and our witness to the world:

> But more importantly, and what would really stand out in the Middle East, and this is the challenge, is that Palestinian believers and Messianic Jews will find a way to come together and show their unity and their ability to cross ethnic lines and the ability of Jew and Gentile to love one another in such a way that it would be such a contrast to the normal way in which these ethnicities relate to one another and these religions relate to one another. That it would stand out like a beacon in the midst of a dark situation.[24]

---

24. Paul Alexander, ed., *Christ at the Checkpoint: Theology in the Service of Justice and Peace* (Eugene, OR: Pickwick Publications, 2012), 123. Bock's full statement is worth noting, because there are some caveats: "So, I probably owe you a little more as a dispensationalist and then I'll be done. I believe that Israel has the right to be here, but I don't believe that she has the right to be here *carte blanche*, that she can do whatever she wants, to whomever she wants, in whatever way she wants. I think she is accountable to God for how she interacts with people who she has stewardship over as a government. I think the land ought to be shared. I think that actually gives Israel the freedom to negotiate with regard to land because she can give it as well. And I think there's probably a pretty good case to be made that she ought to think about that very seriously. That's very surprising coming from a dispensationalist. I don't know how many dispensationalists you've heard say that. In fact, I might get in trouble for saying that when I go home, but I think it's true. But more importantly, and what would really stand out in the Middle East, and this is the challenge, is that Palestinian believers and Messianic Jews will find a way to come together and show their unity and their ability to cross ethnic lines and the ability of Jew and Gentile to love one another in such a way that it would be

While I agree with Dr. Bock's sentiments, it must be recognized that the path to honest and authentic fellowship is all the more treacherous when one side denies the covenantal identity of the other. How can a Messianic Jew embrace a brother or sister who denies his or her existence as part of God's chosen people? Can spiritual unity be found when both sides view the Bible in totally disparate ways? Perhaps there is a way forward, but this way has not been encouraged, as it requires a new openness to the premillennial position, and even a new respect for those who are traditionally dispensationalist on the part of superssionists.

Dr. Katanacho, referring to the Kairos Palestine document, asserts that what is essentially a premillennial theological position is linked to the violation of Palestinian rights.

> Furthermore, we know that certain theologians in the West try to attach a Biblical and theological legitimacy to the infringement of our rights. Thus, the promises, according to their interpretation, have become a menace to our very existence. The "good news" in the Gospel itself has become "a harbinger of death" for us. We call on these theologians to deepen their reflection on the Word of God and to rectify their interpretations so that they might see in the Word of God a source of life for all peoples.[25]

The fundamental infringement and complaint against modern Israel goes far beyond the alleged "taking" of what is viewed as "occupied territories" as simply believing there is a biblical basis for Jewish possession of the land at all is anathema. The historical context, beginning in 1948, regarding wars Israel did not initiate and claiming land after victory for the purpose of national defense are of course not mentioned.

The Palestinian metanarrative and the Kairos document paint Israelis with an evil, menacing, and irreconcilable brush. Palestinian evangelicals who embrace the document, along with Western Christian sympathizers cause irreparable harm to the image of Israelis and their supporters among Western evangelicals, especially among younger adults.

The Kairos document is explicit in its condemnation of Israelis on a spiritual basis, as well as politically.

> Therefore, we also declare that the Israeli occupation of Palestinian land is a sin against God and humanity because it deprives the Palestinians of their basic human rights, bestowed by God. It distorts the image of God in the Israeli who has become

---

such a contrast to the normal way in which these ethnicities relate to one another and these religions relate to one another. That it would stand out like a beacon in the midst of a dark situation. I pray for you all regularly because I can't imagine living in a more difficult social political situation than you all do. I respect you immensely because I think your efforts to try and live faithfully in the midst of this context actually can teach the rest of the church tons. And my prayer is that maybe there'll be some beacons of light in the way the church cares for itself across ethnic lines in this context in such a way that no one can miss it."

25. Katanacho, *The Land of Christ*, 79; cf. Kairos Palestine Document 2.3.3.

an occupier just as it distorts this image in the Palestinian living under occupation. We declare that any theology, seemingly based on the Bible or on faith or on history, that legitimizes the occupation, is far from the teachings of the Church, because it calls for violence and holy war in the name of God Almighty, subordinating God to temporary human interests, and distorting the divine image in the human beings living under both political and theological injustice.[26]

If the above is true as stated without context, then it makes sense that evangelical young people would be more sympathetic to Palestinians than to Jewish Israelis. Therefore, we must recognize that words really do matter. When volatile rhetoric is used, whether of Israelis or of Palestinians, it brings with it a viscerally negative response on the part of the hearers, especially if they are young adults who are advocates for justice and equality for all.

THE POSSIBILITY OF UNITY
AND AUTHENTIC RECONCILIATION

There is unity between Messianic Jews and Palestinian evangelicals who are not supersessionists. They have a common basis leading to a peaceful church and potentially unified nation. Shadi Khalloul, a pro-Israel Christian Arab, expresses his deep concerns about events like Christ at the Checkpoint:

> What is the morality of church leaders who betray the Christian message by serving Islamic propaganda against our country, Israel? It is disturbing to see Christian leaders participating in anti-Israel political conferences like Christ at the Checkpoint because they engage in dishonesty at such conferences. These Christians enjoy full rights and freedom, even the freedom to publicly slander the state without fear. But they suggest otherwise in their public statements at conferences like these, often because of pressure from their Muslim countrymen. Therefore these Christian leaders do not represent the real Christian voices of this land. If they felt free to speak without reprisal from their Muslim neighbors, most Arabic-speaking Aramaic Christians would say they disagree with those Christian leaders who publicly condemn Israel.[27]

He adds,

> So the moral question for Palestinians is this: how can they live in a country, enjoy all types of freedoms and rights, benefit from the system, and still be its enemy from their deepest hearts? This position is immoral, to say the least. It reveals that the hatred of Israel and the Jews has little *to* do with how the state treats Arabs or any other minority but suggests that a certain Islamist theology animates many.[28]

---

26. Ibid.; cf. Kairos Palestine Document, 2.5.

27. Shadi Khalloul, "Theology and Morality: Is Modern Israel Faithful to the Moral Demands of the Covenant in Its Treatment of Minorities?" in McDermott, *The New Christian Zionism*, 298.

28. Ibid., 299.

The ways in which Palestinian evangelicals who affirm the Kairos document and their anti-Christian Zionist Western spokespersons lay a very fragile foundation for unity within the Body of the Messiah, both within the State of Israel and outside.

THE IMPACT OF THE ANTI-CHRISTIAN ZIONIST MOVEMENT ON JEWISH MISSIONS

These views impact the fulfillment of the Great Commission among the Jewish people as it gives Christians a negative view of the Jewish people and provokes anger toward Israel rather than a burden for their salvation. This is especially true among younger evangelicals who attend schools that have been influenced by the Christ at the Checkpoint conferences.

The anti-Christian Zionists—through its spokespersons and proliferation of literature—attempts to take the air out of the historic pro-Jewish and pro-Israel theological sentiments within the broader church. The anti-Christian Zionist movements in Britain and the United States may not be trying to intentionally undermine Jewish evangelism, yet efforts to "re-balance" the influence of "Christian Zionism" creates a disparaging view of Israel and Israelis and damages the cause of Jewish evangelism. Negative rhetoric against Israel produces revulsion toward Israelis and the Jewish people in general. Support for Jewish evangelism becomes collateral damage in these attacks against Israel, led by anti-Christian Zionists and the Palestinian evangelicals on whose behalf they speak. A discussion with one of the proponents of anti-Christian Zionism demonstrates that creating ill will toward Israel and the Jewish people may not been the intention of these authors, yet it is still an unfortunate consequence of their actions.

A PERSONAL STORY

Some time ago, I attended a mission's think tank, attended by Christian leaders of a wide variety of theological and missiological perspectives. The topic addressed was "The Impact of Eschatology on Missions." There were good papers presented and an honest and vigorous discussion took place as a result. However, a few Christian leaders and scholars at this meeting chose to utilize this forum to address the Israeli-Palestinian conflict, which was not on the docket. They had obviously planned to do this because their responses to the plenary papers on eschatology were well prepared ahead of time. Unfortunately, I was unprepared to respond to these issues, as were others, because we did not know these topics would arise. Although the think tank did not justify a platform for the anti-Christian Zionism viewpoint, it was beneficial for me to hear what they had to say. It was disturbing but educational.

I approached one of these brothers, who has written many books on this subject, and asked if we could dialogue for a few moments about what he had said in his paper. I introduced myself and added that I was a Jewish believer who affirmed the right of Israel to exist and possess the land, so that there would be no misunderstanding about my perspective regarding his position. I then asked him if he would be willing to put our differences aside as I wanted to speak to him about some deeper issues arising from his position. He graciously agreed, and I then felt free to dialogue with him quietly and without contention.

I let him know that I felt that his books have had a negative effect on Jewish missions. I quickly added that I also realized that he believes Jewish people need to hear the gospel and accept Jesus as Lord. He smiled and nodded his head, appreciating the fact that I understood that this was his position. I also assured him that I did not necessarily equate his anti-Christian Zionist position with anti-Semitism. I suggested that his books and public lectures had painted the policies of modern Israel so negatively that one could not help but develop a negative view of Israelis from his writings. I added that many Christians could not distinguish between an Israeli political policy and the Jewish people as a whole. He seemed surprised by this. I told him that every time he painted Israel as a *land-grabbing monster*—which I believe, he had done—many Christians unfortunately projected this picture onto the Jewish people in general. Once again, he seemed to be surprised by this. I told him that I believed his books and rhetoric have caused many Christians to have a negative attitude toward Israel and the Jewish people—and that interest in Jewish evangelism, on both sides of our pond, has diminished as a result. Once again, he seemed very surprised at this.

I described the problem in this way: When you paint a picture of one group of people as victims (the Palestinians) in need of help and the others (the Israelis) as aggressors in need of restraint, it is only normal for sensitive kindhearted Christians to sympathize with the group of people in need of help— and you have made an emotional argument that already defines the aggressors and the victims. Many Christians would now view it as their duty to withstand the Israeli aggressors and side with those who are viewed as needing help. I told this brother that, without perhaps intending to, he had charged the evangelical Christian atmosphere with a negative view toward Israel that has spilled over to the Jewish people as a whole. I told him, as gently as possible, that the work of Jewish missions was also suffering because of his negative characterization of Israelis, which in turn led to a broader antipathy by Christians toward the Jewish people as a whole. In effect, this has led to a decreased interest in bringing the Gospel to the Jewish people. Christians want to reach those whom they care about and for whom they have a sense of sympathy. By painting Israelis in such an unflattering manner and the Palestinians as so needy, he had evoked the emotions of Christians who oftentimes feel as if they must favor Palestinians over Israelis—or over Jews, more broadly.

I asked this brother if he might try and do what he can to temper this direction by rebalancing his public rhetoric. I suggested that we might want to have some *back-room* discussions about these issues. I encouraged him to be less aggressive in his rhetoric, both in his writing and lectures, as a way to prevent the evangelical church from becoming increasingly anti-Israel and, unfortunately, more anti-Jewish. I further mentioned that if the church views Jewish missions and ministry among Jews in Israel favorably, and the church is motivated to pray for and support our work, then many more Jewish people will come to know the Lord. When combined with many more Palestinians turning to Jesus, it would undoubtedly have a greater impact on restoring peace to the Middle East. I told him that he was working at cross-purposes with what I knew he wanted most of all—that Christ be glorified in the Middle East.

I could tell he was not in agreement with my position, but he was a gracious listener. I do hope for an ongoing dialogue with him and others who are proponents of this new anti-Christian Zionism, in the hopes that we can find greater unity in the Gospel and tone down any rhetoric that would create ill feelings on the part of Christians toward Palestinians and Israelis. When supersessionism is mixed with a hostile Palestinian metanarrative, it can easily lead to presenting Israel and the Jewish people in a fiercely negative light.

Who wants to evangelize people they dislike? Anti-Christian Zionism makes it more difficult to recruit young people at Christian colleges in the West to go to Israel, reach Israelis in short-term missions, to reach out to Jewish students on campuses, and to recruit a new generation of missionaries to the Jewish people.

CONCLUSION: AN APPEAL FOR BALANCE, RESTRAINT, AND THEOLOGICAL REFLECTION

It is my intention in this chapter to issue a clarion call to rethink the underlying issues that shape the position of today's anti-Christian Zionists, especially the undergirding supersessionism that is currently growing in popularity. Certainly, some of the issues that the anti-Christian Zionists bring to the surface regarding the Middle East crisis must be addressed by Christians who support Israel, which this book as a whole seeks to do.

One of the other issues that needs to be broached is the challenge of racism, which is always wrong, dangerous, and ungodly—whether directed toward Jews or Arabs. As believers in Jesus, we are called to extend his love and grace to all peoples. It is our mandate to proclaim the Gospel to every person: Jew, Gentile, Arab, and Israeli and to demonstrate his love in the most practical terms. Inflammatory rhetoric used by Christians to vilify any race, nation, or social group is always wrong, whether we agree with them or not.

As believers in Jesus, we are called to capture the hearts of fellow believers through our speech and to inspire the body of Christ to love the unlovely and give sacrificially for the evangelization and well-being of those for whom our Savior paid the ultimate price. Anti-Palestinian and anti-Muslim fear-mongering in sermons, books, articles, and activities on the part of some Christian extremists must be tempered. In a similar manner, the ideas, verbal and online messaging, and major publications of anti-Christian Zionists continues to nurture a growing negative view of Israel and the Jewish people and has unfortunately damaged the cause of Jewish evangelism.

The Palestinian Christian voice amplified in the West by their advocates must be tempered, balanced, and cognizant of the damage their statements and "manifestos" like the Kairos Palestine Document are having among Christians. This underlying supersessionism emboldens and seems to justify some evangelicals to speak more harshly about the modern State of Israel than is appropriate.

However, the views of those who believe in Israel's present and future cannot simply be dismissed or ignored as archaic and insensitive. This is disrespectful and harmful to the process of reconciliation. Again, Dr. Darrell Bock writes regarding the biblical pro-Israel position found in The *New Christian Zionism*:

> Christian Zionism is bigger than any denomination, theological tradition or period. It focuses on the character of God and the teaching of Jesus and the apostles. Those at the start of the Christian faith argued that God will keep his promises to Israel. This confidence also provides a basis for assurance about his promises to us. Those promises point to a reconciliation God has worked through his Messiah for the life and the shalom of the world.[29]

I could not agree more as those who affirm the Kairos document and do not believe there is any validity to the continued election of the Jewish people must recognize that reconciliation will not easily take place while the covenant validity of the Jewish people is in question.

As much as the anti-Christian Zionists critics believe that Western Christendom, influenced by premillennialism, Christian Zionism, and dispensationalism have hurt the cause of Muslim evangelism, so today, the promotion of anti-Christian Zionism is fostering a negative view of Israel and the Jewish people within the church, especially among our next generation of Christian young people.

The time has come to pay attention to these trends and temper our rhetoric, calming the waters of antagonism so that the gospel may be preached to both Israelis and Palestinians as all sides agree that Jesus is the only hope for peace in the Middle East. However, it is important to lay our theological cards out on the table and to identify the underlying supersessionism that promotes the theological perspective that the Jewish people rejected Jesus and therefore have been put aside from God's plan and purposes, including the loss of the Promised Land of Israel. An honest discussion, without dismissing the premillennial view as eccentric or even dangerous, must be part of any potentially fruitful discussion about unity and reconciliation.

Anti-Christian Zionists, either intentionally or not, obfuscate the most fundamental issue at stake with calls for political and moral reform. Would the Jewish people have a divine right to the Land if they treated the Palestin-

---

29.   Darrell Bock, "How Should the New Christian Zionism Proceed?" in McDermott, *The New Christian Zionism*, 317.

ians in ways that our critics deem godly? This would not change the underlying theological position that denies the Jewish people a covenantal right to live in the land of Israel. An honest dialogue regarding supersessionism would move the discussion beyond secondary issues and encourage a deeper discussion that could lead to a more authentic reconciliation. Without addressing supersessionism as a theological presupposition, any and all effort toward this end will be fruitless

Yet, the unity Jesus prayed for might very well be within our grasp by the power of his Holy Spirit. I write in hope of a better future for relationships within the body of the Messiah between Arabs and Israelis, and for those who advocate for both. As the apostle Paul writes, it is important to reflect our shared position in the Messiah: "to be specific, that the Gentiles are fellow heirs and fellow members of the body, and fellow partakers of the promise in Christ Jesus through the gospel" (Eph. 3:6, NASB).

ISRAEL AND THE LAND IN THE WRITINGS OF THE CHURCH

MICHAEL J. VLACH

THE COMING SALVATION AND RESTORATION OF ISRAEL, including the permanent return of Israel to the Land of promise, is explicitly taught in many Bible passages (see Deut. 30; Ezek. 36–37). Yet church history shows that it did not take long for the Christian church to adopt a replacement theology position in which the church viewed itself as superseding Israel and Israel's promises to the exclusion of national Israel. Paul himself fought a growing replacement position with his letter to the Romans. In reference to some who viewed Israel as being replaced Paul declared, "God has not rejected His people whom He foreknew" (Rom. 11:2).[1] He also warned Gentile believers by saying, "Do not become arrogant toward the branches [i.e., Israel]" (Rom. 11:18). Yet the growing Gentile church often did not heed Paul's instruction and adopted a replacement position concerning Israel that exists to this day.

But while replacement theology is well-established and documented in church history, not all in the church adopted this perspective. Belief in a restoration of national Israel, including Israel's return to her land, also has historical support. This "restorationism" view is not new nor is it the possession of any one group or denomination. Nor is it the invention of Dispensationalism in the nineteenth century or modern Christian Zionism. While not always the predominant position, restorationism has been affirmed throughout church history. In fact, adherents of various theological eschatological and millennial positions have affirmed the biblical truth that God's plans include the nation Israel and the land of Israel.

This chapter will offer a historical survey of restorationism in church history. By "restorationism" we refer to the view that national Israel remains theologically significant in God's plans. In addition to the current remnant of believing Jews in this age, God will one day restore the nation of Israel who will have a role to play in a coming earthly kingdom when Jesus the Messiah reigns over the earth (see Isa. 2:2; Matt. 19:28; Rev. 19:15). This

---

1. Unless otherwise noted, translation used in this chapter is NASB.

restoration idea includes the idea of Israel returning to and possessing the land of promise.

This chapter comes in three parts. First, it briefly highlights the restoration idea in the first century via the New Testament writings. Second, it mentions factors that led many in the church away from the restoration idea toward a replacement theology view. And third, this chapter surveys those in church history who stood against replacement theology by affirming the restoration of Israel, including the importance of Israel's land. As a result, those who believe in a restoration of national Israel should know that their view is not a recent creation but has been believed by others throughout church history.

RESTORATIONISM IN THE FIRST CENTURY AD

The idea that national Israel would be saved and permanently restored to her Land is well-established in the Old Testament. Concerning a future time God told Israel: "The LORD your God will bring you into the land which your fathers possessed, and you shall possess it; and He will prosper you and multiply you more than your fathers" (Deut. 30:5; cf. Lev. 26; Ezek. 36–27). The restoration expectation also was manifest in the first century AD with the persons and writings of the New Testament. For example, the angel Gabriel told Mary, "The Lord God will give Him [Jesus] the throne of His father David; and He will reign over the house of Jacob [i.e. Israel] forever, and His kingdom will have no end" (Luke 1:32–33). When the disciples asked Jesus about rewards for following Him, Jesus said that when he sits on "His glorious throne," the twelve apostles will "sit upon twelve thrones, judging the twelve tribes of Israel" (Matt 19:28). This reaffirms the future significance of a restored and united twelve tribes of Israel.

While predicting the coming destruction of Jerusalem in AD 70 in Luke 21:20–24, Jesus made clear that Jerusalem's trampling by the Gentiles was only temporary and would be reversed:

> and they [people of Israel] will fall by the edge of the sword, and will be led captive into all the nations; and Jerusalem will be trampled under foot by the Gentiles until the times of the Gentiles are fulfilled (21:24).

The key term in Luke 21:24 is "until" (Grk. *achris ou*) which indicates that Jerusalem's trampling by Gentiles is only temporary and will give way to a restored Jerusalem.

On the day of his ascension into heaven, the apostles asked Jesus, "Lord, is it at this time that you are restoring the kingdom to Israel?" (Acts 1:6). So after forty days of kingdom instruction from the risen Jesus (see Acts 1:3), the apostles expected the kingdom of God to be restored to Israel, an idea that Jesus does not correct. In Romans 9:4–5 Paul affirmed that the "promises," "covenants," and "temple service" given to Israel in the Old

Testament still belong to Israel. Even with Israel currently in unbelief these privileges were not forfeited. Paul also declared that the salvation of all Israel would occur with the second coming of Jesus and then Israel would experience New Covenant blessings just as the prophet Isaiah predicted (Rom 11:26–27; cf. Isa. 59:20–21). Both 2 Thessalonians 2 and Revelation 11:1–2 predict future significance for the Jewish temple in Jerusalem. Revelation 7:4–8 speaks of the salvation of 144,000 people from the twelve tribes of Israel.

The list of examples could go on, but these reveal the fact that the New Testament affirms a coming restoration of Israel, including the land. So what happened to this expectation in the church? Why did many abandon the hope of Israel?

WHY THE CHURCH LARGELY ABANDONED RESTORATIONISM

The biblical expectation of a future for Israel was not entirely lost in the early church, but it was not long before replacement theology developed and hope for national Israel waned. Replacement theology is the view that the Christian church has permanently replaced, fulfilled, or superseded national Israel as the people of God. It holds that Israel's promises and covenants have been taken over or inherited by the Christian church which becomes the new or true spiritual Israel. The result is that Israel and the land of promise are no longer significant in God's purposes. The promises to Israel are either spiritualized or universalized in such a way the particular fulfillment with national Israel will not occur.

Four factors contributed to the replacement theology view and the neglect of Israel's coming restoration. First, as the Christian church became more and more Gentile in its composition belief in Israel's future salvation and restoration began to wane. According to Siker, Jewish Christians "were eventually absorbed into an overwhelmingly Gentile Christianity."[2] As a result, the church increasingly became the *ecclesia ex gentibus* ("church of the Gentiles"). This growing Gentile presence in the church led to "theological questions regarding the status of the Jews before God."[3]

Second, Gentile Christians viewed the destructions of Jerusalem in AD 70 and 135 as God's permanent rejection of Israel. According to Philip S. Alexander, the AD 70 destruction of Jerusalem handed Christians "a propaganda coup" in that it gave them the opportunity to argue that the catastrophe was "a divine judgment on Israel for the rejection of Jesus."[4] The same was also true concerning the failed second Jewish revolt in AD 135. Marcel

---

2. Jeffrey S. Siker, *Disinheriting the Jews: Abraham in Early Christian Controversy* (Louisville: Westminster/John Knox, 1991), 15.195.

3. Ibid.

4. Philip S. Alexander, "'The Parting of the Ways,'" in *Jews and Christians: The Parting of the Ways A.D. 70 to 135*, ed. James D. G. Dunn (Grand Rapids: Eerdmans, 1999), 20.

Simon asserts that the destruction of Jerusalem in 135 "appeared to Christians as the confirmation of the divine verdict on Israel."[5]

The third factor was the church's reappropriation of the Jewish scriptures in such a way that excluded Israel. Wayne House observes, "The church not only appropriated the special status of the Jewish people, it took over their Bible, the Septuagint (LXX)."[6] For example, in addressing Trypho about truths concerning Jesus, the second-century theologian Justin Martyr declared, "Are you acquainted with them, Trypho? They are contained in your Scriptures, or rather not yours, but ours."[7] Thus, the church viewed itself as inheriting Israel's scriptures and Israel's hope.

Fourth, the rise of allegorization of Scripture in the early church contributed to a decline of belief in a literal fulfillment of promises concerning Israel and Israel's land. As House writes:

> By the end of the first century the allegorical method had gained considerable sway in the church. The more literal interpretation of the New Testament authors and post-apostolic fathers gave way to the influence of Greek philosophical interpretation found in Philo and later in *Hermes* and Justin Martyr. By the time of the brilliant Alexandrian theologian Origen, allegory was readily used to move beyond the literal sense of the text.[8]

The historian Jaroslav Pelikan points out that "spiritual exegesis" was applied to the Old Testament Scriptures by the early church.[9] As a result, "There was no early Christian who simultaneously acknowledged the doctrinal authority of the Old Testament and interpreted it literally."[10] There was a tendency to interpret Old Testament texts nonliterally. Tertullian, for example, allegorically interpreted Genesis 25:21–23 and its statement that "the older will serve the younger." For him, this was evidence that national Israel would become subservient to the church:

> Accordingly, since the people or nation of the Jews is anterior in time, and "greater" through the grace of primary favor in the Law, whereas ours is understood to be "less" in the age of times, as having in the last era of the world attained the knowl-

5. Marcel Simon, *Versus Israel: A Study of the Relations Between Christians and Jews in the Roman Empire (135–425)*, trans. H. McKeating (Oxford: Oxford University Press, 1986), 65.

6. H. Wayne House, "The Church's Appropriation of Israel's Blessings," in *Israel, the Land and the People: An Evangelical Affirmation of God's Promises*, ed. H. Wayne House (Grand Rapids: Kregel, 1998), 97.

7. Justin Martyr, *Dialogue with Trypho* 29, *Ante-Nicene Fathers* 1:209.

8. House, "The Church's Appropriation of Israel's Blessings," 98; See also Hans Küng, *Judaism: Between Yesterday and Tomorrow*, trans. John Bowden (New York: Crossroad, 1992), 152.

9. Pelikan, *The Emergence of the Catholic Tradition (100–600)*, vol. 1, The Christian Tradition: A History of the Development of Doctrine (Chicago: University of Chicago Press, 1971), 81.

10. Ibid. Virkler observes, "The allegorical method as practiced by the church fathers often neglected completely the author's intended meaning." Henry Virkler, *Hermeneutics: Principles and Processes of Biblical Interpretation* (Grand Rapids: Baker, 1981), 59.

edge of divine mercy: beyond doubt, through the edict of divine utterance, the prior and "greater" people—that is, the Jewish—must necessarily serve the "less" and the "less" people—that is, the Christian—overcome the "greater."[11]

THE SALVATION OF ISRAEL

Although a replacement view eventually thrived in the early church a consensus of theologians of the Patristic Era affirmed a future salvation of the Jews in accord with Old Testament prophecies and Paul's words regarding Israel in Romans 11. Denis Fahey, in reference to a list from Augustine Lemamn, lists the theologians through the twelfth century who believed "that the Jews will be converted." This list includes: Tertullian, Origen, St. Hillary, St. Ambrose, St. John Chrysostom, St. Jerome, St. Cyril of Alexandria, St. Prosper of Aquitaine, Cassiodorus, Preniasius, St. Gregory the Great, St. Isidore, Venerable Bede, St. Anselm, St. Peter Damian, and St. Bernard.[12] In fact, Fahey points out that the view that "the Jews will be converted . . . toward the end of the world can be proved from the texts of the Fathers, century by century."[13] For example, while often known for his allegorization of Scripture, Origen affirmed a future salvation of Israel:

> For the Church was called between the two callings of Israel; that is to say, first Israel was called, and afterwards when Israel had stumbled and fallen, the Church of the Gentiles was called. "But when the fullness of the Gentiles has come in, then will all Israel, having been called again, be saved."[14]

Cyril of Jerusalem (c. 315–386), when discussing events regarding "the end of the world drawing near," discussed the coming of the Antichrist and his temporary deception of the Jews. For him, the Antichrist will deceive "the Jews by the lying signs and wonders of his magical deceit, until they believe he is the expected Christ."[15] Thus, for Cyril, the coming Antichrist would deceive the Jews for a time until the Jews believed in Jesus.

Augustine, in his *City of God*, linked the salvation of the Jews with the coming of Elijah:

> It is a familiar theme in the conversation and heart of the faithful, that in the last days before the judgment the Jews shall believe in the true Christ, that is, our Christ, by means of this great and admirable prophet Elias who shall expound the law to

11. Tertullian, *An Answer to the Jews* 1, *ANF* 3:151.

12. Dennis Fahey, *The Kingship of Christ and the Conversion of the Jewish Nation* (Kimmage, Dublin: Holy Ghost Missionary College, 1953), 107.

13. Ibid.

14. Origen, *The Song of Songs*, in *Ancient Christian Writers*, eds. Johannes Quasten and Joseph C. Plumpe (Westminster, MD: The Newman Press, 1957), 26:252.

15. Cyril, *Catechetical Lectures*, in William A. Jurgens, *The Faith of the Early Fathers*, 3 vols. (Collegeville, MN: The Liturgical Press), 1:356–357.

them. . . . When, therefore, he is come, he shall give a spiritual explanation of the law which the Jews at present understand carnally, and shall thus "turn the heart of the father to the son," that is, the heart of the fathers to the children.[16]

Significantly, Augustine mentions that his view concerning the salvation of the Jews was "familiar" to believers of his day. Thus, his belief in the salvation of the Jews went beyond just his own personal view. This perspective was common for those of his generation. But did the early church hold out hope for a restoration of national Israel with implications for the land of Israel?

RESTORATIONISM IN CHURCH HISTORY

Belief that many in Israel would be *saved* is not the same as also affirming that Israel as a nation will be *reunited* and *restored* and placed in her land. The restoration of Israel idea was not a majority view in the early church. In fact, the early church did not state much concerning Israel's restoration as a nation and the importance of the land of Israel. In the fourth century the emperor Constantine (274–337) and his mother Helena promoted interest in finding important sites in the holy land. They also encouraged Christians to visit the holy land. Jerome (347–420) viewed pilgrimages to Israel as beneficial, saying, "so we also understand the Scriptures better when we have seen Judea with our own eyes."[17] Yet interest in holy land sites was a far cry from the idea of a restoration of Israel.[18]

Nevertheless, some early theologians still viewed Jerusalem and the tribes of Israel as remaining significant prophetically. For example, Justin Martyr held that the tribes of Israel would be gathered and restored in accord with what the prophet Zechariah predicted:

And what the people of the Jews shall say and do, when they see Him coming in glory, has been thus predicted by Zechariah the prophet: "I will command the four winds to gather the scattered children; I will command the north wind to bring them, and the south wind, that it keep not back. And then in Jerusalem there shall be great lamentation, not the lamentation of mouths or of lips, but the lamentation of the heart; and they shall rend not their garments, but their hearts. Tribe by tribe they shall mourn, and then they shall look on Him whom they have pierced; and they shall say, 'Why, O Lord, hast Thou made us to err from Thy way? The glory which our fathers blessed, has for us been turned into shame.'"[19]

---

16. Augustine, *City of God*, 29, *Nicene and Post-Nicene Fathers*, Series 1, 2:448.

17. Walter Zander, *Israel and the Holy Places of Christendom* (London: Weidenfeld & Nicolson, 1971), 7.

18. See Michael J. Vlach, "Israel in Church History," in *The People, the Land, and the Future of Israel: Israel and the Jewish People in the Plan of God*, eds. Darrell L. Bock and Mitch Glaser (Grand Rapids: Kregel, 2014).

19. Justin, *First Apology*, 52, *ANF* 1:180.

In regard to this comment by Justin, Charles Hauser states, "Justin also links the Jews with the second advent of Christ. It will be at this time that Christ will gather the nation Israel and the Jews shall look on him and repent tribe by tribe."[20] Justin not only held to a future hope for the tribes of Israel, he did so on the basis of Old Testament promises to the nation—in this case, Zechariah. For Justin, the hope for Israel presented in the Old Testament was alive.

Justin Martyr also believed in a coming thousand-year kingdom in Jerusalem, in connection with what the Old Testament prophets predicted:

> I and others, who are right-minded Christians on all points, are assured that there will be a resurrection of the dead, and a thousand years in Jerusalem, which will then be built, adorned, and enlarged, the prophets Ezekiel and Isaiah and others declare.[21]

So in addition to affirming a coming resurrection and kingdom of one thousand years, Justin mentions the physical city of "Jerusalem" as the site of the kingdom. He also states that the city will be built in the way that the prophets Ezekiel and Isaiah discussed, thus expecting a literal fulfillment of what these prophets predicted. Justin was not alone in this understanding pointing out that these were also held by other "right-minded Christians."

Tertullian (155–240) also expected a future restoration of Israel:

> [F]or it will be fitting for the Christian to rejoice, and not to grieve, at the restoration of Israel, if it be true, (as it is), that the whole of our hope is intimately united with the remaining expectation of Israel.[22]

In reference to Joel 3:1–2, Jerome (347–420) espoused a restoration hope with expectation for a return to Jerusalem:

> For those who believe, salvation is in Mount Zion and Jerusalem. In the latter days, the Lord will gather the called remnant from the people of Judah, who with the apostles and through the apostles believed. He will return the captives of Judah to Jerusalem.[23]

While Cyril of Alexandria (378–444) gives a spiritual interpretation of Mount Zion as the church in Obadiah 16,[24] he believes the Jews will possess their land according to Obadiah 19:

> "Those in the south" signifies the area where the Babylonians invaded Jerusalem led by Nebuchadnezzar. The entire province of Judea was laid waste, sinking back

---

20. Charles August Hauser, Jr., "The Eschatology of the Church Fathers" (Ph.D. diss., Grace Theological Seminary, 1961), 112.

21. Justin Martyr, *Dialogue with Trypho*, 80, *ANF*, 1:239.

22. Tertullian, *On Modesty*, 8, *ANF*, 4:82.

23. Jerome, *The Prophet Joel*, in Corpus Christianorum: Series Latina (Turnhout, 1953–) 76, 198.

24. Cyril of Alexandria, *Commentary on Obadiah*, *Patrologia graeca*, 71:591.

into miser so that it was reduced to absolute silence and appeared entirely deserted. However, when God will enter into the misery of the captives, he will return them to the land of their ancestors after his wrath has subsided. In their return from Babylon the entire multitude of Israel will possess the region of the nations that is equal to Edom. This is a sign of blessing from God.[25]

Cyril also spoke of a "migration" of Israel "back to the land":

> At this place in the text, the migration of Israel back to the land is mentioned, more specifically from those Jews taken away into Babylon. . . . Perhaps here he is saying that everything that is to the south and to the north and to the east and to the west will be fully occupied by Israel as they will easily possess the whole region around them. And people will ascend, gathered on top of Zion, which sums up the goal of the prophecy. For the inhabitants of Zion, he says, are saved by God, who will burst through their chains of servitude.[26]

Augustine, who is known as the father of amillennialism, also adopted a literal approach to Zechariah 12:10 in regard to the salvation of Israel. In doing so, he believes some Old Testament prophecies still had continuing relevance in regard to the salvation of Israel:

> "And they shall look upon me because they have insulted me, and they shall mourn for Him as if for one very dear (or beloved), and shall be in bitterness for Him as for an only-begotten." For in that day the Jews—those of them, at least, who shall receive the spirit of grace and mercy—when they see Him coming in His majesty, and recognize that it is He whom they, in the person of their parents, insulted when He came before in His humiliation, shall repent of insulting Him in His passion.[27]

In sum, while the church of the patristic era drifted to a replacement theology position in which they viewed the church as Israel, there was a consensus among the theologians of this era that the Israel would be converted and saved in the last days. And according to some, Israel's salvation would also involve a restoration of Israel, including a restored Jerusalem and the gathering of the tribes of Israel to their land.

MIDDLE AGES

Undeniably, a strong replacement theology view characterized the period we now call the Middle Ages (ca. 500–1500). Belief in a restoration of Israel, including Israel's land, was not common. There was interest in the Holy Land, but this was largely due to the desire to wrest the Holy Land from Muslim control. The Crusades began in 1095 as a way to reclaim the

---

25. Ibid., *PG* 71:593. See *Ancient Christian Commentary on Scripture: OT* 14.125.

26. Ibid., *PG* 71:595–96. See *ACCS: OT 14*.126.

27. Ibid., *NPNF¹*, 2:450.

Holy Land from the Muslims. Pope Urban II, who launched the Crusades, viewed the Crusades as a way of renewing the church and leading to pilgrimages to Israel that allegedly could usher in the return of Christ.

Yet there were some bright spots regarding the idea of the restoration of Israel. One person during this period who affirmed a restoration of Israel was John of Rupescissa (1310–66). Summarizing his views Lerner says: "For him [John] the converted Jews would become God's new imperial nation and Jerusalem would be completely rebuilt to become the center of the purified faith."[28] Another, Gerard of Borgo San Donnino (c. 1255), "taught that some Jews would be blessed as Jews in the end time and would return to their ancient homeland."[29] So while the overwhelming view of the church of the Middle Ages was that of replacement theology and no hope for national Israel, not all went with the replacement view.

REFORMATION PERIOD

The first generation of the Protestant Reformation—including Luther, Calvin, and Zwingli—focused mostly on issues such as the gospel, justification, and the authority of Scripture. Matters concerning Israel were not primary, although Luther explicitly rejected the restoration idea. He stated:

> [A]ll the prophecies which say that Israel and Judah shall return to their lands and have material and unending possession of them have been fulfilled long ago. The hopes of the Jews are utterly vain and lost.[30]

Fortunately, though, not all held such a negative view concerning Israel. William Watson notes that Edmund Bunny (1540–1619), sub-dean of York Cathedral, penned *The Coronation of David* (1588) wherein he hopes for "the imminent restoration of the Jews to their land."[31] In 1585, Cambridge fellow Frances Kett (1547–1589) "called for the Jews to return to their land."[32]

SEVENTEENTH CENTURY

While the restoration of Israel was not a major focus of the Reformation of the sixteenth century, the following century was much more positive toward this idea. The Reformation eventually led to more positive beliefs concerning Israel and Israel's land. This occurred as more people gained access to the Bible and expressed interest in the Old Testament and the Hebrew language. This was especially true of the Puritans. In his study of the

---

28.   Robert E. Lerner, "Millennialism," in *The Encyclopedia of Apocalypticism*, eds. John J. Collins, Bernard McGinn, and Stephen J. Stein. (New York: Continuum, 2000), 2:353.

29.   Thomas Ice, "Lovers of Zion: A Brief History of Christian Zionism," *Voice* (March/April 2005).

30.   Edward M. Plass, ed., *What Luther Says* (St. Louis: Concordia Publishing House, 1959), II 687–88.

31.   Cited in William C. Watson, *Dispensationalism before Darby: Seventeenth-Century and Eighteenth-Century English Apocalypticism* (Silverton, OR: Lampion Press, 2015), 15.

32.   Ibid.

Puritans of the seventeenth century, Iain Murray observed that "belief in a future conversion of the Jews became commonplace among the English Puritans."[33] Smolinski also summarized that, "In fact, Puritan millennialists strongly asserted that the restoration and national conversion of the Jews was a *prerequisite* to the Second Coming. Christ's Second Advent was indefinitely postponed until such time as Israel's 'dry bones' were enlivened and restored to their ancient position of prominence."[34]

Concerning specific examples of a restoration hope, Thomas Brightman (1552–1607), an English clergyman who wrote a commentary on the Book of Revelation, argued that the Jews would return to the Holy Land in fulfillment of the Scriptures: "Shall they return to Jerusalem again? There is nothing more certain: the prophets do everywhere confirm it and beat upon it."[35]

Sir Henry Finch, an English lawyer and politician, also believed in a restoration of Israel. In 1621 he published *The World's Great Restauration, or Calling of the Jews, and with them of all Nations and Kingdoms of the Earth to the Faith of Christ.* He declared, "Where Israel, Judah, Zion and Jerusalem are named [in the Bible] the Holy Ghost meant not the spiritual Israel, or the Church of God collected of the Gentiles or of the Jews and Gentiles both. . . . But Israel properly descended out of Jacob's loynes."[36] In reference to Ezekiel 37–39 Finch referred to Israel being restored to her land: "The bringing of them to their owne country from all the places where they were scattered."[37]

William Perkins (1558–1602), an English cleric and theologian, predicted a future for the nation Israel: "The Lord saith, All the nations shall be blessed in Abraham: Hence I gather that the nation of the Jews shall be called, and converted to the participation of this blessing: when, and how, God knows: but that it shall be done before the end of the world we know."[38]

The English minister John Archer (1598–1682) said that "Israel and Judah" would be under Jesus' kingship "so the Cities of the Tribes shall be built againe, and inhabited by natural Israelites, especially Jerusalem, which shall bee the most eminent city then in the world."[39]

Yet English Puritans were not the only ones affirming a coming restoration of Israel. Wilhelmus à Brakel (1635–1711), a Dutch Reformed minister in Rotterdam, Holland, predicted this as well:

---

33. Iain Murray, *The Puritan Hope: Revival and the Interpretation of Prophecy* (London: Banner of Truth, 1971), 43.

34. Reiner Smolinski, "Israel Redivivus: The Eschatological Limits of Puritan Typology in New England," in *The New England Quarterly,* Vol. 63, No. 3 (September, 1990): 363.

35. Thomas Brightman, *A Revelation of the Apocalypse,* 1615.

36. Sir Henry Finch, *The World's Great Restauration, or Calling of the Jews, and with them of all Nations and Kingdoms of the Earth to the Faith of Christ,* 1621.

37. Cited in Watson, 19.

38. Murray, *The Puritan Hope,* 42.

39. Cited in Watson, 20.

One more question remains to be answered: Will the Jewish nation be gathered together again from all the regions of the world and from all the nations of the earth among which they have been dispersed? Will they come to dwell in Canaan and all the lands promised to Abraham, and will Jerusalem be rebuilt? We believe that these events will transpire. . . . They will be an independent republic, governed by a very wise, good-natured, and superb government. Furthermore, Canaan will be extraordinarily fruitful, the inhabitants will be eminently godly, and they will constitute a segment of the glorious state of the church during the thousand years prophesied in Rev 20.[40]

Note that à Brakel's statement above goes beyond just a salvation of Jews to national restoration. He discusses the "Jewish nation" being "gathered" to "dwell in Canaan" with a rebuilt Jerusalem. Petrus Serrarius (1600–1699) of Amsterdam also expressed belief in both a conversion of the Jews and a restoration of Israel when he said, "The time of the Conversion of the Jews and the restoring of the Kingdom of Israel (of which the Prophets are full) . . . is at hand."[41]

J. Van Den Berg claims that most theologians in the Netherlands affirmed a future for Israel:

For . . . virtually all Dutch theologians of the seventeenth century, 'the whole of Israel' indicated the fullness of the people of Israel 'according to the flesh': in other words, the fullness of the Jewish people. This meant that there was a basis for an expectation of a future conversion of the Jews—an expectation which was shared by a large majority of Dutch theologians.[42]

EIGHTEENTH CENTURY

Like the seventeenth century, expectation of a future restoration of national Israel to the land of promise was strong. Concerning Israel's land, Isaac Newton (1642–1727) said:

This was God's covenant with Abraham when he promised that his seed should inherit the land of Canaan for ever, and on this covenant was founded the Jewish religion . . . it ought to be considered and understood by all men who pretend to the name of Christians.[43]

---

40. Wilhelmus à Brakel, *The Christian's Reasonable Service*, IV, 530–531.

41. Petrus Serrarius, *An Awakening Warning to a Wofull World* (Amsterdam, 1662), 27, 29.

42. J. Van Den Berg, "Appendix III: The eschatological expectation of seventeenth-century Dutch Protestantism with regard to the Jewish people," in *Puritan Eschatology: 1600–1660*, ed. Peter Toon (Cambridge: James Clarke, 1970), 140. According to Van Den Berg, theologians who affirmed a future salvation and/or restoration of Israel include: Samuel Maresius (1599–1673), Simon Episcopius (1583–1643), Jacobus Batalerius (1593–1672), Gisbertus Voetius (1589–1676), Johannes Hoornbeek (1617–1666), Andreas Essenius (1618–1677), Johannes Coccejus (1603–1669), Henricus Groenewegen (1640–1692), Herman Witsius (1636–1708), and Wilhelmus à Brakel (1635–1711) (137–53).

43. Protestantism/Protestants: Dutch Protestantism Witsius, Herman Voetius, Gisbertus Van Den Berg, J.Maresius, Samuel Hoornbeek, Johannes Groenewegen, Henricus Essenius, Andreas Epis-

English theologian and historian William Whiston (1667–1752) also affirmed the importance of Israel's land:

> The Seed or Posterity of Abraham, Isaak and Jacob should conquer and obtain the Land of Canaan. . . . [T]he land of Canaan's being their unalienable Possession and Inheritance, is in the Scripture very frequently and very emphatically expressed.[44]

In eighteenth-century America, optimism concerning Israel also existed. Jonathan Edwards (1703–58), a postmillennialist, argued that the stubbornness of ancient Israel will give way to a national conversion:

> However obstinate [the Jews] have been now for above seventeen hundred years in their rejection of Christ, and however rare have been the instances on individual conversions, ever since the destruction of Jerusalem. . . . Yet, when this day comes, the thick veil that blinds their eyes shall be removed. 2 Cor iii.16. And divine grace shall melt and renew their hard hearts... And then shall the house of Israel be saved: the Jews in all their dispersions shall cast away their old infidelity, and shall have their hearts wonderfully changed, and abhor themselves for their past unbelief and obstinacy. . . . Nothing is more certainly foretold than this national conversion of the Jews in Romans 11.2.[45]

On another occasion Edwards linked the concepts of salvation and restoration for Israel with a literal understanding of the Old Testament and Romans 11:

> Nothing is more certainly foretold than this national conversion of the Jews in the eleventh chapter of Romans. And there are also many passages of the Old Testament that can't be interpreted any other sense, that I can't now stand to mention. Besides the prophecies of the calling of the Jews, we have a remarkable seal of the fulfillment of this great event in providence by a thing that is a kind of continual miracle, viz. the preserving them a distinct [nation] when in such a dispersed condition for above sixteen hundred years. The world affords nothing else like it—a remarkable hand of providence. When they shall be called, then shall the ancient people that were alone God's people for so long a time be called God's people again, never to be rejected more, one fold with the Gentiles; and then shall also the remains of the ten tribes wherever they are, and though they have been rejected much longer than [the Jews], be brought in with their brethren, the Jews.

copius, Simon Coccejus, Johannes Brakel, Wilhelmus à Batalerius, Jacobus Isaac Newton, "Of the Day of Judgment and World to Come," Yehuda MS 6 folio 12r–19r, Jerusalem University Library; in Frank Manuel; *The Religion of Isaac Newton* (Oxford, 1974), Appendix B, 126–27, 130, as cited by Watson, 265.

44. William Whiston, *The Accomplishment of Scripture Prophecies. Being Eight Sermons . . . at the Cathedral* (Cambridge, 1708), 39. As cited in Watson, 266.

45. Jonathan Edwards, *The Works of Jonathan Edwards* (London: Banner of Truth Trust, reprint, 1976), 1:607.

The prophecies of Hosea especially seem to hold this forth, and that in the future glorious times of the church both Judah and Ephraim, or Judah and the ten tribes, shall be brought in together, and shall be untied as one people as they formerly were under David and Solomon (Hos.1:1), and so in the last chapter of Hosea, and other parts of his prophecy.[46]

Note that Edwards believed that all the tribes of Israel, even the lost ten tribes shall be gathered and restored. The return of the Jews to the land is also seen in the following:

And it is the more evident, the Jews will return to their own land again, because they never yet possessed one quarter of the land, which was so often promised them, from the Red Sea to the river Euphrates (Exod. 23:31; Gen. 15:18, Deut. 11:24; Josh. 1:4). Indeed, it was partly fulfilled in Solomon's time, when he governed all within those bounds for a short time; but so short, that it is not thought that this is all the fulfillment of the promise that is to be. And besides, that was not a fulfillment of the promise, because they did not possess it, though they made the nations of its tributary.[47]

A hope for Israel's return to the land can be found Samuel Collet's 1742 work, *A Treatise of the Future Restoration of the Jews and Israelites to Their Own Land*. Collet stated: "The following Treatise being designed to shew, that you, who are the now dispersed among the Nations, will, in a short time, with the rest of the Israelites, be restored to your own Land."[48] In his extensive study William Watson lists more than forty seventeenth- and eighteenth-century authors who "were Philo-Semitic and Expected the Restoration of Israel."[49]

NINETEENTH CENTURY

Riding the wave of the restoration idea of the eighteenth century, the nineteenth century also witnessed great interest in Israel's future and the land. The Calvinist theologian, Charles Haddon Spurgeon (1834–92), taught a restoration of Israel to the land: "It is also certain that the Jews, as a people, will yet own Jesus of Nazareth, the Son of David, as their King, and that they will return to their own land."[50] This expectation coincides with a coming earthly millennial reign. Spurgeon said Jesus "will reign amongst his ancients gloriously, and . . . there will be a thousand years of joy and peace

---

46.   Jonathan Edwards, *Works, A History of the Works of Redemption*, vol. 9, ed. John F. Wilson (New Haven, CT: Yale University Press, 1989), 469–70. Emphases added.

47.   Jonathan Edwards, *Works, Apocalyptic Writings*, vol. 5, 134–35

48.   Cited in Watson, 270.

49.   Watson, 280.

50.   Charles Haddon Spurgeon, "The Harvest and the Vintage," in *The Metropolitan Tabernacle Pulpit*, 50:553–54.

such as were never known on this earth before."[51] Spurgeon's explicit belief in a national restoration of Israel as a governmental entity to her land is seen in his 1864 sermon, "The Restoration and Conversion of the Jews":

> There will be a native government again; there will again be the form of a body politic; a state shall be incorporated, and a king shall reign. Israel has now become alienated from her own land. . . . If there be anything clear and plain, the literal sense and meaning of this passage [Ezekiel 37:1–10]—a meaning not to be spirited or spiritualized away—must be evident that both the two and the ten tribes of Israel are to be restored to their own land, and that a king is to rule over them.[52]

Another unmistakable advocate for a restoration of national Israel was J. C. Ryle (1816–1900). The Reformed English preacher declared:

> I believe that the Jews shall ultimately be gathered again as a separate nation, restored to their own land, and converted to the faith of Christ, after going through great tribulation (Jer. 30:10–11; 31:10; Rom. 11:25–26; Dan. 12:1; Zech. 13:8–9).[53]

Ryle's belief in a literal restoration of national Israel to her land was connected to taking Old Testament prophecies seriously:

> Time would fail me, if I attempted to quote all the passages of Scripture in which the future history of Israel is revealed. Isaiah, Jeremiah, Ezekiel, Hosea, Joel, Amos, Obadiah, Micah, Zephaniah, Zechariah all declare the same thing. All predict, with more or less particularity, that in the end of this dispensation the Jews are to be restored to their own land and to the favor of God. I lay no claim to infallibility in the interpretation of Scripture in this matter. I am well aware that many excellent Christians cannot see the subject as I do. I can only say, that to my eyes, the future *salvation* of Israel as a people, their *return* to Palestine and their national conversion to God, appear as clearly and plainly revealed as any prophecy in God's Word.[54]

The nineteenth century also witnessed the rise of dispensationalism, including the founder of systemtatized dispensationalism—John Nelson Darby. One essential of dispensationalism is its belief that national Israel will be saved and restored, and that God will restore Israel to the land of promise. Yet it should be noted that Darby and Dispensationalism did not invent the restoration-of-Israel idea. William Watson notes that the idea of restorationism concerning Israel "existed in the seventeenth and eighteenth

---

51. Ibid.
52. Spurgeon, "The Restoration and Conversion of the Jews," in *The Metropolitan Tabernacle Pulpit*, 10:426.
53. J. C. Ryle, *Are You Ready For The End Of Time?* (Fearn, Scotland: Christian Focus, 2001), 9; reprint of *Coming Events and Present Duties*.
54. Ibid., 183. reprint of *Coming Events and Present Duties*.

centuries long before John Nelson Darby who is considered the father of modern dispensationalism."[55]

RESTORATIONISM TODAY

Belief in a salvation and restoration of national Israel, including a return to the Land of promise, is well-represented today. This hope has been kindled even further as a result of the Holocaust and Israel becoming a nation again in 1948. Commenting on the events of the Holocaust and the establishment of the Jewish state, Soulen states, "Under the new conditions created by these events, Christian churches have begun to consider anew their relation to the God of Israel and the Israel of God in the light of the Scriptures and the gospel about Jesus."[56] This includes a "revisiting [of] the teaching of supersessionism after nearly two thousand years."[57]

Dispensationalism, in particular, continues to promote the idea of a restoration of national Israel, including the land. But dispensationalists are not alone in this belief. Recent years have also seen the rise of New Christian Zionism. At the forefront of this movement is Gerald R. McDermott and the book he has edited, *The New Christian Zionism: Fresh Perspectives on Israel and the Land.*[58] McDermott and a team of other scholars in this book make clear that New Christian Zionism is not Dispensationalism. Yet like Dispensationalism, adherents of the New Christian Zionism believe the return of Jews from all over the world to Israel and the state of Israel are significant theologically. They also believe in a future restoration of Israel.

Also, some historic premillennialists like Barry Horner and his book, *Future Israel*, promote a restorationist view concerning Israel and the land. Horner is an example of a Reformed theologian who affirms the doctrines of traditional Calvinism and still affirms a future salvation and restoration of national Israel.[59]

Yet while restorationism has many advocates today, it also has a growing list of modern opponents. Scholars such as Gary M. Burge, Stephen Sizer, N. T. Wright and others have strongly opposed the restorationist position, arguing vehemently against a future for national Israel.[60] That is why it is important for those who support a restorationist position to show how this view is supported by Scripture.

---

55. Watson, 2.

56. Soulen, *The God of Israel and Christian Theology*, x.

57. Ibid.

58. Gerald R. McDermott, ed. *The New Christian Zionism: Fresh Perspectives on Israel and the Land* (Downers Grove, IL: InterVarsity Press, 2016).

59. Barry E. Horner, *Future Israel: Why Christian Anti-Judaism Must Be Challenged* (Nashville: B&H Academic, 2007).

60. See Gary M. Burge, *Jesus and the Land: The New Testament Challenge to "Holy Land" Theology* (Grand Rapids: Baker, 2010); Stephen Sizer, *Zion's Christian Soldiers: The Bible, Israel and the Church* (Downers Grove, IL: IVP Press, 2008).

CONCLUSION

As the twenty-first century unfolds, both restorationism and replacement theology are well-represented. For those who affirm a restorationist position concerning Israel and the land, they can know their position has been held by Christians throughout church history. This view is not new. It did not begin the nineteenth century, nor is it the domain of any one group such as dispensationalists. The Bible, not church history, is the ultimate standard for evaluating doctrines, but it should be recognized that restorationism is supported by the testimony of history.

PART 3
YESHUA IN THE MIDST
OF THE CRISIS

THE MESSIANIC JEWISH MOVEMENT IN MODERN ISRAEL

EREZ SOREF

FOLLOWING THE AWAKENING IN ESCHATOLOGICAL interest in Europe in the eighteenth and nineteenth centuries, various groups of Jewish followers of Yeshua (Jesus) appeared in England, Germany, Romania, Hungary, Poland, and more.[1] The nineteenth century through WWI is considered by some as the "Golden Age" of Jewish evangelism, with estimates of some two hundred thousand Jews coming to faith in Jesus, more than 650 missionaries sent to share the gospel with Jewish people and more than 213 agencies focusing on Jewish evangelism.[2]

Notably, in 1841 England and Prussia agreed to establish a Protestant bishop in Jerusalem. Michael Solomon Alexander, a Jewish believer in Yeshua who was formerly rabbi of Norwich and Plymouth and who later served as professor of Hebrew at King's College London, was named the first Anglican bishop of Jerusalem.[3] It is very significant that there was a rekindling of interest in the Jewish people and the land of Israel by major Protestant churches, but even more significant that a *Jewish* believer in Yeshua was appointed as the main Protestant figure in Jerusalem. To many, no doubt, this seemed to be a step toward reestablishing the original Jewish church in Jerusalem—a theme that has resonated from the time of bishop Alexander even through the current Messianic Jewish movement in Israel today. When the British mandate took over the land of Israel in 1917 following WWI, the Anglican Church continued its positive attitude toward Jewish believers in Yeshua in Israel.

---

1. G. Nerel, "Messianic Jews in Eretz-Israel (1917–1967): Trends and Changes in Shaping Self Identity" (in Hebrew, carried out under the supervision of Prof. Gedalyahu Guy Stroumsa, from the Dept. of Comparative Religion, Hebrew University, 1996), 24–32; I. Stanfield, "Messianic Jews in the 19th Century and the Establishment of the 'Hebrew-Christian Alliance' in England, 1866–1871," (MA diss., Hebrew University, 1995), 1–3.

2. S. Perlman and C. D. Harley, *World Evangelization*, vol. 13 no. 43 (Lausanne: Lausanne Committee for World Evangelization, 1986), 1, 3, 4; Dan Cohn-Sherbok, *Messianic Judaism* (London: A. & C. Black, 2000), 15–24.

3. Cohn-Sherbok, *Messianic Judaism*, 15.

Until the end of the British mandate, following the League of Nations (UN) Resolution 181(II), known as the United Nations Partition Plan for Palestine, Messianic Jews met regularly—both openly and in secret—and attempted to define what Israeli Messianic Judaism was. National and regional committees began to form, and the focus was the restoration of the New Testament Jewish church in Israel, independently and separately from the patronage of the Protestant churches.

This attempt by Jewish followers of Yeshua to define themselves vis-à-vis the Protestant church parallels similar developments in the Jewish world in Europe, where advocates of the Jewish enlightenment broke away from traditional Jewish identity to embrace a secular Jewish identity and European education in contrast to a strictly religious Jewish education.

Alongside the Jewish enlightenment, the Jewish "emancipation" in various parts of Europe—seeking equal rights for the Jewish community—necessitated new definitions for religion, society, and nationhood for the Jewish people.[4] As such, new frames of thought and practice, both religious and secular, emerged in the Jewish world, with independent Messianic Judaism as part of it. The main national and regional activities of the Messianic Jews under the British mandate included annual conferences and publications.[5]

"Operation Grace" was a significant event in Messianic Jewish history in Israel. It took place in the few months between the November 1947 UN Partition Plan announcement and the self-declaration of the State of Israel in May of 1948. The purpose of this operation was the evacuation of the Messianic Jews from Israel to the UK under the auspices of the Anglican church. The reason for it was the belief that the Jewish people living in Israel, including the Messianic Jews, would be slaughtered by the outraged Arab countries in the ensuing war. And in the unlikely event that the Jewish people won the war, it was assumed that the Messianic Jews, who were already treated with suspicion by the Jewish people because of their ties to the British, would find themselves without a status in the new Jewish nation. Most Messianic Jews, therefore, left Israel with "Operation Grace," their numbers estimated from several dozen to several hundred.[6]

The few Messianic Jewish families that remained in Israel were scornfully accused by the Jewish community of once again betraying their people and running away to save themselves in a time of peril for all Jews, alluding especially to the Bar Kochba rebellion of AD 132–135. The Messianic Jews of that early rebellion, believing in Yeshua as Messiah, refused to participate in a rebellion led by Bar Kochba, a false messiah, and fled to Transjordan. As a result, the Messianic Jewish community was relatively unharmed by the Romans, while the Jewish rebels were brutally crushed. In many ways, this event marked a climax of the tensions in the Jewish world toward the Messianic

---

4. Stanfield, "Messianic Jews," 3; Nerel, "Messianic Jews," 26–27.

5. Nerel, "Messianic Jews," 82–101.

6. Ibid., 114–123.

Jews that began at the end of the second-temple period and set the tone for these relationships that persists even until today. Bolstered by hundreds of years of ill treatment and persecution of the Jewish people by the traditional churches—mostly Catholic—the Jewish mindset toward Jews who declare faith in Yeshua is extremely negative, since they are viewed as betrayers of their people and their faith. All this surfaced in a dramatic fashion following "Operation Grace," and at some level continues to this day.

Indeed, the Messianic Jews that remained in Israel following "Operation Grace" were also critical of those who fled. "In any case, there is no doubt that 'Operation Grace' is burned in the collective memory of the Messianic Jewish community in Israel as a very traumatic event in their history in Modern Israel."[7]

Directly following the establishment of the State of Israel, the few remaining Messianic Jews attempted to define themselves independently of the foreign Christian mission agencies. The main emphasis, both theologically and practically, was on the reestablishment of the ancient Jerusalem Messianic Jewish community mentioned in the book of Acts. An important event took place in 1957, when a group of Messianic Jews applied to register a nonprofit association called the "Israeli Messianic Community—Jerusalem Assembly." The application letter was based on the proclamation of independence of the State of Israel, and quoted part of it: "[The State of Israel] will ensure complete equality of social and political rights to all its inhabitants irrespective of religion, race or sex; it will guarantee freedom of religion, conscience, language, education and culture."

In light of these foundational statements of the new State of Israel, the letter further stated: "We are a community of Messianic Jews who believe in Yeshua the Messiah who has come and who will come again as the Almighty promised, as mentioned in the Torah, the Prophets and the Writings; We have not changed our religion nor our faith, since the Messiah Himself answered His torturers 'I have not come to abolish the law but to fulfill it.'"[8]

On February 25, 1958, the superintendent of Jerusalem, on behalf of the State of Israel, approved the request to establish the nonprofit. This is significant because it is the first occurrence of a formal recognition of Messianic Jews by the modern State of Israel.

The "Jerusalem Assembly" viewed itself as a national center for Messianic Jews and began to publish a journal called *The Torch: The Journal of the Israeli Messianic Assembly which Is the Renewal of the Ancient Original Assembly/Congregation*. Practically, however, the Jerusalem Israeli Messianic Assembly operated locally in Jerusalem only.[9]

The retaking of Jerusalem in 1967 (the Six-Day War) captured the attention of evangelicals worldwide and provoked significant eschatological

---

7.   Ibid, 122.

8.   Ibid, 172.

9.   Nerel, "Messianic Jews," 171–183; P. Østerbye, *The Church in Israel* (Lund: C. W. K. Gleerup Bokförlag, 1970), 40.

interest. This contributed to the growth and development of the Messianic community in Israel and served as a catalyst for Messianic Jews living in the diaspora to move to Israel.[10]

The immigration of Messianic Jews from around the world to Israel has continued for several decades now, and has contributed to the expansion of the Messianic Jewish community in Israel. A couple of scholarly endeavors to describe the Messianic Jewish community in Israel were conducted in the late eighties,[11] and again in the late nineties.[12] It is fascinating to see the ongoing, longitudinal effort to create and define an independent Messianic Jewish identity while enduring ongoing rejection—an effort that carries over to this day, as we will see.

In his 1989 article, Sibley reports on the establishment of a national gathering of Messianic Jewish leaders starting in 1981, uniting some two-thirds of the community's leaders, as well as general attempts to raise the profile of the Messianic Jewish community in Israel during the seventies and eighties. He further estimates that at the time of his writing, some thirty Messianic Jewish congregations existed in Israel. He comments on the gradual indigenization of the Messianic Jewish congregations, as is evident by the use of Hebrew as the main language, and the music chosen for worship—original songs in Hebrew, as opposed to translated hymns that were common in previous decades.[13]

The Messianic Jewish community's need and desire for biblical and theological training was expressed clearly, but as reported, very few possibilities were available for local believers at that time. Also evident in this period were attempts by the Messianic Jewish community to use legal professionals in the clarification and application of the religious freedoms offered by the State of Israel. This is an obvious corollary of the 1957 precedent.[14]

The overall picture in the late eighties, then, was of a small and young community that was taking steps toward establishing and defining itself in an environment that was somewhat oppressive and resistant.

Kai Kjær-Hansen and Bodil Skøjtt, Danish Protestants, conducted a series of interviews with leaders of Messianic Jewish congregations in Israel a decade later. They published their findings in 1999, in a book titled *Facts and Myths about the Messianic Congregations in Israel*. At that time, Kjær-Hansen and Skøjtt reported eighty-one Messianic Jewish congregations in Israel. The total size of the Messianic community in this report was estimated at five thousand, including children (thirty percent). The common model of leadership is reportedly a

---

10. Cohn-Sherbok, *Messianic Judaism*, 63–66.

11. Jim R. Sibley, "Trends in Jewish Evangelism in Israel," *Mishkan: A Forum on the Gospel and the Jewish People*, Issue 10 (1989), 24–37.

12. Kai Kjær-Hansen and Bodil F. Skøjtt, *Facts and Myths about the Messianic Congregations in Israel* (Jerusalem: United Christian Council in Israel in cooperation with the Caspari Center, 1999). This book actually represents two issues of the journal *Mishkan* published together.

13. Sibley, "Trends in Jewish Evangelism in Israel," 31–32.

14. Ibid., 34.

single pastor/elder; some seventy percent of the leaders were Jewish, and only eighteen percent of the leaders were born in Israel. Very few leaders reported having any biblical-theological training.[15] A later study confirmed this trend.[16]

An overall theme of the Messianic Jewish community in Kjær-Hansen and Skøjtt's study is a tendency to "become more Jewish" in both personal and congregational life and expression, a repetition and progression of Sibley's report a decade prior. Kjær-Hansen and Skøjtt also commented on the commonality of the Messianic Jewish community's experience of persecution by so-called "anti-missionary" organizations. They put it this way: "Harassment and opposition seem to be part and parcel of what it means to be a Jewish believer in Jesus in Israel. The hostility which they face includes posters publicly exposing individuals or groups, unreliable or tendentious newspaper articles on congregations and members, threat of and actual loss of jobs, damage to property, death threats, interruption of meetings or attempts to prevent them from taking place, graffiti, arson, and so forth."[17]

The Messianic Jewish community in the 1990s experienced further expansion in numbers, as well as progression in the formative process of creating an independent Israeli Messianic Jewish identity. To date, there has not been any additional study published regarding the growth and development of the Messianic Jewish identity in Israel.

Much has happened in the last two decades in the Messianic Jewish community in Israel. In an unofficial guide to the Messianic congregations in Israel by a reputable agency requesting to remain anonymous (2017), there are more than three hundred Messianic congregations in Israel today. The growth of the Messianic movement within the last two decades seems significant, and it is no wonder it draws public attention both inside and outside of Israel.

In 2017, Soref and Silver[18] conducted a survey via a web-based questionnaire, the main findings of which are presented below. The questionnaire was first sent to all the Messianic Jewish elders, pastors, and rabbis in Israel with a note from the authors, both personally and in a private email list of that group. Two weeks later, the questionnaire was sent to various Messianic Jewish adult forums online with the note from the authors. The questionnaire was made available in Hebrew (241 participants), English (thirty-nine) and Russian (eighteen), totaling 298 adult participants, seventy-six of whom are leaders. All participants signed an informed consent for participation. The age of participants ranged from eighteen to seventy-three, with thirty-one as the median age. In terms of gender, fifty-three percent were men, and forty-seven percent

15. Kjær-Hansen and Skøjtt, *Facts and Myths*, 24.

16. E. Soref, "Report Summary for ICB's National Leaders' Survey, March–April, 2008," (unpublished manuscript for re-accreditation of Israel College of the Bible, November 2008), 2, 4–5.

17. Ibid, 25.

18. Keren Silver, MA, is the director of the MA program in Counseling at Israel College of the Bible. I am thankful to Mrs. Silver for her help, as I am to Dr. Ilan Roziner from Tel Aviv University for his statistical consultation.

were women (as compared to 49.5 percent men and 50.5 percent women in the general population). Most participants (fifty-six percent) were married, forty-two percent were single, 1.6 percent were divorced and 0.4 percent were widowed. Fifty-six percent of the participants were parents. Sixty-three percent of the participants were born in Israel, a ratio that is slightly smaller than the general population, where seventy-five percent of the Jewish population of Israel was born in Israel.[19] The educational level was sixty percent with up to a high school diploma (forty-four percent with full *Bagrut*, or state high school diploma), and forty percent with an academic education. Of that number, nineteen percent had a graduate degree.

The reported median size of a Messianic congregation was one hundred members, with the largest number reported as six hundred members. Interestingly, the mean congregational size reported by all participants was 130 members (Standard Deviation [SD] = 87), but the congregational leaders reported a mean of 153 members (SD = 129). In other words, the leaders, who likely have a better gauge on the number of members in their congregations, estimated the size of their congregations as bigger. Based on this data and the report of at least three hundred Messianic Jewish congregations in Israel, it is therefore estimated that the Messianic Jewish community in Israel numbers approximately thirty thousand members. As discussed below, sixty percent of participants reported being first-generation Messianic Jews—that is, the majority of the growth of the Messianic Jewish community is from more Jewish people coming to believe in Yeshua, rather than having grown up in a Messianic Jewish family. These numbers represent a significant, even dramatic, growth compared to 1999.

The following table summarizes the growth of the Messianic Jewish community in Israel from 1948 until today, as compares to the general Jewish population in Israel:

YEAR	Jews in Israel	MJ Congregations in Israel	MJs in Israel
1948	600,000[20]	1?	23?
1989	3,688,000	30	1,200?
1999	4,829,000[21]	81	5,000
2017	6,523,000[22]	300	30,000

19. "Then and Now: Selected Data on Life in the State of Israel in the Early Years Compared with Today," April 27, 2017, Israel Central Bureau of Statistics, accessed October 2, 2017, http://www.cbs.gov.il/reader/newhodaot/hodaa_template_eng.html?hodaa=201711113.

20. Selected Annual Data 2017, accessed October 19, 2017, http://www.cbs.gov.il/reader/newhodaot/hodaa_template.html?hodaa=201711279.

21. A query at the website of the Israel Central Bureau of Statistics regarding number of Jewish people in Israel per year, from 1949–2016, http://www.cbs.gov.il/ts.

22. Israel Central Bureau of Statistics, accessed October 19, 2017, http://www.cbs.gov.il/reader/newhodaot/hodaa_template.html?hodaa=201711279.

Most respondents (seventy percent) reported a desire for their congregation to be larger, with leaders desiring growth significantly more than respondents who are not leaders. This sentiment seems to be in line with the current sense of growth the Messianic Jewish community is experiencing, an expression of a desire to be more meaningful in the larger society, a stronger force that is not persecuted. We'll discuss that more in a moment.

It may also reflect the desire of the Messianic Jewish community in Israel to share their faith as Israeli Messianic Jews who are part of the Jewish world, not outsiders or foreign missionaries. This sentiment is not to disparage the many foreign missionaries who have devoted their lives to sharing the gospel with the Jewish people. It is simply to highlight the fact that the Jewish people have tended to treat the message of Yeshua as alien, coming from foreigners who look and speak differently, and are not "of us."

The reality in Israel has changed in the sense that it is Messianic Jews telling their families, neighbors, friends, and communities about Yeshua. One cannot overestimate that difference, and that may explain some of the dramatic growth over the last two decades. This growth and desire for further growth seem to mark a shift in the Messianic Jewish community in Israel. Whereas in previous decades the emphasis seems to have been on survival and protecting one's civil rights, now the Messianic Jewish community is focusing on growth and development, a significant mental transition marking progress in maturity.

The leadership model of congregations was comprised of fifty-six percent with salaried leadership (either one or more elders/pastors/rabbis), and forty-four percent with non-salaried leadership. Forty-five percent of congregations reported functioning mostly independently of foreign financial or ideological support, 17.5 percent reported significant support from abroad, and notably, thirty-eight percent of respondents said they do not know about funding sources. Among the leaders, there was a slightly larger, but statistically significant, sense of financial foreign connections than among respondents that were not leaders. The overall picture continues to demonstrate the progress from previous decades, not just in the maturing of congregations, both in number and in size, but also growing independence, both financially and ideologically.

Most Messianic Jewish congregations indicated that the main language in their services was Hebrew (ninety-two percent), but translations to other languages are still common, mainly into Russian and English. Other translated languages mentioned were Spanish, Amharic, Korean, and German. And holidays (ninety-five percent), most notably Passover (one hundred percent), Rosh HaShana (ninety-three percent); Succoth, or Tabernacles (ninety-three percent); Weeks, or Pentecost (ninety-two percent); Day of Atonement, Purim, and Hannukah (approximately ninety percent). Interestingly, Lag Ba'omer (thirty-three-day count of the omer), a popular nonbiblical, traditional-rabbinical holiday, is celebrated only by thirteen percent. Many participants emphasized a celebration of the feasts with Yeshua at the center, so it is not surprising that a traditional-rabbinical holiday is not typically celebrated.

We asked about respondents' perception of how Israeli their congregation is in terms of culture and general character, an important facet in a land
of (Jewish) immigrants. Ninety-three percent indicated their congregation is
Israeli in character. Of them, Sixty-five percent indicated their congregation
is completely or to a large degree Israeli in culture. The remaining percent
percent indicated their congregation was either somewhat Israeli or slightly
so. Leaders and those attending the congregation more frequently (three to
four weekends a month) both expressed a statistically significant sense that
their congregation is Israeli in character, as compared to those who were
non-leaders or attended less frequently. The same measure (ninety-three percent) indicated their congregation encourages loyalty to the State of Israel,
and ninety-nine percent indicated that military service—a hallmark of Israeli
identity—is encouraged at their congregation. This is important, even if not
surprising; Messianic Jews in Israel see themselves as part of the Israeli society.

As mentioned earlier, Messianic Jews view the return of the Jewish people
to Israel as an act of God, a fulfillment of biblical prophecy, and as part of God's
plan for all nations. Of course, the reemergence of the Messianic Jewish community in Israel is also viewed by the Messianic Jews as part of that plan; therefore, loyalty to the State of Israel is a natural byproduct. The self-perception and
congregational expression of being part and parcel of Israeli society indicates
that the cultural progress over previous decades from a small minority existing under the auspices of foreign mission agencies to a self-defined community
seems to have crossed the point of no return. Israeli Messianic Jews see themselves as an integral part of the Israeli society. In that regard, the struggle and desire expressed by Messianic Jews over the last one hundred years has succeeded.

The Messianic Jewish community exists and thrives on the fringes of two
worlds: the Christian and the Jewish. Many Christians do not understand why
Jewish believers in Jesus do not simply assimilate into the church and pursue
a no-longer-Jewish faith life. As the reasoning goes, once Jewish people come
to believe in Yeshua, they are no longer Jewish, since there is "neither Jew nor
Gentile." The Jewishness of the early church, according to this view, is only a
historical relic with no practical relevance today. Likewise, the general Jewish
world simply does not understand why Jews who believe in Yeshua continue
to insist on belonging to the Jewish people, or how they are able to claim that
believing in Yeshua is the most Jewish thing a Jewish person can do! How do
Messianic Jews exist and thrive in both of these worlds simultaneously?

Over two-thirds (sixty-eight percent) of respondents indicated full to
significant congregational identification with the Jewish world. An additional fifteen percent indicated that their congregation is "somewhat" identified with the Jewish world, and only seventeen percent indicated little or
no such identification.

With regard to identifying with the evangelical worldwide church from
which many Messianic Jews receive encouragement and support, sixty-three
percent indicated their congregation is identified in a complete to significant
manner, nineteen percent see that identification to a certain degree, and eigh-

teen percent see it to a small degree or not at all. So Messianic Jews identify significantly with both the Jewish world, and only slightly less with the evangelical world, simultaneously. This again emphasizes the complex place and identity of the Messianic Jewish community, poised between the Jewish and evangelical worlds.

Israeli Messianic Jews make a meaningful distinction between the evangelical church and general Christendom comprised mainly of traditional churches, such as Catholic and Orthodox. This distinction is made partly because of the painful history of these churches in relation to the Jewish people, as well as for theological reasons. As such, only thirty percent see their congregation as identified significantly with the worldwide Christian church, fourteen percent see it as marginally identified, and fifty-seven percent express no such identification. Leaders expressed a statistically significant higher level of identification with the Jewish world as well as with the worldwide evangelical world, but less with general Christendom.

Interestingly, those who grew up in a Messianic Jewish family—as opposed to first-generation Jewish believers in Yeshua—expressed less identification with the Jewish world, and also less identification with the evangelical world, with no difference on general Christendom. This warrants further investigation, but may be pointing toward the formation of a unique Messianic Jewish identity for those growing up in a Messianic Jewish family in Israel.

Messianic Jews in Israel do not give much weight to religious symbols in their congregations. Only approximately sixty percent of respondents chose to answer questions about religious symbols. Seventy percent indicated they have a menorah in their congregation, forty-six percent have a Torah scroll, and thirty-nine percent have an ark for the Torah scroll. Many participants indicated in their comments that they do not have any religious symbols—something with which they are very pleased. This again may be pointing to the sense of a unique Messianic Jewish identity and expression in Israel.

Almost two-thirds of Messianic Jewish congregations rent their facilities, while one-third are owners. Interestingly, twenty-four percent of respondents indicated it was not important for the congregation to own its facility, while fifty-two percent felt it was important for the congregation to own its facility. (Twenty-four percent did not have a strong opinion.) The ownership of the congregational facility is related not only to financial stability and presence in society, which may explain the majority's desire for ownership, but also to the challenges of persecution. Anti-missionary organizations typically apply pressure on landlords who rent their facilities to Messianic groups. At times, this pressure has resulted in a termination of the rental contract or, in cases where the contracts were being negotiated, a refusal to rent to the congregations.

The Messianic Jewish community in Israel faces an interesting challenge. On the one hand, they very much identify with the Jewish people, both ideologically, religiously, and practically (as shown by motivation to serve in the military, etc.), yet many experience rejection and even persecution by the larger Jewish society.

Statistically, the majority of Messianic Jewish congregations in Israel (eighty percent) have experienced episodes of persecution. Leaders reported a slightly less, yet statistically significant, level of congregational persecution. Further, respondents from ages eighteen to forty-four experienced significantly less persecution than respondents over the age of forty-five. (There was no difference for leaders, by gender, or those growing up in a Messianic home vs. first-generation.) This may be pointing to a perception of persecution by the Messianic Jewish community that is not fully grounded in the reality of living in a democratic country with freedom of speech and freedom of religion, or it may be that persecution has diminished somewhat over time.

Yet forty-three percent of respondents reported having experienced personal incidents of persecution, mostly in the form of threats to their life and activity as Messianic Jews, as well as various forms of slanderous written material warning the general public about their identity as Messianic Jews. The overall picture of persecution seem to portray a slight decline in actual persecution for the Messianic Jewish community, but relative to most other religious groups in Israel's pluralistic democracy, this is still high and remains a factor in the psyche of the Messianic Jewish community.

Israel is called "the start-up nation," referring to the high-tech industry's dramatic growth in Israel.[23] Further, Israelis are the heaviest users of the Internet and of social networks in the world.[24] As such, it may not be surprising that the struggle between the so-called "anti-missionary" organizations and the Messianic Jewish community seems to have shifted online. Hebrew websites telling various strata in the Israeli society about Yeshua abound.[25]

These websites provide Hebrew-speaking Israelis with testimonials of Israeli Jews who have become Messianic Jews, as well as access to the story of Yeshua and apologetics—all in Hebrew, and all by Israelis. There has been a tremendous response and very wide viewership to these websites in the past few years—reportedly over fifteen million views over the past two years(!). General Israeli media, both major television and internet news channels, have noticed this phenomenon and reported on it, further increasing the awareness of the growing Messianic community among the Israeli public.[26]

---

23.   D. Senor and S. Singer, *Start-up Nation: The Story of Israel's Economic Miracle* (New York: Hachette Book Group, 2009).

24.   O. Yaron, "Israelis Lead World in Social Network Use, U.S. Study Shows," *HAARETZ*, December 22, 2011, accessed October 2, 2017, http://www.haaretz.com/israel-news/israelis-lead-world-in-social-network-use-u-s-study-shows-1.402981?v=96EA4D6CA9067B7A60A589943A941924; J. Russell, "Israelis Are Now the World's Biggest Social Network Addicts, Says New Report," 2011, accessed October 2, 2017, https://thenextweb.com/socialmedia/2011/12/22/israelis-are-now-the-worlds-biggest-social-network-addicts-says-new-report/?amp=1.

25.   See for example: www.igod.co.il.

26.   See for example: http://www.mako.co.il/tv-weekend/Article-96fd87403628a41006.htm and https://www.youtube.com/watch?v=XCdyuAOhIp0&list=PLIsG2NQmMGXNIhE8EJUFllex9A D8LEm8T.; https://www.haaretz.com/israel-news/.premium-1.813312.

In response, the so-called "anti-missionary" organizations have created their own websites warning the public not to visit the Messianic Jewish websites and providing testimonials of Jews who have "escaped the Messianic cult" and found their true identity in rabbinic Judaism. But this struggle is not limited to the Internet. In the past few years, a leading "anti-missionary" organization has published a magazine called, *Seeking: A Journal for Jews Who Lost Their Way*, in which they include various articles attempting to prove that Yeshua is *not* the Messiah.

A group of Israeli Messianic Jews responded by publishing a magazine entitled, *Finding: A Magazine for Brothers Who Are Tired from Searching*, answering the claims in *Seeking*. Humorous as this may seem, the important point here must not be overlooked: the Messianic Jewish community in Israel is secure enough in its identity and position in Israeli society to stand its ground, use the civil freedoms the State of Israel provides, and most notably, challenge two-thousand-year-old prejudice and religious control in an intra-Jewish dialogue about the identity of Yeshua.

General Jewish culture places a very high value on education, as the "people of the book." Naturally then, with the noteworthy expansion of the Messianic Jewish movement in Israel, an important consideration has been the training of leaders and biblical-theological scholarship. Previous studies of the community indicate a significant lack of biblical and theological training and a perceived need in that area.

We asked respondents about their perception of the importance of biblical and theological training for leaders. A large majority, eighty-four percent, indicated they view such training as important (forty-two percent as very important), while sixteen percent indicated it was not important (with ten percent of those viewing this as not important at all, and one percent indicating they are against such training). There was no significant difference in that perception between leaders and non-leaders or between men and women, however respondents who were more regular attendees of their congregation (three, four, or more times a month) and respondents under the age of forty-five indicated that biblical and theological training for congregational leaders was significantly more important for them.

This indicates that the committed younger generation of the Messianic Jewish community in Israel puts a high value on biblical and theological training for its leaders. It is likely then that the coming decades will see a substantial rise in the demand for advanced levels of biblical and theological training for Messianic Jewish leaders and scholars.

In terms of commitment and personal dedication to their faith as Messianic Jews, most respondents, an astounding ninety-five percent, indicated they attend services at their congregation at least three to four weekends a month. Additionally, sixty percent indicated they attend a midweek meeting three to four times a month also. In the complex reality described, with pressures from various historical and religious perspectives, the Messianic Jewish community in Israel seems to have members and leaders who are highly committed, and their faith seems to play a central role in their lives.

In terms of political tendencies, the Messianic movement in Israel certainly leans right of center (sixty-three percent of respondents). Only 9.3 percent of respondents indicated being politically left of center. This seems in line with the general tendency in the Israeli Jewish society, as reflected in recent elections.

What are some challenges the Messianic Jewish community in Israel is facing? We asked respondents about challenges in their congregations as well as in the national Messianic Jewish movement. The congregational challenges reported were personal relationships and unity within the congregation (thirty-seven percent), financial needs and poverty (twenty-seven percent), and an unsuitable facility (sixteen percent). Fifteen percent indicated their congregation does not have any struggles. The Messianic Jewish community is comprised of Jewish people coming from a variety of backgrounds and Jewish cultures. This mix, while characterizing Israeli society as a whole, intensifies in a relatively close-knit community, sometimes under various pressures.

Not surprisingly, the perceived challenges in the *national* Messianic Jewish community are similar. Fifty-four percent report relationships as the main challenge, twelve percent view financial challenges as most significant, seven percent see size as the main challenge, and notably, only four percent see persecution as the main challenge. For either question, there were no differences for leaders, generation as believers, gender, or age.

Based on the progression in the last decades, the Messianic Jewish community in Israel is likely to continue to grow and mature, and further secure its place in Israeli society and the Jewish world. With the center of the Jewish world shifting to Israel, at least demographically,[27] the place of the Messianic Jewish community in Israel is likely to be even more central for the worldwide Messianic community.

The thread that ties together the Messianic Jewish movement in Israel has been the ideological renewal of the ancient original Messianic Jewish community found in the pages of the book of Acts in the New Testament. This seems to have been the "scarlet cord" uniting the Messianic Jewish movement in all the studies that have been reviewed. This conceptual yearning expresses a profound process of searching for and formation of identity, since the Messianic Jewish community exists on the fringes of two worlds—Jewish and Christian—that have been in competition and strife. In spite of a painful history of suspicion and misunderstanding, the Messianic Jewish community stands for their reconciliation, in part bridging the gap between them. This is not an easy stance, and is certainly one that to this day has been misunderstood and is not fully accepted by either world.

---

27.   The Jewish Agency for Israel, accessed October 2, 2017, http://www.jewishagency.org/he/content/יהודים-בעולם; Israel's Central Bureau of Statistics, accessed October 20, 2017, http://www.cbs.gov.il/shnaton68/st02_11.pdf.

In spite of these challenges, the Messianic Jewish community in Israel has developed in maturity and security in its identity within Israeli society—especially among the younger generation. While the Messianic Jewish identity in Israel is likely to continue to evolve in the coming decades, a level of stability in terms of presence in society seems to have been achieved. Messianic Jews in Israel view themselves as an integral part of Israeli society's mosaic. The future seems to hold both opportunities and challenges for the Messianic community.

The most significant challenge noted by Messianic Jews is unity. As the movement grows, so do opinions and convictions, which challenge unity. One of the advantages of a small, persecuted minority is that smaller differences are overlooked in the face of difficulty, and a sense of a unified community is achieved. As the movement grows with a larger sense of security, it allows various views to emerge. This too is a sign of maturity, and the challenge of the Messianic Jewish community is to learn to live in unity without expectations of uniformity.

Socially speaking, there seem to be some significant opportunities for the Messianic Jewish community in Israel. The up-and-coming generation of Messianic Jews in Israel seems to be committed to its calling and to the movement, and has high expectations for its leaders, both personally in terms of education and training, and also in terms of desire for social influence. That is promising for a maturing movement. With these trends, we are likely to see an increase in the demand and supply of a broad range of educational services in the Messianic Jewish movement, as well as an increased involvement of Messianic Jews in education and scholarship in Israeli society.

This is especially relevant for biblical studies, an interest not shared by the general Israeli society. This esteem for biblical and theological education and scholarship among Messianic Jews is in direct contrast to the Israeli public at large. Israeli society has been experiencing a significant decline in interest in biblical studies.

Rabbinic Jewish tradition considers actual Bible study to be "for children," and therefore after the age of thirteen young men abandon the study of the Hebrew Bible (OT) to study extrabiblical rabbinic literature—the Mishna and Gemmara (comprising the Talmud). Multiple publications in the Israeli media indicate that non-orthodox Jews report that the Bible (that is, the Hebrew Bible—OT) is the least favorable subject in schools and universities.[28] This situation seems to provide the committed Messianic Jewish community with an opportunity to rekindle an interest in biblical studies in Israeli society, and fill the gap of biblical knowledge and study in Israel. We are likely to see more Messianic Jewish Bible professors in Israeli universities, as well as teachers in Israeli schools in the years to come.

---

28. Y. Amit, "The Rise and Fall of the Hebrew Bible Empire in Israeli Education: National Study Program, 2003: Looking Back and Looking Ahead" (Reches Educational Projects: Even Yeshuah, 2010, in Hebrew), Jewish Agency for Israel, accessed October 19, 2017, http://www.jewishagency. org/he/content/יהודים-בעולם.

Additionally, with the younger generation of Israeli Messianic Jews highly committed to the Messianic movement while feeling part of the Israeli society and eager to influence it, we are likely see many more Messianic Jews in key positions in Israeli society: the military, high-tech, politics, finance, academia, the court system, etc. General education level is likely to increase among Messianic Jews, and these processes are likely to be expressed in a significant economic development in the Messianic Jewish movement. This in turn will provide growing independence for local congregations and national Messianic organizations, paralleled with less dependence on international funding.

The Israeli Messianic Jewish community's development is likely to draw growing attention in Israel and the rest of the Jewish world in the coming decades. Additional studies are needed to gain further insights into other aspects of the Messianic Jewish community in Israel, and also to examine and compare these trends with the Messianic Jewish movement worldwide.

THE 21ˢᵀ-CENTURY PALESTINIAN CHURCH WITHIN ISRAEL

TOM DOYLE

"I AM A PALESTINIAN AND I BELIEVE THE BIBLE is clear that Israel has not been replaced by the church. This might sound strange to hear from me because when Israel became a nation in 1948, my family lost everything. It has not been easy for us by any means, but I hold no grudge against Israel or ill-will whatsoever."

Hanna Massad has lived through more danger than most people have seen on TV. True, it is not strange to see a Baptist church in Israel, or in the West Bank for that matter, but try pastoring one in the Gaza Strip.

While Hanna lived in Gaza as the only evangelical pastor in the Strip, he shepherded the small flock of believers during both the first Palestinian Intifada, which began in 1987, and the second Palestinian Intifada, which launched in 2000.

A visit to the Gaza Strip is akin to stepping onto another planet. The graphic graffiti on buildings is alarming, posters glorifying well-known terrorists too numerous to count, and the deep poverty shocking. High-ranking Hamas leaders just cannot seem to get this distribution thing together, despite the billions of dollars given from the EU and America to alleviate it. The pan-Arab newspaper *Ashara Al-Awsat* made the claim that six hundred millionaires live in the Gaza Strip. Terrorism and corruption have a long-term marriage in Gaza.[1]

Gaza families suffer because of the siphoning of billions of dollars now in Hamas bank accounts. The "gangster takes all" mentality has led to miserable and unbearable living conditions in the eight refugee camps in the Strip.

WHERE'S THE CHURCH IN ALL OF THIS MESS?

So what is the first thing that comes into your mind when you hear the word "Palestinian"? For many people, the word "terrorist" leaps out of their

---

1. Khaled Abu Toameh, "How Many Millionaires Live in the 'Impoverished' Gaza Strip?" Gatestone Institute International Policty Council, August 30, 2012; accessed March 4, 2018, https://www.gatestoneinstitute.org/3308/gaza-millionaire.

mouths. I've asked this question in dozens of churches across America, and I have yet to *not* hear the T-word. I used to say it myself.

But then my wife JoAnn and I went to Gaza. The volatile 6.8-mile-wide and thirty-two-mile-long belt of land in fact does contain a who's who of terrorist groups in the Middle East. Hamas, Islamic Jihad, the Army of Islam, and the al-Aksa Martyr's Brigade lead the pack, with many new groups birthing routinely and in line to follow.

Yet, we also discovered a small group of believers that lived there, with a passion for Jesus we had seen in few American churches.

Our first night in Gaza, in 2002, we felt like we had been transported back to the book of Acts. The Intifada was raging in the streets. American President George Bush and Israeli Prime Minister Ariel Sharon were burning in effigy. That was not exactly the welcome we were expecting. A frenzied young teenage Muslim stood shouting on the corner in Gaza City: "Death to America! Death to Israel!" with the sound of beating drums growing. Soon the ranks swelled and the indignant, violent mob began marching though the streets. The Strip was ready to erupt.

That was outside.

But in an apartment building inhabited by unsuspecting Muslim families, there was another meeting.

A small group of young Gazans secretly worshipped Jesus on the third floor of a nondescript apartment, led by a guitar-playing former Muslim from the West Bank. Another group prayed flat on their faces in heartfelt desperation. Still another group sat on chairs and went over their strategy to advance the gospel among the Muslim fanatics in the refugee camps. The last group was eight to ten women who prayed fervently for godly husbands. With less than two hundred born-again believers in Gaza at the time, I must confess I thought, "What are the chances of that?" Did they ever have faith!

Jesus was in the house.

Palestinians? Palestinians! Despite living in one of the most dangerous locations for believers in the world, these brothers and sisters had a deep, vibrant faith that I longed for. I'd never been in any kind of life-threatening situation just for being a Christian like this. They lived in it.

That was the first shock. *Palestinians can love Jesus, too.*

The second shock was coming.

Ali strummed a nice-looking guitar as he led worship. Except for the bullet holes.

"What's the deal with your guitar, Ali?" I asked.

Ali grinned as he remembered the story and developed it thoughtfully. "I was coming through the Erez Crossing from Gaza to enter back in to Israel and I had my guitar in its case. I was talking with Aaron, the IDF soldier I've gotten to know as I go back and forth to the West Bank when I visit my family. He saw the guitar case and didn't feel right about it. I found out later that the week before, a terrorist tried to transport a bomb in a guitar case that looked just like mine. Out came the robot and soon it was transported about twenty feet away. Within a few seconds, an IDF soldier fired on it and it looked like Swiss cheese.

"Aaron was just doing his job. I didn't get mad and the Lord used it. I was able to tell this young Jewish soldier that I was no longer a Muslim. He asked if that was possible and I said: 'Yeah man, I'm a Jesus follower now. I try to live like he did each day. He was a man of peace and I follow him. The Jewish Messiah changed my life.' Then I hugged him and told him that he had a tough job and that I would be praying for him."

"Aaron was speechless. The Holy Spirit was dealing with him. How privileged I was to tell a young Israeli about Jesus! The bullet holes? Totally worth it."

The other Gaza believers shook their heads in agreement, and prayed for Aaron the soldier.

That was the second shock. *Palestinian believers can love Jews, too.*

So is there peace between Jewish believers and Palestinian believers in Israel today? Or has politics spilled over into the church and spoiled the fellowship?

Is the Palestinian church growing, or are they losing Christians like so many of the surrounding Arab nations? Is the Palestinian church able to rise above failed peace talks to be a dynamic church force in the Middle East? Can it survive escalating tension in the West Bank and Gaza, a predicted third Intifada, while getting caught in the crossfire between Palestinian terror groups and the Israeli Defense Forces, and feeling overlooked by many believers in the West?

Can there be true peace between Palestinian believers and Jewish believers, to show the world what the new man looks like in the most politically divisive area of the world?

This chapter will take you inside today's Palestinian church. The spiritual leaders you will meet live with overwhelming pressure. On the one hand, the Israeli-Palestinian conflict is unending and presents significant challenges to their day-to-day lives. On the other hand, Muslims significantly outnumber Palestinians believers, and the gap is widening. Palestinian families are leaving the West Bank and Gaza in hopes of a better life and who could blame them?

On top of that, Palestinian leaders often feel overlooked, misunderstood, and underappreciated. One Palestinian pastor told me that he was speaking at a church in America some time ago. The pastor introduced him and told the congregation that he was from Israel. One woman didn't realize that he was a Palestinian and when she came to meet him after the sermon, she stuck out her hand and said: "I love Jewish people! It's an honor to meet you." The pastor smiled and replied: "I love Jewish people too! But I'm actually an Arab believer from Israel."

The Palestinian pastor recalled the story and teared up as he looked back at the mix-up. "The woman pulled her hand back, turned her head in disgust, and walked away."

The pastor from East Jerusalem looked down and said: "That one still hurts to this day."

WHAT IS THE STATUS OF THE PALESTINIAN CHURCH WITHIN ISRAEL TODAY?

In Acts 2:11, Luke tells us that Arabs were present and accounted for at Pentecost, the New Testament Church launch event. They heard the mighty works of God in their own Arabic language, and then listened as Peter preached the good news in the universally understood Greek language. Arabs were involved in the church from day one.

Arabs subsequently witnessed a fast start-up church in the region. As an ethnic group, they quickly became an important component in the racially diverse movement and the gospel was anchored within their own culture.

Kenneth Cragg, in his book *The Arab Christian: A History in the Middle East*, supports the idea that Arabs were a major part of the early church: "There are aspects of being Arab that almost necessitate its equation with Islam. That fact has been the burden of Arab Christianity since the seventh Christian century. Yet Christian faith had a long history within Arabia in the six centuries before Islam emerged to dominate the ethnic and cultural determinants of Arab existence."[2]

When thinking of Arabs in the Middle East, this appears to be the lost episodes of their history. Before Islam was conceived, Arab Christianity was potent and spreading throughout the region.

"The first Christian ruler in history was in fact an Arab. Abgar VIII, also known as Abgar the Great, converted to Christianity around the year AD 200 and lived in Edessa, which is in present-day Turkey. Although Turkey is a non-Arab country, Abgar was an Arab living in what was then an Assyrian country. Also, the Nabateans of southern Jordan and northern Arabia converted to Christianity in mass and developed a vibrant church in the region. The Nabateans are best known for their amazing city carved out of the slope of Mount Hor where Aaron the brother of Moses is buried. Petra of Indiana Jones fame is the famous city they built. In Petra's heyday, the population exceeded twenty thousand. Also, the Arabian Tribal Group named the Ghassanids migrated from Yemen to southern Syria, and converted to Christianity. They became a force in the Byzantine church and resisted Islam as it swept through Syria a few centuries later."[3]

Fast-forward to today, and it is obvious that the Palestinian church in Israel is fraught with significant challenges. With the growing hardline Islamic control in Gaza and the West Bank, plus the unending conflict with Israel and the threat of the third Intifada looming, most Palestinians are looking for a feasible exit plan.

The goal of this chapter is not to delineate a new political solution, if there even is one, or to lay out another diatribe about the current Israeli-Palestinian conflict. The aim is to take you inside the Palestinian church by

---

2. Kenneth Cragg, *The Arab Christian: A History in the Middle East* (Louisville: John Knox Press, 1991), 13.

3. Ibid.

meeting some of their own spiritual leaders as they openly speak about the reality on the ground, as it exists today.

Dr. Jack Sara is the President of Bethlehem Bible College trains the majority of Palestinians who serve in ministry in the West Bank. He served as the pastor of the Alliance Church in the Old City of Jerusalem until he was called to replace longtime president Bishara Awad in 2012. Jack received an earned doctorate from Gordon-Conwell Theological Seminary in missions and cross-cultural studies. He speaks in tandem with global Messianic leaders about peace reconciliation in Israel between Arabs and Jews who are born-again believers. Jewish and Palestinian clergy have a deep love and respect for each other.

However, when the subject of politics enters the picture, the camaraderie can change in a nanosecond. The geopolitical issues that divide Jews and Palestinians are scrutinized, discussed, editorialized, and debated daily by news outlets, politicians, national governments, and spiritual leaders. Amazingly, people who have never visited Israel and the West Bank often form their opinions with no firsthand experience. How can we expect people who live in the midst of the conflict to remain neutral and be any different?

The "great divide" between believing Israelis and believing Palestinians is clearly visible at the "Christ at the Checkpoint" biennial conference hosted by BBC in Bethlehem at the college. The purpose of the conference, according to the Bethlehem Bible College website, is:

> The mission of "Christ at the Checkpoint" is to challenge Evangelicals to take responsibility to help resolve the conflicts in Israel/Palestine by engaging with the teaching of Jesus on the Kingdom of God.[4]

All one has to do is do an Internet search on "Christ at the Checkpoint," and you get a feel for the controversy that is associated with the weeklong conference. For many Messianic leaders in Israel, because of some of the political statements that are made at the conference, and the lineup of the speakers over the last few years, the conference is viewed as a rallying cry for Palestinians, resulting in significant divisiveness between Jewish and Palestinian believers.

In fairness to Bethlehem Bible College, one of the core values of the conference is "an openness to diverse perspectives." The majority of the speakers come from a pro-Palestinian perspective, as one would expect, but there is room for opposing views. In 2010, Darrell Bock defended Israel's right to be a nation in the land based on Scripture. In 2012, Pastor Wayne Hilsden, of the largest Messianic congregation in Israel, spoke at the conference. In 2018, the conference lineup features Michael Brown, a Messianic leader, conservative radio and TV host, author, and professor.

---

4. "Christ at the Checkpoint," Bethlehem Bible College, accessed October 23, 2017, https://bethbc. edu/christ-at-the-checkpoint.

The purpose of this chapter is not to discuss the conference but the Palestinian Church in general. I sat down with Bethlehem Bible College (BBC) president Jack Sara, and asked him candid questions about the reality "on the ground" for Palestinian believers today, and what the future looks like.

Tom: *Jack, you used to be involved in with Messianic pastors speaking about peace between Arabs and Jews in Israel throughout Europe and the US. Did you come to any common ground?*

Jack: *I still am privileged to do these events. About a month ago, I was part of a small consultation with seven Arab pastors and seven Jewish leaders, and the topic was the new unity that we see emerging. There is a wave toward unity in spite of our differences and political disagreements. Believe me, it is not easy. But I believe when people are going in the wrong direction, the church needs to go in the right direction. And the right direction is always in love and unity despite our conflicting theologies and ideologies. That is hard, I must confess, because I want to sympathize with my people and I have a right to do so. My Jewish brother wants to sympathize with his own people and he has the right to do so. But in the midst of our sympathies with our own people, can we truly have empathy with each other and work together toward providing healing to each other?*

Tom: *How are churches doing in the West Bank? You're at the forefront of training the students that become pastors. Do you see growth and good things happening?*

Jack: *I believe there are signs of hope. Any time we see the next generation rising up and committing to study that Word of God, it's always a sign of hope.*

Tom: *One of the signs of a healthy movement is when people are willing to give of themselves, despite their own situation. The students of BBC have been a part of reaching out to Syrian refugees in Jordan. How has that helped the BBC students?*

Jack: *Many of the Palestinians that we work with are refugees. So that means that many of them have to have permission to go outside of the wall that is around the West Bank. But once they went to serve the refugees from Syria and Iraq who had fled to Jordan, God changed our students forever. One student said to me recently, "Pastor, I cannot believe what happened to me today. Thank you for sending me here!" I asked him what happened and filled with joy he continued, "Today I was visiting a family that are refugees from Syria and not Christians. We gave them food, and listened to their story, and then we shared the gospel with them. Pastor, all of them came to faith in Christ!"*

Tom: *Jack, are the Palestinian churches growing?*

Jack: *They are steady, but not seeing great growth.*

Tom: *How many Palestinian evangelical Christians live in the West Bank, Gaza, and Israel?*

Jack: *I estimate that there are approximately five thousand in total.*

Tom: *If you could send a message to evangelical believers in the West who perhaps have not discovered that there are Palestinian brothers and sisters in Christ, what would you say to them?*

Jack: *It seems to be a "eureka" moment when Christians in the West discover that there is actually such a thing as a Palestinian Christian. The term is not in their vocabulary. It's assumed that all Palestinians are Muslims, as many assume that all Israelis are Jews and there is nothing in between. Arab believers have been here since the beginning of the church, yet along the way, Arab Christians became very nominal and traditional. But the good news is that God is now reviving his church.*

Tom: *Have you been threatened because of your faith in Christ, living in a predominately Muslim culture?*

Jack: *Yes I have been threatened, but not recently.*

Tom: *OK Pastor Jack, one last question: If you could ask American believers who will read this book to pray for you, how would you ask them to pray?*

Jack: *We need wisdom to know how to go through all the challenges we are facing. The church here is struggling spiritually because as much as God loves this country, Satan hates it. The spiritual warfare is so intense and possibly more intense than anywhere else. This is the land of Jesus, where he was born, where he died for our sins, where he was buried, and where he rose from the dead. He went to heaven and then sent the Holy Spirit so the church would be born. But yet, after two thousand years, it's ironic that the people of this country, regardless of their ethnic or religious background are unreached. How can it be that so many in this land have not experienced the risen Christ in the very place that he was risen from?*

As Palestinians, we ask for prayers of protection as well. We do feel that we're between a rock and a hard place. The Israelis are not easy on us. Our own people are not easy on us. Our numbers are small, but we are praying for a breakthrough in order that all Palestinians and Jews will hear the good news and that Jesus' salvation will be known throughout this land.

FROM GAZA WITH LOVE

Sami Abbasi (cover name used for security) is one unique individual. Growing up in the Gaza Strip as a Palestinian youth and embroiled in the first

Intifada is not the resume you would expect for an evangelist to the Jews of Israel. For Sami, everything changed at salvation.

"When I came to faith in Christ, I decided I wanted to be a 'full disciple.' I could not just pick and choose the commands of Christ that I wanted to obey. If I was to follow Jesus, I wanted to do all that he told his disciples to do. Loving you enemy was by far the biggest challenge for me.

"Israel was my nemesis, and the evil enemy of my people. I lived in Gaza, and the most dangerous label to be attached to a person living there is 'Zionist' or 'Jew-lover.'

"That's what Palestinian Muslims accuse Palestinian Christians of. In Gaza, it was a given that you hate Israel and Jews as a people. Christians are also often accused of being spies for Israel. I've seen men hung in public for merely being *suspected of collaborating* with Israel in any way.

"What was I to do? Above all else, I had to give my ultimate allegiance to my Savior. Jesus never gave us the luxury of hating our enemies. But the clashes between the IDF and my people were vivid images in my mind and hard to forget or let go of. As a young boy, I threw a rock at an Israeli jeep patrolling in downtown Gaza. It was my best throw ever! It hit the windshield and cracked it. The soldier jumped out and chased me. But I knew the back roads and he didn't. I remember bragging to my friends at school about my feat. I expected that in a few years I would use something that could do more damage than a rock.

"After Jesus entered my life, I hadn't been a believer long when I was reading through the Sermon on the Mount and the Spirit of God convicted me. I had heaviness in my heart and it was because of my loathing of the State of Israel and Jewish people. In my mind, Israel was the reason for everything that was negative in my life. All news was slanted against them and they were the ultimate scapegoat.

"They certainly qualified as *my enemy.* I expected Jesus to forgive me for my hatred and to change my heart in the process. He could do that of course, but I thought I might merely tolerate Jews and that would be the end of that.

"I was not prepared for the complete fulfillment of this prayer. Jesus not only took away my hatred for Israel and the Jews but he replaced it with a love for them. This was unexpected. How could I love Jewish people while living in the Gaza Strip? If anyone found out about my change of heart and told some of the radicals that lived around me, well this was my death sentence."

Sami's life changed forever on an October day when his close friend Rami Ayyad was given a death sentence, and the edict was carried out in the Gaza Strip.

For Christians, the stream of blood that flows from the heroes of our faith has been constant since the birth of the church in the first century. Martyrdom has been growing ever since the stoning of Stephen in Jerusalem. The year 2015 was declared the Year of the Martyr. Even secular media outlets[5] recognized this growing global phenomenon that Jesus predicted in John 16:1–3:

> All this I have told you so that you will not fall away. They will put you out of the synagogue; in fact the time is coming when anyone who kills you will think they are offering a service to God. They will do such things because they have not known the Father or me.

Throughout the history of Jesus' church, heroes of the faith have given their lives rather than deny their Master. In heaven, thousands upon thousands will be given the martyr's crown for paying the ultimate price for their commitment to Christ.

For believers, the word "martyr" is connected to a rich tradition of those who gave their all and ended up losing their lives. Like the Master who bought them with a price, these men and women voluntarily surrendered their lives rather than succumb to the fear of men. Martyrs are choice saints of the true God.

In these days of moral equivalence, what is the difference between a Christian martyr and an Islamic one? According to most news sources, there is no difference. But the reality is, there is no comparison between the two.

For Islamic suicide bombers, men, women, and children are all targets. When this is carried out in Israel for the sole reason to kill or maim Jews, this brings pleasure to Allah. In the Gaza Strip, *shaheed* ("martyrs" in Arabic) are given prominent displays. Monuments such as the one to the Turkish "flotilla martyrs" that attacked IDF soldiers in 2010 are erected on placed on major intersections. They are heroes in Gaza. Christian martyrs, on the other hand, are not the ones who do the killing. Their lives are given freely, taken from them because of their abiding love for Jesus Christ.

Rami Ayyad was one such martyr—the first known Palestinian to lose his life for Christ.

As he closed the Bible Society doors in downtown Gaza in the late afternoon of October 7, 2007, Rami headed for home. His wife Pauline waited for him with their two children and she was pregnant with their third. Rami noticed two men parked outside of the Bible Society that day, and it was somewhat strange to see this on the traffic clogged downtown street. He had seen the men before, so he called Pauline. Rami told his wife that he was *going to be with his people for the next couple of hours,* and if he did not see her then, he might not be seeing her for a while.

So with his killers waiting for him outside the downtown building, he did not head the back door but walked toward them as he entered the street—and then he entered into eternity.

5. Samuel Smith, "2015 Deadliest Year for Christians Worldwide, Open Doors World Watch List Finds," *The Christian Post,* January 13, 2016; accessed March 4, 2018, https://www.christianpost.com/news/open-doors-world-watch-list-2015-deadliest-year-christians-killed-for-faith-jesus-christ-154875.

One young Palestinian woman eloquently put it this way: "Rami's earthly home was a mere fifteen minutes away, yet he was on his way to his heavenly home."

The next morning, at 2 am, his dead body was thrown from a car near the Bible Society, and Islamic terrorist group self-named The Righteous Swords of Islam immediately claimed the killing.

Sami Abbasi still cries as he talks about his dear friend's death. "I did not believe it. I could not fathom that this happened. I went to the morgue to look at the body myself. Now that I look back over late-night conversations that I had with Rami, I remember that he said that the Lord had shown him that persecution was coming and that we should be bold with our faith even if we were called on to give our lives for Jesus."

In a touching display of unity, Palestinian churches, along with Messianic congregations in Israel, collected funds and helped establish a trust for Pauline and the children. Rami's martyrdom drew all the believers together.

Sami continues; "At the funeral, the coroner who performed the autopsy asked to address the congregation. This was unexpected but he was given his chance to speak. He was a Muslim so when he told his side of the story, we were given a peak into the final moments of Rami's life. The coroner told the funeral crowd that he tested Rami's adrenaline levels and they had no elevation whatsoever. He said, "Rami died in perfect peace and that when they found him, he had a smile on his face. Rami was already safe in his savior's arms. Rami was with Jesus."

After Rami's death, life in Gaza was changed forever for the small group of believers. Young couples like Sami and his wife Adelle were the future of the evangelical church in the Strip—but they were begged by their parents to leave Gaza for good. With Hamas now the ruling government, Christians were considered fair game for the several Islamic terrorist groups. Living in Gaza often doesn't leave many options for immigration, but because of the extreme situation for Christians in Gaza, Israel approved the relocation for the young men and women of the Gaza Baptist Church.

GO, WEST BANK, YOUNG MAN

Sami picked up with his story: "My life changed after that. I was born in Gaza and I figured that I would die there, too. But saying goodbye to my parents and Adelle's too at the Erez Crossing was one of the hardest things I ever had to do.

"But soon we settled into our new mission field, the West Bank. Bethlehem had considerably more freedom than the Gaza Strip and we could even apply for permission to go to Jerusalem. I could've never imagined that my feet would ever stand inside the Old City gates of Jerusalem.

"The distance from Gaza to Jerusalem is only about seventy miles, but the differences are startling. In Gaza, the only Jewish people that I saw were Israeli defense forces. But when I went to Jerusalem, the first time there I was watching orthodox men with side curls and black hats praying at the Western Wall. I'd only seen them on TV. I'm glad that Jesus cleansed my heart from all my Jewish hatred when I was a new believer, because if I had waited to ask him to do that once I got to Jerusalem, I might not have asked. I was shocked at the pushing and shoving of the crowds in the Old City.

"By the time I reached Jerusalem though I'd read through the Scriptures several times. How could I doubt that God loved the Jewish people? It was all over the Bible!"

Today, Sami is passionate about reaching Jews. He is learning Hebrew and has a heart to reach out to Orthodox Jewish men.

"Jesus has called Jews and Arabs in Christ to serve Him together. This is deep within the heart of God. I used to hate Jews and run from them. Now I run to them. God has called me, a humble Palestinian, to reach the lost sheep of Israel. I have trouble fathoming this at times!

"Recently, I shared with an Orthodox Jewish man on a bus. I told him that I was from Gaza and I used to hate him and all Jews. But then Jesus, the Jewish Messiah came into my life and he gave me a deep love and respect for Jewish people."

"I think he was in absolute shock. He finally asked me if I would come to his house that night and share my story with his family. I did come, and I was overwhelmed with the opportunity to share Jesus with an Orthodox family at their Sabbath meal. Me, a Palestinian from Gaza in an observant Jewish home in Israel and being invited to tell them about Jesus? Only God could have orchestrated this one!"

In Bethlehem, I visited with Sami and Adelle to hear more of their story:

Tom: *Sami, tell us about your ministry now that you're in the West Bank.*

Sami: *I have a call from God to reach out to Muslims and to Jews as well. I grew up as a nominal Christian. Most people when they hear that I am from Gaza assume that I am Muslim. I was not a Muslim, but by virtue of living in the Strip I thought like one. I was, I guess you could say, "under the influence of Islam." My thinking was that of a Muslim.*

Tom: *Which of the two groups are harder to reach?*

Sami: *I think Jews are harder to reach. When it comes to Islam, many young Muslims are thoroughly fed up with their religion. Gazans barely tolerated Hamas. In fact, that's one thing Palestinians and Jews agree on: We'd all be better off without Hamas. But privately, Muslims talk about how much they are disgusted with their leaders, and we're talking both political ones and spiritual ones. Corruption is corruption. It doesn't matter if it's a leader in the Hamas government or an imam from the mosque; Muslim people know that they are being lied to.*

In Gaza, I led Muslims to faith in Christ and also in the West Bank as well. So many of them were ready and waiting to hear about Jesus. I think the phenom-

enon of Muslims having dreams about Jesus is growing. So you combine this with the overall distrust that Muslims have with their political leaders and spiritual leaders, you can see why we are in the midst of the great Muslim harvest today.

But Jews, on the other hand, have such a bias against Jesus to begin with. At least for Muslims, Jesus is a part of their religion as a respected prophet. For many Orthodox Jews, Jesus is ignored or hated vehemently. I was quite shocked by this.

Tom: *So Sami, how do you and Adelle share with observant Jews when you are given the chance?*

Sami: *I think so many Jews in Israel have heard the Gospel before. It's often aimed at them and how they need the Messiah who has come to save them. But I don't do that. I aim the Gospel at me, and tell them how Jesus changed me and took away my hatred for Jews and the State of Israel.*

Adelle: *Jews are God's chosen people, but they are like everyone else. They want to be loved. Can you imagine being Jewish and seeing how anti-Semitism is growing in Europe and, of course, soaring in the Middle East? Their list of enemies is endless.*

Sami: *That's right, Adelle! Then to have someone confess their hatred to him or her from Gaza like us and ask for their forgiveness! Wow! The question I am always asked is "What caused your change of heart? Was it being in the West Bank and actually seeing Jews for the first time other than just soldiers?" Then I tell them that my change of heart happened when I lived in Gaza. "The Jewish Messiah set me free from my hatred of Jews and Israel." I ask them to forgive me and tell them that I am honored to meet them. That's why I believe I'm called to a life of reaching out to the Jews of Israel. Adelle and I have this deep burden for Jews to come to know Yeshua!*

Tom: *Your team that you serve with and lead in the West Bank has many former Muslims. Do they have the same heart you have to reach Muslims and Jews?*

Sami: *Yes! One of the brothers on the team named Mahmoud is also learning Hebrew like us. He shocked me one day when he lifted his sleeve and showed me his new tattoo. He had the Shema tattooed on his forearm in Hebrew! Can you imagine that? I'm telling you now that is a statement when he shares the Gospel with Jewish people! He has their confession of faith permanently written on his body. It's hard for Jewish people to fathom this on a former Muslim.*

Tom: *Is the Palestinian Church growing?*

Sami: *I think it is stable. But the numbers are hard to quantify because of what's happening with Muslims. If a Muslim in the West Bank or Gaza comes to faith in Christ, they have to go underground. If their own family even saw them stepping into a church, they would be taking their life into their hands. So they meet* *in underground churches. They have to.*

Tom: *You did this even in while living in Gaza, didn't you?*

Sami: *Yes, we met privately in homes or neutral sites. One day I was discipling a few brothers who were former Muslims, and this was during the summer. The heat was scorching. In Gaza, the electricity is usually only on for an hour or two a day and so we had the windows open. We were studying the Bible and praying and the next thing we knew, someone opened fire. The bullets sailed through the windows and hit the wall that we were leaning against. We hit the floor and then we crawled to a back exit and escaped. Discipling former Muslims in the Gaza Strip and the West Bank is dangerous business.*

Tom: *Sami, how can we pray for you, Adelle, and your family?*

Sami: *I have been in meetings where Jewish believers and Muslim background believers came together to worship the Lord Jesus in secret, and I have never felt the power of God any stronger. It was beautiful, touching, and the room was filled with hope. All of this was because of Jesus. This is the new man that the apostle Paul talked about. If the world can see Jews and Arabs come together in love, peace, and harmony in Israel because of our Jesus . . . how can they doubt that this is a work of God? Pray for a great revival in Israel. We're asking God for an awakening that hasn't been seen here since the second chapter of Acts. Would you pray for that with us?*

What if Israel became a model of peace and stability in the Middle East, because of what Jesus accomplished in the lives of Palestinians and Jews through a massive miraculous reconciliation? The United Nations could not pull this off. Only Jesus could get the credit. And he deserves it. Just look at what he did in my life—a Palestinian from the Gaza Strip who is called by God to reach Jews in Israel!

THE SHEPHERD FROM GAZA

In the opening, I mentioned Hanna Massad, at one time the only pastor in the Gaza Strip. Here is my interview with him:

Tom: *Pastor Hanna, after so many of the young adults left Gaza after the death of Rami Ayyad, how many evangelical believers remain in Gaza?*

Hanna: *Maybe fifty to sixty believers are still living in Gaza. Traditional Christians and evangelicals are moving out, as the situation has worsened during Israel's war with Hamas. Please pray for the remnant of faithful believers in Gaza and for God bring growth instead of decline.*

Tom: *I've known you since 2001 but never once have you brought up that story of your family and the land that they lost until I asked you about it today. Can you tell us what happened?*

Hanna: *My family owned about seventy dunams of land near Ashkelon, which is about seventeen acres. When Israel became a nation we lost it, and were relocated to Gaza as refugees. My father was a good man, and he prayed that there would be peace between Palestinians and Israelis in his lifetime. He died without seeing it.*

Tom: *Pastor Hanna, though you do not live in Gaza currently, you founded the Christian Mission to Gaza many years ago and you travel into the Strip several times a year. What are some of the challenges you face when you come back out of Gaza through the Erez Crossing?*

Hanna: *One time, as I was leaving Gaza because of security issues, I was not able to get out. My family was in Jordan and I could not get permission to leave for Jordan for forty-four days. I have dual citizenship and an American passport, too, but it didn't matter. I finally was granted permission to leave, but my wife had even a tougher time. She is Jordanian and we were living in Gaza when she went home to see her family in Amman. She was not allowed back into the Israel for several months, and so we finally went to the Supreme Court of Israel and she was granted permission. It took nine months and we were so thankful to God to be reunited. I give the credit to Jesus for keeping me from not becoming bitter through things like this.*

Tom: *Hanna, you have a special love for your Jewish brothers and sisters in Christ. Humanly speaking, this is remarkable in light of the difficulties in your life that you could've become bitter about. But you never did. Why is that?*

Hanna: *I knew in my heart that God was not finished with the Jewish people because of what I read in the Scriptures. But God used an event in my life that I will never forget. I was in a conference in the Philippines and there were Christians from Gaza, the West Bank, and Messianic believers from Israel. Here is the prayer that one Messianic believer stood up and prayed publicly in that meeting. He said: "Lord, give me so much love for my Palestinian brother here that I would be willing to die for him."*

I was speechless. I nhad ever heard a prayer like that in my life. But it wasn't over. A Palestinian brother then stood as well and said: "Lord, give me so much love for my Jewish brother that I would be willing to die for him, too."

Now that is the Body of Christ in action! Ever since then, every time I meet with my Messianic brothers and sisters, I feel a special blessing. The presence of the Lord falls on us when we're together and we are overwhelmed by the love of God.

Politicians tell us that there will never be peace between Jews and Palestinians. But I've seen it . . . and it is beautiful to behold.

BIBLICAL RECONCILIATION
BETWEEN JEWS AND ARABS

DARRELL BOCK

THE BUSINESS OF SALVATION IS ABOUT more than individuals. It is also about groups and bringing them together, including formerly hostile groups. At its root is a plan to restore creation and bring it back to its intended goal. Life on earth is designed to be a place where people could flourish in their relationship to God and each other. Some people may ask what that has to do with the Middle East and Israel today. The short answer is a great deal. God's plan for the kingdom is a designed to restore humanity to its rightful place. People who image God are called to manage well the garden of the world God has created. Our rebellion and detachment from God not only has resulted in a world full of chaos, it has produced the kind of tribalism that feeds war and devastation. This essay considers the structure of the kingdom and focuses on a goal the kingdom program has to bring people together in a reconciled relationship with God and each other. In that space is the hope for all kinds of restoration, including that in the tangled world that is the Middle East.

The idea that the kingdom program of God in Jesus is already-not yet is not a recent creation as some charged.[1] This already-not yet feature of the kingdom is an important preamble to considering the topic of reconciliation and the role of the church in reflecting that call. It is a program that runs parallel to how salvation itself works where we are saved but also expect more

---

1. The positive case has been made by Kümmel, *Promise and Fulfillment* and his article, "Futurische und präsentische Eschatologie im ältesten Urchristentum," *NTS* 5 (1958–59): 113–26. Some of the elements are even earlier in the work of Johannes Weiss, *Jesus' Proclamation of the Kingdom of God* (Philadelphia; Fortresss, Press, 1971 reprint of 1892 German edition), 66–67, 129. His view is that Jesus proclaimed the kingdom as imminent, (but in some texts as already dawned), but not yet fully actualized. This tension of inaugurated but not yet consummated always leaves the church looking forward to more to come. Still the roots of restoration and reconciliation are already laid in what Christ has done. The church is called to be a preview of what is to come at a corporate level in its engagement as a community both among those of faith and in the world. Our failure to appreciate and seek to carry out the ethical and corporate roots of this dimension of salvation has hurt the church and its testimony severely bringing damage to the credibility of the church and its witness in the world.

to come in our salvation. It is deeply rooted in biblical teaching and perspective. It points to a program that is deeply ethical and vision casting for how the church is to live out her calling. In this essay, we first look at key texts in Luke-Acts that make this distinction, and point to hope for a reconciliation that involves both Jews and the nations, including the Arab world. It is a textual reading showing the stewardship of God's management of salvation. It reveals a program coming in distinct stages. Such stewardship is what a dispensation is all about, as it shows both the intent of God's program, provides a hermeneutical key for seeing the program of God, and lays the groundwork for appreciating the core relational and ethical call of Scripture. That call focused on reconciliation between God, individuals and corporate groups has application to even the most complex of human relationships, including the Middle East.[2] So what does God's kingdom program look like, and what promises lie within it?

LUKE'S TWO-STAGE PROGRAM

A look at Luke's eschatology shows a fundamental two-part structure (promise/fulfillment), with the second half of fulfillment divided into three parts. The basic division between promise and fulfillment (Luke 7:28; 16:16) means that eschatology in Scripture, the entry into the last days, started with Jesus' life and ministry on earth (Heb 1:1–2). In the "period of anticipation of promise" are the OT promises and the ministry of John the Baptist.[3]

---

2. At its core, a dispensation is not about a theological system of reading, but looks to the structure of the way God manages his program of salvation. Stewardship has its roots in Genesis 1 and the call for humans to manage creation well, to subdue the earth, a pre-Fall mandate given to people as the image the creation and sustaining work of God who made people in his image. God reflects such management in how he also organizes his plan. That is what this essay traces by looking at how God planned (1) to keep his commitments to Israel while (2) blessing the world through those commitments (Gen 12:1–3).

3. This reading of Luke's structure having two parts and not three stands in contrast to the famous reading of Lucan eschatology by Conzelmann, *Theology of St. Luke.* He has a period of promise, the church, and the end. He sees Luke's major concern as the delay of the return, as he argued that Luke opted for salvation history in place of eschatology. This reading requires that Conzelmann ignore the infancy material of Luke 1–2. It also misread the position of John the Baptist presented as a bridge figure between only two periods, the old era and the new. Luke 7:28 shows this most clearly with John being connected to the old era and differentiated from all who are a part of the new era, which shows fulfillment's fundamental unity as an era for Luke. Luke 16:16 also has this core twofold breakdown. Nor do we accept the idea that Luke wished to arouse end-time hope of a return as John Carroll argues in *Response to the End of History.* This makes too much of consummative eschatology in Luke. Our position is that Luke uses eschatology to motivate for mission and ethical accountability. This motivation occurs in the context of a present and future dimension to eschatology that looks ahead to vindication by God in the end. This position is rooted in the treatment by Kümmel, *Promise and Fulfillment* and his article, "Futurische und präsentische Eschatologie im ältesten Urchristentum," *NTS* 5 (1958–59): 113–26. This position is most recently argued for by Anders E. Neilsen, *Until It Is Fulfilled* (WUNT 2/126; Tübingen: Mohr/Siebeck, 2000). His study looks at eschatology through the lens of the farewell discourses of Luke 22:1–39 and Acts 20:17–35. See also John Nolland, "Salvation History and Eschatology," in *Witness to the Gospel,* 63–81, esp. 68–70. As Nolland notes, the claim of a present initially realized kingdom would seem empty if it were not linked to the comprehensive victory to come in the future. Our look at hope will cover similar ground.

John's ministry is a bridge into the new era of fulfillment. It represents a transition preparing for Jesus and the arrival of kingdom hope, but technically he is the last of the old era. The forerunner was a part of the promise period (see Luke 7:19–20, 28; 16:16). Luke 7:28 reads, "I tell you, among those born of women there is no one greater than John; yet the one who is the least in the kingdom of God is greater than he." The difference between the two core eras of promise and fulfillment is that great. Here is the best evidence of the Lucan breakdown of history into two core eras. A new level in the program is reached after John the Baptist with the coming of Jesus. Those who are in the new era are far better off than anyone in the former period.

Luke 10:23b–24 has Jesus teach, "Blessed are the eyes that see what you see. For I tell you that many prophets and kings longed to see what you see but did not see it, and to hear what you hear but did not hear it." Jesus is very clear that with him, promise has turned into the beginning of arrival. It is kingdom and salvation hope that he is discussing here.

Luke 16:16 reads in a similar way, "The Law and the Prophets were proclaimed until John. Since that time the good news of the kingdom of God is being preached, and everyone is forcing their way into it."[4] In this rendering, the kingdom comes with much struggle. To opt for the kingdom and belief in it is to go against the flow of opinion in the world. An alternative reading sees people being urged to enter into the kingdom. Either way, the invitation is to step into arriving kingdom hope. Again, a twofold breakdown appears with the kingdom now preached as present and available. These two texts are the most important passages when it comes to showing the core twofold structure of Luke's view of eschatology.

The picture of fulfillment is more complex. With Jesus' ministry one enters the "period of realization" for kingdom promise. This fulfillment has three parts: (1) transition tied to Jesus' earthy ministry (where Jesus' authority is established and his message of arrival and invitation goes out); (2) the "already" period (church age of the indwelling Spirit as the product of an already provided forgiveness that was tied to New Covenant promises to Israel); and (3) the "not yet" period (Christ's return to reign and bring the period of peace in the movement to the total establishment of righteousness and justice).[5] Let us look at each period as Luke presents it.

---

4. The meaning of βιάζεται (*biazetai*, "is forcing") is much discussed but not directly relevant to this discussion on eschatology. The term normally describes struggle, but in a middle/passive can refer to being urged in with a note of struggle. For details, see BAGD, 140–41, and my discussion of this term in *Luke 9:52–24:53*, 1351–53.

5. For Luke, there are no stages to the final consummation. He simply presents it as a unit. Differentiation of this final stage of the eschatological calendar is something Paul reveals in the Thessalonian letters, which is why he speaks of a word of the Lord in a mystery in 1 Thessalonians 4:16. Such periodization also gains detail in Revelation 20, as well as in much of the rest of the Apocalypse. These later details reveal to us a premillennial view for Scripture, where there is an intermediate earthly kingdom (often called the millennium), and then the new heavens and new earth.

The transition period into arrival and authority is shown in passages such as Luke 11:20 and 17:21. Luke 11:20 reads, "If I drive out demons by the finger of God, then the kingdom of God has come upon you." Luke 17:21 says, "Nor will people say, 'Here it is,' or 'There it is,'" for the kingdom of God is in your midst." God's current activity for his people has taken on a new level of intensity with Jesus' coming as Luke 7:28 also argued. The kingdom is within their present reach; it has arrived. One can speak of the kingdom arriving, in that the King was exercising his power and reflecting his authority, especially over the reversal of the presence of evil in the world, showing the ultimate full potential of the kingdom. The presence of the kingdom reflects a transition at this point, because the covenant's salvific blessings (most notably the forgiveness of sins and the coming of the Father's promise of the Holy Spirit) have not yet been distributed. Jesus' coming requires his death to provide for the forgiveness that in turn cleanses so that the Spirit can occupy clean, sanctified vessels.[6]

These benefits were not yet available to any who believed in the Old Testament and had to await the key work Jesus would do in death and in God's resurrection of him (Luke 3:15–18; 24:49). It is why the New Covenant is called new and is distinguished form the Mosaic Covenant that was the management arrangement of the nation of Israel. Jeremiah 31:31–34 is explicit that this New Covenant is not like the Mosaic Covenant. So the promise of the New Covenant (22:20) could not be realized until the covenant was activated by Jesus' sacrifice. The arrival of the central promised blessings of the period of realization did not come until the Spirit arrived and the rule of God could be enabled from within his people through this indwelling. It gave people a capability to walk with God they previously had lacked. It makes possible the movement toward the kingdom realization in terms of how people live and act in the world. The Spirit's arrival in Acts 2 completed the period of transition, in terms of bringing initial fulfillment of the promised blessings that grew out of forgiveness. It makes possible reconciliation with God and with others. These blessings were for those who acknowledged that Jesus is the promised Messiah, those who sought the forgiveness and enabling life he offered.

Since it is the already part of the program that is often most disputed or misunderstood, we now focus on this idea in Luke-Acts. It involves thinking about the kingdom program as outlined in those two books, a discussion often ignored in kingdom discussions.[7]

---

6. The relationship between forgiveness, cleansing and the provision of the indwelling Spirit as a result of salvation I develop in detail in a biblical theology of the gospel in my *Recovering the Real Lost Gospel* (Nashville: Broadman & Holman, 2012).

7. In this criticism I have in mind some covenantal handlings of these themes by writers such as Gary Burge, Steve Wellham, and Peter Gentry. Ignoring Luke-Acts leads to an undervaluation of the role of Israel in the program of God, especially in the consummation. It sets up a claim of Christ as a fulfillment of promise that sidesteps what the fulfiller actually taught, leaving a serious lacuna in the resulting description of the program of God and a hole in how God executes reconciliation. A more direct, fuller critique of such approaches can be found in my "Israel in Luke-Acts," in *The People,*

LUKE'S KINGDOM PROGRAM, AND A CLOSER LOOK AT "ALREADY" TEXTS

The rule of Jesus is reflected in Luke's writing by what is done "in his name" or "through Jesus." To do something "in Jesus' name" is to do it in his authority—that is, in view of the fact that he reigns. Such texts are limited to Acts, which shows how important a turning point his resurrection is. The fact Jesus is acting also shows that kingdom rule has begun, pointing to the "already" period.

Numerous passages speak of salvation or forgiveness of sins in his name (Acts 2:21 [this refers to Jesus, cf. v. 38]; 4:12; 10:43). Others speak of baptism in Jesus' name (2:38; 8:16; 10:48; 19:5). These references to water baptism refer to the public confession of Jesus that expresses concretely the presence of inner faith in Christ. Water baptism pictures the spiritual washing that comes from forgiveness as well as the coming of the Spirit. This public identification with Jesus pictures God's saving act. This identification showed that the one who comes to be baptized acknowledges what God has done in Jesus. In the first century, the rite of baptism and what it represented are seen as a unit and are interchangeable (1 Peter 3:21–22 is similar in perspective). A third group of passages speak of healing done in Jesus' name (Acts 3:6, 16; 4:9–10), and a fourth group refers to signs and wonders through his name (4:30). Some preach in his name (8:12) or speak boldly in his name (9:27–28). All of this shows the "already" authority of Jesus and his activity. We may note in passing that Romans 6 says the same thing in the same way from Paul, and Hebrews 1:1–2 does it in introducing Jesus before moving to the promise of Jesus having the name "Son" as part of Hebrew Scripture promise. In other words, this "already" theme is not Luke's alone.

The kingdom program is already-not yet in Luke. Some texts point to its presence and arrival with Jesus. Others look to its consummation in his future return, often with allusion to a role for Israel that she currently lacks.

Luke 11:20. Two texts emphasize the kingdom's presence. Luke 11:20 deserves a close look. It reads, "If I cast out demons by the finger of God, then the kingdom of God has come upon you." It is no exaggeration to see this passage as a crucial text for establishing Luke's view of the kingdom (see also 9:27; 10:9, 18; 17:20–21). The meaning of the passage is disputed.

Clearly the conditional clause alludes to God's work, as seen in the mention of God's finger. It is seen contextually as a reference to Jesus' miraculous activity as power points, audio-visuals of the authority Jesus has to reverse the effects of sin and evil. If God is acting through Jesus, then the kingdom has overtaken you. Interestingly, Matthew 12:28 agrees verbally with Luke except at this point, where he refers to God's Spirit. Luke, who normally emphasizes the Spirit, does not refer to him here. However, their point is the same: God is the source of power for the exorcism and other miracles Jesus performs. Most

---

the Land, and the Future of Israel: Israel and the Jewish People in the Plan of God, eds. Darrell L. Bock and Mitch Glaser (Grand Rapids: Kregel, 2014).

see in the reference to God's finger an allusion to Exodus 8:19 [8:15 MT], where pagan magicians recognize divine work in their opponent Moses. The image is often used for God's activity and intervention, whether in creation, miracles, or the giving of the law (Deut. 9:10; Ps. 8:3 [8:4 MT]).[8] In the Lucan context, Jesus is arguing that if Satan is not behind his work, God is. So the kingdom and its reversal of the fall is breaking into the world.

The main dispute involves the term ἔφθασεν (ephthasen). Does it mean "come near" or "arrive"? The difference is crucial.[9] Jesus is either teaching that the kingdom draws close in the present activity or that it arrives. At stake is whether an inaugural kingdom is present in Jesus' first coming or whether "kingdom" functions as it did in the OT and intertestamental Judaism as an eschatological term referring exclusively to the consummation of God's rule on earth through Israel. The idiom "kingdom of God" itself was not used in the OT, though the concept is found in the prophets. It was found later among the rabbis. But the concept of God's physical rule in a great age of fulfillment was expected both in the OT and in Judaism. This expectation took two forms: the prophetic hope that God would bring this promised age to pass on earth through sociopolitical rule, and the apocalyptic hope that he would usher it in with heavenly signs.[10]

Those who argue for the kingdom being "near" suggest that behind the reference is the same Aramaic term translated by ἐγγίζω (engizō, "to be near") in Mark 1:15. This verb can carry such a sense (Matt. 26:45; Luke 15:1). In Judaism, "kingdom" is an apocalyptic, eschatological term, so the idea of its arrival without apocalyptic and political elements is not possible if traditional usage applies. However, against this understanding and in favor of the idea that the kingdom "arrives" is the normal meaning of φθάνω (phthanō) when linked to ἐπί (epi). Also for the idea of arrival is a passage such as Luke 10:18, which clearly ties Satan's fall to the disciples' miraculous activity. In addition, there is the immediacy of the image that follows in Luke 11:21–22. The stronger man is defeating Satan and is passing out the spoils.

Above all considerations, however, stands the prepositional reference in 11:20 to "upon you" (ἐφ' ὑμᾶς, eph' hymas), which because of its personal object cannot look at approach, but must refer to arrival. Jesus' activity gives evidence of the arrival of God's kingdom.[11] That arrival is vividly evident in his miraculous power, which his followers also exhibit. Jesus' work and demonstration of saving authority in their midst must be dealt with. It calls for decision. Twelftree brings out how Jesus' exorcisms and claims are unique, though he seems to underplay their messianic dimension, given their delivery and end-time character.[12]

---

8. Schlier, *TDNT*, 2:20–21.

9. Although Fitzer, *TDNT*, 9:91–92, minimizes it.

10. G. von Rad, K. Kuhn, and K. Schmidt, *TDNT*, 1:566–76, 580–89.

11. Schrenk, *TDNT*, 1:610.

12. G. H. Twelftree, *Jesus the Exorcist: A Contribution to the Study of the Historical Jesus* (WUNT 2/54; Tübingen: Mohr-Siebeck, 1993).

If the kingdom has come in an initial but not yet consummative form, what does its current form involve? The portrait of Luke-Acts provides a good answer. Jesus is perceived as ruling over God's many salvation benefits. He has authority to distribute them to anyone who responds to his message (Luke 3:15–17 [where "the more powerful" one brings the Spirit, which shows he is the Messiah and the new age has come]; Acts 2:16–39). In addition, he provides the Spirit as a sign of the arrival of the promised age and as a source of enablement and guidance over those he rules, which is why the Spirit is connected to the idea of power (Luke 24:44–49; Acts 2). The emphasis of the kingdom picture in the present phase is not on realm, but on rule.

Nonetheless, a realm is envisioned. Jesus' realm is the world as it is manifested in his scattered followers. That realm will involve people of many nations, not just Israel (Luke 24:47). The kingdom is contained in Jesus' total authority over salvific blessing, an authority that is present over everyone (Acts 10:42–43; 17:31: Jesus is Lord of all, so the gospel goes to all; salvation comes through this one figure appointed by God for this task). The presence of his rule in believers anticipates his coming to earth to rule physically, when he will exercise dominion and judgment over the earth.

This theme of reign and authority is expressed in various ways in Luke-Acts: 1) Acts associates the concept of Jesus' universal lordship and rule with the initial fulfillment of Davidic promise (Acts 2:30–39; 13:32–39; see also Luke 1:68–79). 2) Acts 3:19–24 makes clear that the program is not yet consummated or completed but will come to pass *as the OT prophets taught.* Nothing is what lies ahead has been altered from what the OT declared. There is more detail and more to it now with more NT promise revealed, but we never lose what God committed himself to do in the teachings of the OT. Gentile inclusion does not mean Israelite exclusion. Reconciliation looks to both groups united in Christ, as the story of Acts also depicts. 3) Acts 10:42–43 and 17:31 show Jesus' authoritative rule over salvation and his ultimate function as judge over all humans, living and dead. 4) Jesus' parables speak of the Son's going away to receive a kingdom and so look at his present authority.

The rule expressed in Luke 11 is the first phase of this kingdom program, what we might call the "invisible kingdom." The kingdom in Acts is expressed in the ministry of the Spirit during the time of Jesus' seeming physical absence (thus the term *invisible*) from the earth. It is this rule that Jesus says is arriving now and that is pictured in his work of exorcism. The result of his presence is powerfully evident in the transformed people over whom he rules in the church, even though he is not physically visible.

The first phase of his rule is really put in place with the resurrection-ascension and the distribution of salvation's benefits (Acts 2:30–39), the roots of which are in the promise of the new covenant (Luke 22:19–20; 24:49; Acts 1:7–8). However, this power is also shown in Jesus' ministry, so that Jesus could speak of its presence with the divine activity that was worked through him in ministry. Still, the real benefits and provisions in forgiveness and the Spirit await his death and vindication to establish the covenant that opened up these core provisions of the new era. From the time of his divine vindication on, Jesus rules from God's right hand. He is not present on earth for all to see, but rules through the benefits he bestows on those who come to him to receive the life Jesus brings.

The Spirit reflects God's presence in people as well as God's work of power and his promise. Humans are now able to live as God would desire because they respond to his Spirit, so that his rule becomes evident in their lives. This group of disciples, which becomes the church, is not all there is to the kingdom, nor is it all there is to God's plan and promise, but it is a microcosm of what the kingdom will be when OT promises are completely fulfilled at Jesus' return. The Spirit is the down payment of the redemption to come (Eph 1:13–14).[13] The one new man is made up of Jew and Gentile together (Eph 2:11–22).

Luke 17:21. A second significant "already" text is Luke 17:21. A closer look reveals an important exegetical issue. What does ἐντὸς ὑμῶν (*entos hymōn*) mean? Three options are available.

1) Does it mean "inside of you"? Many, including numerous ancient interpreters, take the phrase to mean that the kingdom is "inside you" (Ps. 39:4 [38:4 LXX]; 103:1 [102:1 LXX]; 109:22 [108:22 LXX]; Isa. 16:11). This view has two major problems. Contextually, Jesus is addressing the Pharisees, who are the last group of people whom Jesus would say has the kingdom in them (Luke 11:37–52, esp. 11:52). It would be strange if Jesus said this to the Pharisees and never to his disciples! Moreover, nowhere else in the NT is the kingdom spoken of in internal terms. Granted, the Spirit is sent as a token of God's promise and does relate people to the kingdom. Marshall, however, is right when he says that in the NT people enter the kingdom, but the kingdom does not enter people.[14] The Spirit is a sign that one has come into the kingdom, but his presence does not equal the kingdom. The kingdom is a community of residence, blessing, and enablement, while it is the Spirit who marks one for membership.

2) Does it mean "in your grasp or reach"? Others argue on the basis of its usage in the papyri that the phrase means this—that the kingdom's coming is related to one's power to repent as a response to Jesus' message. This view is possible, but the case made for it from the papyri is challenged by Riesenfeld and Wikgren, who argue that the phrase could mean "in your presence or domain."[15] Also against this view is that it could be regarded as a non-answer. On this view, Jesus has said it is not by signs that the kingdom comes, but it is within your grasp. But the essential question still remains, "Where is it so that I can obtain it?" Thus, this option does not really supply a sufficient answer to deal with the question. A clearer way to state that the kingdom comes through

---

13. Bock, *Luke 9:51–24:53*, 1079–82.

14. Marshall, *Gospel of Luke*, 655.

15. H. Riesenfeld, "'Εμβολεύειν–'Εντός," *Nuntius* 2 (1949): 11–12; A. Wikgren, "'Εντός," *Nuntius* 4 (1950): 27–28.

one's choice is to mention directly the need to repent, which Jesus often says to the Pharisees (Luke 5:31–32; 11:29–32). Meier rejects the reading, arguing that it puts the stress on human control and calculation when the context argues for God's manifesting his presence in his sovereign way.[16] In addition, to say that the kingdom is within one's grasp in the present is to say in effect that it is present, since one can reach for it now. Nonetheless, this sense conceptually ends up being very similar to the next view.

3) Does it mean "in your presence"? A final option argues that the phrase means "in your presence" or "before you" (Isa. 45:14 ["God is among you"]).[17] The emphasis here would be that the Pharisees confront the kingdom in Jesus. They do not need to look all around for it because its central figure is in front of their eyes. Mattill objects that Luke has a more common phrase for this idea (ἐν μέσῳ [en mesō, "in the midst"] in Luke 2:46; 8:7; 10:3; 21:21; 22:27, 55; 24:36; Acts 1:15; 2:22; 17:22; 27:21).[18] But Mattill understates the synonymity of the phrases. Since Jesus and his authority are the major obstacles in the Pharisees' way, this view fits the context nicely. To see the kingdom, look to Jesus and what he offers.[19]

As noted earlier in the discussion on the kingdom, Jesus' future rule is described primarily in terms of his already noted work as judge, when he returns to gather his people (Luke 17:22–37; 21:5–36; Acts 1:11; esp. 3:19–23; 10:42; 17:31). Luke does not give much detail about God's future program other than to make one important point, namely, that Jesus will fulfill the rest of the promise in the Hebrew Scriptures about the restoration of all things at that time (Acts 3:20–21).[20]

So here is the "already" part of Jesus' program. If we add a text like Luke 4:16–21 and Jesus' appeal to Isaiah 61, we can see that this activity is tied to promises out of God's program made to Israel. There is no separate program here, only initial fulfillment.

The Arrival of Salvific Benefits. The descent of the Holy Spirit on Pentecost, made possible by Jesus' resurrection-ascension, marks the arrival of the "already" period of promise in terms of salvific benefits to its recipients. Jesus functions now as Lord-Messiah, distributing blessings promised in the Hebrew Scriptures and holding all people accountable for responding to him.[21] Acts 11:15 referred back to the event on the day of Pentecost as "the begin-

---

16. John P. Meier, *A Marginal Jew: Rethinking the Historical Jesus,* vol. 2: *Mentor, Message, and Miracles* (ABRL; New York: Doubleday, 1994), 427.

17. Danker, *Jesus and the New Age,* 292; Marshall, *Gospel of Luke,* 655; Ellis, *Gospel of Luke,* 211.

18. A. J. Mattill, Jr., *Luke and the Last Things: A Perspective for the Understanding of Lucan Thought* (Dillsboro, NC: Western North Carolina Press, 1979), 196–97.

19. Bock, *Luke 9:51–24:53,* 1415–17.

20. The remarks in Acts 3:18–26 are the result of what Peter saw and heard in 1:6–11. Nothing about what is said in either text indicates that the restoration of Israel has been set aside, even though this is a popular position in expounding Acts 1. Peter in Acts 3 says that the program has already been revealed and can be read about in the Hebrew Scriptures.

21. "From now on," Luke 22:69; "exalted to the right hand of God" as Psalm 110 promised.

ning." Here the hope of the new covenant was inaugurated, made possible by Jesus' death (Luke 22:20; Acts 20:28). These current blessings are part of the eschaton because in Luke's view they represent the initial line of OT promises that God fulfilled. In the Holy Spirit, God is at work in his people. Jesus rules with sovereignty over these benefits as the Mediator of divine blessing.

This is the point Peter makes in his speech, that Israel can know God has made Jesus both Lord and Messiah (Acts 2:36), because the Spirit has come to God's believing people. This verse says: "Let all the house of Israel know with assurance that both Lord and Christ God has made him, the Jesus whom you crucified" (pers. trans.).[22] The kingdom has come because the power of God is expressed through Jesus by means of the Holy Spirit working in his people.

Not Yet Texts. But there also is a "not yet" element in Luke's eschatology. Here Luke presents the hope of consummation, in which God's promises will be brought to full realization. All the prophetic promises made to Israel will be fulfilled (Acts 3:19–21) as God will restore everything: "Repent, therefore, and turn for the washing of your sins, so that times of refreshing might come from before the Lord and he might send the Christ appointed for you, Jesus, whom it is necessary that heaven receive until the times of restoration of all things which God spoke about through the mouth of his holy prophets of old" (personal trans.). Note how the prophets speak with a singular voice (note it is one "mouth"). God speaks through them about his program. Also important is that what is left to be done is already described in the prophets. To see what God will do one need only to go back and read them. There is no hint here of a reconfiguration of anything as a result of Jesus' coming. He realizes what was always promised and revealed. What was said is still the case.

In Acts 3:20, "the times of refreshing" (καιροὶ ἀναψύξεως, *kairoi anapsyxeōs*) is a NT *hapax* expression. It looks to a period of time that includes rest and refreshment. The term ἀνάψυξις (*anapsyxis*) refers to a "cooling" to relieve trouble or to dry out a wound ("refreshment" in NLT; "refreshing" in NIV, RSV, NET; BDAG 75).[23] In the LXX, the only use of ἀνάψυξις is in Ex 8:11 LXX (= 8:15 Eng.), where it refers to relief from the plague of frogs. The verb ἀναψύχω (*anapsychō*, "to refresh") is used of the Sabbath rest of slaves and animals and the soothing of Saul by David's music (Exod. 23:12; 1 Sam. 16:23).[24] The arrival, then, is of a period of mes-

---

22. I have kept the word order in the translation to show the emphasis with which the point is made. The idea of being made Lord and Christ is not the appointment to a new role but reflects the obvious public display of the point. The infancy narrative already has Jesus in this role. The point is like Romans 1:2–4, where Jesus is "horizoned" or "marked out" as Son in power.

23. Schweizer, *TDNT*, 9:664; Fitzmyer, *Acts of the Apostles*, 288, "to cool by blowing" is the idea of the related verb.

24. Johnson, *Acts of the Apostles*, 69.

sianic refreshment, the "definitive age of salvation."[25] The idea has parallels in Judaism (*2 Esdr.* [*4 Ezra*] 7:75, 91, 95; 11:46; 13:26–29; *2 Bar.* 73–74; *1 En.* 45.5; 51.4; 96.3) and is traditional in its origin.[26] It refers to entry into a new and unending eschatological life before the Lord. The closest parallel in the NT is the concept of "rest" in Hebrews 3–4.[27] One wonders if ἀνάψυξις alludes to the Spirit's washing work in the messianic age that points to the start of spiritual refreshment.

The reference to times and seasons contains terms that appear in Luke 21:24 ("times [καιροί, *kairoi*] of the Gentiles"—the current era) and Acts 1:6–7. The question in Acts 1 receives a reply that it is not for Peter's hearers to know the "times or dates"—a reply that uses both terms for "time" (καιροί and χρόνοι, *chronoi*). In other words, their repentance opens up the possibility of both times of refreshment and times establishing all things God promised.[28] There is nothing about the question about whether this is the time the kingdom will be restored to Israel that suggests the question is wrong or reflects a poor premise. Jesus simply says this is in the Father's timing. Jesus had just spent forty days with the disciples and explained the hope of the Scripture to them. They still have this hope. Apparently, they are right to have it, but the timing is not theirs to know. All of this takes place before the Lord, before his presence.

Peter's exposition in Acts 3 is a reflection of what they learned from the Acts 1 exchange with Jesus. This entry into refreshment is the completion of God's plan with Christ's return. Peter urges repentance so that one can participate in God's entire planned program from start to finish. A key aspect of that program is Jesus' return, when the Christ will exercise judgment on behalf of righteousness and complete God's promise already outlined in the prophetic teaching of the Hebrew Scriptures. Nothing Peter says indicates that anything promised there has been changed, including what is said about Israel. There may be additions and expansions of those ideas in light of revelation in the period tied to Jesus, but in the rest of what Jesus brings he will complete what also was already revealed.[29] The timing of the consummation comes down the road, but what will happen has been described in those texts. Peter speaks of God's sending the Christ "appointed" (προκεχειρισμένον, *prokecheirismenon*) for

25. Schweizer, *TDNT*, 9:664.

26. Bruce, *Acts of the Apostles*, 144. This is against the argument of Kremer that the language is Lucan (see his discussion in *EDNT*, 1:95).

27. R. Pesch, *Die Apostelgeschichte (Apg 1–12)* (EKKNT 5/1; Zurich: Benzinger/Neukirchen-Vluyn: Neukirchener, 1986), 155.

28. Barrett, *Critical and Exegetical Commentary on the Acts of the Apostles*, 1:205.

29. This point is made against those who argue Jesus reconfigured the end events by what he said and did in his initial coming. What Jesus did was to add to an existing portrait, not change or reconfigure promises that had been made already to a specific people. The implication of this observation is that hope for Israel remains as the completion of promises at the end of time will include her as it also does the reconciliation of the world. That plan for her is revealed in the Hebrew Scriptures.

all of them (Acts 3:20).[30] The two other occurrences of this verb in Acts are about Paul as a "chosen" servant of God (22:14–15; 26:16–18).

This Christ is received in heaven for now. Here is another way to portray the experience of ascension. Heaven holds Jesus at God's side until the day he is revealed to the world in power in his return (Luke 21:25–28). Jesus is not passive until the return, however, for Acts 2 shows that Jesus is active now in salvation by distributing the Spirit, and Acts 3 shows him as the source of the healing of the crippled man. This is executive messianic, kingdom authority that Jesus is exercising from heaven as he blesses those who come to him with forgiveness and the Spirit. As Bruce notes, "Jesus must reign at God's right hand until all hostile powers are overthrown" (1 Cor. 15:24–28).[31]

Nevertheless, with his return comes "the seasons of the restoration of all things" (lit. trans. of 3:21; χρόνων ἀποκαταστάσεως πάντων, chronōn apokatastaseōs pantōn), yet another NT *hapax* expression. The term ἀποκατάστασις (*apokatastasis*, "establishment") does not appear in the LXX.[32] The end is reestablishing the original creation's pristine character. This restoration is what Jesus will bring with his return, an idea given later development in Revelation 19–22 but whose roots Peter declares here are already evident in that of which "God promised long ago through his holy prophets." The relative pronoun ὧν (*hōn*, "of which") could refer back to "the seasons" of which God spoke[33] or to "all things" of which God spoke.[34] Acts 3:24 appears to highlight the period of time being addressed by the promise ("these days"), but it is the content that is being highlighted here—that all things will be restored (i.e., taking πάντων as the antecedent of ὧν).[35] The new world and the messianic creation appear in a final and complete restoration.

In the NT, this idea is discussed in Matthew 19:28; Romans 8:18–23; and Hebrews 2:5–8. The point is that God has already indicated what the end will be like. So, to learn about the future, Peter urges the people to note what God has already said through the prophets about the new era that the eschaton will bring. The expression about the prophets is like Luke 1:70. Texts such as Isaiah 65–66 are in view, where Israel is restored to fullness (also Isa. 34:4; 51:6; Jer. 15:18–19; 16:15; 23:8; 24:6; Ezek. 17:23; Amos 9:11–12).[36] Isaiah 2:1–4 and 19:23–25 look to Israel and Jerusalem as the center of this activity. Isaiah 19 speaks of a highway running from Egypt through Jerusalem to Assyria. A physical kingdom on earth will span the

---

30. Note that the second-person pronoun "you" (ὑμῖν, *hymin*) is plural.

31. Bruce, *Book of Acts*, 185.

32. Müller, *EDNT*, 1:130.

33. Otto Bauernfeind, *Kommentar und Studien zur Apostelgeschichte* (WUNT 22; Tübingen: Mohr-Siebeck, 1980), 69.

34. Conzelmann, *Acts of the Apostles*, 29; Barrett, *Critical and Exegetical Commentary on the Acts of the Apostles*, 1:206. It is the nearest referent.

35. So Oepke, *TDNT*, 1:391.

36. Jervell, *Apostelgeschichte*, 167, n. 358.

globe. The two expressions for time—καιροί and χρόνοι—probably look at one period, as opposed to distinct periods of time. However, it is seen as one great, extended period (thus the plurals) whose high point is Christ's return, and so the stress is on what participation in the period of messianic blessing ultimately will yield.[37]

In sum, three blessings are offered in Acts 3:19–21: the forgiveness of sins, the promise of times of refreshing that includes the prophets hope for the nation, and the opportunity to participate in the return of the Messiah. Jesus brings all of this over time, and the core story is told in the writings from the prophets of old.

THE RESULT: RECONCILIATION TO COME WITH JEW AND GENTILE

So what is foreseen by these texts Peter refers to in Acts 3? The time to come will be a period of reconciliation for the world. Jews and Gentiles, including Arabs, will be brought together. Here are a few key texts from the Hebrew Scripture that show what Acts 3 was alluding to in referring to the restoration to come.

Isaiah 2:1–4: Nations Gathered with Israel. The prophet Isaiah is in the midst of challenging a stubborn people caught in disobedience. He offers this word of hope in 2:1–4. The entire section is called "a word from the Lord." This marks it out as an important message. This *ḥāzâ* points to an utterance giving divine insight (Lam. 2:9; Ezek. 7:26). It is a special disclosure from God.[38]

Isaiah gives a message about Judah and Jerusalem. He announces that the mountain of the Lord's temple will endure into the latter days (Deut. 4:30; Jer. 23:20; Ezek. 38:16; Hos. 3:5).[39] This time period for Isaiah is simply the last days of human history. He has no more detailed calendar of events than this. This is when full deliverance finally comes in all its fullness. In that time he declares, nations will stream to Jerusalem. They will worship on the Lord's high mountain and come to learn the Lord's standards. Zion will be the center for instruction. Literally, the Torah will go out from there. Torah in this context is about God's will and ways as the previous parallelism shows. Cases will be settled among nations there. Swords will be beaten into plowshares and spears into pruning hooks.[40] They will no longer train for war. The picture is of a world at peace before the one God. All the nations, side by side, gathered before the one God. This reconciliation to peace involves all the nations and Israel is at its center. Judah and Jerusalem in the

---

37. Marshall, *Acts of the Apostles*, 93–94.

38. Gary Smith, *Isaiah 1–39*. The New American Commentary (Nashville: Broadman & Holman Publishing Group, 2007), 128.

39. Joseph Blenkinsopp, *Isaiah 1–3*. The Anchor Yale Bible 19 (New Haven, CT: Yale University Press, 2008), 190.

40. Interestingly, this text is prominently displayed in New York City at the United Nations.

midst of the nations will have this role. In the context of the book, such hope to come should lead to faithfulness within Israel now (Isa. 2:5).

This is an important text. While other OT texts speak of judgment of the nations as righteousness comes, this text pictures the aftermath and result of what God will bring, a reconciliation that includes righteousness, instruction, and peace. It is not a melding in of people, but a gathering of nations who no longer battle as they had. Also significant is that this note of hope comes at the beginning of the prophetic book. It is a note of introduction that is to abide in one's thinking, as one moves through Isaiah and all the ideas it raises.

Another note from this text is important. This redemption comes to this earth and this history. This is not a dualistic vision of something happening above or in a newly created physical reality emerging out of what had been. It is an account of God's resolution of conflict in the current stream of history and reality. Other OT texts travel this same road, speaking to this same reality (Isa. 14:1–2; 45:22–23; 49:26; 56:7; 60:1–14, 66:18–21; along with the texts that follow). As Watts puts it, "Jerusalem has an abiding place in God's future."[41]

Isaiah 19:23–25: Blessing with the World. The picture of Isaiah 2 is reinforced by images in Isaiah 19. The reference opens with a discussion of "that day," the period when God is delivering and Egypt is pulled into the fold as he both strikes and heals them (19:21–22). These two "vectors" are a part of OT hope. Israel will be victorious, but it will not be a victory that leads to vanquishing but to reconciliation.[42] Here we have a highway running from Egypt to Assyria. People will travel back and forth, interacting openly in all kinds of ways. Those nations will worship together. Assyria and Egypt, former enemies, will bow alongside of Israel to God. That Assyria, an even more threatening neighbor than Egypt, is included in this vision is even more surprising. Israel, in a middle position between them. She will be a third member of the group and will be a recipient of blessing in the midst of the earth. This is still about events on earth in the midst of current history. There is no above and below dualism here. Egypt will be blessed as my people. Assyria will be affirmed as the work of God's hands. And God's inheritance, Israel, will also be blessed in the land/earth.[43] Nothing in this language foresees the absorption and disappearance of Israel as a people and nation. In fact, the identification of Israel as an inheritance pictures them as a people possessed by God and as beneficiaries of that relationship. The picture is of a reconciliation between peoples whose identity remain even in the midst of their gathering together as one. The two nations most hostile to Israel up to the time of Isaiah are now seen as allies and cohorts.

Isaiah 55–56: The Nation with the Nations. This is all tied into a covenantal blessing in Isaiah 55–56. Here the promises of David are portrayed

---

41. John D. W. Watts, *Isaiah 1–33,* rev ed. Word Biblical Commentary 24 (Nashville, Thomas Nelson, 2005), 49.

42. Blenkinsopp, *Isaiah 1–39,* 320, speaks of two vectors in prophetic hope.

43. Watts, *Isaiah 1–33,* 317, speaks of a reminder of Genesis 12:3 here. The reference to earth here is ambiguous, as the positon of Israel between Egypt and Assyria looks at her specific location as well.

as sustaining water that rescues the thirsty as they are handed over to the people. God will cut a covenant of duration with the people, just like the "firm" covenant made with David (55:3). This is language of surety. Watts speak of a covenant that is "unconditioned and 'sure,'" in contrast to the conditioned covenant made to Moses that required obedience.[44] God is making a commitment he will keep. The result will be nations running to Israel as a sign of honor to them. This hope becomes the basis for an appeal to the nation to turn and receive forgiveness, much like we saw in Isaiah 2:1–5, where the hope of verses 1–4 led to the response in verse 5. There are core themes at work here.

In 55:11–13 the point is made that God keeps his promises and they do not return to him empty as he brings a peace that causes creation to rejoice. As McKenzie says, the dynamic word of Yahweh, "never returns with its mission unaccomplished."[45] The application in Isaiah 56 is to preserve justice and do righteousness (56:1–2). This inclusion of blessing should lead the blessed people to be a blessing to others. This hope includes foreigners who turn to God, as 56:3 argues. They will not be excluded and neither will the eunuch (two groups traditionally seen as on the outside of God's blessing). These foreigners also will be brought to God's holy mountain to be followers of God who serve him. They will share in the worship of God.

The picture is a consistent one in Isaiah of a hope that encompasses all the nations and where Israel has a visible role as the gathering place for the presence of the peace of God.

One question remains. Does Israel have a future according to other texts in the New Testament? Has anything changed the picture we get from the prophets? Here we consider two key New Testament texts.

THE REALIZATION OF PROMISE AND THE HOPE OF RECONCILIATION

These two texts show that God brings people together into a new entity but does not give up on hope for Israel.

Romans 11: The Regrafting Back into Promise and Blessing. Perhaps no claim introduces more conversation about Israel than the idea that Israel has now becomes a reference to the church. That approach argues that what was said of Israel is now true of the church. That new entity is the people of God and has a relationship to Jesus, the Messiah, who is the ultimate seed and the center of fulfillment of promise. There is much truth in this claim. Jesus is at the center of fulfillment. He is the ultimate seed in whom promise is realized, as Galatians 3 makes abundantly clear. As those who Jesus has brought near, Gentiles and any member of the church became coheirs of promise because

44.   John D. W. Watts, *Isaiah 34–66,* The Word Biblical Commentary 25. rev ed. (Nashville: Thomas Nelson, 2005), 817.

45.   John L. McKenzie, *Second Isaiah,* The Yale Anchor Bible 20 (New Haven, CT: Yale University Press, 2008), 144.

of the grace shown through Jesus. In saying they have been brought near to promise, they have been made citizens of the promises God made (Eph. 2:11–22). In this way, the promise that always looked to involve the world has brought those responding to Jesus into blessing.

However, inclusion of Gentiles does not mean the exclusion of Israel. The problem of significant Jewish rejection was so painful in the first century for Jewish believers that Paul wrote about it. It is clear in Romans 9–11 that Paul is discussing ethnic Jews. He opens Romans 9 by noting he wishes himself accursed for the sake of his fellow Jews who have rejected Jesus (v. 3).[46] He goes on to discuss the benefits Jews have: adoption as sons, the glory, the covenants, the giving of the law, the temple and—the promises, the patriarchs, and the Christ. He is discussing ethnic Israel in this section, not Gentile believers. The problem he raises is about what happened and what will happen? If God does not keep his commitments to Israel, then can we be sure he will keep them for us? After noting that not everyone in Israel is Israel and the existence of a remnant, as well as the fact that many Jews have a zeal for God that is not according to knowledge, the rest of the exposition in Romans 9–11 has Paul urge a preaching of the gospel that does not reflect ethnic favoritism. In Chapter 11, this includes a warning to Gentiles not to be arrogant about their access to the gospel, because Gentile inclusion is designed in part to make Israel jealous (11:11). Paul's making this point means he is still hoping for a response by the mass of Jews.

In Romans 11:12, he turns his attention to the possibility of restoration for them. He raises the question whether they stumbled so as to fall beyond recovery and answers with an emphatic, "By no means!"

In verse 15, he hopes for their future acceptance. That acceptance means life from the dead, resurrection. Now if we are sensitive to what Paul is invoking here, he is harking back to the dry-bones picture of Ezekiel 37, a nation risen from the dead.[47] He then goes on to discuss branches broken off from

---

46.   Douglas J. Moo, *The Epistle to the Romans*. The New International Commentary on the New Testament (Grand Rapids: Wm. B. Eerdmans Publishing Co., 1996), 555, makes this very clear with this statement on 9:1–5, "Paul begins his exposition of the gospel and Israel with an impassioned assertion of his own concern for his 'kindred according to the flesh' (vv. 1–3). Implied by this concern, as the word 'accursed' in verse 3 makes especially clear, is a circumstance well known among the Roman Christians: The great majority of the Jewish people have not responded in faith to the Gospel. But Paul's concern is not the result only of a natural love for his own people; nor is it directed only to their salvation. As the rehearsal of Israel's privileges in verses 4–5 makes clear, Paul is also concerned that Israel's unbelief has ruptured the continuous course of salvation history: the people promised so many blessings have, it seems, been disinherited. It will be Paul's task to show that this is not the case."

47.   It is often argued that there is a choice here between a reference to Israel's restoration and the idea of a reference to a general resurrection at the end of salvation history. So Moo, *Romans*, arguing for a preference for the latter (694–95). We would ask why must one choose between the two? The restoration of Israel would mean a decisive step toward the end of salvation history. In addition, the former point about resurrection and the end of salvation history alone does not advance the argument about Israel that is the concern of the section. Unprecedented blessing in the world would be the point of a reference to general resurrection, but that really does not treat the theme in view, especially since the following verses use the picture of unnatural grafting in of Gentiles and a potential new grafting in of Jews.

an olive tree, along with others now grafted in. In verse 17, Paul notes how some branches were broken off, and that "you" (i.e., Gentiles) as a wild shoot were grafted in with some of the original branches. They all now share in the richness of the olive root. The exhortation to Gentiles is not to boast over their access, as promise is a root with Jewish connections that supports them. The prospect exists that the whole reversal process could itself by reversed if ethnic arrogance surfaces. If natural branches were not spared, unnatural ones also could be at risk and cut off if they do not learn from God's grace.

In verse 24, things turn back. Paul raises the question that natural branches can be grafted into their own olive tree. The impression is this is easier than the previous grafting in of unnatural branches. In verse 25, he wants them to understand a mystery and not be conceited. That mystery is a partial hardening has taken place to Israel *until* the full number of Gentiles has come in.

Two points cannot be missed here: 1) Israel *has* to be ethnic Israel here because of the contextual contrast to the Gentiles and the image of being reconnected for this non-Gentile group. 2) The crucial term *until* tells us that things as they are now will once again change, and that change anticipates the grafting in of natural branches Paul has been discussing leading into this point. Partial and permanent hardening is not the fate of Israel. A reversal of that hardening is coming. This the content of the mystery Paul is revealing here. In this way, Israel, the Israel he has been talking about consistently in these three chapters will be saved. The picture is of a Messiah associated with Zion who will regather his people and there will be no ungodliness left in Jacob (v. 26). The language here recapitulates the picture of texts like those we saw from the Hebrew Scriptures. The language comes from such texts, including Isaiah 27:9, Isaiah 59:20–21, and Jeremiah 31:33–34. All the Isaiah texts cited do is develop the hope already expressed in texts like Isaiah 2, 19, and 55–56. These are other texts of Jewish eschatological hope.[48] God will perform his covenant with them. Paul believes God will keep his word and promise. God will forgive Israel's sins (vv. 26–27). The everlasting covenant of peace made with Israel will be realized for her, just as it has been with Gentiles. The picture is of reconciliation pure and simple, a reconciliation that leaves no room for ethnic arrogance on either side.

Why does God do it? God acts in this way because of the Fathers (the patriarchs) and because the gifts and callings of God are irrevocable (vv. 28–

---

48.   Once more I cite Moo, *Romans*, who makes this point well (724): "the hope of a spiritual rejuvenation of the nation of Israel is endemic in the OT prophets and in Jewish apocalyptic. This rejuvenation is often pictured as a regathering of Jews that reverses the judgment of Israel's exile and that ushers in the eschatological age. Paul—and the rest of the NT—teaches that the coming of Christ has brought the fulfillment of many of these prophecies about Israel's renewal. But Paul's language in Rom. 11 seems deliberately calculated to restate this traditional hope for Israel's renewal. His point seems to be that the present situation in salvation history, in which so few Jews are being saved, cannot finally do full justice to the scriptural expectations about Israel's future." He goes on to argue that this will come through faith in Jesus and not in any special way for Jews, precluding any idea of a view of Jewish salvation in the NT that has a unique path for Jews apart for Christ.

29). God keeps his promises. Faithfulness to his character and commitments mean there is every reason to hope for the restoration of Israel, because only her presence in significant numbers can paint the picture of reconciliation that is a core result of the gospel with its hope for peace not just with God but with others. The goal is to show mercy to all (vv. 30–32). The consideration of the entire sequence of hope leads Paul to praise God for the depths and riches of his wisdom and knowledge (vv. 33–36). The reversal that comes with grace at an ethnic level is itself pointing to a repeat in the opposite direction so all nations can share in God's blessing without favoritism. This emphasis exists because all have the same need for God.

At a corporate level, Paul repeats a theme he raised as early as Romans 3, all have the same need for a Savior. All get access to God on the same basis. All get access to all the same blessings. The one people is made up of the reconciled many in Christ. No wonder the Hebrew Scripture saw a day when all would come to Jerusalem and worship God together. It will be their capital one day and they will share one King.

Ephesians 2:11–22: Jew and Gentile Together and Reconciled. Paul also develops this reconciliation in Ephesians 2. Here he goes the other way. He starts with how Gentiles were far off and detached from promise. They were the uncircumcision, without Messiah, alienated from citizenship of Israel, strangers to the covenants of promise, without hope and without God (vv. 11–12). Now the blood of Christ has brought them near, which here clearly means has brought them in (v. 13). Christ has become peace for Jews and Gentiles in which hostility has been destroyed and commandments nullified as God has made of the two entities one new man, making peace. It takes two to make peace. God through Christ has become the middle man in that transaction between Jews and Gentiles as all get access to the Spirit through Christ (vv. 14–18). The result is that Gentiles are no longer foreigners and noncitizens, but fellow citizens with the saints as members of the house of God, a sacred people compared to a cleansed temple (vv. 19–22).

We do the church much damage if we understate what is in view here. This reconciliation is one of the primary means by which we see the power of the gospel and testify to God's amazing work. That work is not just with us as individuals but between peoples. The Gospel makes claims and shows itself in a thorough reclamation of the creation and its structures. One of the ways that is shown is by how enmity between people should be removed when Christ resides among the lives of peoples.

THE IMPLICATIONS OF ISRAEL AS A NATION FOR ALL, INCLUDING ARABS, AND THE THEME OF RECONCILIATION

For the Middle East. The idea that Israel has a future as a nation and a right to the land has major implications for the Middle East.[49] The attempt

---

49. A more detailed case for a future for Israel in the land appears in Gerald R. McDermott, ed., *The*

by some to eliminate her presence as a nation there is illegitimate on various grounds. Theologically, the nation has had a right to the land because it is a part of God's promise to Israel. However, for many it also is hers by legal right, something a careful retracing of the complex history of the region from the Balfour Declaration on can show. The failure of many of her neighbors to recognize her right to exist is part of what has created the tension in the Middle East. Such recognition should be a given in the effort to make political progress in the region.

The emphasis on reconciliation also should make one careful not to turn this right into a defense of a kind of nationalism at the expense of God's care and concern for others. This has significance because it means Israel does not have a *carte blanche* to do whatever she desires in the region. She is responsible for justice concerns because of the prophet's call for justice from those who claim ties to Israel's God as well as out of respect for all made in God's image.

The Middle East is a tangled mess, as anyone knows. Part of the pressure on justice concerns comes from the deep hatred that has motivated much violence from some opposed to Israel's presence in the region. Many of her actions are part of an attempt to pursue self-defense in the face of those who seek to harm or eliminate the nation. The idea that Israel has a right to exist and to be treated with the rights and protections of any nation means these attempts should be seen not as conflicts of liberation but as violations of international law. The suppression of such a recognition for Israel in the Middle East does nothing to advance the cause of peace there. Only such a recognition and the protection that goes with it allow for an environment that then can more easily pursue peace.

All of this is a direct implication of the recognition of Israel's right to exist as a people and an understanding that behind all the legal and political wrangling stand theological concerns. Any theological perspective that excludes Israel as a part of the divine promise program only clouds things in the Middle East and sets the background for a defense of the kind of violence we see from both sides.

Yet the emphasis on reconciliation means that the presence of Israel should not be seen as a threat to Arabs. The divine program foresees a nation that eventually turns back to God and that becomes part of a larger reconciliation program of God. It is not an affirmation of nationalism to affirm a role for Israel. On Christ's return, she is to be a source of global blessing that all will welcome. It is clear this is a deeply theological claim. Only seeing this direction for the program of God in Christ allows one to see this potential trajectory for the Middle East.

For the Church. The church is designed to be a place that previews where things are headed. It is to show a commitment to faithfulness to God's word, a love for God and for others, and to be a community that gives evidence

---

New Christian Zionism: Fresh Perspective on Israel and the Land (Downers Grove, IL: IVP Academic, 2016). This book involves essays from people of a variety theological traditions showing it is not merely the product of one particular theological tradition.

of the reconciliation to come. We have not always done this well, in part because of the already-not yet character of salvation, where growth is what takes place not a leap to perfection. The church should be characterized by an evenhandedness and sense of justice that not only pursues righteousness, but is appropriately self-critical as it responds to God's commitment to grow us as individuals and as the body of Christ. That means there will be success and failure, but the aims of the church should be to reflect the product of the gospel in terms of truth and relationally. If the goal of salvation is the regaining of a flourishing before God and the presence of genuine *shalom*, then the church should be an example of how that works and should argue for moves toward such reconciliation between people as they urge them to respond to what God has designed for the peoples of the world. To paraphrase Galatians 6:10, those in the church are to do good to all people, especially those of the faith. That also means being concerned about justice toward all, including those of the faith. God is a God of all nations. The church needs to be careful to reflect that commitment alongside its discussion of God's revealed plan.

For Divine Promise and Character. In many ways, this point stands at the core of the thesis for this essay. What is at stake in the future for Israel and the reconciliation of the nations in Christ is not only related to the status of a particular people and nation, but a reading about the character of God and his revelation as he acts on behalf of the world. Many of the texts we cited, especially in the Old Testament discuss the certainty of God's word. The completion of this promise reveals God's character to be faithful and shows that he keeps his word to those to whom he originally made it. The veracity of God and the clarity of his communication are both in play. In many ways, he stakes his reputation upon completing this promise. The prophets compare the promise's certainty to remarks about the surety of the creation. The connection serves to underscore the prophets' view about the promise's realization. It will take place and all nations will share in the unity and joy it brings to humanity. This hope is not about nationalism. Nor is it only about reconciliation. It is about God's grace and character as rooted in his promises. It is about his word and character. It is about what Craig Blaising's essay calls Redemptive Kingdom Theology. God's faithfulness to Israel is actually also a picture of his faithfulness to all his children. What is true for Israel is true for all who belong to God. In Israel's future as a nation, we see our own future as well—and we see a reconciliation that cancels out our nationalisms and tribalisms. Real hope in the Middle East can only come with a comprehensive program involving redemption and the uniting of all the nations in conjunction with promises made long ago with Abraham. The realized and culminated work Messiah, including a hope for national Israel and the long-revealed promises of God, unites us as one. It also shows a God who keeps his word and is worthy of honor as the designer of that amazing global grace.

PART 4
CURRENT CHALLENGES
TO PEACE IN ISRAEL

SHOULD CHRISTIANS SUPPORT THE MODERN STATE OF ISRAEL?

MARK L. BAILEY

THE QUESTION ABOUT WHETHER AN EVANGELICAL Christian should support the modern state of Israel is a certainly a current issue and a debatable one, for sure. According to a poll conducted by the Pew Research Center, eighty-two percent of white evangelicals think God gave the land of Israel to the Jewish people. Less than half as many Jewish Americans or Catholic Americans agree.[1] And according to a Bloomberg poll, almost sixty percent of evangelicals say the US should support Israel even if its interests diverge with American interests.[2] A recent LifeWay research poll found that sixty-seven percent of evangelicals in the United States have a "positive perception" of Israel.[3]

Central to the discussion are the nuanced definitions of the term "support." Since neither God nor the Hebrew prophets ever condoned the sins of the covenant people, blind support for anything or everything a country or state like Israel does is certainly not what is meant by the term "support" in this essay. As examples, neither laws that would prohibit sharing of the Gospel nor hateful treatment of Jesus-followers by the orthodox Jews of Israel should be excused as acceptable. Likewise, support does not imply agreement with all political policies or actions of Israel. Not everyone, even in Israel, agrees with all government policies. What it does mean is support for their belief that the land of Israel is the land God promised them.

"Zionism" is a term that has been used of a modern Jewish movement committed to Jewish resettlement in the land of Israel. What makes Christian Zion-

---

1. Michale Lipka, "More White Evangelicals Than American Jews Say God Gave Israel to the Jewish People," Pew Research Center, October 3, 2013; accessed January 12, 2018, c.

2. Margaret Talev, "Bloomberg Politics National Poll Finds Deep Partisan Split on Israel and Iran." *Bloomberg Politics*, April 15, 2015; accessed January 12, 2018, https://www.bloomberg.com/news/articles/2015-04-15/bloomberg-politics-national-poll-finds-deep-partisan-split-on-israel-and-iran.

3. LifeWay Research, "Evangelical Attitudes toward Israel: Representative Survey of 2,002 Americans with Evangelical Beliefs," accessed February 10, 2018, http://lifewayresearch.com/wp-content/uploads/2017/12/Evangelical-Views-on-Israel.pdf.

ism Christian is the biblical basis to which those in support of Israel appeal. Both Jewish and Gentile believers in Jesus who recognize support the reestablishment of the nation of Israel, in the land of Israel, do so because they believe it is in keeping with God's promises to Abraham and his descendants long ago, and the prophetic expectation of a future in which the Jewish people as God's chosen people are entitled to possess the land of Israel in God's time and for all time. Therefore, like all nations under the providential control of God (Dan. 2:21), the modern nation of Israel in particular is a nation under God's sovereign oversight in preparation for the fulfillment of their prophetic destiny.

There are biblical reasons and practical reasons to support the modern State of Israel. Biblical bases include the covenants God made with Israel, the centrality of Christ, and the obedient pursuit of Christian values. Among the practical arguments for supporting the state of Israel are Israel's right to exist, their setting as a refuge of security and defense for the Jewish people, the incredible global contributions they have and continue to make in multiple fields of expertise, and the values they share with others in promoting freedom, protection, and democracy for its citizens.

BIBLICAL REASONS FOR SUPPORT

God's Promises to Israel—Covenant Faithfulness

God's covenant promises recorded in the Pentateuch are rooted in the Abrahamic and Mosaic (or Sinaitic), covenants. The Abrahamic Covenant contains unconditional elements, which reveal what God has bound himself to do for the nation Israel. The Mosaic Covenant reveals conditional elements, which specify the conditions upon which the Israelites as a nation and Jews as individuals may receive the benefits of the covenant.

For no other explanation than his very character, God chose to love and choose Israel to be a light to the nations, a channel of blessing in the Messiah, and a repository of the truth of divine revelation. Several passages reference Israel as the "apple of God's eye" (Deut. 32:10; Zech. 2:8). The first speaks of the immediate work of God in the origin of Israel, and the second speaks of both a historical return after the exile and a culminating future when the Lord comes to dwell on the earth. Zechariah 2:7–11 reads:

> Up! Escape to Zion, you who dwell with the daughter of Babylon. For thus said the LORD of hosts, after his glory sent me to the nations who plundered you, for he who touches you touches the apple of his eye: "Behold, I will shake my hand over them, and they shall become plunder for those who served them. Then you will know that the LORD of hosts has sent me. Sing and rejoice, O daughter of Zion, for behold, I come and I will dwell in your midst, declares the LORD. And many nations shall join themselves to the LORD in that day, and shall be my people. And I will dwell in your midst, and you shall know that the LORD of hosts has sent me to you."[4]

---

4.   All Scripture references will be taken from the English Standard Version unless otherwise noted.

Isaiah 54:10 states that this covenanted love is as secure and permanent as creation itself. "For the mountains may depart and the hills be removed, but my steadfast love shall not depart from you, and my covenant of peace shall not be removed, says the LORD, who has compassion on you." Likewise, Jeremiah 31:3 states, "I have loved you with an everlasting love; therefore I have continued my faithfulness to you." Such expectations come from almost every one of the writing prophets of Hebrew Scripture. For example, Amos proclaimed:

> "Also I will restore the captivity of My people Israel, and they will rebuild the ruined cities and live in them; they will also plant vineyards and drink their wine, and make gardens and eat their fruit. I will also plant them on their land, and they will not again be rooted out from their land which I have given them," says the Lord your God (Amos 9:14–15).

This looks beyond the postexilic return to a time when Israel will permanently possess their Promised Land. Since this has not yet occurred, the fulfillment must still be future.

That God has made unconditional and eternal covenants to the nation of Israel is foundational to a support for what God is doing with his chosen people. Because others in this volume will discuss these issues with more depth, we will limit the discussion their past and future implications. The promises of the Abrahamic covenant were directed to Abraham, Isaac, Jacob, and their descendants. It is repeated to them twenty times in Genesis.[5] Besides personal blessings for Abraham as an individual, the provisions of the Abrahamic Covenant included specific promises of the land (of Canaan), a seed, and through that seed (see Gal. 3:16) blessing would come to the rest of the world. Saving the second two for the moment, it seems inconceivable to understand Genesis 12:7; 13:14–17; 15:18–19 as anything other than the promise of a literal land to a literal people for a literal time termed forever.

Even though God promised to bless Abraham's descendants, he singled out only one branch of his family for covenant blessing. The land was promised to the descendants of Isaac, and not to the descendants of Ishmael (Gen. 17:18–21). The land was promised to the descendants of Jacob and not Esau. In Gen. 28:13–15; 35:11–12; and 48:3–4, God personally assures Jacob of his covenant and particularly in relationship to the promise of land. The covenant made with Abraham promised his descendants the land of Canaan, located "from the river of Egypt as far as the great river, the river Euphrates." (Gen. 15:18) This covenant was later restated to Isaac (Gen. 26.2–5), and then to Jacob (Gen. 28:13; 35.12). After the Exodus, God made this same covenant with Israel, as a nation:

---

5. Gen. 12:1–3, 7–9; 13:14–18; 15:1–18; 17:1–27; 22:15–19; 26:2–6, 24–25; 27:28–29, 38–40; 28:1–4, 10–22; 31:3, 11–13; 32:22–32; 35:9–15; 48:3–4, 10–20; 49:1–28; 50:23–25.

For My angel will go before you and bring you in to the land of the Amorites, the Hittites, the Perizzites, the Canaanites, the Hivites and the Jebusites; and I will completely destroy them. . . . And I will fix your boundary from the Red Sea to the sea of the Philistines, and from the wilderness to the River Euphrates; for I will deliver the inhabitants of the land into your hand, and you will drive them out before you (Exod. 23:23, 31).

Israel's right to the Land includes the promise that Israel's sin and eventual captivity did not abrogate God's land promise[6] since God's *hesed* (loyal covenant love) and his plans for Israel's future are said to be as certain as the sustained existence and function of the universe itself (Jer. 31:35–37).

The Bible makes a distinction between the fact that God has sovereignly given the land of Israel to the Jewish people as seen in the many repetitions of the Abrahamic Covenant and the conditions required for them to possess that land. Unconditional covenants provide humanity with God's sovereign decrees of what he has planned for human history, while the conditional Mosaic Covenant provides us with the means and methods he will use to get to that point of fulfillment.

The Mosaic Covenant was a conditional covenant specifying the conditions under which Israel would enjoy the blessings or curses of the covenant stipulations spelled out in Deuteronomy 28–30. God promised what would happen to Israel if they obeyed him and warned them about the prospective discipline if they failed to obey him. The specific details are given in Leviticus 26 and Deuteronomy 28. The ultimate penalty was the temporal judgment of being removed from the land of promise with the resultant exilic servitude to others (Lev. 26:33). Yet, the promise of restoration was always securely available, since God swore he would never permanently reject them: "Yet for all that, when they are in the land of their enemies, I will not spurn them, neither will I abhor them so as to destroy them utterly and break my covenant with them, for I am the LORD their God" (Lev. 26:44; see also Jer. 31:35–37; Lam. 4:22; Mic. 7:18–20). As Walter Kaiser counted, "sixty-nine times the writer of Deuteronomy repeated the pledge that Israel would one day 'possess' and 'inherit' the land promised to her."[7]

The New Covenant is rooted in the everlasting love and unconditional faithfulness of God to keep the promises he made to Abraham (Jer. 31:3). The return of the Jews will be from the north in particular and from the farthest parts of the world (Jer. 31:8). There will be a genuine repentance of Israel at some point in the future (Jer. 31:9). The God who scattered them is the One who will bring them back (Jer. 31:11–12). Jeremiah 31:17 states, "There is hope for your future, declares the LORD, and your

---

6. Lev. 26:40–45; Deut. 30:1–5; Jer. 16:15; 31:10; Isa. 43:5–7; Amos 9:14–15.

7. Walter C. Kaiser Jr., *Toward a Theology of the Old Testament* (Grand Rapids: Zondervan, 1978), 124–25.

children shall come back to their own country." One should not miss the fact that postexilic ownership of the land is assured for Israel. The promise of the New Covenant is as sure as creation itself (Jer. 31:36–37). The final promise in that great chapter speaks to the permanent restoration of Jerusalem (Jer. 31:38–40).

The Scriptures are replete with prophesies of a future for Israel. While many pre-exilic and exilic prophesies may find a measure of fulfillment in the anticipated return of the Jews from the Babylonian exile, many more anticipate a more distant and final future return that includes both a regathering of the Jews and a spiritual regeneration of the nation. God said the people of Israel would be exiled from their land due to disobedience, but he promised to bring them back a "second time" (Isa. 11:11). This mention of the regathering is the more distant view since the regathering is said to be from all over the world, and not just the Babylonian captivity. Isaiah 14:1–3 also mentions a second choice of Israel by God with a final settlement in the land in a prominent position and a permanent peace. Speaking of the final stages, Isaiah says the people will be "righteous and they will possess the land forever" (Isa. 60:21). The scene of such a restoration is earthly as can be seen by the worship references in Isaiah 66:20, as there will be no temple in heaven (Rev. 21:22). This must take place in time, and in Jerusalem, during the future earthly kingdom of the Messiah. According to Ezekiel 39:28, the regathering of Israel to the land will extend ultimately to every single person with not one single Jew left dispersed among the nations. Such a fulfillment has obviously not yet occurred and therefore must be future.

This argues well against the idea that God has given up his work with Israel and has permanently canceled the land promises of his covenant. At no time in Israel's history up to this point has the land promises been totally fulfilled. To name just one example, the Euphrates River has never yet been Israel's eastern border as promised to Abraham (cf. Gen. 15:18–21).[8] Zechariah, following the return from the Babylonian captivity, speaks of a future restoration of Israel to the land, thus suggesting that Israel's past restorations did not ultimately fulfill the land promise given to Abraham, Isaac, and Jacob (Zech. 8:4–8, 10:11–15). The restoration of Israel to the land was a constant theme of the Hebrew prophets.[9]

Some have argued that passages such as Joshua 11:23; 21:43 and 1 Kings 4:20–21 suggest the land promise has already been fulfilled. While Joshua repeatedly affirms the faithfulness of God to give Israel the land, that Israel would possess the land has yet to be fulfilled. Donald K. Campbell writes in response:

---

8. For a biblical description of the boundaries of the land anticipated during the earthly reign of the Messiah during the millennium, see Ezekiel 47:15–20.

9. Isa. 11:1–9; 12:1–3; 27:12–13; 35:1–10; 43:1–8; 60:18–21; 66: 20–22; Jer. 16:14–16; 30:10–18; 31:31–37; 32:37–40; Ezek. 11:17–21; 28:25–26; 34:11–16; 37:21–25; 39:25–29; Hos. 1:10–11; 3:4– 5; Joel 3:17–21; Amos 9:11–15; Mic. 4:4–7; Zeph. 3:14–20; Zech. 8:4–8; 10:11–15.

Some theologians have insisted that the statement in Joshua 21:43 means that the land promise of the Abrahamic Covenant was fulfilled then. But this cannot be true because later the Bible gives additional predictions about Israel possessing the land after the time of Joshua (e.g., Amos 9:14–15). Joshua 21:43, therefore, refers to the extent of the land as outlined in Numbers 34 and not to the ultimate extent as it will be in the messianic kingdom (Gen. 15:18–21). Also though Israel possessed the land at this time it was later dispossessed, whereas the Abrahamic Covenant promised Israel that she would possess the land forever (Gen. 17:8).[10]

Anticipation of a heavenly city does not mean there was not the expectation of an earthly promise for God's people. Even with the clear teaching of Jesus about the prospect of heaven, the early disciples still expected a literal restoration of the kingdom to Israel in history prior to eternity. This hope was to be a physical reality and an expectation to be experienced on earth before eternity as anticipated in Amos 9:11–13 (Acts 1:6).

Centrality of Christ—A Jewish Savior for the World

In choosing Israel, God was forming and fashioning a people through whom He would reach the world through the seed of Abraham. Revelation 19:10 states that Jesus is the spirit of prophecy. In John 4, when Jesus addresses the Samaritan woman, it is interesting that—even with the failures of Israel's leaders upon whom the woes of Jesus were pronounced of Judaism, and the hypocrisy of some of her key leaders, who will ultimately be complicit in his arrest, trials, and death—Jesus is supportive of the Jews in contrast to the Samaritans when he says, "You worship what you do not know; we worship what we know, for salvation is from the Jews" (John 4:22). When faced with a contrast between the rejecting leaders who opposed Jesus versus a spurious Middle Eastern faith based on human writings that may even be held by the Samaritans as sacred, Jesus sided with his own people Israel as a better option for truth about worship. With the obvious parallels to the present situation, why would anyone choose to side with Muslim people who adhere to Islam and the false prophet Mohammed, against the Jews and their Hebrew Scriptures? To connect to the latter, Jesus summarized all three sections of the Hebrew canon as leading toward him (Luke 24:44). Why would one not want to show support for a country where the Hebrew Scriptures are still held in honor and the opportunity to witness from multiple millennia of revealed truth? If the OT Scriptures were the Bible that could lead a person to Christ in his day, what an advantage to then finish the "second story" on top of the "first story" of the Hebrew Bible by introducing the NT and its prophetic fulfillment of what the Hebrew Scriptures promised?

---

10.   Donald K. Campbell, "Joshua," in John F. Walvoord and Roy B. Zuck, eds., *The Bible Knowledge Commentary: Old Testament* (Wheaton, IL: Victor Books, 1985), 364–65.

A commitment to Christ and the Gospel will result in a passion for Jewish evangelism. While the order of "to the Jews first and also to the Greek" in Romans 1:16 may reflect a chronological sequence as evidenced in how God has worked in history, and even how Paul functioned in his missionary ministry, it would seem that Paul's passion, as reflected in the rest of the book of Romans, may indicate that there is more—a category of God's interest that might be phrased "especially to the Jews." Such an emphasis may very well have been necessary in light of the rejection of Jesus by the majority of Jews at his first coming. Paul seems to go out of his way to assure the Roman readership that God, who had privileged Israel with so many blessings—all of which were to help them in their role as a light to the nations—has not rejected them forever, nor forgotten his promises to them. They are still very much a part of his future plan.

Paul is quite clear in his reference in Romans 9:1–5 to Israel as an ethnic people distinguished from Gentiles by his explanatory reference to "my brothers, my kinsmen according to the flesh." After rehearsing their advantages of adoption, the glorious revelation of God, the covenants, the law, the worship, *the promises* (emphasis mine), the Patriarchs, the Messiah via the incarnation is also identified as God. Paul's attitude as a postresurrection Jewish Christian is that he would risk his own salvation for that of his Jewish brethren (Rom. 9:2). They are still a people in need of salvation (Rom. 10:1). While most of those who were part of the generation of Jesus rejected him, God has not rejected them (Rom. 11:2). This is God's heart, and should be ours as well for the people of Israel. Paul then asks the great rhetorical question: "For if their rejection means the reconciliation of the world, what will their acceptance mean but life from the dead?" (Rom. 11:15). This centrality of Christ and God's plan of salvation, which includes Israel and the nations, calls upon Christians in every age to support the proclamation of the Gospel among the Jewish people anywhere and everywhere, even in Israel.

Christian Love—A Genuine Display of Impartiality

To raise the question of support for Israel seems to force a bifurcating choice between Israelis and Palestinians. If limited to the question of ultimate the rightful possession of the land, that is one issue. If the choice involves how one values and treats people of differing ethnicities or economic status, then that is another matter. The Bible speaks to the ethics of how we should treat one another (Eph. 2:11–22; Jas. 2:1–9). The biblical commandment, from Moses to Jesus, is to love others as we love ourselves and is binding across all political and geographical lines.

This principle is illustrated in the parable of the good Samaritan. In this parable, Jesus places emphasis on how one should act as a good neighbor, rather than trying to overdefine the question of "Who is my neighbor?" Christ followers should be good neighbors and encourage others—Israelis, Arabs, and all peoples—to do the same.

Gentile Christians should have a deep concern for Israel and especially for the Messianic Jewish saints living in the holy land. They are a part of the "one another" (others of the same kind) community Jesus commanded to be loved in the same way He loves (John 13:34–35). They must be included according to Galatians 6:9–10: "So then, as we have opportunity, let us do good to everyone, and especially to those who are of the household of faith." Paul even argues that help for the saints in Jerusalem in his day illustrated the principle of reciprocal blessing that included material support and not just spiritual. Paul's explanation of the ways in which Gentile Christians are indebted to their Jewish brothers and sisters who helped launch a world-wide ministry was used by the Apostle to motivate further generosity on the part of those living in Macedonia and Achaia (Rom. 15:26–27).

Ironically, there will again be a refocus on this Abrahamic fountainhead of blessing in the *eschaton* (Rom. 11:25ff. Gen. 12:3). The prophets predict Israel will be central among of nations and the Word of the Lord will extend the knowledge of the Lord to the ends of the earth, starting from Jerusalem and. Further, when Messiah returns He will reign in peace and righteousness in Jerusalem. (Isa. 2:2–4; Jer. 31:36).

PRACTICAL REASONS TO SUPPORT ISRAEL

Besides the biblical reasons a Christian should support God's agenda for Israel, there are also many practical ones as well. These would not be just limited to Christians; they can apply to the people of the world in general and the citizens of the United States in particular. Four specific reasons to mention include Israel's right to exist; their need for a setting of refuge, security, and defense; the incredible contributions they make in multiple fields of expertise enjoyed by the rest of the world; and the values they share with others promoting freedom and democracy for its citizens.

The Right of Israel to Exist

One of the most hotly debated political issues today in light of the Middle East conflict is the question of whether or not Israel has a right to exist. The drive to self-determination and independence in the formation of nations, especially in the last hundred years, is perhaps at the heart of the current conflict. Often shifting boundaries resulting from of war, whether in Europe, Africa, or the Middle East has lead to this quagmire of national formation. One of the most famous statements pertinent to this issue was declared by Menachem Begin, after assuming the premiership of Israel in 1977:

> Our right to exist—have you ever heard of such a thing? Would it enter the mind of any Briton or Frenchman, Belgian or Dutchman, Hungarian or Bulgarian, Russian or American, to request for its people recognition of its right to exist? . . . Mr. Speaker: From the Knesset of Israel, I say to the world, our very existence per se is our right to exist! [11]

---

11. "Statement to the Knesset by Prime Minister Begin upon the Presentation of His Government, June 20, 1977," Volumes 4–5:1977–1979, Israel Ministry of Foreign Affairs.

This is an argument from the principle of self-determination. Another argument can be made from historical continuity. From the time of the Romans through the Ottoman Empire, there has always been a continuous presence of Jewish people residing in what is now called Israel. The Jews were the last indigenous people to rule in Israel before being conquered by the Romans (142–63 BC). Since then six governing powers ruled in the land, but always from a home base outside the land: Roman/Byzantine (63 C–AD 636); Arabian (636–1099); Crusaders (1099–1291); Mameluke (1291–1516); Ottoman (1516–1917); and British (1917–1948). Even while dispersed outside the land, the Jews longed to return to the promised land, in order to preserve the nation and practice their faith. Long before the state of Israel became a reality, multiple movements of Jews returned to the region to take up residence, purchase land at high prices, and develop wastelands into productive farms with an intensive work ethic borne of a desire to both survive and thrive in their ancient homeland.

A third argument that can be advanced is that of international recognition. Ironically, the name Palestine was given to the land by the Roman emperor Hadrian after the second Jewish revolt under Bar-Kochba (AD 132–135). His purpose was an attempt to somehow eliminate the memory of any Jewish religious and social involvement with the land. After being passed back and forth between the Gentile powers for centuries, World War I witnessed the victory by the British and French over Germany and the Ottoman Empire along with their territories. The San Remo Conference of 1920 was an international meeting held following the conclusion of World War I that determined the precise boundaries for dividing up the territories captured by the Allies. At San Remo, the Allies confirmed the pledge contained in the 1917 Balfour Declaration concerning the establishment of a Jewish national home in Palestine.[12]

The League of Nations also recognized the importance of the Balfour Declaration and included the text in their mandatory award to Britain in 1922, and made the decision as to who would have the sovereign right to exist and occupy the region. The United General Assembly voted in 1947 to partition the land on the western side of the Jordan River into two states, one Jewish and one Palestinian. This vote led to Israel's recognition by the international community. The Arabs were given a majority portion of the land, with Britain and France retaining ultimate control. The British Mandate and the Balfour Declaration "viewed with favor the establishment in Palestine of a national home for the Jewish people, and will use their best endeavors to facilitate the achievement of this object."[13] "Whether or not the League of Nations was wrong to decide that Palestine should become a

---

12.   "Pre-State Israel: The San Remo Conference." *Jewish Virtual Library*, accessed January 22, 2018, http://www.jewishvirtuallibrary.org/the-san-remo-conference.

13.   "The Balfour Declaration," *History*.com, accessed January 23, 2018, http://www.history.com/topics/balfour-declaration.

Jewish homeland, the effect of that decision led to hundreds of thousands of Jews who came to Palestine from the creation of the Mandate in 1922 until the birth of the State of Israel in 1948 came pursuant to the international law that existed at the time."[14]

The 1967 United Nations Resolution 242 requires that all states in the area recognize Israel's "right to live in peace with secure and recognized borders free from threats or acts of force."[15] Therefore, the 1917 Balfour Declaration, the 1922 League of Nations Mandate, the 1947 UN Partition Plan, and Israel's 1949 admission into the UN all evidence Israel's right to exist in the Jewish homeland. In 2014, the 113rd US Congress passed HR 938, which classified Israel as a "major strategic partner" of the United States. This was an unusual affirmation not even extended to other nations. The bill unanimously passed the Senate and was signed into law by then-president Barack Obama on December 19, 2014.[16] The Arab countries and those who identify as Palestinians argue that the UN Security Council Resolution 242 requires that Israel evacuate all territories acquired in 1967, as they also reject the League of Nations Mandate to create a Jewish homeland in the region. However, "Lord Caradon of England, and Eugene Rostow of the U.S., two of the principal diplomats responsible for negotiating the Resolution, and most independent international legal experts, agree that Resolution 242 was not intended to, and does not, require Israel to return to the '67 borders."[17]

Historical antecedence is often the argument used to demonstrate that Palestinians have a superior rights to the territory controlled by Israel. A number of arguments can be advanced to counter this line of reasoning.

First, Jewish kingdoms existed for centuries in the territory well before any modern identities. Jerusalem has been identified as the capital for the Jewish nation for three thousand years or since the time of David. Throughout the centuries there have always been Jewish people living in the land. Second, the Arabs have millions of square miles and plenty of room to live in seventeen different countries of their choice, whereas the Jews have a small piece of real estate to live out their ideals. No one, including the Arab countries, ever thought of the land as a separate Arab country until the Jews began returning the region. Third, the Jews need a homeland they can protect for their own self-determination and security. Fourth, the Jewish ideal is not the elimination of the Arab peoples, but the ideal of the more radical arms of Islam is to see Israel "driven into the sea"—one of the most well known challenges to Israel attributed to Gamal Abdul Nasser, then-president of Egypt,

---

14.   "What the Fight in Israel Is All About," *Simple to Remember.com/Judaism Online*, accessed January 13, 2018, https://www.simpletoremember.com/articles/a/what-the-fight-in-israel-is-all-about.

15.   "The Meaning of the UN Security Council Resolution 242," *Jewish Virtual Library*, accessed January 22, 2018, http://www.jewishvirtuallibrary.org/the-meaning-of-un-security-council-resolution-242.

16.   "H.R. 938 United States-Israel Strategic Partnership Acts of 2014," accessed January 23, 2018, https://www.congress.gov/bill/113th-congress/house-bill/938.

17.   "What the Fight in Israel Is All About."

who denied making the statement. Yet, this sentiment characterized many of the leaders who were part of various Arab coalitions at the time.[18]

Fifth, a fact often overlooked, hundreds of thousands of Jews dispersed throughout the Arab world were forced from their homes and had their property confiscated because of the conflicts in the land of Israel. Sixth, and still a consternation, is the fact that countries with a population ten times that of Israel repeatedly refuse to accept any Arab refugees from Israel, even though they speak the same language, share the same culture, and practice the religion of Islam.

Finally, it is compelling to realize that Jerusalem, though viewed as the third most holy site after Mecca and Medina, was never thought to be the capital of the Islamic religion. In contrast, the Jewish people historically understood Jerusalem, based upon the Hebrew Scriptures to be the past, present, and future capital of the holy land (Isaiah 2:1–3).

Israel as a Place of Haven and Refuge for the Jewish People

From the north, Israel faces the threat of Hezbollah and from the south, terrorism is spawned and sourced in Hamas. From the other side of both the river and the country of Jordan is the continued hatred and nuclear threat of Iran. Outside the region antisemitism abounds. According to the FBI, the Jewish community in the United States are annually subjected to the most hate crimes of any religious group. During the last decade in Europe, the Jewish people were the target of fifty-one percent of racist attacks in France in 2014, for example.[19]

Well over a century ago in 1896, Theodor Herzl, considered the father of Zionism, envisioned the founding of a future independent Jewish state. He argued that a Jewish homeland would be the best way to be safe from the threats of antisemitism in Europe.

Politically, from the Jewish perspective, an argument for support for Israel in the land of Israel is warranted to create a place where Jews can live without being persecuted or treated like scapegoats as they have been throughout history. Many Arab leaders have continually called for the eradication of Israel, resulting in a perpetual existential fear on the part of Israel for their own security. History has shown that any proposed solution, even a two-state solution in the region, seems to be doomed because of the Arab opposition to the idea of an independent sovereign Jewish state. Most Arabs have refused to recognize the international mandates and plans for the region since to do so would require recognizing Israel as a legitimate entity. To this

---

18.   Elder of Ziyon, "Did Arab States Really Promise to Push Israel into the Seas? Yes!" accessed February 11, 2018, *The Algemeiner*, https://www.algemeiner.com/2014/02/20/did-arab-states-really-promise-to-push-jews-into-the-sea-yes.

19.   Yar Rosenberg, "Five Myths about Antisemitism." *The Washington Post* February 3, 2017; accessed February 8, 2018, https://www.washingtonpost.com/opinions/five-myths-about-anti-semitism/2017/02/03/a8de59e2-e884-11e6-b82f-687d6e6a3e7c_story.html?utm_term=.6e4037663824.

very day, groups like Hamas, who control Gaza, do not recognize the legiti-macy of Israel's claim to the land.

The hope of the land is foundational to the Jewish religion as expressed in the daily prayers of the Jewish people and the liturgy of the synagogue. The longing for the land helps to preserve Jewish history, it unites the children of Israel in dispersion, and is foundational to having a safe place to rediscover, preserve, and practice the Jewish faith. So much of the religious practice of the Jewish faith is tied to the land. The location of Jerusalem is important as the site of the central sanctuary and the only place of legitimate sacrifice, should there ever be a temple rebuilt. This hope is imbedded in the fabric of Jewish identity and practice. The conclusion of the Zionist pamphlet, *The Jewish State*, expressing the dreams of Theodor Herzl seem appropriate to quote here as a conclusion to this section and an introduction to the next:

> Let me repeat my opening words again: The Jews who wish, will have their state. We shall live at last as free men on our own soil, and die peacefully in our own home-land. The world will be freed by our liberty, enriched by our wealth, magnified by our greatness. And whatever we attempt to accomplish there for our own welfare will have a powerful and beneficial effect for all people.[20]

Israel's Blessing to the World

In a relatively short time, Israel has become a world leader in so many ways and is, without a doubt, a global epicenter of invention and innova-tion. "Tel Aviv is also the home of 'Silicon Wadi,' the second largest startup ecosystem in the world. It has more startups per capita than any other region, and is home to 95 companies on the NASDAQ, which is more [than sic] Europe, China, Japan, and Korea combined."[21] The following factors have been assembled from a variety of sources. [22]

Israeli entrepreneurs have invented numerous technologies considered crucial to modern society, such as cell phones, the Intel chip, the flash drive, the Waze app, and modern drip irrigation.

Voice over Internet protocol (VoIP) technology was pioneered in Israel,

---

20. Theodor Herzl, *The Jewish State*, accessed February 5, 2018, http://www.zionism israel.com/js/Jew-ish_State_tc.html.

21. Jake Gould, "Why Americans Should Support Israel," *United with Israel*, October 2, 2017; accessed January 23, 2018, https://unitedwithisrael.org/why-americans-should-support-israel.

22. The listed contributions have been culled from a variety of articles and websites, including Jim Eck-man, "Israel: "A Channel of God's Blessing," in Grace University's *Issues in Perspective* (June 1, 2003):1; "Cool Facts about Israel." *Greater Miami Jewish Organization*, accessed January 23, 2018, http://jew-ishmiami.org/about/departments/missions/coolfacts.pdf; Jake Gould, "Why Americans Should Sup-port Israel," *United with Israel*, October 2, 2017; accessed January 23, 2018, https://unitedwithisrael.org/why-americans-should-support-israel; David Brooks, "The Tel Aviv Cluster," *The New York Times*, January 12, 2010, A:23; "Israel's Contribution to the World." *The Herald*, September-October 2015; accessed January 24, 2018, herald-magazine.com/2015/09/01/israels-contributions-to-the-world-potential-for-blessing; "18 Ways Israel is Changing the World." *Israel 21c.*, accessed January 20, 2018, https://www.israel21c.org/exhibition/18-ways-israel-is-changing-the-world.

and Intel's double-core processor was completely developed at its design facility in Israel. The cell phone was developed in Israel by Motorola, which has its largest development center in Israel. Most of the Windows NT operating system were developed by Microsoft-Israel. The technology for AOL Instant Messenger (ICQ) was developed in 1996 by four young Israelis. The first PC anti-virus software was developed in Israel in 1979. Israeli engineers are behind the development of the largest communications router in the world, launched by Cisco. Israel has designed and manufactured the first flight system to protect passenger and freighter aircraft against missile attack.

Israel has also set high marks for its medical innovations. An Israeli company has designed a blood test that can diagnose heart attacks over the telephone. They are testing stem-cell technology to regenerate heart tissue. Given Imaging is a company which invented a ingestible video camera small enough to fit inside a pill, so that doctors are able to view the small intestine from the inside; the micro camera allows doctors to diagnose cancer and other digestive disease. An Israeli company has developed a self-injecting system so patients can administer insulin themselves; another company is the world's leading sleep-disorder sensors manufacturer. Israeli technology also designed the device that helps nurses locate hard-to-find veins.

As far as education is concerned Israel, has the highest per capita ratio of university degrees in the world. Israel produces more scientific papers per capita than any other nation by a large margin, as well as one of the highest per-capita rates of patents filed. Businesswise, in proportion to its population, Israel is second only to the US in the total number of startup companies (3,500, mostly in high-tech). Israel has the third largest number of companies trading on Wall Street, after the US and Canada, and attracts as much venture capital as France and Germany combined.

Israeli humanitarian efforts have been among the most noteworthy. Over the last twenty-six years, Israel has sent out fifteen emergency aid teams to give help to countries struck by natural disasters. Over the years of its existence, Israel has extended international humanitarian aid and assistance to more than 140 countries. In 1984 and 1991, Israel safely airlifted a total of 22,000 Ethiopian Jews in Ethiopia to Israel. Efforts include relief to New Orleans after Hurricane Katrina, rapid response teams and aid in for the 2004 tsunami in Indonesia, and eighty-two tons of relief to Sri Lanka alone. A one-hundred-member Israeli delegation flew to Kenya in 2006 to rescue survivors of a building collapse. Israel's team of more than two hundred relief agents took the lead after the earthquake of January 2010 in Haiti. Israel was also one the first to send aid at request of the Japanese government in their typhoon disaster of 2017.

As to some other sample achievements, Israel makes up 0.2 percent of the world population, and yet has produced fifty-four percent of the world chess champions; twenty-seven percent of Nobel physics laureates and thirty-one percent of the medicine laureates; twenty-one percent of Ivy League student bodies; twenty-six percent of Kennedy Center honorees; thirty-seven percent of Academy Award-winning directors; thirty-eight percent of those on a recent *Business Week* list of leading philanthropists; and fifty-one percent of the Pulitzer Prize winners for nonfiction. Between 1980 and 2000, Egyptians registered seventy-seven patents in the US; Saudis registered 171. Israelis registered 7,652. One could go on and on about the rapid advances in the life sciences, cost-efficient yet quality healthcare, global pioneering pharmaceuticals, unique designs in biotechnology with an array of prosthetic devices helping remobilize the diseased and disabled to functionality and productivity. The modern State of Israel places a high value on education, teamwork, and creative solutions to the problems of the world.

Global support from non-Israelis, especially from Christians, helps the Jewish nation flourish and enjoy God's blessing leading to her being a blessing to the world. Humanitarian support for Israel is also needed, as the defense budget swallows up so much of the national budget. Christian support and friendship toward Israel is helping to change the negative impression Jewish people have about Christianity. There is no doubt that Israelis do see evangelicals as their friends, and this change in the historic relationship between Jews and Christians opens the doors to many discussions, not the least of which is the "why" of the Gospel of Jesus the Messiah.

Israel's Shared Values with Other Democracies in the World

In many ways Israel is a unique expression of democracy in the Middle East. It allows significant freedoms and a pluralism of political and religious expression unlike many, if not all, of the surrounding countries. The concepts of democracy, the rule of law, freedom of religion, speech, and human rights are core values shared by the United States and a limited number of other countries. As a document penned by AIPAC comments:

> Both nations were founded by refugees seeking political and religious freedom. Both were forced to fight for independence against foreign powers. Both have absorbed waves of immigrants seeking political freedom and economic well-being. And, both have evolved into democracies that respect the rule of law, the will of voters and the rights of minorities.[23]

As a political ally, the United States has had a long-standing connection with Israel. In response, Israel has maintained position as a strong US ally. For both economic and military purposes, the US-Israel partnership has been important. Both the United States and other countries benefit from Israel by improving relations with the Middle East.[24]

---

23. "Shared Values," *AIPAC: America's Pro-Israel Lobby*, accessed January 28, 2018 https://www.aipac.org/learn/us-and-israel/shared-values.

24. Jamie Ganet, "Six Reasons Why Everyone Should Support Israel," *Philos Project,* June 22, 2016; accessed February 5, 2018, https://kehilanews.com/2016/06/23/six-reasons-why-everyone-should-support-israel.

Throughout its existence it has sought to create a safe and protected environment that extends not just to the Jews but to all its citizens. The opportunity to live and flourish in Israel is not limited to Israel's Jewish majority population, but extends to Palestinians and other immigrants in the country. Arabs in Israel serve in many professional fields such as business, medicine, judgeships, city mayors, agriculture, and especially tourism. They are also represented in the coalition government of the Israeli Knesset. This government by the people and for the people can support the modern nation of Israel.

CONCLUSION

There are a number of inadequate reasons why a Christian should support Israel. First, it should not be because of an eschatological desire to see the battle of Armageddon come soon. Knowing the judgments to come, our heart should be set on reaching and discipling the nations. Second, it should not be primarily for the selfish benefits of American prosperity. While God promised to bless those who bless Israel (Gen. 12:3), the material blessings may be a byproduct, but should never be a primary motive. A third illegitimate reason is an unbiblical bias against the Arab people. If one is not careful, one will look through the colored lens of politics and end up despising either the Arabs or the Jews, or both. A proper gaze through a biblical lens will engender a genuine love for Palestinians, Arabs, Israelis, and Jews alike as people created in the image of God, the object of his love, and all viable candidates to receive the love of Christ through our proclamation of the Gospel message.

THE LEGAL ISSUES AT THE NEXUS OF THE CONFLICT

CRAIG PARSHALL

September 30, 2017

IT WAS MAY 1948. The profound question facing the member nations of the United Nations was the existence of the state of Israel. The Arab League nations vehemently opposed it and emotions were running high. In the White House, President Harry Truman was committed to the idea of Israel's statehood, a position backed by political precedent. After all the precursor to the UN had previously recognized a Jewish homeland in "Palestine," and following that, a joint resolution was passed in both houses of the United States Congress that expressed the same sentiment.[1]

But Truman's Secretary of State had a very different idea. George Marshall favored a United Nations "trusteeship" to be imposed over the territory of present-day Israel, and tasked his State Department to pursue it within the UN.[2]

Enter Philip Jessup, a former American professor of international law and the US Ambassador to the United Nations. As Jessup hustled toward the podium in the UN's General Assembly, he held a message in his hand. Ruth Gruber, a *New York Times* reporter present at the time describes the scene this way:

> I knew, after talking to his aides, that in [Jessup's] hand he had a speech supporting trusteeship, not statehood, for Israel. The State Department was about to betray the president.[3]

---

1. The March 2017 proceedings of the US Senate and House Concurrent Resolution No. 1014 confirm that "the legal basis for the establishment of the modern state of Israel was a binding resolution under international law, which was unanimously adopted by the League of Nations in 1922 and subsequently affirmed by both houses of the United States Congress." https://www.congress.gov/congressional-record/2017/3/23/senate-section/article/S1972-1.

2. Ruth Gruber, "The Birth of a Nation, 1948," *The New York Times*, May 18, 2008, https://mobile,nytimes.com/2008/05/18/opinion/18gruber.html.

3. Ibid.

But Jessup never made it to the podium, nor did Secretary Marshall's message. Jessup was greeted with an Associated Press dispatch reporting that President Harry Truman had just beaten the State Department to the punch, publicly declaring that the United States of America formally recognized the State of Israel.[4] Eventually, the UN would follow suit.

But that is where the story takes a turn. In the subsequent decades, criticism of Israel has grown to a fever pitch. It is now routine for the UN and others to allege international law violations against Israel. In November 2016, for instance, UN committees adopted ten different resolutions against Israel in a single day.[5]

Of course, international law can play a role as a basis to collectively contain lawless nations like Iran or North Korea, or to minimize the collateral damage from failed states like Afghanistan. But the broad, unwieldy nature of international law makes it a blunt axe, best reserved for use against outlaw regimes, rather than nations like Israel that display a history of self-governance under the rule of law. Additionally, international law is largely unenforceable unless the nations at issue have either previously agreed to make it binding, or the day ever arrives when global law is actually mandated.[6] But that doesn't stop allegations against Israel from being used strategically, applying geopolitical pressure on the tiny country.

Current international law threats against Israel invariably relate to the Palestinian people or the Palestinian Authority. For example, a 2016 UN Security Council resolution, where the US abstained rather than vetoed, repeated an old refrain that Israel was in "flagrant violation of International law" by allowing Jewish settlements in the "West Bank" area of Israel ever since its victory in 1967 during the Six-Day War.[7] Yet, Israel's military decimation of the impending invasion from its Arab neighbors had been in self-defense. Keeping control of the sector to the west of the Jordan River that it gained in that war, including Jerusalem, was equally necessary for Israel's security. UN resolutions like this illustrate how the use of the broad axe of international law can swing past the facts, particularly those that are politically incorrect.

I agree with the assessment of fellow lawyer Robert Nicholson, who describes the international law charges against Israel as "notoriously ambiguous."[8] The UN's West Bank resolution not only ignored the fact that

---

4. Ibid.

5. "UN Committees Adopt 10 Resolutions against Israel in a Single Day," *The Times of Israel*, November 9, 2016, https://www.timesofisrael.com/un-committees-begin-voting-on-10-resolutions-against-israel-in-a-single-day.

6. International law has historically been "voluntaristic" in nature. See Henry J. Steiner and Philip Alston, *International Human Rights in Context—Law, Politics, Morals* (Oxford: Oxford University Press, 1996) 150–151. The dire alternative to that is discussed at the end of this chapter.

7. "Israel's Settlements Have No Legal Validity, Constitute Flagrant Violation of International Law, Security Council Reaffirms," UN Meetings Coverage and Press Releases, December 23, 2016, https://www.un.org/press/en/2016/sc12657.doc.htm.

8. Robert Nicholson, "Theology and the Law," in *The New Christian Zionism: Fresh Perspectives on Israel & the Land*, ed. Gerald R. McDermott (Downers Grove, IL: InterVarsity Press, 2016), 260.

Israel defended itself against "existential threats from the surrounding Arab states," it was also based on shaky international law grounds: the West Bank could reasonably qualify as a "disputed" rather than an "occupied" territory where different legal rules apply, and even if deemed "occupied," Israel's control over it still comports with international law standards.[9]

Michael Oren, former Israeli ambassador to the United States and currently a member of the Knesset and Deputy Minister in the prime minister's office, crystalizes the issue: "[T]he Israeli-Palestinian conflict has never been about territory Israel captured in 1967. It is about whether a Jewish state has the right to exist in the Middle East at all."[10]

Israel's right to exist is the relevant international law question. For if it is a legitimate state, then it should be accorded the same respect for its sovereign decisions and actions as any other nation on the earth.

To address that issue, I suggest the exact international law standard advanced in 1948 by the United States and uniformly accepted by other nations of good will. Unlike much of international law, that standard remains relatively clear, comprised of only four conditions that needed to be met in order to validate Israel's claim for statehood.

Among the statements describing the four traditional requirements under international law for the existence of "statehood," none was more concise or timely than the declaration made by the United States representative to the United Nations Security Council, Philip C. Jessup. He delivered it in December of 1948, eight months after the US State Department abandoned its "trusteeship" idea in the wake of President Truman's public recognition of Israel's right to exist. This time Jessup made it to the podium, though his address wasn't one of vague geopolitics or diplomatic compromise. Instead, it was a statement of the four basic international law principals for statehood, and a declaration that Israel satisfied all four of them:

> We are all aware that, under the traditional definition of a State in international law, all of the great writers have pointed to four qualifications: first, there must be a people; second, there must be a territory; third, there must be a government; and, fourth, there must be a capacity to enter into relations with other states of the world.[11]

Referring to those standards of international law that are implied in the United Nations Charter, Jessup concluded:

> My government considers that the State of Israel meets these Charter requirements.[12]

---

9.   Ibid., 265, 268–279.

10. "One Hundred Thirty-Two Hours & Fifty Years: A Conversation with Michael Oren," *Providence*, no. 7 (Spring 2017): 7, 13.

11. 3 U.N. SCOR, 383 Mtg., Dec. 2, 1948, No. 128, 9–12.

12. Ibid.

During debate, Jessup mentioned the near universal acceptance among the state members that three out of the four international law conditions for Israel's statehood were clearly met, with the remaining dispute limited to the Arab nations' complaints about Israel's "territory."

Sadly, in the years since then, many of the accusations against Israel have exceeded rational bounds.[13] If objectivity is to prevail, and if international law is to be the measure, then what better standard to use than the same test that was applied to Israel's status in 1948?[14]

As we are about to see, all four of the established international law elements for statehood and the right to exist as a sovereign nation were not only satisfied by Israel in 1948, they continue to be met by Israel today. We examine each of those four elements below.

A PEOPLE

For purposes of statehood, international law requires that a nation must possess a "permanent population." Such an identifiable group can exist even if numbers of nomads among them travel in and out of its territory.[15] Thus, even though Israel openly accommodates nomadic Arab Bedouins within its borders, that doesn't lessen the legitimacy of its status as a national state.

History shows that for millennia there has been a Jewish presence in Eretz Israel—the term for the widest borders of biblical Israel.[16] Of course, during the Old Testament period, the Jews incurred occupation under the Assyrians and the Babylonians, and later under the Roman Empire in the New Testament epoch and by other national occupiers for centuries beyond. Regardless, under established international law, occupation by a foreign power does not prevent them from qualifying as a "people" worthy of recognition as a nation.[17]

Before examining more about the Jewish "people," a word must be said about the "Palestinian people." It is helpful to contrast the ancient, historical claim of the Jews as a people group, from the relatively recent nomenclature about the "Palestinians." Israel is filled with wonderful Palestinians, both Christian and Muslim alike, and I have had the pleasure of fellowshipping with many of them. The problem arises however, when international law becomes a mere weapon of pressure politics. Factually, the identity of the Palestinians as an Arab subgroup is of recent vintage, and its claim to the land on the "western bank" of the Jordan River is historically suspect. The

---

13. As only one example, the publication *Middle East Eye* has even gone so far as to equate Zionism with white supremacy; http://www.middleeasteye.net/columns/birds-feather-1463289527.

14. Those four international law conditions for statehood continue to be recognized. They were applied in 1991 by the Arbitration Commission established by the Peace Conference on Yugoslavia in dealing with the breakup of the Socialist Federal Republic of Yugoslavia.

15. Restatement of the Law of the Foreign Relations of the United States (Third), § 201, Comment *c*.

16. *Collins English Dictionary*, "Eretz Yisrael," or "Eretz Israel."

17. Restatement, § 201, Comment *b*.

existence of the Jewish people, on the other hand, runs through history like a river, and the evidence supporting their claim to biblical Israel is impressive. The name Palestine comes from "Philistia," which means "land of the Philistines," and originally corresponded to a small geographical area where the ancient Philistines dwelled.[18]

Yossef Bodansky, a former senior consultant to the US departments of state and defense, summarizes the lack of historical basis for the claim of a Palestinian land in Israel:

> One of the ironies in the Arab-Israeli dispute over "Palestine" is the oft-neglected fact that there is no Palestine in the Muslim or Arab tradition. Neither *Filastin* (Palestine) nor *al-Quds* (Jerusalem) is mentioned in the Koran. During more than a millennium when Muslims (both Arabs and Ottoman Turks) ruled the Middle East—from about 633 to 1917, with the exception of the century of the Crusaders' reign (1099 to 1187)—there was never a separate entity encompassing the general area of today's Israel/Palestine.[19]

The rise of a Palestinian movement didn't occur until 1974, when the Arab League met in Morocco and passed a resolution recognizing a Palestinian right to "self-determination," which was followed that same year by UN Resolution 3236, recognizing the existence of the Palestinian people.[20]

By contrast, extensive historical evidence points to the long national history of the Jewish people migrating to, and then living within Eretz Israel.

The identity of the Jews as a "people" begins with Abraham, who followed God's command and migrated from the land of Ur to Canaan, in Eretz-Israel, where Abraham's "favorite" residence became Hebron, approximately nineteen miles south of Jerusalem.[21] Remarkably, because Hebron is a heavily populated by Palestinians now, UNESCO's World Heritage Committee has deemed it to be not a Jewish historical site but a "Palestinian world heritage site," even though the tombs of the Old Testament Jewish patriarchs and matriarchs—Abraham, Isaac, Jacob, Sarah, Rebecca ,and Leah—are all located there.[22] History more than four millennia must now apparently yield to politics only decades old.

The biblical account of Abraham reaching the land of Canaan and initially settling in the hill country, and avoiding the dangerous Canaanite for-

---

18. Leon J. Wood, *A Survey of Israel's History*, revised, David O'Brien (Grand Rapids: Zondervan Publishing House, 1986), 8.

19. Yossef Bodansky, *The High Cost of Peace: How Washington's Middle East Policy left America Vulnerable to Terrorism* (New York: Prima Publishing, 2002), 2.

20. David Brog, *Reclaiming Israel's History* (Washington, DC: Regnery Publishing, 2017), 154–155.

21. *The Zondervan Pictorial Encyclopedia of the Bible*, Vol. I, ed. Merrill C. Tenney (Grand Rapids: Zondervan Publishing House, 1976), 20–21.

22. "UNESCO Decision on Hebron Holy Site Angers Israel Officials," *CBS News*, July 7, 2017, https://www.google.com/amp/s/www.cbsnews.com/amp/news/unesco-decision-hebron-holy-site-angers-israel-officials.

tified cities of the plains authenticates its reliability. Oxford historian Ian Wilson concludes that regarding "the credibility of this information there can be no doubt," noting the twenty-five thousand cuneiform tablets from 1800 BC that prove the existence and location of the Canaanites who, the Bible indicates, were "in the land at the time."[23]

Scholarly studies in ancient languages also point to the authenticity of the declaration in Exodus 1:1 regarding "the sons of Israel," including Jacob, traversing to Egypt. This reference to Jacob, Abraham's grandson, as one of the "sons of Israel" is significant linguistically. Use of "the sons of " phrase signified people groups who functioned as nations. That phrase is utilized some 613 times in the Old Testament, identifying the "sons of Israel" as both a people and a nation, and paralleling similar phrases used by their contemporaries, the Canaanites, as well as by the inhabitants of an ancient city-state in Syria, who called themselves the "sons of Ebla."[24]

Then there is that well known, second seminal event in the history of the Jewish people, the Exodus from Egypt. Intriguing historical evidence corroborates the Exodus story: an ancient text from the Egyptian sage Ipuwer during the Middle Kingdom period describes plagues very similar to the Biblical account; the evidence of "a sudden evacuation of a Semitic slave population" in a region of Egypt; and an account from an Egyptian writer at the relevant time period admitting how "a powerful god acted in Egypt's history and delivered a deadly blow."[25] As for the conquest of the land of Canaan in the books of Joshua and Judges and the massive destruction of those cities by the invading Israelites, even a jaded expert archaeologist in Israel had to admit that digs have revealed that "destruction, amazing destruction" occurred to that Canaanite civilization during that general period.[26] Renowned archaeologist Yohannan Aharoni notes evidence of Israelite settlements appearing in Eretz-Israel during the "Late Canaanite Period, roughly around 1200 BC."[27]

A third epoch of ancient Jewish nationalism is apparent during the reigns of King David, and his son, Solomon. Not surprisingly, skeptics have assailed the historicity of those facts, even doubting whether David was an existing monarch at all. But they are on the losing side of history. As Hershel Shanks, editor of *Biblical Archaeology Review*, has stated: "Archaeologists have now found an inscription that actually refers to David's dynasty. So that's settled."[28] Discoveries continue to pour in. In 2005 immense stone

---

23. Ian Wilson, *The Bible Is History* (Washington, DC: Regnery Publishing, Inc., 1999), 25–26.

24. Giovanni Petinato, *The Archives of Ebla* (Garden City: Doubleday & Company, Inc., 1981), 281.

25. Timothy P. Mahoney, Steven Law, *Patterns of Evidence: Exodus, a Filmmaker's Journey* (St. Louis Park: Thinking Man Media, 2015), 227.

26. Ibid. 231.

27. Anson F. Rainey, *The Archaeology of the Land of Israel*, trans. Yohanan Aharoni (Philadelphia: Westminster Press, 1978), 153.

28. "Jesus of History versus Jesus of Tradition: BAR Interviews Sean Freyne," *Jesus & Archaeology*, Biblical Archaeological Review, special issue (Easter 2016), 104.

structures south of the Temple Mount in Jerusalem were excavated, exactly in the spot where the Bible locates the palace of King David.[29]

All this illustrates the vast historical support for the existence of a Jews as a "people," and their deep ties to the land of Israel, an issue we explore next.

A TERRITORY

The story of the Jewish people is a tale inexorably tied to precise geography, whether it is called The Promised Land, Eretz Israel, or the Holy Land. The Bible describes the boundaries of the land that God promised "on oath to Abraham, Isaac, and Jacob," and Abraham's "descendants," as Moses viewed it from the mountaintop (Deut. 34:1–4). The land described there not only included all of current Israel from the Jordan River west to the sea, but part of present-day Jordan (Moab) as well.

In 1948, Ambassador Phillip Jessup was clear that of the four legal qualifications for Israel's statehood, one was virtually unanimous among the UN members, two others were uncontested, and the real sticking point was the precise "territory" that belonged to Israel.[30] How interesting that Israel's critics have continued to object to this day over Israel's right to exercise national sovereignty over its land grant from God.

Disputes about Israel's exercise of dominion over the so-called "West Bank" are continual. Even as Israeli Prime Minister Benjamin Netanyahu was preparing in 2017 to celebrate the fiftieth anniversary of Israel's victory in the Six-Day War, a conflict that began and quickly ended in a single week in 1967, harsh voices of criticism were raised. Antonio Guterres, Secretary General of the United Nations, took the occasion to denounce as "occupation" Israeli housings in the West Bank and Jerusalem, arguing that such actions fuel "recurring cycles of violence and retribution" with Palestinians.[31]

In response, Israel's ambassador to the UN Danny Danon pointed out the illogic of the position of the UN's chief: "The attacks on Israel by our neighbors did not begin in 1967 and any attempt at a moral equivalency between [Palestinians] killing innocent people and the building [by Israelis] of homes is absurd."[32]

Moral logic dictates that land disputes over boundaries and territorial control, the gist of UN head Guterres' comments, must bow to the legitimate right of a nation like Israel to defend itself against terror attacks, the point made by Ambassador Danon.

Regardless, international law does not demand precise, undisputed boundaries for a nation to exercise its rights as a sovereign state. That point

---

29. Dore Gold, *The Fight for Jerusalem* (Washington: Regnery Publishing, Inc., 2007), 39.

30. 3 U.N. SCOR, 383 Mtg., Dec. 2, 1948, No. 128, 9–12.

31. Danille Ziri, "UN Chief Denounces '50 Years of Israeli Occupation' on Six Day War Anniversary," *Jerusalem Post*, June 5, 2017, http://m.jpost.com/Arab-Israeli-Conflict/UN-chief-denounces-50-years-of-Israeli-occupation-on-Six-Day-War-anniversary-494924.

32. Ibid.

was made to the UN in December 1948 when US Ambassador Jessup noted how America's early nationhood was never questioned after its War of
Independence, even though there were lingering questions about its exact
borders, including its "indeterminate claims" to the western territories as
against the claims of France, England, and Spain, while in "the North, the
exact delimitation of the frontier with the territories of Great Britain was not
settled until many years later."[33]

In the case of Israel, it is fascinating to look at maps drawn from scholars
who have studied the land controlled by biblical Israel during various periods
in the Old Testament. Whether it is the geographical sectors won from the
Canaanites during the Conquest period, or the territory controlled during the
time of King Saul, or the expansive Israelite landmass that comprised the kingdom under David and Solomon that stretched into present-day Jordan and
to the north past Damascus, or the divided kingdom or Josiah's kingdom, the
maps show an intriguing fact: with only minor variations, biblical Israel during
these periods covered at least the geography of present-day Israel.[34]

While we can easily recognize how God's law transmitted to the Jewish people in the Old Testament had a *moral* dimension, it is less obvious
how God's commands to the people of Israel were also *territorial*. If God's
people observed God's moral law, God has promised to bless them *internally*
within the Promised Land, both "in the city" and "in the country" (Deut.
28:3). Likewise, *externally* (which would also mean, internationally) God has
promised also to bless Israel "high above all the nations of the earth" (Deut.
28:1). We should not miss the territorial distinction between these two kinds
of blessings, separately stated in Scriptures, one internally within Israel's borders, and the other externally among the other nations. If God takes national
boundaries seriously, so should we.

In God's word, the Jewish people are not just a migratory race, a mere
thread in the vast tapestry of the global community. Just the opposite: They
are a people anchored to a God-granted homeland. The necessary corollary
is that their homeland is a distinct nation-state entity that, by virtue of its
providential identification with the Jewish people and its historical boundaries, must be viewed legally and territorially as separate from the rest of "all
the nations of the earth."

In addition, the legal case for the right of the nation of Israel to exist and
to pursue its own national interests is also buttressed by its fidelity to the rule
of law and government, which we examine next.

A GOVERNMENT

The requirement of a functioning government as a prerequisite for a nation's "statehood" under settled international law does not mandate that such

---

33.   3 U.N. SCOR, 383 Mtg., Dec. 2, 1948, No. 128, 9–12.

34.   *Dictionary of Old Testament Historical Books*, eds. Bill T. Arnold and H. G. M. Williamson (Down-
      ers Grove, IL: InterVarsity Press, 2005), 319–326.

a government function perfectly, or even fairly, although the stated goal of the UN is to encourage and persuade nations to aspire to, and practice, universal norms regarding human rights. For instance, in 1981 the UN issued a declaration setting out those basic human rights, which all nation-states are encouraged to recognize and protect. Its Declaration on the Elimination of all Forms of Intolerance and of Discrimination Based on Religion or Belief requires, among other things, the "right to freedom of thought conscience and religion," and proclaims opposition to any "coercion" against any person "which would impair his freedom to have a religion or belief of his choice."[35]

Regrettably, most of us can rattle off the names of countries, many of them neighbors of Israel, which are members of the UN and yet openly violate with impunity those fundamental rights of their citizens and of others.

Israel, on the other hand, has a long history of protecting freedom and liberty. Its courts regularly render decisions designed to enforce human rights standards rather than to satisfy political ends. As I wrote this chapter, Israel's high court issued an order temporarily halting the enforcement of an Israeli law that would have favored Israeli settlors who had built homes on the private lands of Palestinians.[36] Such a "pro-Palestinian" decision by an Israeli court is a hallmark of a nation with a respect for the rule of law, regardless of the political outcome.

Israel's respect for fundamental human rights is so well known that even a Saudi Arabian journalist has praised it, writing that the high standard of "justice" in Israel is the "secret of the Zionist entity's advantage over his neighbors," where "injustice" is too often the norm.[37]

Respect for the rule of law within the court system in Israel and which flows all the way to its Supreme Court, is on a par with the American judiciary. Though Israel has no written constitution, its "Basic Law" provides the foundation for the protection of fundamental liberties. As the US State Department has noted: "The Supreme Court [of Israel] has repeatedly held that the Basic Law on Human Dignity and Liberty protects freedom to practice religious beliefs, and its rulings incorporate the religious freedom provisions of international human rights agreements into the country's body of law. The Basic Law describes the country as a 'Jewish and democratic state' and cites the Declaration of the Establishment of the State of Israel, which promises freedom of religion and conscience and full social and political equality, regardless of religious affiliation."[38]

35. U.N. G.A. 55 (XXXVI) (1981), 21 I.L.M. 205 (1982), Article 1, sections 1, 2, adopted by the UN Assembly, November 25, 1981.

36. Tovah Lazaroff and Yonah Jeremy Bob, "Court Freezes Law that Retroactively Legalized Unauthorized Settler Homes," *Jerusalem Post*, August 17, 2017, http://www.jpost.com/Israel-News/Politics-And-Diplomacy/High-Court-freezes-law-confiscating-private-Palestinian-property-502679.

37. Rebecca Montag, "Saudi Columnist Praises Israeli Justice System," *Jerusalem Post.com*, August 8, 2017, http://m.jpost.com/Arab-Israeli-Conflict/Saudi-columnist-praises-Israeli-justice-system-501878.

38. US Department of State, "2012 Report on International Religious Freedom: Israel and the Occupied Territories," May 20, 2013, https://www.state.gov/j/drl/rls/irf/2012/nea/208392.htm.

Media reports of violence between Israeli security forces and Palestinian insurgents or Hamas terrorists often place the moral responsibility on Israel. The sad reality is that terror attacks are a fact of life in Israel. As the US State Department noted in its 2016 report on Israel's human rights record: "[A] ccording to the Ministry of Foreign Affairs, Palestinians committed 12 terror attacks within the Green Line that led to the deaths of seven Israelis and one foreign citizen, as well as injuries to 62 Israelis. According to the Ministry of Foreign Affairs, Palestinian militants fired 46 projectiles into Israel, and there were 21 incidents of mortar fire or cross-border shooting from Syria."[39] Tragically, 2017 saw several Israeli police murdered by Palestinians.

Despite this, the U.S. State Department describes how Israel continues to grant Palestinians access to the Israeli court system for legal redress and relief: "By law, Palestinians may file suit to obtain compensation through civil suits in some cases, even when a criminal suit is unsuccessful and the actions against them considered legal."[40]

Israel's record for protecting civil rights may be the reason why oppressed persons seek sanctuary there. When Iranian journalist Nada Amin, who was stationed in Turkey, was about to be deported back to Iran where she would almost certainly face the death penalty for her writings critical of the regime, she sought asylum in Israel, where she was welcomed with open arms.[41]

In June of 2017 I witnessed firsthand Israel's regard for civic inclusion when my wife Janet and I visited a session of the Knesset in Jerusalem— Israel's legislative congress. At the time, a member of the Knesset at the podium was arguing passionately for added police protection in his city. What struck me as remarkable was the fact that this Israeli citizen who was addressing the 120-seat Knesset that day was not only a full, participating member of the Israeli legislature; he was also an Arab. Arab and Muslim citizens have been permitted to serve in the Knesset from its inception. In 2013 there were twelve Arab MKs (Members of Knesset).[42] Currently there are seventeen Arabs serving there.[43]

In Israel, organizations like the Jerusalem Institute of Justice—a legal group dedicated to protecting the rights not only of Jews but also of Christians, Muslims, and Druze—flourish and operate openly. Contrast that with other nations. In Egypt, civil rights lawyer Karim Hamdy was tortured to

---

39. US Department of State, "Israel 2016 Human Rights Report," 1, https://www.state.gov/documents/organization/265712.pdf.

40. Ibid. 17.

41. "Iranian Journalist Facing Death Penalty Arrives in Israel Seeking Asylum," *Forward*, August 10, 2017, http://forward.com/fast-forward/379547/iranian-journalist-facing-death-penalty-arrives-in-israel-seeking-asylum.

42. Deroy Murdock, "Arabs Are Prominent in Israel's Government," *National Review*, November 25, 2013, https://www.nationalreview.com/article/364746/arabs-are-prominent-israels-government-deroy-murdock.

43. "List of Arab Members of the Knesset," *Wikipedia*, https://en.m.wikipedia.org/wiki/List_of_Arab_members_of_the_Knesset.

death in a Cairo police station by police officers, and dozens of other attorneys have been arrested because of the controversial clients they represented.[44] In Iran, lawyer Mohammad Mostafaei, who defended a woman sentenced to death by stoning, had his family arrested and his office ransacked.[45] In China, the government has rounded up and subjected to interrogation dozens of human rights attorneys.[46]

Israel's high regard for the rule of law and justice is no accident. It is impossible to understand Israel without grasping the notion that its history, people and nation, are tightly bound to the rule of law. The Pentateuch speaks exhaustively about the need for a practical application of justice within the Jewish people, and for an orderly administration of law. Deuteronomy 16:18–20 addresses the appointment of "judges and officers" who are to "judge with righteous judgment," meaning that in the process of judging they must avoid "distort[ion]" and shall not be "partial."

These Old Testament mandates are not just abstract principles. God's declaration to Israel about the rule of law was fixed to the very land that God had given to his people. The process of judging was to take place "*in all your towns* which the Lord your God is giving you, according to your tribes" (Deut. 16:18, emphasis added). The overall description of that land that God granted to the Jewish people is exacting and precise (Num. 34:1–15; Deut. 1:7–8). Deductively, this means that God's rule of law that the Jewish people were to administer was to be implemented in the context of a precise territorial (i.e., land-based) jurisdiction.

So, we have seen that the Jewish people exist, that they are divinely and historically connected to a specific land, and that even their rule of law and form of government harken us back to God's pronouncements about their land.

THE CAPACITY TO ENGAGE IN INTERNATIONAL RELATIONS.

The fourth international law precondition for the statehood of Israel, or any other country, requires that it must have the capacity to engage in relations with other nations. US Ambassador Jessup told the UN in 1948, "On this point, I believe that there would be unanimity that Israel exercises complete independence of judgment and of will in forming and in executing its foreign policy."[47] It is ironic that Israel's spirit of "independence of judgment" in its geopolitical policies was lauded as a reason for recognizing

---

44. "Egypt Policemen Jailed over Death of Lawyer Karim Hamdy," *BBC News*, December 12, 2015, http://www.bbc.com/news/world-africa-35082987.

45. Saeed Kamali Dehghan, "Iran Stoning Case Lawyer Mohmmad Mostafaei's Relatives Arrested," *The Guardian*, July 25, 2010, https://www.theguardian.com/world/2010/jul/26/iran-stoning-case-lawyers-relatives-arrested.

46. Violet Law, "Human Rights Lawyers, Staffers Detained in Widespread Crackdown across China," *Los Angeles Times*, July 11. 2015, https://www.latimes.com/world/asia/la-fg-human-rights-lawyers-staffers-detained-across-china-20150711-story,amp.html.

47. 3 U.N. SCOR, 383 Mtg., Dec. 2, 1948, No. 128, 10.

Israel's statehood in 1948, yet today that same spirit of independence has become a thorn in the side of the internationalists.[48]

While the pressure against Israel from the international community seems objectively disproportionate, could it be warranted? A review of current history compels a "no" answer.

At the outset, Israel was quite willing to bargain away some of its territory. As *New York Times* reporter Ruth Gruber observed firsthand in 1947–1948, even before formal recognition of Israel as a nation, first by America and then later by the United Nations, a committee of the UN had proposed a compromise which then led, she recounts, to a "General Assembly vote of Nov. 29, 1947, to partition Palestine into separate Jewish and Arab entities."[49] The response from the Jewish representatives, and from the Arab contingent, is telling. Gruber notes, "The Jews accepted this proposal, but the Arabs stormed out and threatened war."[50] In fact, war did come from the Arab nations when they attacked Israel shortly after Israel declared itself to be a state on May 14, 1948.

In the subsequent decades, not much has changed.

A quick review of the peace talks between Israel and the Palestinians plus their Arab proxies illustrates that Israel has "given peace a chance," but in return has often received war. In 1967, the "imprecise language" of a UN proposed settlement stopped any progress; in the 1973 Yom Kippur war, Egypt and Syria coordinated a military assault on Israel while the Arab League imposed an oil embargo; in 1975–1977, President Jimmy Carter pushed for a resolution and called for a Palestinian "homeland," resulting in the 1978–1979 Camp David Accords, in which Israel agreed to withdraw from the Sinai Peninsula—and in fact did, giving it back to Egypt—and called on the Arab nations to join in peace negotiations, but none responded; in 1987 the terror group Hamas was founded as it fueled the First Intifada (violent uprising) against Israel, consistent with its charter calling for the destruction of Israel and the creation of an Islamic Palestinian state through violent jihad; in 1993–1994, the Oslo Accords forged a framework with Israel agreeing to, and accepting, the creation of the Palestinian Authority inside the borders of biblical Israel; in 2000, the Camp David negotiations understandably collapsed when Palestinian terrorists mounted a second violent Intifada against Israel; in 2007, after six years of various attempts at peace, and after Israel had withdrawn from Gaza in the south, jihadist Hamas filled the power vacuum there; in 2008 Hamas violence led to Israel's incursion into Gaza to stop the rocket attacks; in 2009–2010, President Obama secured concessions from Israel to stop any further settle-

---

48.   Note for example this headline in the December 31, 2016 *Irish Times* article reporting on the UN's criticism of Israel's policies on settlements in the West Bank: "World View: Is Israel Really Prepared to Accept Isolation?" The first sentence in the article paints Israel's position as "characteristically belligerent."

49.   Gruber, "The Birth of a Nation, 1948."

50.   Ibid.

ments in the West Bank for ten months during negotiations, but later told Israel to retreat back to the borderlines that existed before it won the 1967 Six-Day War while the Palestinians pursued statehood in the UN, creating a zero-sum game, with Israel gaining nothing in terms of security.[51]

It is easy to understand why Michael Oren says, "the Second Intifada demonstrated that Palestinians were not going to accept Israel on any borders. . . . Israel ripped up all [its] settlements, ripped up 21 settlements and moved back to the 1967 lines. It didn't get peace. It got Hamas—and tens of thousands of rockets."[52]

ISRAEL'S FUTURE IS OUR FUTURE

The evidence is overwhelming that Israel is a legitimate nation. It deserves more respect than the international critics have afforded it. It was founded by a people group with thousands of years of history, and with unique biblical ties to their land, who exhibit a heritage of governance and respect for the rule of law and have shown the willingness to enter into good faith negotiations with only one, unyielding condition: that its people must be kept safe from the crucible of terror that surrounds it.

That one condition is not only the universal right of every nation, it was also enshrined in the Preamble of our own Constitution, a document designed to "insure domestic tranquility [and] provide for the common defense." There is much truth in the adage that Israel is valuable friend to the US because it is the only true democracy in the Middle East. But Israel's importance goes far beyond that. There is a troublesome clamor for a global enforcement mechanism either through "new institutions" or "strengthening existing institutions" to compel all national states to obey "a law above states."[53]

If that happens, Israel will not be the only target. The US has already been subjected to scathing criticism from the UN regarding its domestic policies.[54] Will sovereign freedom-loving nations like Israel and America continue to have the liberty to solve their own domestic problems and to pursue peace, free from either the boot of global masters or from the tethers of a thousand international laws? If so, then America may have Israel to thank for it, for in this struggle to retain national sovereignty, that tiny nation fights for us all.

---

51. Uri Friedman, "The 'Peace Process': A Short History—Chronicling Israel and Palestine's path to becoming a catchphrase," *Foreign Policy*, February 27, 2012, http://foreignpolicy.com/2012/02/27/the-peace-process-a-short-history.

52. "One Hundred Thirty-Two Hours & Fifty Years," 7, 15.

53. Steiner and Alston, *International Human Rights in Context—Law, Politics, Morals*, 151.

54. Natasja Sheriff, "US Cited for Police Violence, Racism in Scathing UN Review on Human Rights," *Al-jazeera America*, May 1, 2015, http://america.aljazeera.com/articles/2015/5/11/us-faces-scathing-un-review-on-human-rights-record.html.

IS IT SINFUL TO DIVIDE THE LAND OF ISRAEL?

MIKE BROWN

IS IT A SIN TO DIVIDE THE LAND OF ISRAEL TODAY? Does the Bible address the question of a two-state solution? Is there a particular stance on these issues that followers of Jesus should take based on the testimony of Scripture? In order to answer these questions, we need to review the relevant biblical passages in context, first asking if there is a consistent, biblical position on the land of Israel being divided and second, asking how those biblical statements apply to Israel today.

Many evangelicals believe that Joel 3:2 gives a definitive answer to the question of a two-state (= divided-land) solution: God will judge those who seek to divide the land. As stated in Joel 3:1–3 (ESV; cf. Heb. 4:1–3), "For behold, in those days and at that time, when I restore the fortunes of Judah and Jerusalem, I will gather all the nations and bring them down to the Valley of Jehoshaphat. And I will enter into judgment with them there, on behalf of my people and my heritage Israel, because they have scattered them among the nations and have divided up my land, and have cast lots for my people, and have traded a boy for a prostitute, and have sold a girl for wine and have drunk it."

Although it is notoriously difficult to date the book of Joel with certainty, the text appears to be speaking of an eschatological judgment for sins committed at different times in ancient Israel's history.[1] We can therefore ask if Joel 3:2 makes a categorical statement that God will judge those who have divided his land. There is no real ambiguity in the verb "divide" (*ḥillēq*), but does it mean divide in the sense of split into two, with part of the land going to Israel and part of it going others (as in a two-state solution)? Or does it mean divide in the sense of foreigners dividing the land up between themselves?

---

1. Radak explains the scattering of Israel here as the destruction of the land and scattering of the people under Titus.

Among modern versions, the NJPSV[2] is unique in rendering it, "For they divided My land among themselves." This is not reflected in the ancient versions (Septuagint [LXX], Targum, Peshitta, or Vulgate), but it is reflected in some traditional Jewish commentaries. Metzudat David[3] explains "they divided" to mean "they divided between themselves," while Malbim[4] writes that it is "as if they acquired the land as an inheritance, since they thought that the people of Israel were their servants, and whatever the servant acquires, his master acquires."[5]

Other commentators agree with the understanding that "they divided" means "they divided between themselves." For example, H. W. W. Wolff, looking back at Israel's history, notes that, "The deportations were the precondition for the new distribution of the soil, now without owner, among the conquerors and the new settlers," with reference to Micah 2:4, Lamentations 5:2, and 2 Kings 17:24.[6] So, with the people of Israel exiled from their land, foreigners divided it up for themselves. Similarly, Duane A. Garrett writes, "The two specific offenses mentioned at the end of this verse (scattering the Israelites and taking their land) both refer to foreign invasion and exile."[7]

Clearly, it is wrong to separate "they divided" in Joel 3:2b from the preceding "they have scattered" (p-z-r), meaning that the nations that God will judge were guilty of exiling his people from the land and dividing it up for themselves. At the same time, this is *God's land* they are tampering with, a very common theme in the Old Testament the land of Israel is the Lord's land, his inheritance, his special possession. David A. Hubbard, in his commentary regarding Joel 3:2 highlights how this is a common theme throughout Scripture.[8]

The bigger question, then, would seem to be this: Do the nations have any right at all to the land of Israel? Is it up to them to decide what part of the land belongs to the Jewish people and what part (if any) belongs to others? Is it just as sinful to scatter Israel from its homeland as it is to parcel out the land?

---

2. The New Jewish Publication Society Version of the Bible (1985)

3. Commentary on the Prophets and Writings written by Rabbi David Altschuler in the 18th century.

4. Written and published between 1845 and 1870 by Rabbi Meir Leibush ben Yehiel Michel Wisser (Malbim).

5. See, conveniently, https://www.sefaria.org/Joel.4.2?lang=bi&p2=Malbim_on_Joel.4.2.1&lang2=bi.

6. Hans Walter Wolff, *Joel and Amos: A Commentary on the Books of the Prophets Joel and Amos* (Hermeneia; Philadelphia: Fortress Press, 1977), 77.

7. Duane A. Garrett, *Hosea, Joel* (NAC; Nashville: Broadman & Holman Publishers, 1997), 380.

8. "The *basis* on which Yahweh will *enter into judgment* (Heb. *špṭ* in reflexive stem; cf. Isa. 66:16; Jer. 2:35; Ezek. 17:20) with them is their ruthless treatment of my *land* (Heb. *ḥlq* in intensive stem means *divide* and parcel out, as though they, not Yahweh, had full right of ownership; cf. Josh. 13:7; Ps. 22:19; Isa. 52:12) and the people of Judah, to whom, with his jealousy ablaze (cf. 2:18), he shows his special relationship—'my people'; *my* heritage'; '*my* land'. His legal rights to ownership had been violated by the scattering (Heb. *pzr*, used of Israel's scattering and isolation in Esth. 3:8; Jer. 50:17); of the people and the occupation of the land (for *heritage* and *people* in parallel, cf. 2:17; Pss 28:9; 78:62, 71; 94:5; 106:40; Isa. 47:6; Mic. 7:14)." David A. Hubbard, *Joel and Amos: An Introduction and Commentary* (TOTC; Downers Grove, IL: InterVarsity Press, 1989), 79.

It is clear from the Scriptures that the Lord has a unique and particular jealousy for the land of Israel, as seen from the language used in these verses (with my emphasis):

- "And I brought you into a plentiful land to enjoy its fruits and its good things. But when you came in, you defiled *my land* and made *my heritage* an abomination" (Jer. 2:7).
- "But first I will doubly repay their iniquity and their sin, because they have polluted *my land* with the carcasses of their detestable idols, and have filled *my inheritance* with their abominations. (Jer. 16:18).[9]
- "Therefore thus says the Lord GOD: Surely I have spoken in *my hot jealousy* against the rest of the nations and against all Edom, who gave *my land* to themselves as a possession with wholehearted joy and utter contempt, that they might make its pasturelands a prey" (Ezek. 36:5).
- "You will come up against *my people* Israel, like a cloud covering the land. In the latter days I will bring you against *my land*, that the nations may know me, when through you, O Gog, I vindicate *my holiness* before their eyes" (Ezek. 38:16).
- "I will break the Assyrian in *my land*, and on *my mountains* trample him underfoot; and his yoke shall depart from them, and his burden from their shoulder" (Isa. 14:25).
- "For a nation has come up against *my land*, powerful and beyond number; its teeth are lions' teeth, and it has the fangs of a lioness" (Joel 1:6).

As I noted in my commentary on Jeremiah 2:7, with reference to the verses just cited:

> Interestingly, in all these verses (i.e., outside of Jeremiah), the texts here are addressing *other nations* and how the Lord will deal with them or use them (either *in* his land or with reference *to* his land). Only the Jeremianic texts deal with *Israel's sins* against the Lord's land—a land that was fertile (*'ereṣ hakarmel*) and verdant (cf. the common, "flowing with milk and honey" in 11:5); yet Israel's sins made the land *unclean* (*ṭ-m-*), turning it into something *detestable* (*tô'ēbâ*). These two terms have clear legal overtones, speaking of ritual defilement and pollution, either by sexual sin, idolatry, violence or various unclean acts (cf., e.g., Gen. 34:5; Lev. 18:29–30; 19:31; 20:3; Num. 5:20; see also Num. 35:33). Thus, Yahweh's land became dirty to him, and Israel's sin against the land was a sin against him (this could be termed a spiritual ecology). Cf.

---

9. Note that both Jeremiah 2:7 and 16:8 have *naḥalātî* for ESV's "my heritage" and "my inheritance," respectively; for *naḥalātî* elsewhere in Jeremiah in relevant contexts, see Jeremiah 12:7–9; 50:11. Note also Isaiah 47:6, speaking to Babylon: "I was angry with my people; I profaned my heritage; I gave them into your hand; you showed them no mercy; on the aged you made your yoke exceedingly heavy."

Lev 18:24–28, summarized with the warning that ". . . if you defile [*t-m-*] the land, it will vomit you out as it vomited out the nations that were before you" (Lev 18:28).[10]

Commenting on the same verse in Jeremiah, William L. Holladay writes,

> And the land was not given to Israel, it is "my land," Yahweh's land. This view of the land is consonant with Lev 25:23 and is rather different from the more common affirmation that the land is a gift (Exod 20:12 and constantly in Deuteronomy and elsewhere). The parallel, "inheritance" (נַחֲלָה), means "land, (inalienable) property," usually family property gained by inheritance; compare 3:19; 12:7–10. The hearers defiled Yahweh's land and made it loathsome.[11]

The imagery is striking and the message is clear: Neither Israel nor the nations can defile or destroy the Lord's personal "inheritance"—his land—without severe consequences. And so, even when it is viewed as his gift to his people, it is a sacred stewardship for them, a gift not to be scorned. As expressed by Matthew Henry, "It was God's land; they were but tenants to him, sojourners in it, Leviticus 25:23. It was his heritage, for it was a holy land, Immanuel's land; but they *made it an abomination*, even to God himself, who was wroth, and greatly abhorred Israel."[12]

Both Holladay and Henry (among others) cite Leviticus 25:23, which reads, "The land shall not be sold in perpetuity, for the land is mine. For you are strangers and sojourners with me." Rashi[13] comments on the phrase "for the land is mine," stating, "Your eye shall not be evil toward it (you shall not begrudge this) for it is not yours." The midrash[14] even claims that, when the prepositional phrase *lî*, is used ("to me, for me," meaning "mine") with reference to the Lord, it refers to this world and the world to come, with Leviticus 25:23 cited as one example (see Midrash Tanchuma Buber, Terumah 3:1). Thus the land of Israel belongs to the Lord in eternal perpetuity.[15]

Deuteronomy 32:8 in the Masoretic Text is relevant in this context (cf. also Targum and Peshitta; contrast the reading found in the Dead Sea Scrolls, and see the LXX): "When the Most High gave the nations their inheritance

---

10. Michael L. Brown, "Jeremiah," in *The Expositors Bible Commentary, Revised Edition* (Grand Rapids: Zondervan, 2010), 86–67.

11. William L. Holladay, *Jeremiah 1: A Commentary on the Book of the Prophet Jeremiah, chapters 1–25* (Hermenia; Philadelphia: Fortress Press, 1986), 87–88.

12. Matthew Henry, *Matthew Henry's Commentary on the Whole Bible: Complete and Unabridged in One Volume* (repr., Peabody, MA: Hendrickson, 1994), 1221.

13. Rabbi Shlomo Yitzchaki (Rashi, 1040–1105), one of the most famed of all Jewish Bible commentators.

14. A collection of sermon-like Bible commentaries and explanations dating from several centuries after Jesus.

15. See further Gerhard von Rad, "The Promised Land and Yahweh's Land in the Hexateuch," in idem, *The Problem of the Hexateuch and Other Essays* (New York: McGraw-Hill, 1966), 79–93; Walter Brueggemann, *The Land: Place as Gift, Promise and Challenge in Biblical Faith* (Philadelphia: Fortress, 1977).

and divided the human race, He set the boundaries of the peoples according to the number of the people of Israel" (CSB[16]; verse 9 continues, "But the LORD's portion is His people, Jacob, His own inheritance.").[17] As explained by the medieval commentator Ibn Ezra (1089–1164), "The traditional commentators have explained the passage beginning *When the Most High allotted inheritances to the peoples* as referring to the Generation of the Dispersion. It was during that time that the land became scattered, and it was then that God decreed that the land of the Seven Nations would be Israel's (and that it would be sufficient to their population—hence, *to the number of the children of Israel).*"[18]

So, then, from the very start, when the Lord apportioned certain lands to certain peoples, his plan was for Israel to have this particular land. At first, other nations would dwell there, but ultimately, the land was designated for Israel, its only rightful possessor. As noted in the *IVP Bible Background Commentary,* "In Israelite theology Yahweh had assigned each nation its inheritance ([Deuteronomy] 5:2, 9, 19; Amos 9:7), though there is also some accommodation to the concept that each god gave territory to his people (Judges 11:24). It was not uncommon for kings in the ancient Near East seeking expansion of territories to claim that deity had assigned or delivered land to them. In Israel the territorial assignment was uniquely based on a covenantal bond with Yahweh."[19]

All this, then, would suggest that: 1) no one has the right to decide who inhabits the land of Israel other than the Lord himself, since the land belongs to him; 2) the Lord has designated this land for the people of Israel; 3) it is, therefore, wrong for anyone to take any portion of the land from Israel and designate it for someone else, as would be the case in a two-state solution.

But are these the only conclusions to draw? What about the times when Israel went into exile because of sin? And what of the fact that Israel, to this very day, has never possessed the totality of the land that was promised? Why should we assume that Israel is entitled to full possession of the land today? The majority of the nation is secular while the ultra-Orthodox militantly oppose faith in Jesus the Messiah. On what basis, then, does Israel have a "right" to the land at this point in time, other than the sovereign choice of God? And if it is based on his choice, perhaps he wants the land divided until the time of Israel's full repentance?

---

16. Christian Standard Bible

17. ESV and NET are among the versions that follow DSS and LXX, rendering, respectively, "When the Most High gave to the nations their inheritance, when he divided mankind, he fixed the borders of the peoples according to the number of the sons of God"; "When the Most High gave the nations their inheritance, when he divided up humankind, he set the boundaries of the peoples, according to the number of the heavenly assembly." Cf. also NLT. The KJV, which did not have the evidence of the DSS, naturally followed the MT; other versions following MT include NKJV; NASB; NIV; CJB.

18. Following the translation of Ibn Ezra on Sefaria.com to Deuteronomy 32:8.

19. V. H. Matthews, M. W. Chavalas, and J. H. Walton, *The IVP Bible Background Commentary: Old Testament* (Downers Grove, IL: InterVarsity Press, 2000), electronic ed., to Deut. 32:8.

We will explore these questions one at a time, asking first, "What about the times when Israel went into exile because of sin?" To be sure, the Jewish people have been driven out of the land by God, the ultimate landowner and this has happened because of their persistent acts of rebellion and transgression. As the Lord warned in Leviticus 18, with primary reference to sexual sins,

> Do not make yourselves unclean by any of these things, for by all these the nations I am driving out before you have become unclean, and the land became unclean, so that I punished its iniquity, and the land vomited out its inhabitants. But you shall keep my statutes and my rules and do none of these abominations, either the native or the stranger who sojourns among you (for the people of the land, who were before you, did all of these abominations, so that the land became unclean), lest the land vomit you out when you make it unclean, as it vomited out the nation that was before you (Lev. 18:24–28).

As a result of Israel's disobedience, which included violation of the Sabbath laws, God said that "the land shall be abandoned by them and enjoy its Sabbaths while it lies desolate without them, and they shall make amends for their iniquity, because they spurned my rules and their soul abhorred my statutes" (Lev. 26:43). Throughout the OT, there are repeated references to the people of Israel being exiled for sin, and Jesus in the NT speaks to this as well (see Luke 21:24, and note 19:41–44, which speaks of the destruction of Jerusalem without mentioning exile). At the same time, the God who scattered Israel is the one who promised to regather, and he has done what he promised to do, first in the aftermath of the Babylonian exile, and second, in the last one hundred-plus years (see, e.g., Jer. 30:10–11; 31:7–14; 32:37–44; Ezek. 36:7–38; 37:21–28; Isa. 40:9–11; none of these promises were fully realized with the return from Babylonian exile; they are being gradually fulfilled in our day).

Some would object here, saying that we cannot really know if the modern day return is an act of God. Biblical logic, however, would say that it must be. Simply stated, we know that when God blesses no one can curse and when he curses no one can bless (e.g., Num. 22:12; 23:8). When he heals no one can smite and when he smites no one can heal (Exod. 15:26; 23:25–26; Deut. 7:12–15; conversely, Deut. 28:58–61). When he opens a door no one can shut it and when he shuts a door no one can open it (Isa. 22:22; Rev. 3:7–8). Consequently, if the Lord scattered his people in his wrath, Israel cannot regather herself, nor can the nations of the world regather Israel, nor can Satan regather Israel. To do so would be to overrule and overpower God. The fact that six million Jews now live in the land of Israel—birthed out of the ashes of the Holocaust at that—is testimony to the fact that God is regathering his people. And so, just as Israel was exiled because of sin, Israel is being regathered because of mercy.

What of the fact that Israel, to this very day, has never possessed the totality of the land that was promised? Why should we assume that Israel is entitled to full possession of the land today? These are fair questions that, generally speaking, are often neglected in contemporary, Christian Zionist discussion.

When the Lord made a covenant with Abram in Genesis 15, he said, "To your offspring I give this land, from the river of Egypt to the great river, the river Euphrates, the land of the Kenites, the Kenizzites, the Kadmonites, the Hittites, the Perizzites, the Rephaim, the Amorites, the Canaanites, the Girgashites and the Jebusites" (Gen. 15:18–21). However, Gordon J. Wenham states that "there is an element of hyperbole here, for the land of promise is identified with Canaan, whose boundaries are more restricted (see Num. 34:2–12). Only in Solomon's day did Israel's boundaries approach the limits specified here (1 Kings 5:1 [4:21]), but it seems unlikely that they extended as far west as the Nile even then (A. Malamat, *JNES* 22 [1963] 1–17)."[20] Similarly, Derek Kidner observes that, "Only in David's reign were the boundaries of verse 18 attained, and then as an empire rather than a homeland."[21]

Consider also the laws concerning the cities of refuge, which are mentioned in the Torah in Exodus 21:13; Numbers 35:9–15; and Deuteronomy 4:41–43; 19:1–13 (see also Josh. 20; 1 Chron. 6). Of particular importance is Deuteronomy 19:8–9: "And if the Lord your God enlarges your territory, as he has sworn to your fathers, and gives you all the land that he promised to give to your fathers—provided you are careful to keep all this commandment, which I command you today, by loving the Lord your God and by walking ever in his ways—then you shall add three other cities to these three."

Did that promised expansion ever take place? Ramban[22] begins his lengthy comment to Deuteronomy 19:8 by noting that, "This passage is future," connecting its fulfillment to other verses which speak of God circumcising the heart of his people (Deut. 30:6) and giving them a single heart to serve him (Jer. 32:39).[23] So, when Israel will walk in complete obedience to God's commands, which has not happened to date and which will not happen until the Messianic era, Israel will enjoy the fullness of its inheritance.

According to the Rambam (Maimonides):

> It is a positive commandment to set aside cities of refuge, as Deuteronomy 19:2 states: "You shall set aside three cities." The practice of setting aside cities of refuge applies only in Eretz Yisrael.

> There were six cities of refuge. Three Moses our teacher set aside in TransJordan, and three Joshua set aside in the land of Canaan.

---

20. Gordon J. Wenham, *Genesis 1–15* (WBC; Dallas: Word, 1998), 333.
21. Derek Kidner, *Genesis: An Introduction and Commentary* (TOTC; Downers Grove, IL: InterVarsity Press, 1967), 136. See further Samuel E. Loewenstamm, "The Divine Grants of Land to the Patriarchs," *JAOS* 91 (1974), 509–510.
22. A Spanish-born medieval commentator who lived from 1194–1270.
23. See, conveniently, https://www.sefaria.org/Deuteronomy.19.8?lang=bi&with=Commentary&lang2=en.

None of the cities of refuge served as a haven until they were all set aside, as implied by Numbers 35:13: "There shall be six cities of refuge for you." And so, Moses informed us that the three cities of refuge in TransJordan did not serve as a haven until the three in the land of Canaan were set aside.

If so, why did Moses set them aside? He said: "Since a mitzvah came to my hand, I will fulfill it."

In the era of the King Mashiach, three other cities will be added to these six, as Deuteronomy 19:9 states: "And you shall add three other cities to these three cities."[24]

So, then, according to one of our great Rabbinic commentators, Israel will not enjoy its full inheritance of the land until the Messianic era. Why press the issue now?

Returning to Genesis 15, even if the land description is not taken literally, Israel today hardly occupies all the land that Israel and Judah occupied during the reigns of David and Solomon.[25] Why then should it be assumed that Israel should not accept, say, the 1967 borders? We are not asking this question based on pragmatism or security; we are asking it theologically and biblically. Why assume that there cannot be a two-state solution until the Messiah comes? Or, perhaps less drastically, why assume that Israel's present borders are sacrosanct?

Many evangelical Christians recognized God's sovereign hand of restoration in 1948 and his hand of deliverance and even expansion in 1967, yet, to my knowledge, there were few who protested when Israel returned most of the Sinai Peninsula to Egypt in 1982. What makes Israel's current borders any more fixed than its borders in 1948 or 1967?

Even some advocates of a one-state solution, like Caroline Glick, have left Gaza out of the equation, thereby accepting a separate Palestinian territory on some of Israel's divinely promised land. As she explains, "Gaza is not part of the plan, for several reasons. First, Israel withdrew its military forces and civilian population from Gaza in 2005, arguably renouncing its legal claim to the area. Second, there is no significant Israeli constituency for absorbing Gaza into Israel. Third, the strategic advantage that Israel would gain from dislodging Hamas from power in Gaza would be outweighed by the strategic price it would pay in terms of the likely need to fight an insurgency within Gaza."[26]

---

24. Mishneh Torah, Hilkhot Rotzeach uShemirat Nefesh, 8:1–4, as translated on the Chabad website, http://www.chabad.org/library/article_cdo/aid/1088924/jewish/Rotzeach-uShmirat-Nefesh-Chapter-Eight.htm.

25. See, conveniently, http://seekingtruth.co.uk/israel_borders.htm.

26. Caroline Glick, *The Israeli Solution: A One-State Plan for Peace in the Middle East* (New York: The Crown Publishing Group, 2014; Kindle edition), locs. 206–209. Of course, Glick's concerns are political more than theological, and so the question of divinely promised borders would not concern her in this context.

Evidently, even some one-state proponents derive their stance on the borders of Israel based on modern geopolitics rather than a strict application of Israel owning all of the promised land before Jesus returns.

In sum: 1) the people of Israel have never possessed the entirety of the promised land; 2) the Scriptures indicate that Israel will not do so until the fullness of the Messianic era; and 3) Israel is in the land today by grace not by merit (meaning, Israel has not fulfilled the Sinai requirement of repentance, as laid out in Leviticus 26:40–45 and many other passages). Accordingly, this brings us back to the last two questions posed above, viz., On what basis, then, does Israel have a "right" to the land at this point in time, other than the sovereign choice of God? And if it is based on his choice, perhaps he wants the land divided until the time of Israel's full repentance?

Viewed from this angle, it becomes difficult to argue that Israel cannot be divided into two states until Jesus returns and reigns from Jerusalem. We can only say that this is God's decision, not man's, and that the nations that want to parcel out his land, the land over which he is particularly jealous, better do so with caution, knowing what happened to past nations that tampered with the Lord's inheritance.

Perhaps, however, there is one more factor to consider. What if the Scriptures indicate that there must be Jewish sovereignty of the land *before* Jesus returns? Could that indicate that supporting a two-state solution would mean standing against the purposes of God? The most relevant passages appear to be Zechariah 12–14 (with the possible exception of 13:7–9)[27] and Ezek. 38–39. The former passages point to a Jewish Jerusalem (also required by Matt. 23:39), with frequent mention of Judah (Zech. 12:2, 4–7; 14:14, 21), which would almost certainly refer to Judah as Zechariah knew it.[28] The latter passages speak of an end time invasion of Israel when it is dwelling safely and securely in its land (Ezek. 38:14). Note in particular Ezekiel 38:11, where the invader says, "'I will go up against the land of unwalled villages. I will fall upon the quiet people who dwell securely, all of them dwelling without walls, and having no bars or gates.'"

Of course, it quite treacherous to make contemporary political decisions based on eschatological prophecy, especially when the texts are couched in typical prophetic language.[29] But even if we agree that: 1) the descriptions in Zechariah and Ezekiel are largely literal; 2) they refer to the end of the age; and 3) they speak of the Jewish people dwelling safely in the land, with Jerusalem the national center, that would still not mean that there could not be a temporary two-state solution. That is because Israel today in no way fits Ezekiel's description of an unwalled nation living in peace and safety, which means that the fulfillment of Ezekiel's prophecies awaits a still future

---

27.   See Mark J. Boda, *Zechariah* (NICOT; Grand Rapids: Eerdmans, 2016), 734–742.

28.   For further discussion, see Boda, ibid., to the verses in question, for the larger context and background.

29.   More broadly, see Carl E. Amerding and W. Ward Gasque, eds., *A Guide to Biblical Prophecy* (repr., Eugene, OR: Wipf & Stock, 2001).

time. So, it is quite plausible that there could be a two-state solution in the near future, leading to a single-state solution in the more distant future, at which time there will be a false sense of peace that settles on the land (see 1 Thes 5:1–3). In short, while the passages in Zechariah and Ezekiel speak of a sovereign Jewish land at the end of the age, it is probably unwise to use those passages in a political debate concerning Israel's borders today.

What, then, can we say as Bible believers in response to the question, "Is it a sin to divide the land?" To review: 1) All parties involved must remember that the land of Israel is God's land, not their land. 2) Because of this, all nations which mistreat the people of Israel and misuse the land of Israel will be accountable to him. 3) Yet Israel is not entitled to full possession of the land without full repentance and full obedience, which has not happened so far in the nation's history and is certainly not happening today. 4) Consequently, Israel does not have a "right" to be in the land; rather, Israel has been regathered by the mercy of the Lord. 5) At the same time, it is undeniable that the Lord has regathered and reestablished the nation, which indicates clearly that he is in the act of bringing his eternal purposes to pass. 6) Before Jesus returns, it appears clearly that there will be a sovereign, secure, Jewish state with Jerusalem as its center.

In light of this, I would suggest that while we cannot dogmatically say that it is a sin to support a two-state solution, such a solution would only be short-term, at best, and those who support it must read carefully, remembering that the land is God's land in a special and unique way.[30]

---

30. We have not addressed here the question of compassionate and fair treatment of the Palestinians, since that was outside the purview of this chapter. That being said, there are many verses that address this, and the question is: What is best for the Palestinians? Many would argue that a two-state solution is not the answer. For varied perspectives, see Mae Elise Cannon, ed., *A Land Full of God: Perspectives on the Holy Land* (Eugene, OR: Cascade Books, 2017); Salim J. Munayer, ed., *The Land Cries Out: Theology of the Land in the Israeli-Palestinian Context* (Eugene, OR: Wipf & Stock, 2011); David Brog, *Reclaiming Israel's History: Roots, Rights, and the Struggle for Peace* (Washington, DC: Regnery, 2017).

THE LIFEWAY SURVEY

INTRODUCTION TO THE LIFEWAY SURVEY

EVANGELICAL ATTITUDES TOWARD ISRAEL AND THE JEWISH PEOPLE

WE ARE CELEBRATING THE 70TH ANNIVERSARY of the birth of the modern State of Israel in 2018! This is the genesis for this book and for the surveys included in this section. We know that Jewish people have discovered that evangelical Christians are the best friends of Israel. Personally, I recognized this soon after becoming a believer and was encouraged by it. It became an avenue of testimony to my Jewish family and friends. Remember that Jewish people live in the shadow of the Holocaust. Unfortunately, most Jewish people believe that "Christians" perpetrated the Holocaust. I cannot imagine a real Christian persecuting a Jewish person, but this is the perception of the Jewish community based upon events like the Crusades, Russian pogroms, and the Holocaust.

It is not easy to change these perceptions within the Jewish community, but they are changing. A few years ago a Pew Foundation survey found that thirty-four percent of the Jewish people surveyed believe you can be Jewish and believe in Jesus. That is amazing to me, as I think about how my family responded in 1971 when I told them I had come to faith in Jesus.

Yet, we do see the landscape changing and wanted to get a more objective view of the current attitudes of evangelical Christians towards the Jewish people, Israel, and Jewish evangelism.

A number of key evangelical leaders joined forces to try and tangibly measure how evangelical Christians view the Jewish people and the nation of Israel and asked LifeWay Research to prepare and administer the survey. LifeWay completed the survey in the fall of 2017, utilizing a random sampling of 2,002 individuals who responded to four critical questions describing evangelical beliefs. In other words, LifeWay did not simply ask, "Are you an evangelical Christian?" Questions were formulated and asked that demonstrated whether the participants were true Bible believing Christians who had a fervent desire to see Jews and Gentiles receive Jesus as their Messiah.

As you will see, the results of the survey are generally favorable toward Israel. There also seems to be a good degree of sympathy for Palestinians, especially those Christians who are struggling in hostile environments where they are either persecuted or face regular attempts to restrict their religious freedom.

On the other hand, along with all of the positive news, we discovered some critical challenges as well.

According to the survey, millennials and the generations after them are not quite as pro-Israel as their parents and grandparents. There are many reasons for this and I can instantly think of three. First of all, our young people did not personally experience the devastation of the Holocaust, which led to the foundation of the state of Israel. As some have said, "Israel was born out of the ashes of the Holocaust." Sympathy for the Jewish people is not part of the millennial DNA.

Additionally, our young people are socially sensitive and justice-oriented—which is a good thing—yet, they only know Israel as a well-formed nation with a strong economy and professional army. They were not around for the founding of the State of Israel and cannot easily appreciate the struggles of the modern State of Israel, the wars fought or the terrorism endured; from the Munich massacre of Israeli athletes to the Ma'alot debacle in May 1974 when twenty-five innocent Israelis were murdered by Palestinian terrorists.

From 1948 until the late 1970s, most Christians and even most Americans viewed the modern State of Israel as the "underdog" and became deeply concerned for the future of the nation. During these years, most evangelical Christians also viewed the formation of the modern State of Israel as the fulfillment of biblical prophecy. I am happy to report that eighty percent of those surveyed believe that God's promises to Abraham are inclusive of the preservation of the Jewish people and the "divine deed" to the Land. This includes many millennials and this shows that our young people are grappling with biblical truth!

However, during the last couple of decades there seems to be a revival of *replacement theology*, or what theologians traditionally call *supersessionism*. Simply put, this theological perspective envisions Israel as permanently set aside by God, replaced by the Church and the promises of God to Abraham mostly transferred from Israel to the Church. In other words, the Church has inherited spiritual blessings rather than actual land. This viewpoint tends to view the land promises as non-literal. This perspective on Scripture, held by a growing number of godly evangelical Christians, shies away from a more literal interpretation of the Old Testament through Abraham, thereby removing the biblical and theological significance God granted to the Jewish people and the modern State of Israel.

This is one reason why Chosen People Ministries has helped form a new group called the *Alliance for the Peace of Jerusalem*, which affirms God's ongoing plan for the Jewish people. This broader community of theologians, pastors, and lay leaders support the biblical connection with the modern State of Israel and plan to encourage Christians to pray for the peace of Jerusalem, to love both Jews and Arabs, and to remain committed to bringing the Gospel to all the peoples of the Middle East—"to the Jew first and also to the Gentile" (Romans 1:16). The Alliance already has plans to produce additional materials and hold conferences designed to help Christians gain a better understanding of what God is doing in the Middle East—especially in Israel.

We also surveyed evangelical Christian attitudes about Jewish evangelism and found that eighty-six percent of evangelical Christians believe sharing the Gospel with the Jewish people is important. This is a very encouraging number. However, the survey also indicated that sixty percent of the
Christians surveyed have not shared the Gospel with a Jewish friend in the
last year. That is a number that I am especially concerned about. Also, only
thirty-five percent of Christians with Jewish friends have prayed for the salvation of their Jewish loved ones in the last week.

Another of our concerns is that a new generation of Christians is growing less interested in Israel than previous generations.

We released the results of the survey at the Press Conference, held on
December 4, 2017 at the National Press Club in Washington DC. Joel
Rosenberg made the following statement at this event:

> Millennials are sending the Church a sobering message. At the moment, they're
> not against Israel. Not at all. But the survey makes it clear that many of them
> really don't understand Israel's place in the biblical narrative. Thus, their sup-
> port for Israel is nearly twenty points less than their parents and grandparents.
> Now, extrapolate that going forward. Unless the Church gives younger believ-
> ers a healthy, balanced, solidly biblical understanding of God's love and plan
> for Israel, overall Evangelical support for the Jewish State could very well plum-
> met over the next decade as Millennials represent an ever-larger percentage
> of the overall Church body. That said, I'm cautiously optimistic. I've agreed
> to be part of the founding leadership council of "Alliance for the Peace of
> Jerusalem" because I see a real need to educate the Church—and particularly
> younger evangelicals—about God's love and plan for both Israel and her Arab
> and Persian neighbors, and to mobilize them to seek peace, pray for peace, and
> be peacemakers in a dark and troubled region.

We also discovered, through the survey, that the number of evangelical Christians who claim a Jewish parent, parents, or grandparents (only two percent
of our survey), comes out to between 800,000 and 1 million evangelicals
with Jewish ethnicity, if we identify between 50 and 70 million evangelical
Christians in the US. This is a far higher number of Jewish people who believe in Jesus in the US than we ever thought of.

I am sure you will enjoy reading the survey results. The full survey is
printed in the pages to follow.

EXECUTIVE SUMMARY

Perceptions of Israel
- 67% of those with evangelical beliefs have a positive perception of Israel.
- 45% say that the Bible has most influenced their opinions about Israel the most.

Right to the Land
- 19% agree and 46% disagree that Palestinian people have a historic right to the land of Israel.
- 69% agree that Jewish people have a historic right to the land of Israel.
- 41% agree that Jewish people have a biblical right to the land of Israel, but also have a responsibility to share the land with Palestinian Arabs.
- 63% disagree that biblical passages about Jewish people having a right to the land of Israel no longer apply today.
- 80% agree that God's promise to Abraham and his descendants was for all time.
- 76% agree that Christian should support Jewish people's right to live in the sovereign state of Israel.
- 51% disagree that the Jewish people lost the promise of the land because they rejected Jesus.

Support for the existence, security, and prosperity of the State of Israel
- 42% support the existence of the State of Israel, but don't feel the need to support everything Israel does.
- A majority of supporters indicate the reason for their support includes:
  - 60% Israel is the historic Jewish homeland.
  - 63% The Bible says God gave the land of Israel to the Jewish people
  - 52% Israel is important for fulfilling biblical prophecy.
- The majority of those with evangelical beliefs attribute the primary reason for their support of Israel to the Bible including 33% who select select "the Bible says God gave the land of Israel to the Jewish people"; 12% selected "The Bible says Christians should support Israel."
- 71% say that their support for the State of Israel has stayed the same over the last five years.

Modern State of Israel
- "When you think of the modern rebirth of the State of Israel in 1948 and the regathering of millions of Jewish people to Israel,"

80% say these events were fulfillments of Bible prophecy that show we are getting closer to the return of Jesus Christ, and 20% say these were simply interesting geopolitical events.

- 23% agree but 46% are not sure if the state of Israel should sign a peace treaty that allows Palestinians to create their own sovereign state.
- 14% agree, 50% disagree, and 36% are not sure if the modern rebirth of the State of Israel has been an injustice to the Arab people.
- 22% agree, 41% disagree, and 37% are not sure if modern Israel has been unfair to the Palestinian people.

Christians and Israel
- 59% agree that Christians should do more to love and care for Palestinian people.
- 73% agree that Christians should support Israel's defense of itself from terrorist and foreign enemies.
- 73% are concerned for the safety of Christians in areas controlled by the Palestinian Authority.
- 41% disagree that the Christian church has fulfilled or replaced the nation of Israel in God's plan.

Jewish people and the Gospel
- 86% agree (71% strongly) that sharing the Gospel with Jewish people is important.
- 55% agree that the Bible teaches that one day most or all Jewish people, alive at that time, will believe in Jesus.
- 47% agree that Jesus will return when the Jewish people accept Jesus
- 72% wish they knew more about what the Bible teaches about Israel's future.
- 30% have Jewish friends, 17% have Muslim friends, and 6% have Palestinian friends.
- 35% of those with Jewish friends have prayed for the salvation of their Jewish friends in the last week.
- 60% of those with Jewish friends have not shared the Gospel with any of them in the last year.

US and Israel
- 97% have not traveled to Israel.
- 51% of those who have never been to Israel are interested or very interested in traveling to Israel.
- 31% of all those with Evangelical Beliefs believe the US does the right amount to help Israel.

METHODOLOGY

The Evangelicals Attitudes towards Israel Research Study was sponsored by Chosen People Ministries and The Joshua Fund.

LifeWay Research conducted the study September 20–28, 2017. The survey was conducted using the web-enabled KnowledgePanel®, a probability-based panel designed to be representative of the US population. Initially, participants are chosen scientifically by a random selection of telephone numbers and residential addresses. Persons in selected households are then invited by telephone or by mail to participate in the web-enabled KnowledgePanel®. For those who agree to participate, but do not already have Internet access, GfK provides at no cost a laptop and ISP connection.

Sample stratification and weights were used for gender by age, ethnicity, region, education, and household income to reflect the most recent US Census data. The completed sample is 2,002 surveys. The sample provides ninety-five percent confidence that the sampling error does not exceed plus or minus 2.7 percent. Margins of error are higher in sub-groups.

Respondents were screened to only include adults with evangelical beliefs. Evangelical beliefs are defined using the NAE LifeWay Research Evangelical Beliefs Research Definition based on respondent beliefs.

Respondents are asked their level of agreement with four separate statements using a four-point, forced choice scale (strongly agree, somewhat agree, somewhat disagree, strongly disagree). Those who strongly agree with all four statements are categorized as having evangelical beliefs:

- The Bible is the highest authority for what I believe.
- It is very important for me personally to encourage non-Christians to trust Jesus Christ as their Savior.
- Jesus Christ's death on the cross is the only sacrifice that could remove the penalty of my sin.
- Only those who trust in Jesus Christ alone as their Savior receive God's free gift of eternal salvation.

QUANTITATIVE FINDINGS

PERCEPTIONS OF ISRAEL

67% have a positive perception of Israel

Table 1: "Overall what is your perception of the country of Israel today?"
n=1,997

Very Positive	23%
Positive	27%
Somewhat Positive	17%
Somewhat Negative	6%
Negative	2%
Very Negative	1%
Not sure	24%

Those age 65+ are the most likely age group to select "Positive" (76%) followed by age 50–64 (69%), age 35–49 (64%) and age 18–34 (58%). Males (76%) are more likely to select "Positive" than females (61%). Those in the South (69%) and West (72%) are more likely to select "Positive" than those in the Northeast (61%) and Midwest (61%). Black, Non-Hispanics are the least likely ethnic group to select "Positive" (50%). Those who have a bachelor's (75%) or a graduate degree (76%) are more likely to select "Positive" than those who are high school graduates or less (64%) or have some college (67%).

Those who have travelled to Israel are much more likely to select a "Positive" response (95%). Those with Jewish friends (77%), Muslim friends (73%), and Palestinian friends (76%) are more likely to select a "Positive" response. Those who attend church services once a week or more (73%) are more likely to select "Positive" than those attending one to three times a month (65%) or less than once a month (53%). Protestants (71%) are more likely to select "Positive" than Catholics (53%). Republicans (77%) are more likely to select "Positive" than Independents (66%) or Democrats (53%).

"Which of the following have influenced your opinions about Israel?"

Table 2: "Which of the following have influenced your opinions about Israel?" n=1,995

The Bible	56%
The media	27%
Your local church	25%
Friends and family	18%
National Christian Leaders	15%
Personal experiences with Jewish people	11%
Positions of elected officials	7%
Teachers or professors	4%
Personal experiences with Muslim people	3%
Not sure	22%

The Bible
Those in the South (58%) and West (60%) are more likely to select than those in the Northeast (48%) and Midwest (50%). Those age 65+ are the most likely age group to select (65%), followed by those age 50–64 (58%). White non-Hispanics (60%) and Hispanics (55%) are more likely to select than Black non-Hispanics (45%). Those with a bachelor's degree (64%) are more likely to select than those who are high school graduates or less (52%) or with some college (56%).

The media
Those age 65+ are the least likely age group to select (22%). Those with some college (29%) or a Bachelor's Degree (35%) are more likely to select than those who are high school graduates or less (24%).

Your local church
Those age 35–49 are the least likely age group to select (18%). Black, Non-Hispanics are the least likely ethnic group to select (13%).

Friends and family
Those age 18–34 are the most likely age group to select (26%). Black non-Hispanics are the least likely ethnic group to select (5%). Those with a bachelor's degree are most likely education group to select (32%).

National Christian leaders
Those age 35–49 are the least likely age group to select (10%). White non-Hispanics (18%) are more likely to select than Black non-Hispanics (9%) and Hispanics (13%).

Personal experiences with Jewish people
Those age 65+ (13%) are more likely to select than those 18–34 (8%). Those who are high school graduates or less are the least likely education group to select (6%), followed by those with some college (10%).

Positions of elected officials
Those age 50–64 (9%) and 65+ (9%) are more likely to select than those 18–34 (4%).

Teachers or professors
No significant differences.

Personal experiences with Muslim people
Those age 18–34 (5%) are more likely to select than those 50–64 (2%) and 65+ (2%).

45% say that the Bible has influenced their opinions about Israel the most

Table 3: "Which one of the following has influenced your opinions about Israel the most?" n=1,995

The Bible	45%
The media	15%
Friends and family	4%
Your local church	4%
Personal experiences with Jewish people	3%
National Christian Leaders	2%
Positions of elected officials	2%
Personal experiences with Muslim people	1%
Teachers or professors	<1%
Not sure	25%

Those age 65+ are the least likely age group to select "The media" (11%). Those age 50–64 (49%) and 65+ (56%) are more likely age group to select "The Bible" than those 18–34 (35%) and 35–49 (39%). Hispanics (20%) and other ethnicities (24%) are more likely to select "The media" than White non-Hispanics (12%). White non-Hispanics (49%) are more likely to select "The Bible" than Black non-Hispanics (36%) and Hispanics (42%).

RIGHT TO THE LAND

Table 4: "Palestinian people have a historic right to the land of Israel." n=1,981

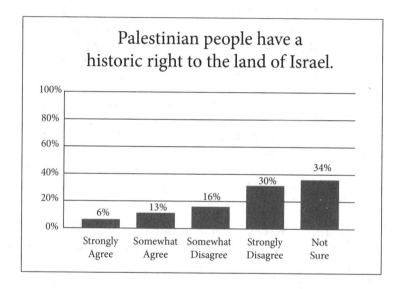

Males (53%) are more likely to disagree than females (41%). Those in the West are most likely to disagree (58%). Those age 50–64 (48%) and 65+ (53%) are more likely to disagree than those 18–34 (41%) and 35–49 (41%). White non-Hispanics (53%) and other ethnicities (58%) are more likely to disagree than Black non-Hispanics (28%) and Hispanics (40%). Those with a bachelor's degree (53%) or a graduate degree (54%) are more likely to disagree than those who are high school graduates or less (44%) or with some college (45%).

Table 5: "Jewish people have a historic right to the land of Israel."
n=1,982

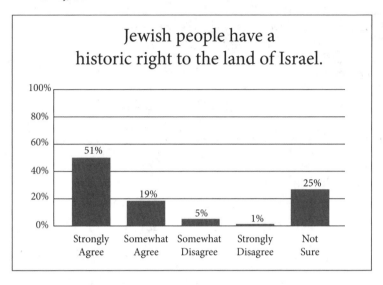

Males (74%) are more likely to agree than females (66%). Westerners (75%) are more likely to agree than Midwesterners (67%) and Southerners (68%). Those age 50–64 (72%) and 65+ (80%) are more likely to agree than those 18–34 (61%) and 35–49 (62%). Black non-Hispanics are the least likely ethnic group to agree (54%).

Table 6: "Jewish people have a biblical right to the land of Israel, but also have a responsibility to share the land with Palestinian Arabs."

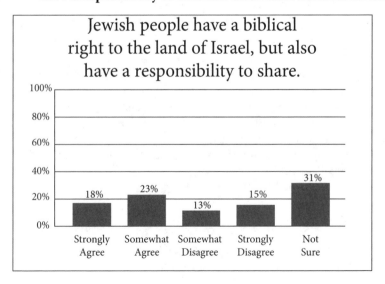

Those age 65+ (48%) are more likely to agree than those 18–34 (37%). White non-Hispanics are the least likely ethnic group to agree (38%). Those with a graduate degree (49%) are more likely to agree than those who are high school graduates or less (40%) or with some college (39%).

Table 7: "Biblical passages about Jewish people having a right to the land of Israel no longer apply today." n=1,982

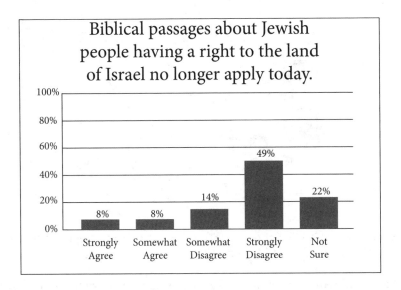

Those in the Northeast (22%) are more likely to agree than those in the South (13%) and West (14%). Those age 50–64 (65%) and 65+ (72%) are more likely to disagree than those 18–34 (58%) and 35–49 (55%).

Black non-Hispanics (20%) and other ethnicities (23%) are more likely to agree than White non-Hispanics (13%). White non-Hispanics are most likely to disagree (70%). Those who are high school graduates or less are the least likely education group to disagree (57%)

Table 8: "When God promised Abraham and his descendants the land of Israel, the promise was for all time." n=1,980

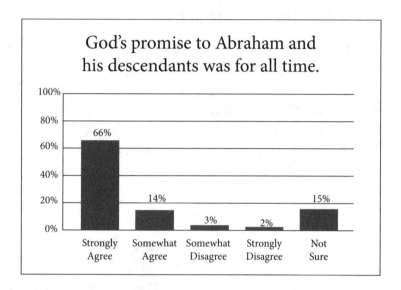

Those age 50–64 (83%) and 65+ (86%) are more likely to agree than those 18–34 (72%) and 35–49 (75%).

Table 9: "Christians should support the right of the Jewish people to live in the sovereign state of Israel." n=1,983

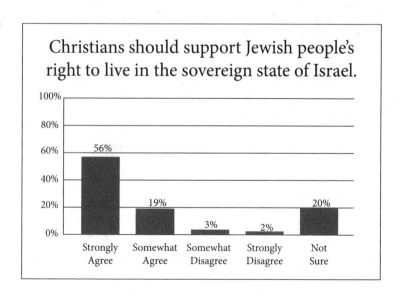

Those age 50–64 (77%) and 65+ (86%) are more likely to agree than those 18–34 (68%) and 35–49 (68%). Other ethnicities are the most likely ethnic group to agree (90%), followed by White non-Hispanics (78%).

Table 10: "The Jewish people lost the promise of the land because they rejected Jesus." n=1,980

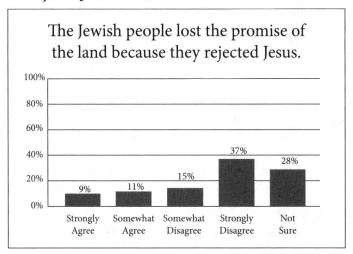

Those in the Northeast (27%) are more likely to agree than those in the Midwest (18%) and South (20%). Those age 35–49 are the most likely age group to agree (27%). Those age 50–64 (56%) and 65+ (61%) are more likely to disagree than those 18–34 (45%) and 35–49 (40%). White non-Hispanics are the least likely to agree (16%).

SUPPORT FOR THE EXISTENCE, SECURITY, AND PROSPERITY OF THE STATE OF ISRAEL

42% support the existence of the State of Israel, but don't feel the need to support everything Israel does.

Table 11: "Which of the following statements best represents your personal views?" n=1,987

I support the existence, security, and prosperity of the State of Israel no matter what Israel does.	24%
I support the existence, security, and prosperity of the State of Israel but don't feel the need to support everything Israel does.	42%
I do not support the existence, security, and prosperity of the State of Israel.	1%
I have no strong views about the State of Israel.	32%

Females (39%) are more likely to select "I have no strong views about the State of Israel" than males (25%). Those in the West (49%) are more likely to select "I support the existence, security, and prosperity of the State of Israel but don't feel the need to support everything Israel does" than those in the Northeast (38%) and South (39%). Those age 65+ (29%) are more likely to select "I support the existence, security, and prosperity of the State of Israel no matter what Israel does" than those 18–34 (22%) and 35–49 (22%). Those age 65+ are the most likely age group to select "I support the existence, security, and prosperity of the State of Israel but don't feel the need to support everything Israel does" (48%). Those age 18–34 (41%) are more likely to select "I have no strong views about the State of Israel" than those 50–64 (33%) and 65+ (22%).

Black non-Hispanics are the least ethnic group likely to select "I support the existence, security, and prosperity of the State of Israel no matter what Israel does" (14%) and the most likely to select "I have no strong views about the State of Israel" (52%). White non-Hispanics (46%) are more likely to select "I support the existence, security, and prosperity of the State of Israel but don't feel the need to support everything Israel does" than Hispanics (38%) and Black non-Hispanics (32%). Those with a bachelor's (57%) or a graduate degree (56%) are more likely to select "I support the existence, security, and prosperity of the State of Israel but don't feel the need to support everything Israel does" than those who are high school graduates or less (34%) or with some college (43%). Those who are high school graduates or less are the most likely education group to select "I have no strong views about the State of Israel" (39%)

"Which of the following reasons, if any, contribute to your support for the modern State of Israel?"

Table 12: "Which of the following reasons, if any, contribute to your support for the modern State of Israel?" n=1,314

The Bible says God gave the land of Israel to the Jewish people.	63%
Israel is the historic Jewish homeland.	60%
Israel is important for fulfilling biblical prophecy.	52%
Every nation has a right to exist.	49%
Israel is the United States' closest ally in an unstable region.	43%
The Bible says Christians should support Israel.	42%
Jesus was a Jewish person.	36%
Other	2%
None of these	1%
Not sure	4%

The Bible says God gave the land of Israel to the Jewish people.
Those age 50–64 (66%) and 65+ (68%) are more likely to select "Yes" than those 35–49 (55%). White non-Hispanics (66%) and other ethnicities (68%) are more likely to select "Yes" than Black non-Hispanics (52%).

Israel is the historic Jewish homeland.
Those in the West (67%) are more likely to select "Yes" than those in the Northeast (56%) and South (58%). Those age 35–49 are the least likely age group to select (50%). White non-Hispanics (62%) and other ethnicities (72%) are more likely to select "Yes" than Black non-Hispanics (48%). Those with a bachelor's degree (69%) are more likely to select "Yes" than those who are high school graduates or less (56%) or have a graduate degree (58%).

Israel is important for fulfilling biblical prophecy.
Those age 65+ (60%) are more likely to select "Yes" than those 18–34 (47%) and 35–49 (42%). White non-Hispanics (53%) and other ethnicities (61%) are more likely to select "Yes" than Black non-Hispanics (43%).

Every nation has a right to exist.
Those in the Northeast (58%) are more likely to select "Yes" than those in the South (46%). Those age 18–34 (54%) and 50–64 (51%) are more likely to select "Yes" than those 35–49 (43%). Hispanics (58%) and other ethnicities (59%) are more likely to select "Yes" than White non-Hispanics (46%). Those with a bachelor's (53%) or a graduate degree (55%) are more likely to select than those who are high school graduates or less (45%).

Israel is the United States' closest ally in an unstable region.
Males (50%) are more likely to select "Yes" than females (36%). Those age 65+ (49%) are more likely to select "Yes" than those 35–49 (39%) and 50–64 (41%). Black non-Hispanics are the least likely ethnic group to select "Yes" (27%), followed by Hispanics (37%). Those with a bachelor's degree (49%) or a graduate degree (49%) are more likely to select "Yes" than those who are high school graduates or less (40%).

The Bible says Christians should support Israel.
Those age 18–34 (45%) and 50–64 (47%) are more likely to select "Yes" than those 35–49 (37%). Other ethnicities (51%) are more likely to select "Yes" than Black non-Hispanics (36%) and Hispanics (38%).

Jesus was a Jewish person.
Those age 35–49 are the least likely age group to select "Yes" (28%). Hispanics (43%) are more likely to select "Yes" than White non-Hispanics (33%). Those who are high school graduates or less are the most likely education group to select "Yes" (41%).

33% select "the Bible says God gave the land of Israel to the Jewish people" as their primary reason for support.

Table 13: "Which of the following reasons is the most important reason for your support for the modern State of Israel?" n=1,310

The Bible says God gave the land of Israel to the Jewish people.	33%
Every nation has a right to exist.	16%
The Bible says Christians should support Israel.	14%
Israel is important for fulfilling biblical prophecy	12%
Israel is the historic Jewish homeland.	8%
Israel is the United States' closest ally in an unstable region.	7%
Jesus was a Jewish person.	3%
Other	1%
None of these	1%
Not sure	5%

Those in the Northeast are most likely to select "Every nation has a right to exist" (30%). Those in the South (35%) and West (37%) are more likely to select "The Bible says God gave the land of Israel to the Jewish people" than those in the Midwest (26%).

Those age 35–49 (20%) are more likely to select "Every nation has a right to exist" than those 65+ (13%). Those age 18–34 are the most likely age group to select "The Bible says Christians should support Israel" (24%). Those age 50–64 (36%) and 65+ (37%) are more likely to select "The Bible says God gave the land of Israel to the Jewish people" than those 35–49 (26%). Those age 18–34 are the least likely age group to select "Israel is important for fulfilling biblical prophecy" (6%).

Hispanics (21%) and other ethnicities (24%) are more likely to select "Every nation has a right to exist" than White non-Hispanics (14%). Those with a graduate degree (14%) are most likely to select "Israel is the United States' closest ally in an unstable region."

Those who attend church services one to three times a month (13%) are more likely to select "Israel is the historic Jewish homeland" than those attending once a week or more (8%) or less than once a month (6%). Those who attend church services once a week or more (36%) are more likely to select "The Bible says God gave the land of Israel to the Jewish people" than those attending one to three times a month (22%) or less than once a month (26%). Those attending church services less than once a month (16%) are more likely to select "Israel is important for fulfilling biblical prophecy" than those attending once a week or more (11%) or one to three times a month (9%).

71% say that their support for the State of Israel has stayed the same over the last five years.

Table 14: "Which of the following best represents your personal views? My support for the existence, security, and prosperity of the State of Israel has" n=1,970

Increased over the last 5 years	24%
Stayed the same over the last 5 years	71%
Decreased over the last 5 years	5%

Those age 65+ (29%) are more likely "Increased over the last 5 years" to select than those 18–34 (19%) and 50–64 (23%). Those age 18–34 (75%) are more likely to select "Stayed the same over the last 5 years" than those 65+ (67%).

MODERN STATE OF ISRAEL

Personal views on the modern rebirth of the State of Israel in 1948

Table 15: "When you think of the modern rebirth of the State of Israel in 1948 and the re-gathering of millions of Jewish people to Israel, which of the following statements best represents your personal views?" n=1,956

| These events were fulfillments of Bible prophecy that show we are getting closer to the return of Jesus Christ. | 80% |
| These events were interesting geopolitical events but they were not the result or fulfillment of biblical prophecy. | 20% |

Those age 50–64 (82%) are more likely to select "These events were fulfillments of Bible prophecy that show we are getting closer to the return of Jesus Christ" than those 35–49 (76%). Other ethnicities are the most likely ethnic group to select "These events were fulfillments of Bible prophecy that show we are getting closer to the return of Jesus Christ" (91%). Those who are high school graduates or less (82%) or with some college (81%) are more likely to select "These events were fulfillments of Bible prophecy that show we are getting closer to the return of Jesus Christ" than those with a graduate degree (73%).

Table 16: "The state of Israel should sign a peace treaty that allows the Palestinians to create their own sovereign state in the West Bank and Gaza." n=1,978

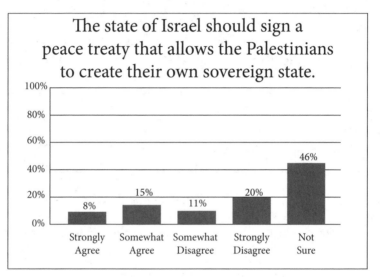

Those in the Northeast (32%) are more likely to agree than those in the Midwest (23%) and South (21%). Those in the West are most likely to disagree (42%). Those age 50–64 (36%) and 65+ (34%) are more likely to disagree than those 18–34 (25%) and 35–49 (27%). White non-Hispanics are the least likely ethnic group to agree (20%).

Table 17: "The modern rebirth of the State of Israel has been a terrible injustice to the Arab people in the Middle East." n=1,968

Males (58%) are more likely to disagree than females (43%). Those in the West (57%) are more likely to disagree than those in the Northeast (43%) and South (48%). Those age 55–64 (55%) and 65+ (62%) are more likely to disagree than those 18–34 (34%) and 35–49 (43%). Those age 18–34 (19%) and 35–49 (17%) are more likely to agree than those age 50–64 (13%) and 65+ (9%).

White non-Hispanics (59%) and other ethnicities (55%) are more likely to disagree than Black non-Hispanics (22%) and Hispanics (43%). Those who are high school graduates or less are the least likely education group to disagree (43%).

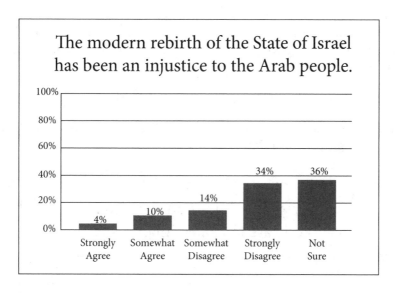

The modern rebirth of the State of Israel has been an injustice to the Arab people.

Table 18: "Modern Israel has been unfair to the Palestinian people."
n=1,969

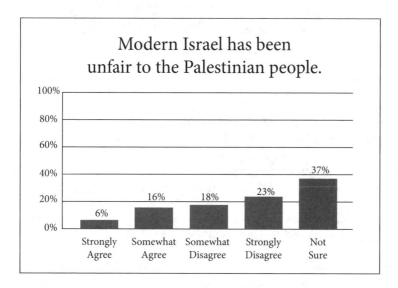

Modern Israel has been unfair to the Palestinian people.

Males (48%) are more likely to disagree than females (35%). Those in the West (50%) are more likely to disagree than those in the Northeast (34%) and South (39%). Those age 50–64 (45%) and 65+ (49%) are more likely to disagree than those 18–34 (32%) and 35–49 (35%).

White non-Hispanics are the least likely ethnic group to agree (17%). Black non-Hispanics are the least likely ethnic group to disagree (18%). Those who are high school graduates or less are the least likely education group to disagree (36%).

CHRISTIANS AND ISRAEL

Table 19: "Christians should do more to love and care for Palestinian people." n=1,965

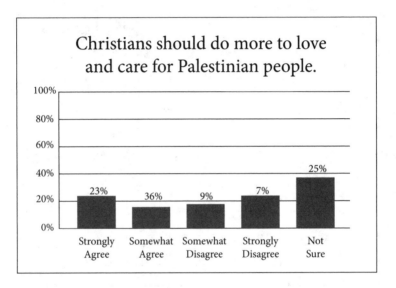

Christians should do more to love and care for Palestinian people.

Those in the Northeast (66%) and the West (66%) are more likely to agree than those in the South (55%). Those age 18–34 (66%) are more likely to agree than those 50–64 (57%) and 65+ (54%). Black non-Hispanics are the least likely ethnic group to disagree (7%). Those who are high school graduates or less are the least likely education group to agree (53%).

Table 20: "Christians should support Israel's defense of itself from terrorists and foreign enemies." n=1,972

Males (81%) are more likely to agree than females (67%). Those in the West are most likely to agree (82%). Those age 50–64 (74%) and 65+ (83%) are more likely to agree than those 19–34 (66%) and 35–49 (67%). Black non-Hispanics are the least likely ethnic group to agree (57%). Those a bachelor's (83%) or a graduate degree (86%) are more likely to agree than those who are high school graduates or less (69%) or with some college (72%).

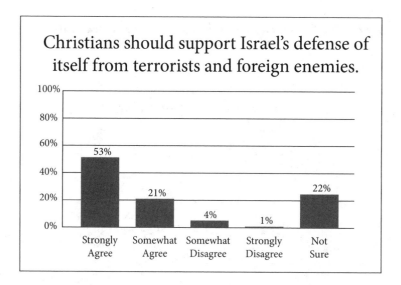

Christians should support Israel's defense of itself from terrorists and foreign enemies.

Table 21: "I am concerned for the safety of Christians in areas under the control of the Palestinian Authority." n=1,967

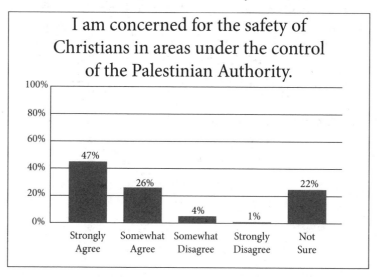

I am concerned for the safety of Christians in areas under the control of the Palestinian Authority.

Males (80%) are more likely to agree than females (68%). Those in the West (80%) are more likely to agree than those in the Midwest (71%) and South (70%). Those age 50–64 (76%) and 65+ (75%) are more likely to agree than those 18–34 (68%). Black non-Hispanics are the least likely ethnic group to agree (59%). Those a bachelor's (84%) or a graduate degree (81%) are more likely to agree than those who are high school graduates or less (68%) or with some college (73%).

Table 22: "The Christian church has fulfilled or replaced the nation of Israel in God's plan." n=1,956

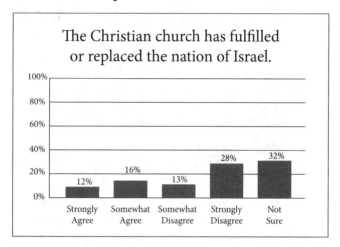

Those in the Northeast are the most likely to agree (39%). Those age 18–34 (34%) and 35–49 (31%) are more likely to agree than those 50–49 (24%) and 65+ (23%). White non-Hispanics are the most likely ethnic group to disagree (45%). Those with a bachelor's (46%) or a graduate degree (55%) are more likely to disagree than those who are high school graduates or less (37%).

JEWISH PEOPLE AND THE GOSPEL

Table 23: "Sharing the Gospel with Jewish people is important." n=1,967

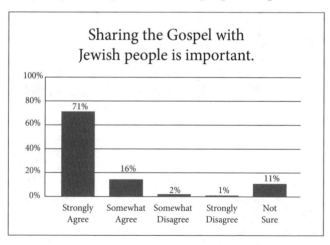

Those in the Northeast (92%) and West (92%) are more likely to agree than those in the Midwest (83%) and South (85%). Those age 65+ (91%) are more likely to agree than those 18–34 (82%) and 35–49 (84%). Other Ethnicities are the most likely ethnic group to agree (97%). Those who are high school graduates or less are the least likely education group to agree (83%).

Table 24: "The Bible teaches that one day most or all Jewish people, alive at that time, will believe in Jesus." n=1,963

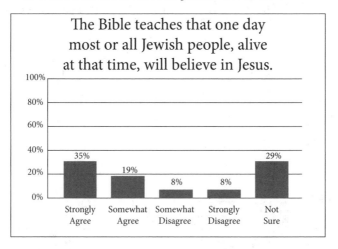

Those in the Midwest are least likely to agree (48%). Those age 50–64 (59%) and 65+ (62%) are more likely to agree than those 18–34 (47%) and 35–49 (47%). Those with bachelor's degrees are the least likely to agree (42%).

Table 25: "Jewish people continue to be significant for the history of redemption as Jesus will return when the Jewish people accept Jesus." n=1,956

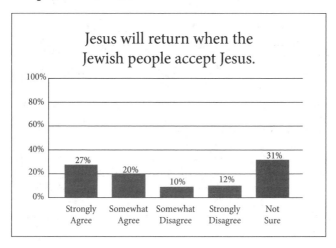

Those age 50–64 (51%) are more likely to agree than those 18–34 (44%) and 35–49 (44%). White non-Hispanics are the least likely ethnic group to agree (42%). Those who are high school graduates or less (48%) or with a graduate degree (54%) are more likely to select than those with a bachelor's degree (40%).

Table 26: "I wish I knew more about what the Bible teaches about Israel's future." n=1,962

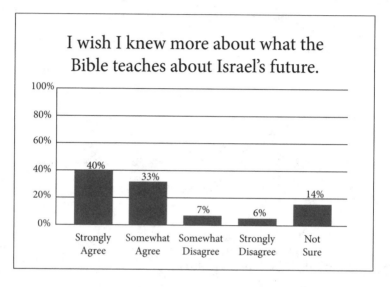

Those age 65+ are the most likely age group to agree (79%). Other ethnicities are the most likely ethnic group to agree (87%).

46% do not have Jewish, Muslim, or Palestinian friends.

Table 27: "Currently, do you have any…" n=1,988

Jewish friends	30%
Muslim friends	17%
Palestinian friends	6%
None of these	46%
Not sure	19%

35% of those with Jewish friends have prayed for the salvation of their Jewish friends in the last week.

Table 28: "In the last week have you prayed for the salvation of your Jewish friend(s)?" n=591

Yes	35%
No	60%
Not sure	5%

60% of those with Jewish friends have not shared the Gospel with any of them in the last year.

Table 29: "In the last year have you shared the Gospel with any of your Jewish friends?" n=588

Yes	32%
No	60%
Not sure	9%

U.S. AND ISRAEL

97% have not traveled to Israel.

Table 30: "Have you ever traveled to Israel?" n=1,998

Yes	3%
No	97%

51% of those who have never been to Israel are interested or very interested in traveling to Israel.

Table 31: "How interested would you be to travel to Israel if it was financially possible?" n=1,925

Very Interested	34%
Interested	17%
Somewhat Interested	19%
Not Interested at All	21%
Not sure	10%

31% believe the US does the right amount to help Israel.

Table 32: "Which of the following best describes your views on American involvement in Israel?" n=1,985

The U.S. does too much to help Israel	6%
The U.S. is doing the right amount to help Israel	31%
The U.S. does not do enough to help Israel	24%
Not sure	38%

DEMOGRAPHICS

Political ideology of participants

Table 33: "Which description best represents your political ideology?" n=1,989

Progressive/Very Liberal	2%
Liberal	6%
Moderate	15%
Conservative	39%
Very Conservative	18%
Libertarian	2%
Not sure	19%

Political affiliation of participants

Table 34: "In which party are you registered to vote or do you consider yourself to be a member?" n=1,989

Democrat	29%
Republican	46%
Independent	16%
Libertarian	1%
Green	<1%
Constitution	1%
Other	7%

Jewish parents or grandparents

Table 35: "Are one or more of your parents or grandparents Jewish?" n=1,989

Yes	2%
No	93%
Not sure	5%

Worship service attendance of participants

Table 36: "How often do you attend worship services at a church?" n=1,976

Once a week or more	65%
Three times a month	5%
Twice a month	4%
Once a month	2%
Several times a year	7%
Rarely	14%
Never	4%

Denomination of Protestant and non-denominational participants

Table 37: "What specific religious group or denomination type do you prefer?" n=1,740

Assemblies of God	3%
Baptist	32%
Christian & Missionary Alliance	2%
Church of Christ	3%
Church of God	3%
Evangelical Free	2%
Lutheran	5%
Methodist	5%
Non-denominational	19%
Pentecostal	7%
Presbyterian	3%
None	5%

Denominations receiving one percent or less: African Methodist Episcopal (AME), Anglican, Apostolic, Brethren, Calvary Chapel, Christian Methodist Episcopal, Church of God in Christ, Congregational, Disciples of Christ, Episcopal, Evangelical Covenant Church, Foursquare Gospel, Mennonite, Messianic Jewish, Nazarene, Reformed, Seventh Day Adventist, Vineyard Church, Wesleyan, Other

Gender of participants

Male	44%
Female	56%

Region of participants

Northeast	10%
Midwest	20%
South	54%
West	16%

Age of participants

18–34 years old	20%
35–49 years old	23%
50–64 years old	33%
65 years or more	25%

Education level of participants

High school graduate or less	49%
Some college	28%
College graduate	14%
Graduate degree	8%

Ethnicity of participants

White, Non-Hispanic	62%
Black, Non-Hispanic	20%
Hispanic	13%
Other	5%

ALLIANCE FOR THE
PEACE OF JERUSALEM

STATEMENT

THE ALLIANCE FOR THE PEACE OF JERUSALEM is an organization dedicated to facilitating a better public understanding of the complexities of the Middle East including its roots in history and the Bible. The group, which is comprised of key faith leaders, scholars, authors, and pastors, strives to educate Millennials and others about Israel's role in the biblical narrative—past, present, and future—while also affirming God's concern for Palestinians and all people's of the Middle East.

THE PURPOSE OF THE ALLIANCE IS:

1. To unite Pro-Israel Evangelicals in concerted action to counterbalance the growing Supersessionist trends within the global Evangelical movement.

2. To promote a theology that gives Israel a proper place in the story of the Bible and that is relevant and sensitive to the theological and social issues of the Middle East conflict and engenders a greater degree of respect among the broader movement of Evangelicals.

3. To create a theological position that is positive towards Israel, demonstrates concern for the spiritual well being of Palestinians and all citizens of the Middle East that younger Evangelicals may more easily embrace.

4. To stimulate theological discussion, conferences, and the production of resources, books, websites, videos, podcasts, etc., at both an academic and popular level to impart this theological perspective within the "academy" and among pastors and Christian leaders.

5. To better define and respond to the theological and ethical issues of the Israeli-Palestinian Conflict leading to authentic dialogue and more genuine reconciliation in the region.

OUR HOPE FOR PEACE
A Statement on Israel, the Nations and the Gospel
By the Alliance for the Peace of Jerusalem

Affirmations

In General:

1. We affirm that God is faithful, unchanging, and keeps His covenants and promises to individuals and nations. (Num. 23:19; Deut. 7:8–9; Lam. 3:22–23; Rom. 4:21; 11:29; 2 Thess. 5:24; 2 Tim. 2:13; Heb. 13:8; Rev. 1:8)

2. We affirm these covenants include the restoration of creation, the formation and preservation of the Jewish people; the promise of a land for the physical descendants of Abraham, Isaac and Jacob; and blessings for all nations through Jesus the Messiah. (Gen. 12:1–3; 15:18–21; Isa. 49:5–6; Luke 2:29–32)

3. We affirm that Jesus, the promised Messiah, is Jewish and lived in the land of Israel—a necessary, important, and critical part of the gospel narrative. (Matt. 1:1–2; Rom. 1:3; 9:4–5)

4. We affirm that God loves Jews, Arabs, those who live in the Middle East, and all humanity, and that He sent His Son, Jesus the Messiah, to redeem and reconcile them to Himself and to one another. (Isa. 19:20–25; Jer. 31:1–3; 49:38–39; Joel 2:32; John 17:22–23; 2 Cor. 5:18–20)

5. We affirm that Jesus, Messiah of Israel, Son of David, and Lord of all nations, died for sins, was buried, and rose from the dead on the third day, so that through Him, forgiveness and cleansing from sins, personal renewal and everlasting life is given as a gift from God to all who believe in Him, whether Jew or Gentile. (Pss. 2:1–12; 16:5–11; Isa. 28:16; 52:13–53:12; Hos. 6:1–3; John 3:14–17; 7:37–38; 8:34–36; 10:27–30; Rom. 1:16–17; 1 Cor. 15:3–4)

6. We affirm the importance of the Great Commission, to "make disciples of all nations"—so Jews, Arabs, those who live in the Middle East, and all humanity may receive forgiveness of sins and eternal life by trusting in Jesus as Messiah and Lord. (Matt. 28:18–20; Mark 1:14–15; Luke 24:45–49; John 1:9–13; 3:16; 14:6; Acts 1:8; Rom. 1:16; 10:9–10)

7. We affirm that Jewish and Gentile followers of Jesus retain their unique identities in the Messiah, even as they form the spiritual unity Jesus prayed for and created through His death and resurrection, reflecting the full shalom of God. (John 17:20–23; Eph. 2:11–22; Rev. 5:9–10; 7:9)

The Present:

8. We affirm that the preservation of the Jewish people despite centuries of persecution and violence, and the return of millions of Jewish people to the Land of Israel, demonstrate that God is capable of keeping His promises and fulfilling His covenants. (Jer. 31:31–37; 33:19–26; Rom. 11:25–29)

9. We affirm that all efforts to bring the message of Jesus to Israel and the nations should be characterized by respect for ethnicity and culture, communicated with unconditional love, honesty, and clarity. (Matt. 4:23–25; 9:35–38; Rom. 1:16; 10:9–17)

10. We affirm and fully support the growing Messianic movement in Israel and around the world, whereby Jewish followers of Jesus cherish and express their Jewish identity in Jesus the Messiah. (Rom. 11:1–2, 5)

11. We affirm that Jesus said, "blessed are the peacemakers"—thus, the Church should faithfully pray for and humbly work towards peace, security, justice, and reconciliation between Israel and her Arab neighbors, and encourage a culture of love, respect, and unity among all followers of Jesus the Messiah in the Holy Land. (Pss. 122:6; 133:1; Mic. 6:8; Matt. 5:9; John 13:34–35; 17:20–23)

The Future:

12. We affirm that God will keep His promises to Israel, that one day "all Israel will be saved" by turning to Jesus, and the Messiah Jesus will return to establish His kingdom for Israel and all the nations of the world with blessings for all. (Isa. 2:1–4; 11:6–12; Matt. 23:37–39; Rom. 11:11–15, 25–29)

13. We affirm that the "all Israel" who will be saved in the future specifies those Jewish people alive on the earth who believe in Jesus as Messiah at the time of His return—therefore, faithful gospel proclamation among the Jewish people in preparation for that day has great significance for all followers of the Messiah Jesus. (Zech. 12:10–13:1; Rom. 1:16; 10:1; 11:25–29)

Denials

Theological:

1. We deny that God rejected the Jewish people forever because the Jewish people in general rejected Jesus as Messiah—to the contrary, God has faithfully preserved a remnant during the last 2,000 years and is drawing more Jewish people to faith in Yeshua today than ever before. (Ezek. 37:1–14; Rom. 11:1–5, 25–29)

2. We deny that God has replaced Israel with the Church in His plan for the ages—to the contrary, the God of the Bible is both a promise-maker and a promise-keeper. (Rom. 11:29; Rev. 21:10–14)

3. We deny the notion that flawed theology regarding the Jewish people is without consequence—to the contrary, the chronic pattern of theologians removing ethnic Israel from God's plan has led to virulent anti-Semitism bringing great harm to the Jewish people, and hindering the proclamation of the gospel to the Jewish people, for which the Church should repent. (Rom. 11:17–24, 28–29; 15:25–27)

4. We deny that Muslims are unresponsive to the Gospel—to the contrary, the gospel is the power of God for salvation to everyone who believes, and we rejoice in the great number of Muslims who have recently come to faith in Jesus the Messiah. (Joel 2:32; John 3:16; Rom. 1:16)

5. We deny that the Great Commission may be fulfilled in the Middle East without a global prayer movement because the physical and spiritual warfare in the region demands that followers of Jesus be "faithful in prayer." (Luke 11:2; Rom. 12:12; Eph. 6:10–18)

Ethical:

6. We deny that hostility towards Palestinians, or any other peoples in the Middle East, is congruent with expressing love and support for Israel. (Matt. 19:19; 5:43–45; Luke 6:27–28; John 15:12–13; Eph. 6:10–20)

7. We deny that the Church can effectively bear witness for Jesus in the Middle East without showing compassion towards the poor, vulnerable, and suffering—to the contrary, Jesus commands the Church to care for widows, orphans, prisoners, the physically weak, and the impoverished. (Matt. 9:35–36; 25:31–46; Mark 6:33–44; 8:1–21; Luke 10:25–37; James 1:27–2:26)

8. We deny the validity of any attempt to coerce a Jewish or Muslim person to follow Jesus as Messiah and Lord—to the contrary, every person has a God-given right to religious freedom, and thus should be permitted to make his or her own decision to receive or reject Jesus as Messiah, free from intimidation. (John 1:12; Acts 26:28–29; Rev. 22:17)

9. We deny that spiritual unity and fellowship between Jewish and Arab believers is impossible due to the political challenges and theological differences of the Middle East—to the contrary, our unity is rooted and grounded in our shared allegiance to the Messiah. (Luke 1:37; John 13:34–35; 17:20–23; Rom. 12:18; Phil. 4:1–7, 13)

10. We deny that an affirmation of God's love and ongoing plan for Israel requires uncritical, wholehearted agreement with all policies of the modern state of Israel—to the contrary, the Church is to "speak the truth in love." (Prov. 3:3; Eph. 4:15; Col. 4:6)

11. We deny that an affirmation of God's love for Palestinians, Syrians, Jordanians, Egyptians, Iranians, and other peoples in the Middle East requires uncritical, wholehearted agreement with all the policies of their governments—to the contrary, the Church is to "speak the truth in love." (Prov. 3:3; Eph. 4:15; Col. 4:6)

12. We deny that any affirmation of suicide bombings or acts of terrorism as heroic are appropriate for followers of Jesus—to the contrary, support for terrorism is immoral and counterproductive to the pursuit of authentic peace, justice and reconciliation in the region. (Pss. 33:5; 34:14; Isa. 61:8; Rom. 12:17; 2 Peter 3:9)

13. We deny that an enduring peace in Israel and the Middle East is possible unless the Prince of Peace reigns on His rightful throne, yet this does not negate the value and responsibility of believers in Jesus to prayerfully and practically pursue peace today. (Isa. 9:6–7; Rom. 12:18–19; Col. 3:14–15; Heb. 12: 14)

A CONCLUSION AND WAY FORWARD

DR. DARRELL BOCK

THE RELATIONSHIP BETWEEN ISRAEL, THE CHURCH, and the Middle East has a long and complicated history. It began with the God of Israel fulfilling his covenants with the people he created and chose by sending his promised Messiah, Jesus of Nazareth. His coming and work of redemption created a new first-century movement among the Jewish people who lived in the land of Israel. Yet this Spirit-infused Messianic Jewish movement could not be contained within Jerusalem, her capitol city where the Messiah died and rose for our sins, nor in the Galilee where he was born and conducted so much of his ministry. The movement spread quickly among the nations, as God always intended to use the Jewish people as his bridge of redemption to a sinful and broken world.

The members of the movement Jesus founded preached the Good News in synagogues throughout the Diaspora, initiating a call to global missions mandated just prior to his ascension (Matt. 28:19–20, Acts 1:8). Some centuries later, another monotheistic religion emerged, Islam, which also traced its spiritual heritage back to Abraham, as did Judaism and Christianity. This new faith would challenge both Judaism and Christianity and solidly established itself in the region as well. A spiritual and political tug of war ensued within the region, including disruptive and tragic events like the Crusades, and continues to this very day reflected in the disputes between the three major Abrahamic faiths over holy sites in Jerusalem and other parts of the Holy Land.

More recently, the rise of the Zionist movement, events tied to the aftermath of World War I, the horror of the Holocaust in World War II, the return of vast numbers of Jewish people to the Promised Land, and the establishment of Israel in 1948 placed a renewed Jewish state in the midst of a largely Islamic world. The political, social, and religious tensions between Jews and Arabs remain unresolved to this day. In general, the church in the West, especially Bible believing Christians, were and continue to be sympathetic to the right of the Jewish people to settle in their historic homeland. Historically, this support helped pave the way for the emergence of the modern State of Israel.

This long and tangled history is the context for this book as it has looked at the issues erupting after 1948 from a biblical, legal, and socio-historical perspective. These diverse vantage points are essential to understand the region as anyone who travels to the Holy Land is immediately confronted with this global mix of faiths and competing stories which undergird the current tensions.

Our hope is that this volume has presented the current complexities of the region in a way that affirms Israel's place in the Middle East. Israel has been, and is, an essential part of God's unfolding plan to bless and heal our world so desperately in need of redemption (Gen. 12:1–3). In fact, our authors have tried to make it clear that it is impossible to understand the future God has prepared for the world he created without understanding the role of Israel and the Jewish people in the midst of the story. Yet, we have also emphasized the great love the Creator has for the nations of the world, especially in the Middle East.

Our authors agree that the conflict between Israel and her neighbors in the region is caused by a fundamental rejection of Israel's right to exist as a Jewish nation. Our authors contend that the Bible does teach that the land of Israel belongs to the Jewish people. This does not mean that every policy and decision of the modern State of Israel is without flaw, as every nation is tainted by the Fall. Yet, Israel is all too often viewed as a stain on what is regarded as Muslim territory. At the same time, we respect the dignity of all people present in the holy land. This tension between differing people of distinct beliefs is particularly acute in Jerusalem, where holy sites of all three faiths reside. It is the recognition of this complexity and desire to clarify the issues by seeing them through the lens of Scripture that was the genesis for the book. Our authors remind all who read the book that our views about Israel, the nations, and the current Middle East conflict must be rooted and grounded in Scripture.

A SUMMARY OF THE CHAPTERS

The following attempts to summarize the critical arguments of the chapters from a theological, historical, and socio-political perspective.

THE THEOLOGICAL ISSUES
AT THE HEART OF THE CONFLICT

At a theological level, we recognize that the covenantal commitments of God and the fact that he faithfully keeps his promises that drives the story of Scripture regarding the Jewish people and the nations of the world. Mark Yarbrough urges readers to see the Bible as God's unfolding story about his intention to use Israel as his instrument of grace in restoring a fallen world. Israel is the chosen means through which God will bless the entire world through the nation he has created, called, and commissioned.

God's commitment to restore and redeem our broken world goes back to Genesis 12:1–3 and his promise to Abraham that his descendants would become a blessing to the world. It is ironic that this relationship created for the benefit of the nations has become, in our fallen world, a source of divisiveness. That was not God's intent in calling Israel as a people for the sake of his greater and global purposes.

This understanding of Israel's universal calling may also be seen in Walter Kaiser's reflections on Isaiah 19. He points out that God created Israel to be the nexus of salvation and reconciliation for the world, described by the prophet in terms of a highway connecting Egypt with Assyria through Israel with all three nations sharing in the worship of the same, one true God together. This vision for Israel predates the coming of Jesus by centuries, yet it is consistent with the understanding many Christians have of the full reconciling work of Jesus on the cross. This chapter is another one of many portions of the Hebrew Scriptures emphasizing the great theme of redemption and reconciliation ultimately through the work of Christ, a consistent and ongoing theme our authors weave together throughout the book as clearly presented throughout the full expanse of Scripture.

This way of reading the Hebrew Scriptures raises the issue of hermeneutics and how to understand those texts that focus on Israel's role in the story of the Bible. These concerns are particularly acute in various eschatological passages. Underscoring how God will be faithful to the promises he made to the Jewish people, Michael Rydelnik argues against reading the Bible in ways that divest or replace those intended to be the literal recipients of his promises. The mistake often made throughout church history and today, as the blessings of redemption are extended to the nations, is to remove or redefine the original recipients instead of including them as part of God's plan. Dr. Rydelnik showed us how a supersessionst reading of Scripture only exacerbates the biblical issues related to the conflict.

Richard Averbeck's walk through the covenants provides greater and finer details to the consistent and comprehensive plan of God painted by the writers of the Old Testament. He juxtaposes the idea of permanent promise and ongoing obligation with a call to faith and obedience in order to appropriate these promises. Dr. Averbeck illustrates the need for Israel to repent in order to enjoy the totality of God's promised covenantal blessings. He reminds the reader of the expectation that one day national Israel will accept God's offer of forgiveness through Jesus, according to Paul's explanation in Romans 11:25–29. At that time the natural branches will regrafted back into the "olive tree," a metaphor used by the apostle Paul to again remind us of God's hope for Jewish-Gentile unity.

In New Testament terms, I show how the hope of the kingdom points to a reconciliation that will be enjoyed by the nations of the world. One of God's goals for the gospel message is that Israel and the nations are brought together and share an appreciation of the grace God has extended to them through Jesus. All of this may sound distant in light of the social and political realities of the region today, but it is in fact the very biblical foundation for transforming the current hostilities into the *shalom* he always intended for mankind.

Craig Blaising takes a step back and looks at the overall relationship between Israel and the church. Rather than fusing them together, Blaising sees
the two as distinct entities designed by God for distinct periods of time, with
a unique set of purposes, while sharing some commonalties of identity as the
people of God. He warns against so flattening out the reading of Scripture
across time that we forget the distinctions Scripture also reveals regarding
Israel and the church. God's plan for the ages affirms both unity and diversity
which is clearly seen in the relationship between Israel and the church and
within the Body of Christ as well.

THE HISTORICAL REALTIES OF THE CONFLICT

So how did the story of Israel within the biblical story of covenants
and salvation get lost? Michael Vlach addresses this by looking at how the
Church Fathers handled the nation of Israel and the promise of the land. He
details the ways Christians lost an appreciation for the theme of Israel's restoration in both the Old and New Testaments, especially in regards to the land
promises. The rise of Gentiles as the core interpreters of the text contributed
to this loss by means of allegorizing and spiritualizing the interpretation of
key texts. Vlach's historical observations amplify Dr. Rydelnik's conclusions
as well by pinpointing the hermeneutical erasure of ethnic Israel from the
plan of God. In tracing this history, Vlach also notes how the original vision
of restoration accepted by many Church Fathers included Israel, a literal and
physical kingdom, and the fulfillment of land promises further affirmed by
some Church divines throughout the centuries. However, the early church's
recognition of the critical role in God's plan of Israel's restoration is now
either unknown or marginalized.

Craig Parshall examines the actual case for Israel's legal right to make decisions regarding her own security as a sovereign and modern nation in light
of international court opposition and the threat of United Nations sanctions.
As a lawyer, he looks at the foundations of Israel's nationhood and how Israel
responds to the challenges of a hostile global political environment. In particular, Parshall takes on efforts to marginalize the Jewish state and those allied to
her by rewriting the historical and legal facts of the emergence of the nation
in 1948. The chapter establishes an important context for understanding and
answering the legal challenges hurled at Israel by the international community.

One of the encouraging realities in Israel today is the dynamic growth of
the Israeli messianic movement. Dr. Erez Soref traces this growth and reflects
on the pressures of living as a believer for the Messiah in Israel. Dr. Soref
details the results of a recent survey of Messianic Jews in Israel regarding the
number of believers and the ways in which this growing movement reflects
the realities of modern Israel. The indigenous Israeli Messianic movement
harkens a major shift from the past when the Christian presence in Israel
was mostly comprised of people from other countries. The future for the
Gospel is bright, according to Dr. Soref, who is the leader of a Bible college
training both Israeli Jewish and Palestinian pastors and Christian workers for

the work of the Gospel in the Holy Land. In itself, this effort stands as a role model for reconciliation within the Israel.

Tom Doyle, a frequent visitor to Israel with a ministry throughout the Middle East, takes a look at the group that probably gets the least attention in the region, Palestinian evangelicals. This includes Palestinian Christians who recognize Israel's right to be a nation and to live in the Land promised them by God. He reminds us that not all Palestinians are hostile or affirming of terrorism, challenging a common stereotype. Doyle introduces the reader to a group of believers who may be a key source for peace in the region. Yet this group faces distinct challenges that make their life difficult, including threats on their lives from Palestinians who are hostile towards any support of Israel and oppose the work of the Gospel among Muslims.

An awareness of this group is a key part of the Middle Eastern puzzle. Their story also shows how Christ can make a difference in changing the direction of one's life, especially in terms of violence as the chapter closes describing Jewish and Palestinian believers who fellowship together as they are able. Amazingly, they are not restricted by fear of reprisal by more radical fundamentalist elements within their societies.

Michael Brown wrestles with one of the political elephants in the room by discussing the suggested two-state or one-state solution in solving the conflict from a biblical perspective. He walks the reader through the wide variety of issues and factors that one should take into consideration as part of this particularly challenging discussion. Dr. Brown calls for sensitivity and nuance in applying the Bible to the question as the issues are not so cut and dry. Dr. Brown encourages the reader to balance the biblical teaching on the topic with the immediate sense so many possess simply to bring the hostiles to an end. His study of the Hebrew Bible gives us some insights to some passages that many assumed teach that the Land may never be divided according to Scripture. I am sure readers find his chapter to be both challenging and helpful in shaping views on this issue within Scriptural boundaries.

Mitch Glaser writes as president of Chosen People Ministries, an international mission to the Jewish people. Dr. Glaser provides a counterbalance to the Doyle chapter, by reviewing the beliefs of Christian groups who oppose the presence of Israel in the Land, which has damaged efforts to bring the Gospel to the Jewish people. He also analyzes views he deems extreme that too easily excuse the role of violence in the region. The flaws of the Kairos Document come in for attention, as well as its foundational supersessionism. Replacement theology invalidates any ongoing theological existence to Israel and the Jewish people, resulting in great harm in efforts to bring the Gospel to Jewish people as well as efforts to bring authentic reconciliation among Jews and Arabs. The existence of these views complicates our efforts find solutions in the region. There is an appeal for balance and restraint in the chapter that needs to be heard.

Mark Bailey, the president of Dallas Theological Seminary, underscores the relevance of trusting in Scripture's promises and God's character as we think about the region. Bailey reiterates the importance of acknowledging that the ways in which we understand God's faithfulness to Israel impacts the confidence we have in our own faith. He makes the biblical case for why Christians should support Israel. That support comes not because one is for Israel as one who can do no wrong, but because God chose the Jewish people for his glory and holy purposes. Bailey argues that the land is not incidental to God nor to the Jewish people. So the land should not be treated as less important by Christians today.

Additionally, the encouragement to share the Good News with others reflects God's commitment and love for all people as reflected in the Great Commission. It also grows out of a commitment to follow the Great Commandment to love God and one's neighbor. All these themes are central to how we view events in the region, making our personal reflections on the Middle East crisis and conflict relevant. No Christian should ignore the commands and the issues tied to them.

CONCLUSION

Anyone reading the chapters in this book immediately senses the web of complexities the region presents. Multiple millennia of conflicts and proposed solutions will certainly not be reversed overnight. With so many faiths present, establishing productive and irenic dialogue, as well as trust, is a significant challenge. Because violence is so often an act of first resort peaceful solutions have proven to be elusive. Nonetheless, it is the conviction of the authors of these chapters that there is a way forward—which begins with a deeper understanding of the role of Israel in God's plan. Once Israel's role becomes clear, an understanding of God's plans for the nations comes easier, as does the path to real and comprehensive reconciliation.

Our hope is ultimately in the Gospel because we believe in a God who always keeps his promises. The existence of Israel and the perseverance of the Jewish people is a visible reminder of God's faithfulness. We are especially encouraged by the growth of the global Messianic movement and for the growth of the Palestinian church. It is our hope that followers of Jesus will lead the way in showing what a humanity united in Christ looks like. This necessitates our praying for and doing all we can to bring the Good News of Jesus the Messiah to the peoples of the Middle East, beginning with the Jew (Rom. 1:16).

God has shown how genuine reconciliation is possible. We contend that recognizing that God's faithfulness to his promises through the Messiah also shows how both Israel and the nations can find true shalom in a situation that seems humanly impossible. It is because of this hope that we can pray for the peace of Jerusalem.

BIBLIOGRAPHY

à Brakel, Wilhelmus. *The Christian's Reasonable Service,*. 4 vols. Grand Rapids: Reformation Heritage Books, 2015.

Alexander, Paul, ed. *Christ at the Checkpoint: Theology in the Service of Justice and Peace.* Eugene, OR: Pickwick Publications, 2012.

Alexander, Philip S. "The Parting of the Ways," In *Jews and Christians: The Parting of the Ways A.D. 70 to 135*, edited by James D. G. Dunn. Grand Rapids: Eerdmans, 1999.

Alexander, T. Desmond. "Further Observations on the Term 'Seed' in Genesis." *Tyndale Bulletin* 48 (1997).

_____. "Royal Expectations in Genesis to Kings: Their Importance for Biblical Theology." *Tyndale Bulletin* 49 (1998).

_____. *From Paradise to the Promised Land: An Introduction to the Pentateuch.* Third edition. Grand Rapids: Baker, 2012.

Allis, Oswald T. *Prophecy and the Church.* Philadelphia: Presbyterian and Reformed, 1947.

Amerding, Carl E., and W. Ward Gasque, eds. *A Guide to Biblical Prophecy.* Reprint. Eugene, OR: Wipf & Stock, 2001.

Arnold, Bill T., and H. G. M. Williamson, eds. *Dictionary of Old Testament Historical Books.* Downers Grove, IL: InterVarsity Press, 2005.

Augustine. *City of God.* Nicene and Post-Nicene Fathers, Series 1, 2:448: 29.

Averbeck, Richard E. "Law." In *Cracking Old Testament Codes: A Guide to Interpreting the Literary Genres of the Old Testament.* Nashville: Broadman and Holman, 1995.

_____. "The Egyptian Sojourn and Deliverance from Slavery in the Framing and Shaping of the Mosaic Law." In *"Did I Not Bring Israel Out of Egypt?" Biblical, Archaeological, and Egyptological Perspectives on the Exodus Narratives*, Bulletin of Biblical Research Monograph Series, edited by James Hoffmeier, et al. Winona Lake, IN: Eisenbrauns, 2016.

_____. "The Cult in Deuteronomy and Its Relationship to the Book of the Covenant and the Holiness Code." In *Sēpher Tôrat Mōšeh: Studies in the Interpretation of Deuteronomy*, edited by Daniel I. Block and Richard L. Schultz. Peabody, MA: Hendrickson, 2017.

Barrett, C. K. *Critical and Exegetical Commentary on the Acts of the Apostles.* London: Bloomsbury T & T Clark, 2004.

Bartholomew, Craig G. "Covenant and Creation: Covenant Overload of Covenantal Deconstruction." *Calvin Theological Journal* 30 (1995).

Bauernfeind, Otto. *Kommentar und Studien zur Apostelgeschichte.* WUNT 22. Tübingen: Mohr-Siebeck, 1980.

Beale, G. K. *The Temple and the Church's Mission: A Biblical Theology of the Dwelling Place of God.* New Studies in the Biblical Theology. Downers Grove, IL: IVP, 2004.

Blaising, Craig A. "Premillennialism." In *Three Views on the Millennium and Beyond,* edited by Darrell L. Bock. Grand Rapids: Zondervan, 1999.

————. "A Case for the Pretribulational Rapture." In *Three Views on the Rapture: Pretribulation, Prewrath, or Posttribulation,* edited by Alan Hultberg. Grand Rapids: Zondervan, 2010.

————. "Israel and Hermeneutics." In *The People, the Land and the Future of Israel: A Biblical Theology of Israel and the Jewish People,* edited by Darrell L. Bock and Mitch Glaser. Grand Rapids: Kregel, 2014.

————. "Dispensation, Dispensationalism." In *The Evangelical Dictionary of Theology,* edited by Daniel J. Treier and Walter A. Elwell, 3rd edition. Grand Rapids: Baker, 2017.

Blaising, Craig A., and Darrell L. Bock, *Progressive Dispensationalism.* Reprint. Grand Rapids: Baker Books, 2000.

Blenkinsopp, Joseph. *Isaiah 1–39.* The Anchor Yale Bible 19. New Haven, CT: Yale University Press, 2008.

Bock, Darrell. *Luke 9:51–24:53.* Baker Exegetical Commentary on the New Testament. Grand Rapids, Baker, 1996.

————. "Covenants in Progressive Dispensationalism." In *Three Central Issues in Contemporary Dispensationalism: A Comparison of Traditional and Progressive Views,* edited by Herbert W. Bateman IV. Grand Rapids: Kregel, 1999.

————. *Recovering the Real Lost Gospel.* Nashville: Broadman & Holman, 2012.

————. "Israel in Luke-Acts." In *The People, the Land, and the Future of Israel: Israel and the Jewish People in the Plan of God,* edited by Darrell L. Bock and Mitch Glaser. Grand Rapids: Kregel, 2014.

Boda, Mark J. *Zechariah.* NICOT. Grand Rapids: Eerdmans, 2016.

Bodansky, Yossef. *The High Cost of Peace: How Washington's Middle East Policy Left America Vulnerable to Terrorism.* New York: Prima Publishing, 2002.

Brightman, Thomas. *A Revelation of the Apocalypse* (1611). EEBO Editions, ProQuest, 2010.

Brog, David. *Reclaiming Israel's History: Roots, Rights, and the Struggle for Peace.* Washington, DC: Regnery, 2017.

Brooks, David. "The Tel Aviv Cluster." *The New York Times,* January 12, 2010, A:23.

Brown, Michael L. "Jeremiah." In *The Expositors Bible Commentary,* revised edition. Grand Rapids: Zondervan, 2010.

Bruce, F. F. *Acts of the Apostles: The Greek Text with Introduction and Commentary.* NICNT. Grand Rapids: Eerdmans, 1990.

Brueggemann, Walter. *The Land: Place as Gift, Promise and Challenge in Biblical Faith.* Philadelphia: Fortress, 1977.

Buchanan, George Wesley. "To the Hebrews." In *The Anchor Bible*, Vol. 36. New York: Doubleday, 1972.

Burge, Gary. *Whose Land? Whose Promise?: What Christians Are Not Being Told about Israel and the Palestinians*. Cleveland: Pilgrim Press, 2003.

_____. *Jesus and the Land: The New Testament Challenge to "Holy Land" Theology*. Grand Rapids: Baker, 2010.

Campbell, Donald K. "Joshua." In *The Bible Knowledge Commentary: Old Testament*, edited by John F. Walvoord and Roy B. Zuck. Wheaton, IL: Victor Books, 1985.

Cannon, Mae Elise, ed. *A Land Full of God: Perspectives on the Holy Land* Eugene, OR: Cascade Books, 2017.

Carson, D. A. "Matthew." In *The Expositor's Bible Commentary*, Vol. 8. Grand Rapids: Zondervan, 1984.

_____. *The God Who Is There: Finding Your Place in God's Story*. Grand Rapids: Baker Books, 2010.

Chafer, Lewis Sperry. *Systematic Theology*. 8 vols. Dallas: Dallas Seminary Press, 1948.

Chapman, Colin. *Whose Promised Land?* Grand Rapids: Baker, 2002.

_____. *Whose Holy City?* Oxford: Lion, 2004.

Chester, Tim. *From Creation to New Creation: Making Sense of the Whole Bible Story*. Purcellville, VA: The Good Book Company, 2010.

Cohn-Sherbok, Dan. *Messianic Judaism*. London: A. & C. Black, 2000.

Conzelmann, Hans. *Acts of the Apostles: A Commentary on the Acts of the Apostles*. Hermeneia. Minneapolis: Fortress, 1988.

Cragg, Kenneth. *The Arab Christian: A History in the Middle East*. Louisville: John Knox Press, 1991.

Cranfield, C. E. B. *The Epistle to the Romans*, Vol II. The International Critical Commentary. Edited by J. A. Emerton and C. E. B. Cranfield. Edinburgh: T & T Clark, 1979.

Cyril of Alexandria. *Catechetical Lectures*. In William A. Jurgens, *The Faith of the Early Fathers*. 3 vols. Collegeville, MN: The Liturgical Press.

_____. *Patrologia Graeca*, 71:593, 595–596.

_____. *Ancient Christian Commentary on Scripture*, 14.125–126.

_____. *Nicene and Post-Nicene Fathers*, 2:450.

Danker, Frederick W. *Jesus and the New Age*. Philadelphia: Fortress, 1988.

Davies, W. D. *The Gospel and the Land: Early Christianity and Jewish Territorial Doctrine*. Berkeley: University of California Press, 1974.

Duvall, J. Scott, and J. Daniel Hays. *Living God's Word: Discovering Our Place in the Great Story of Scripture*. Grand Rapids: Zondervan, 2012.

Eckman, Jim. "Israel: A Channel of God's Blessing." *Issues in Perspective* June 1, 2003.

Edwards, Jonathan. *The Works of Jonathan Edwards*. Reprint. London: Banner of Truth Trust, 1976.

_____. *Works, A History of the Works of Redemption*, vol. 9. Edited by John F. Wilson. New Haven, CT: Yale University Press, 1989.

Ellis, E. Earl. *The Gospel of Luke*. Eugene, OR: Wipf and Stock, 2003.

Fahey, Dennis. *The Kingship of Christ and the Conversion of the Jewish Nation*. Kimmage, Dublin: Holy Ghost Missionary College, 1953.

Fairbarn, Patrick. *The Interpretation of Prophecy*. Edinburgh,:T. and T. Clark, 1865.

Feinberg, Paul D. "The Case for the Pretribulation Rapture Position." In *The Rapture: Pre-, Mid-, or Post-Tribulational?*, edited by Richard Reiter, et al. Grand Rapids: Zondervan, 1984.

Finch, Sir Henry. *The World's Great Restauration, or Calling of the Jews, and with them of all Nations and Kingdoms of the Earth to the Faith of Christ*. London: Edward Griffin, 1621.

Fitzmyer, Joseph A. *Acts of the Apostles*. The Anchor Yale Bible Commentaries. New Haven, CT: Yale University Press, 1998.

France, R. T. *The Gospel of Matthew*. NICNT. Grand Rapids: Eerdmans, 2007.

Garrett, Duane A. *Hosea, Joel*. NAC. Nashville: Broadman & Holman Publishers, 1997.).

Gentry, Peter J., and Stephen J. Wellum. *Kingdom through Covenant: A Biblical-Theological Understanding of the Covenants*. Wheaton, IL: Crossway, 2012.

Glick, Caroline. *The Israeli Solution: A One-State Plan for Peace in the Middle East*. New York: The Crown Publishing Group, 2014.

Goitein, S. D. *Jews and Arabs: Their Contact through the Ages*. New York: Schocken, 1964.

Gold, Dore. *The Fight for Jerusalem*. Washington, DC: Regnery, 2007.

Greengus, Samuel. "Covenant and Treaty in the Hebrew Bible and in the Ancient Near East." In *Ancient Israel's History: An Introduction to Issues and Sources*, edited by Bill T. Arnold and Richard S. Hess. Grand Rapids: Baker Academic, 2014.

Grudem, Wayne. *Understanding the Big Picture of the Bible: A Guide to Reading the Bible Well*. Wheaton, IL: Crossway, 2012.

Gundry, R. H. *A Commentary on His Literary and Theological Art*. Grand Rapids: Eerdmans, 1982.

Guthrie, Donald, "Galatians." In *New Century Bible*. London: Oliphants, 1974.

Hamilton, Victor P. *The Book of Genesis Chapters 1–17*. NICOT. Grand Rapids: Eerdmans, 1990.

Haran, Menahem. "The *Bĕrît* 'Covenant': Its Nature and Ceremonial Background." In *Tehillah le-Moshe: Biblical and Judaic Studies in Honor of Moshe Greenberg*, edited by Mordechai Cogan, et al. Winona Lake, IN: Eisenbrauns, 1997.

Hauser, Charles August Jr. "The Eschatology of the Church Fathers." Ph.D. diss., Grace Theological Seminary, 1961.

Helm, David R. *The Big Picture Story Bible*. Wheaton, IL: Crossway, 2010.

Henry, Matthew. *Matthew Henry's Commentary on the Whole Bible: Complete and Unabridged in One Volume*. Reprint. Peabody, MA: Hendrickson, 1994.

Hess, Richard S. "The Slaughter of the Animals in Genesis 15: Genesis 15:18–21 and Its Ancient Near Eastern Context." In *He Swore an Oath: Biblical Themes in Genesis 12–50*, edited by R. S. Hess, et al., second edition. Grand Rapids: Baker, 1994.

Holladay, William L. *Jeremiah 1: A Commentary on the Book of the Prophet Jeremiah, Chapters 1–25*. Hermeneia. Philadelphia: Fortress, 1986.

Holsteen, Nathan D., and Michael J. Svigel, gen. eds. *Exploring Christian Theology*. Minneapolis: Bethany House, 2015.

Horner, Barry E. *Future Israel: Why Christian Anti-Judaism Must Be Challenged*. Nashville: B&H Academic, 2007.

House, H. Wayne. "The Church's Appropriation of Israel's Blessings." In *Israel, the Land and the People: An Evangelical Affirmation of God's Promises*, edited by H. Wayne House. Grand Rapids: Kregel, 1998.

Hsieh, Nelson S. "Abraham as 'Heir of the World': Does Romans 4:13 Expand the Old Testament Abrahamic Land Promises?" *The Master's Seminary Journal* 26/1 (Spring 2015).

Hubbard, David A. *Joel and Amos: An Introduction and Commentary*. TOTC. Downers Grove, IL: InterVarsity Press, 1989.

Ice, Thomas. "Lovers of Zion: A Brief History of Christian Zionism." *Voice* (March/April 2005).

Jerome. *The Prophet Joel*. Corpus Christianorum: Series Latina. Turnhout: Brepols, 1953–.

Jervell, Jacob. *Die Apostelgeschichte*. Gottingen: Vandenhoeck & Ruprecht, 1998.

Justin Martyr. "First Apology." In *The Ante-Nicene Fathers,* 1:180.

———. "Dialogue with Trypho." In *The Ante-Nicene Fathers* 1:209, 239.

Kaiser, Walter C. Jr., *Toward an Old Testament Theology*. Grand Rapids: Zondervan, 1991.

———. "The Land of Israel and the Future Return." In *Israel: The Land and the People: An Evangelical Affirmation of God's Promises,* edited by H. Wayne House. Grand Rapids: Kregel, 1998.

———. "Nasi." In *Theological Wordbook of the Old Testament*, edited by R. Laird Harris, Gleason L. Archer, Jr., and Bruce K. Waltke. 2 vols. Chicago: Moody Press, 2003.

———. *Preaching and Teaching the Last Things: Old Testament Eschatology for the Life of the Church*. Grand Rapids: Baker Academic, 2011.

Katanacho, Yohanna. *The Land of Christ: A Palestinian Cry*. Eugene, OR: Pickwick Publications, 2013.

Kidner, Derek. *Genesis: An Introduction and Commentary*. TOTC. Downers Grove, IL: InterVarsity Press, 1967.

Kik, J. M. *Matthew Twenty-Four: An Exposition*. Philadelphia: Presbyterian and Reformed, 1948).

Kitchen, Kenneth A. *On the Reliability of the Old Testament*. Grand Rapids: Eerdmans, 2003.

Kitchen, Kenneth A., and Paul J. N. Lawrence. *Treaty, Law, and Covenant in the Ancient Near East*. 3 vols. Wiesbaden: Harrassowitz, 2012.

Kittel, Gerhard, and Gerhard Friedrich, editors. *Theological Dictionary of the New Testament*. 10 vols. Grand Rapids, Eerdmans, 1977.

Kjær-Hansen, Kai, and Bodil F. Skøjtt. *Facts and Myths about the Messianic Congregations in Israel*. Jerusalem: United Christian Council in Israel in cooperation with the Caspari Center, 1999.

Knoppers, Gary N. "Ancient Near Eastern Royal Grants and the Davidic Covenant: A Parallel?" *JAOS* 116 (1996).

Kümmel, Werner Georg. *Promise and Fulfillment: The Eschatological Message of Jesus*. London: SCM Press, 1957.

————. "Futurische und präsentische Eschatologie im ältesten Urchristentum." *NTS* 5 (1958–59).

Küng, Hans. *Judaism: Between Yesterday and Tomorrow*, translated by John Bowden. New York: Crossroad, 1992.

Lerner, Robert E. "Millennialism." In *The Encyclopedia of Apocalypticism*, edited by John J. Collins, Bernard McGinn, and Stephen J. Stein. New York: Continuum, 2000.

Lewis, C. S. *Reflections on the Psalms*. New York: Harcourt, Brace and World, 1958.

LiVecche, Marc. "One Hundred Thirty-Two Hours & Fifty Years: A Conversation with Michael Oren." *Providence* 7 (Spring 2017).

Loewenstamm, Samuel E. "The Divine Grants of Land to the Patriarchs." *JAOS* 91 (1974).

Longman, Tremper III, *Genesis*. The Story of God Bible Commentary. Grand Rapids: Zondervan, 2016.

Lucado, Max, and Randy Frazee. *The Story: The Bible as One Continuing Story of God and His People*. Grand Rapids: Zondervan, 2011.

Luter, A. Boyd. "The Continuation of Israel's Land Promise in the New Testament: A Fresh Approach." *Eruditio Ardescens* (Spring, I:2).

Mahoney, Timothy P., and Steven Law. *Patterns of Evidence: Exodus, a Filmmaker's Journey*. St. Louis Park: Thinking Man Media, 2015.

Marshall, I. Howard. The *Gospel of Luke*. The New International Greek Testament Commentary. Grand Rapids: Eerdmans, 1978.

Marty, William H. *The Whole Bible Story: Everything That Happens in the Bible in Plain English*. Minneapolis: Bethany House, 2011.

Matthews, V. H., M. W. Chavalas, and J. H. Walton. *The IVP Bible Background Commentary: Old Testament*. Downers Grove, IL: InterVarsity Press, 2000.

Mattill, A. J. Jr., *Luke and the Last Things: A Perspective for the Understanding of Lucan Thought*. Dillsboro, NC: Western North Carolina Press, 1979.

McCullough, Donald. *If Grace Is So Amazing, Why Don't We Like It? How God's Radical Love Turns the World Upside Down*. San Francisco: Jossey-Bass, 2005.

McDermott, Gerald. *Israel Matters*. Grand Rapids: Brazos Press, 2017.

McDermott, Gerald R., editor. *The New Christian Zionism: Fresh Perspectives on Israel and the Land*. Downers Grove, IL: InterVarsity Press, 2016.

McKenzie, John L. *Second Isaiah*. The Yale Anchor Bible 20. New Haven, CT: Yale University Press, 2008.

Meier, John P. *A Marginal Jew: Rethinking the Historical Jesus, Vol. 2: Mentor, Message, and Miracles.* ABRL. New York: Doubleday, 1994.

Moo, Douglas J. *The Epistle to the Romans.* NICNT. Grand Rapids: Eerdmans, 1996.

Müller, Paul-Gerhard. *EDNT*, 1:130.

Munayer, Salim J., editor, *The Land Cries Out: Theology of the Land in the Israeli-Palestinian Context.* Eugene, OR: Wipf & Stock, 2011.

Murray, Iain. *The Puritan Hope: Revival and the Interpretation of Prophecy.* London: Banner of Truth, 1971.

Neilsen, Anders E. *Until It Is Fulfilled.* WUNT 2/126. Tübingen: Mohr/Siebeck, 2000.

Nelson, David. "The Story of Mission: The Grand Biblical Narrative." In *Theology and Practice of Mission: God, the Church, and the Nations,* edited by Bruce Ashford. Nashville: B&H, 2011.

Nerel, G. "Messianic Jews in Eretz-Israel (1917–1967): Trends and Changes in Shaping Self Identity." PhD diss., Hebrew University of Jerusalem, 1996.

Nolland, John. "Salvation History and Eschatology." In *Witness to the Gospel: The Theology of Acts,* edited by I. Howard Marshall. Grand Rapids: Eerdmans, 1998.

Origen. *The Song of Songs.* In Ancient Christian Writers, edited by Johannes Quasten and Joseph C. Plumpe. Westminster, MD: The Newman Press, 1957.

Østerbye, P. *The Church in Israel.* Lund: C. W. K. Gleerup Bokförlag, 1970.

Paul, Ian. "Metaphor." In *Dictionary for Theological Interpretation of the Bible,* edited by Kevin J. Vanhoozer. Grand Rapids: Baker 2006.

Pelikan, Jaroslav. *The Emergence of the Catholic Tradition (100–600), Vol. 1: The Christian Tradition: A History of the Development of Doctrine.* Chicago: University of Chicago Press, 1971.

Perlman, S., and C. D. Harley, *World Evangelization,* vol. 13, no. 43. Lausanne: Lausanne Committee for World Evangelization, 1986.

Perrin, Nicholas. *Jesus the Temple.* Grand Rapids: Baker, 2010.

Pesch, R. *Die Apostelgeschichte (Apg 1–12).* EKKNT 5/1. Zurich: Benzinger/Neukirchen-Vluyn: Neukirchener, 1986.

Petinato, Giovanni. *The Archives of Ebla.* Garden City: Doubleday & Company, Inc., 1981.

Piper, John. "Land Divine?" *World,* May 11, 2002.

Plass, Edward M. editor. *What Luther Says.* St. Louis: Concordia Publishing House, 1959.

Poythress, Vern S. *Symphonic Theology: The Validity of Multiple Perspectives in Theology.* Grand Rapids: Zondervan, 1987.

Rainey, Anson F. *The Archaeology of the Land of Israel,* translated by Yohanan Aharoni. Philadelphia: Westminster Press, 1978.

Rashi. "Bereishis." In *The Metsudah Chumash/Rashi,* vol. 1, translated by Avrohom Davis. Hoboken, NJ: Ktav, 1993.

Riesenfeld, H. "Ἐμβολεύειν–Ἐντός." *Nuntius* 2 (1949).

Roberts, Vaughan. *God's Big Picture: Tracing the Storyline of the Bible*. Downers Grove, IL: InterVarsity Press, 2002.

Ross, Allen P. *Creation and Blessing: A Guide to the Study and Exposition of the Book of Genesis*. Grand Rapids: Baker, 1988.

Rydelnik, Michael. *Understanding the Arab-Israeli Conflict: What the Headlines Haven't Told You*, revised and updated. Chicago: Moody Publishers, 2007.

Rydelnik, Michael, and Michael VanLaningham, editors. "Genesis." *The Moody Bible Commentary*. Chicago: Moody Publishers, 2014.

Ryken, Leland. *Words of Delight*. Grand Rapids: Baker, 1992.

———. *The Literature of the Bible*. Grand Rapids: Zondervan, 1974.

Ryle, J. C. *Are You Ready for the End of Time?* Reprint of *Coming Events and Present Duties*. Fearn, Scotland: Christian Focus, 2001.

Saucy, Robert L. *The Case for Progressive Dispensationalism: The Interface between Dispensational and Non-Dispensational Theology*. Grand Rapids: Zondervan, 1993.

Schreiner, Thomas R. *Romans*, Baker Exegetical Commentary on the New Testament. Grand Rapids: Baker Books, 1998.

Senor, D., and S. Singer. *Start-up Nation: The Story of Israel's Economic Miracle*. New York: Hachette Book Group, 2009.

Serrarius, Petrus. *An Awakening Warning to a Wofull World*. Amsterdam: n.p., 1662.

Shanks, Hershel. "Jesus of History vs. Jesus of Tradition: BAR Interviews Sean Freyne," *Biblical Archaeological Review*, November/December 2010.

Sibley, Jim R. "Trends in Jewish Evangelism in Israel." In *Mishkan: A Forum on the Gospel and the Jewish People*, Issue 10 (1989).

Siker, Jeffrey S. *Disinheriting the Jews: Abraham in Early Christian Controversy*. Louisville: Westminster/John Knox, 1991.

Simon, Marcel. *Versus Israel: A Study of the Relations Between Christians and Jews in the Roman Empire (135–425)*, translated by H. McKeating. Oxford: Oxford University Press, 1986.

Sizer, Stephen. *Christian Zionism: Roadmap to Armageddon*. Leicester: InterVarsity Press, 2004.

———. *Zion's Christian Soldiers: The Bible, Israel and the Church*. Downers Grove, IL: IVP, 2007.

Smith, Gary. *Isaiah 1–39*. The New American Commentary. Nashville: Broadman & Holman Publishing Group, 2007.

Smolinski, Reiner. "Israel Redivivus: The Eschatological Limits of Puritan Typology in New England." In *The New England Quarterly*, Vol. 63, No. 3 (September, 1990).

Soref, E. "Report Summary for ICB's National Leaders' Survey, March–April, 2008." Unpublished manuscript for reaccreditation of Israel College of the Bible, November 2008.

Soulen, R. Kendell. *The God of Israel and Christian Theology*. Minneapolis: Fortress, 1996.

Spurgeon, Charles Haddon. "The Harvest and the Vintage." In *The Metro-*

politan Tabernacle Pulpit. Edinburgh: Banner of Truth, 1987.

_____. "The Restoration and Conversion of the Jews." In *The Metropolitan Tabernacle Pulpit*.

Stanfield, I. "Messianic Jews in the 19th Century and the Establishment of the 'Hebrew-Christian Alliance' in England, 1866–1871." MA dissertation, Hebrew University, 1995.

Stein, Robert. *A Basic Guide to Interpreting the Bible*. Grand Rapids: Baker, 1994.

Steiner, Henry J., and Philip Alston. *International Human Rights in Context—Law, Politics, Morals*. Oxford: Oxford University Press, 1996.

Stek, John H. "'Covenant' Overload in Reformed Theology." *Calvin Theological Journal* 29 (1994).

Stetzer, Ed. "The Big Story of Scripture: Creation, Fall, Redemption, Restoration." *Christianity Today*, November 2012.

Tasker, R. V. G. *The Gospel according to Matthew*, Tyndale New Testament Commentary. Grand Rapids: Eerdmans, 1961.

Tenney, Merrill C., editor. *The Zondervan Pictorial Encyclopedia of the Bible*, Vol. I. Grand Rapids: Zondervan Publishing House, 1976.

Terry, Milton. *Biblical Hermeneutics*, 2nd ed. 1883; reprint edition. Grand Rapids: Zondervan, 1999.

Tertullian. "*An Answer to the Jews, 1*," In *The Ante-Nicene Fathers*, 3:151.

_____. "*On Modesty, 8*," In *The Ante-Nicene Fathers*, 4:82.

Toussaint, Stanley D. *Behold the King*. Portland, OR: Multnomah Press, 1980.

Turner, D. L. *Matthew*, Baker Exegetical Commentary on the New Testament. Grand Rapids: Baker, 2008.

Twelftree, G. H. *Jesus the Exorcist: A Contribution to the Study of the Historical Jesus*. WUNT 2/54. Tübingen: Mohr-Siebeck, 1993.

Van Den Berg, J. "Appendix III: The eschatological expectation of seventeenth-century Dutch Protestantism with regard to the Jewish people." In *Puritan Eschatology: 1600–1660*, edited by Peter Toon. Cambridge: James Clarke, 1970.

Van Groningen, Gerard. "Covenant." In *Evangelical Dictionary of Biblical Theology*, edited by Walter A. Elwell. Grand Rapids: Baker, 1996.

VanLaningham, M. G. "Matthew." In *The Moody Bible Commentary*. Chicago: Moody Publishers, 2014.

Virkler, Henry. *Hermeneutics: Principles and Processes of Biblical Interpretation*. Grand Rapids: Baker, 1981.

Vlach, Michael. *Has the Church Replaced Israel?: A Theological Evaluation*. Nashville: B&H, 2010.

_____. "Israel in Church History." In *The People, the Land, and the Future of Israel: Israel and the Jewish People in the Plan of God*, edted by Darrell L. Bock and Mitch Glaser. Grand Rapids: Kregel, 2014.

von Rad, Gerhard. *The Problem of the Hexateuch and Other Essays*, translated by E. W. Trueman Dicken. London: Oliver & Boyd, 1966.

Watson, William. *Dispensationalism before Darby: Seventeenth-Century and Eighteenth-Century English Apocalypticism*. Silverton, OR: Lampion Press, 2015.

Watts, John D. W. *Isaiah 1–33*. The Word Biblical Commentary 24, revised edition. Nashville, Thomas Nelson, 2005.

———. *Isaiah 34–66*. The Word Biblical Commentary 25, revised edition. Nashville: Thomas Nelson, 2005.

Wax, Trevin. *Counterfeit Gospels*. Chicago: Moody, 2011.

Weiss, Johannes. *Jesus' Proclamation of the Kingdom of God*. Reprint of 1892 German edition. Philadelphia: Fortress Press, 1971.

Wellum, Stephen J., and Brent E. Parker, editors. *Progressive Covenantalism*. Nashville: B&H Academic, 2016.

Wenham, G. J. "The Symbolism of the Animal Rite in Genesis 15: A Response to G. F. Hasel," *JSOT* 19 (1981).

———. *Genesis 1–15*. WBC. Dallas: Word, 1998.

Westbrook, Matthew C. *The International Christian Embassy, Jerusalem, and Renewalist Zionism: Emerging Jewish-Christian Ethnonationalism*. Madison, NJ: Drew University Press, 2014.

Westermann, Claus. *Genesis 12–36: A Commentary*, translated by John J. Scullion, S. J. Minneapolis: Augsburg, 1985.

Whiston, William. *The Accomplishment of Scripture Prophecies. Being Eight Sermons . . . at the Cathedral*. Cambridge, 1708.

Wikgren, A. "Ἐντός," *Nuntius* 4 (1950).

Williamson, Paul R. *Abraham, Israel and the Nations: The Patriarchal Promise and its Covenantal Development in Genesis*. JSOTSup 315. Sheffield, England: Sheffield Academic Press, 2000.

———. "Covenant." In *Dictionary of the Old Testament: Pentateuch*. Downers Grove, IL: InterVarsity Press, 2003.

———. *Sealed with an Oath: Covenant in God's Unfolding Purpose*. NSBT 23. Downers Grove, IL: InterVarsity Press, 2007.

———. "Covenant." In *NIV Study Bible*, second edition. Grand Rapids: Zondervan, 2015.

Wilson, Ian. *The Bible Is History*. Washington, DC: Regnery, 1999.

Witsius, Herman Voetius, et al. "Of the Day of Judgment and World to Come." Yehuda MS 6 folio 12r–19r, Jerusalem University Library; in Frank Manuel, *The Religion of Isaac Newton* (Oxford: Oxford University Press, 1974), Appendix B.

Wolff, Hans Walter. *Joel and Amos: A Commentary on the Books of the Prophets Joel and Amos*. Hermeneia. Philadelphia: Fortress Press, 1977.

Wood, Leon J. *A Survey of Israel's History*, revised by David O'Brien. Grand Rapids: Zondervan Publishing House, 1986.

Wright, N. T. *The New Testament and the People of God*. Minneapolis: Fortress, 1992.

Yarbrough, Mark. *How to Read the Bible Like a Seminary Professor*. New York: FaithWords, 2016.

Zander, Walter. *Israel and the Holy Places of Christendom*. London: Weidenfeld & Nicolson, 1971.

SCRIPTURE INDEX

NAME INDEX

SUBJECT INDEX

ALSO AVAILABLE

FOREWORD BY
JOEL C. ROSENBERG

THE PEOPLE, THE LAND, AND THE FUTURE OF ISRAEL

ISRAEL AND THE JEWISH PEOPLE IN THE PLAN OF GOD

EDITORS
DARRELL L. BOCK AND MITCH GLASER